A SONG in the NIGHT

Rebecca Bryan-Howell

ISBN: 978-1-7325959-1-0
Library of Congress Control Number: 2018910651

Book and cover design: Kat Paul

Printed in Meridian, Idaho, United States of America
by Rebecca Bryan-Howell

This book is dedicated
To my Wonderful Mother;
A True Story woven together
with her words,
from her heart.

To all who hope to live, as she has,
Happily Victorious!

Contents

CHAPTER ONE

Ancestry: My Beginnings

The pages of history brim with stories of people young and old, rich and poor, powerful and common; and of places domesticated and untamed; fertile and barren, near and far away. There will never be an end of writing the multitudinous accounts made up of the ever-emerging combinations of scenes, characters, circumstances and eras played out on the world stage. Never will mankind be able, on his own, to extract the depth of meaning embedded in human history—this story that God has ordained: *His-story* as his people have fondly named it.

History comes down, however lofty its reputation, to people's lives; records of their pilgrimage from birth to death. Whether or not one's journey is recorded, we all have a part in "His-story"; and here are the strands that began the weaving of mine.

Mussell Roots

My grandfather, Jacob Mussell, was raised in Upper Canada, now Ontario, where John Mussell—his grandfather and a British soldier—had been awarded a land grant from the Crown for his service in the War of 1812.[1] I learned that Jacob's dad, my great-grandfather William Mussell, was born in Coventry, England and died when Jacob was only four years old. My grandpa was one of sixteen children born to William Mussell and Jemima Lundy.[2] His mother, Jemima, was a godly woman who taught him to pray and to serve the Lord. His father died of blood poisoning following a logging accident, leaving Jemima to raise nine children alone[3] while eking out a living on their rocky piece of land. Four of her sons became ministers of the gospel, my Grandpa Jacob being one of them!

In 1877, although Jacob may have been as stimulated as any other young Englishman to discover gold or silver in the Idaho Territory, his reason for heading west was simply to build a cheese factory for his cousin, Henry.[4] With his mother's permission[5] he set off with Henry by train to Winnemucca, Nevada. He tells a funny story about the speed of the train: "One day when I was leaning out the train window to get a better view of the country, I accidentally dropped my ticket! Instantly I jumped out, retrieved my ticket and climbed back on!"[6]

The boys took the stage on to Silver City, Idaho; but Henry didn't see enough cows there to support his cheese-making so he went back home.[7] Jacob stayed and took a job for forty dollars per month on a cattle ranch, which was good money in those days! He arrived just as the Bannock Indians were going on the warpath and for two months he slept with his Winchester by his bed[8] while working for his employer as a lookout in case of Indian raids. In 1880, while breaking horses, he also broke his ankle. Having only a fifth grade education,[9] he decided he should prepare for a different career. He sent away for school books and studied many hours each day while recuperating.[10] Then he moved to Silver City to take a job at a local mercantile as a bookkeeper. The story goes that when the owner of the store saw how much money Jacob was saving him, and how dependable and honest he was, he decided to fire two other clerks and make Jacob the manager.[11]

He also worked as a bookkeeper at the Dewey Mines and led the Silver City band. Grandpa Jacob was from a talented family of self-taught musicians, and played the violin.[12] He was also a prolific writer who, throughout his life, wrote many poems and many gospel hymns—both words and music. Grandpa owned 5,000 sheep at the young age of twenty-two, and he was the first Idaho rancher to ship wool to Boston.[13]

While in the Silver City mining community he met his wife, Ada Norton. This beautiful sixteen-year old was the daughter of Sprowel and Lucy Norton. Mr. Norton was a wagon maker whose ancestry dated back to Martha's Vineyard, Massachusetts in the early 1600s. They had traveled west by wagon train to Winnemucca, carrying on the pioneer tradition.[14] But when Jacob met Ada, her father owned a furniture store in Silver City and was using his honed carpentry skills to make and sell fine furniture. Their family was very refined and quite concerned that Ada should marry a worthy man who was able to take good care of her. When Ada's parents saw that Jacob Mussell was a responsible and hard-working man with a stellar reputation in the community, they decided to give their consent for their daughter to marry him. My mother said that Ada Mussell was a kind and gentle woman whom she loved very much, but Grandma Ada died when my parents were newlyweds.

After their marriage in 1883, Jacob and Ada migrated down to Owyhee County and homesteaded 400 acres of land on Succor Creek along the Idaho-Oregon border. They built a two-story house with lumber hauled from Middleton and ferried across the Snake River. They transported the wagon by removing the wheels so it would float across like a skiff. Grandpa Jacob dug a ditch two miles long to irrigate his farm, fruit trees and garden. He also introduced alfalfa to the State of Idaho, bringing the seed from San Francisco to plant on his land.[15]

Later on they moved to the banks of the Snake River and founded the town of Homedale. To name the new town, settlers placed suggestions in a hat and Grandma Ada's choice of "Homedale" was drawn! Here Jacob Mussell established his home place, which tripled as the schoolhouse, post office—where Grandma Ada was the first Postmistress—and stage stop for their small community. Stage drivers took mail and passengers between Jordan Valley, Oregon and Caldwell, Idaho, stopping once each day to deliver the mail and switch their horses for fresh ones at Grandpa's stage stop. Since all this activity happened at their house, my Aunt Mamie kept notes about it. They were filled with the wonder of it all through the eyes of a young girl who watched the goings on from the upstairs bedroom window. She described how the passengers were dressed in winter, with their thick woolens, knitted headscarves or caps with earflaps, and buckled overshoes. She noted how big and burly the drivers had to be in order to dig the stage out of a mud hole or snowbank along the route. She marveled at how courteous these rough men treated the women as they tucked fur robes around them and nodded words of assurance muffled beneath their big handlebar moustaches! Meals were only served to travelers when the coaches were held up by a storm; Grandpa Jacob offered this benefit at no charge.[16]

Grandpa Jacob also built a ferry boat and operated Mussell's Ferry across the Snake River for nearly ten years. He made roads by dragging a V-shaped railroad iron through the sagebrush to expose the sand.[17] The current bridge at Homedale, Idaho, which was built in 1970, is directly over the old ferryboat crossing.[18]

They had lots of pioneer stories and narrow escapes to tell about. One winter when the temperatures dropped to 30 and 40 degrees below zero, the Snake River was so frozen that Grandpa drove his wagon with a four-horse team across on the ice! He lost many sheep that year because their wool froze into the snow when they lay down so that they couldn't get back up! [19]

Once when a cattleman named Spanish Charlie threatened to kill him, Grandpa's efforts to talk about it ended in a confrontation where Charlie was shot and killed. Grandpa Jacob was so grieved over it that he surrendered to the authorities in Baker City, Oregon. He was acquitted by a grand jury for self-defense, after which he built Charlie a coffin and preached his funeral! [20]

Hostile Indians shot at Grandpa many times; he was hit a few times, but survived. Once when he was driving the stage coach to Jordan Valley a band of Indians attacked; by God's grace he was able to escape and make it back to the Snake River and to safety. It was always dangerous for any settlers to get far from their homes where they were vulnerable and might be seen as easy prey.

Jacob Mussell was a prominent citizen, recorded in Idaho history books. He did, in fact, receive his education and ordination with the Methodist church, traveling throughout the region as a circuit-riding preacher who ministered in Methodist out-stations, school houses, grange halls and wherever people met for worship. Later in life, some of his poems and songs were published by Moody Press, and in Methodist hymnals.[21]

My grandparents, Jacob and Ada—or Ma and Pa, as my parents called them—already had six of their twelve children when they came to the banks of the Snake River to build their multi-functional residence! But this amazing house in Homedale is where my daddy, Jules LaVerne Mussell, was born on February 16, 1907. My father was the youngest of twelve children, nine girls and three boys. The girls were Myrtle, Mamie, Cora, Pearl, Alma, Ruth, Lillian, Ethel, and little Ada who died at two. All the boys were named "J" and they each got to choose their own name when they got older: J. Sherman, John Edgar, and Jules LaVerne. Daddy had read the classic science fiction novel, *Twenty Thousand Leagues Under the Sea*, by Jules Verne and decided from that story to adopt the name "Jules" for himself. Meanwhile, as Jules LaVerne's boyish pilgrimage was beginning to take its course at the Mussell Ferry Stage Stop, a little girl appeared on the horizon just over the Oregon border.

Bunt Roots

Addie Alice Bunt was born on June 22, 1908 in Ontario, Oregon; the third daughter of nine children fathered by William Taylor Bunt. My grandmother, Nancy Jane (Royce) Bunt, had already borne nine children (two of which had died in childhood) by her first husband who had left her a widow and, imagine, a single mother of seven!

Grandma Bunt had a hard life. Her mother died when she was only ten years old, and her mean and cruel father made her prepare the body for burial while he was gone to town. She was married at age fifteen to William Hall, a cattleman who would be away on cattle drives for three months at a time, leaving her to fend for herself and the children. She learned to do everything imaginable by herself: treating all kinds of sickness, administering emergency First Aid, delivering her own babies, chopping wood and building fires for warmth and cooking, preparing food for winter, making clothing, and hiding from hostile Indians in the territory, while doctoring the babies of friendly ones. We were always fascinated by her stories of life as a real pioneer among the Indians on the frontier in the early days of the Wild West! She said the only way to live among the Indians was to make friends with them, do kind things for them and to give them gifts. She became a midwife for them and cared for their sick children. They thought her mustard plasters were like magic!

One story that I remember hearing is about some Indians who were chasing her on horseback. She got far enough ahead that she was able to get off the beaten path to hide behind a deserted barn. Her horse was restless and breathing hard but she was trying to keep him quiet, for if he whinnied the hostile Indians would hear him and find her. Her heart pounded as they wandered the area looking for her. God must have made that old barn invisible because soon enough the wild band rode away, leaving her very frightened but perfectly safe!

My mother said Grandma would sometimes tell them stories of her past before bedtime. She told about her grandparents—my great-great grandparents—coming to Oregon in a covered wagon. Mama's journal says:

> They were staying in a log house with a small window away up high
> in the end of the house. Her grandma was sitting in a chair one time,
> and there was an Indian with all those feathers on his head looking in
> through that window! Her grandma wore false teeth and knew that the
> Indians were superstitious; so she let her teeth fall out of her mouth onto
> her lap. She scared that Indian! He got down real quick, and left. Her
> grandparents left that place soon after that; but ... they never saw any
> Indians come around again while they were there.[22]

Grandma's first husband, Bill, decided they should drive their cattle to Idaho and settle there. She drove a wagon packed with all of their belongings and her seven living children; Bill rode a horse and drove the cattle. When they got to Mountain Home, Idaho Bill got sick with Rocky Mountain spotted fever (from tick bites) and was hospitalized there until he died.

Enter my grandfather, a brave and compassionate soul to take on such a brood to raise; not to mention adding nine more later to make it an even eighteen pregnancies for the amazing Nancy Jane! The story goes that William Bunt was a nurse, for in those days they took volunteers from the community to help at the hospital. After Bill died, Grandma had to sell their cattle to pay for the funeral and to care for her large family. Three of her first nine children had died by this time, so when she met Grandpa she had Beth, Effie, Fay, Bill, Lula, and Nancy Jane. Grandpa saw that this young widow was alone with no one to help her, and offered to drive them back to Sacramento, California with Bill Hall's mother, who had come to Idaho for her son's funeral.

So he packed up the Grandma, the Mama, and six children into a horse-drawn wagon and headed for California. On the way, Mrs. Hall told Nancy Jane that she would have to put the children in an orphanage because she couldn't keep "all those kids"! William saw Nancy Jane's terrible distress and told her that he would send Mrs. Hall alone to Sacramento by train. He told my Grandma that he would take her back to Idaho and marry her so she could keep her family together! So Nancy Jane Hall became Mrs. William Bunt; and soon more children were added to this happily blended family.[23]

My mother was the third child of William Taylor and Nancy Jane Bunt. The first of God's great miracles in her life, as she puts it, happened when she

was three years old. Her father was one of the workers hired to build Holy Rosary Hospital in Ontario, Oregon. The weather had turned cold and little Addie became very ill with pneumonia. She was the very first patient at the new hospital, but her parents were told that she would probably die. Although her birth name was Addie Alice, the priest baptized her as "Addie *Catherine* Bunt" during the last rites ceremony; but her father, William, asked him to pray for her to get well, and he agreed. The nurses made a half-circle at the bedside, while the priest and Addie's parents stood at the head of the bed. The priest put his hand on her head and prayed. Then he turned to William, with a good-natured punch on his shoulder, and said, "Go home, my good man! You will have your daughter in a few days." She improved right away and two days later they took her home, and changed her name from Addie *Alice* to Addie *Catherine*, as the priest had christened her at baptism.

Mama's siblings were May, Sadie, Amy—who died at birth—John, Mary, Jim, Joe and Sarah Ellen. They lived in Ironside, Oregon in the early days, and Mama remembers a frightening event about that house. One day while her papa was at work, her mama was cooking and spotted smoke pouring out at the ceiling near the pantry. Realizing that there was a fire upstairs, she ran outside with all of the kids, slamming the door! She rushed them out into the sagebrush away from the house, and laid a quilt on the ground, telling them all to stay on that quilt until she got back. They could hear the fire crackling fiercely! High above the roof, the smoke was barreling into the sky with large flames underneath. They watched their mama run back into the burning house, and come right back out with an armload of rifles she had snatched from a corner. Everything else was lost, including their little yellow dog, Fanny, who had run underneath the house. A kind family who owned a large ranch nearby invited the Bunts to move in with them until they could find another place to live.[24]

Mama talks about all the places they lived and all their amazing adventures as settlers of the Wild West; from killing rabid coyotes on the front porch to Grandma Bunt chopping up huge rattlesnakes with a shovel. One time Mama looked out the kitchen window and saw something flopping around in the shallow waters of the nearby creek. Grandma ran down there with the .22 rifle to see what it was and came back with a huge salmon for dinner!

She talked about the "ice tent" that Grandpa always kept. He knew how to keep ice frozen between layers of sawdust. She said that their family always had ice that her papa cut from the frozen pond in the winter. They even had enough in the summer to make homemade ice cream! One day after they had all enjoyed their ice cream with visiting neighbors, one of the boys got a rattlesnake by the tail and swung it above his head several times. Then he gave it a snap and off came its head, which flew through the air and hit Grandma Bunt in the ankle. When the neighbors left and she finally told Grandpa, he had to cut her shoelaces with a knife in order to remove her shoe from her badly swollen foot. The nearest hospital was in Baker City, sixty miles away and too far for a buggy ride. He sat beside her all night, reading the Bible and changing her tobacco poultice regularly until morning. She lived; but it was a miracle because many people died from snake bites in those days. Many years later, Grandma showed Mama those two fiery-red dots on her ankle; a lifelong reminder of God's protection in tough times.[25]

When they moved from Oregon to southern Idaho, Grandpa rented two boxcars for the trip. In one car, all their household furniture was placed at one end and all the cows were loaded in the other end! The second boxcar held Grandpa's horses in one end while his wagons, buggy, tools and such were packed on the other side! One brother, and a brother-in-law, each rode in one of the boxcars to care for the livestock; they went ahead of the family who later came by train.[26]

Everyone worked hard in those days because there was a lot to do and each family member had to pitch in. Mama even helped graze their cattle when she was only eleven! She rode her saddle horse out to the grazing land early in the morning where Grandpa had built a corral. Grandma sent her a small lunch and a water bag tied to her saddle. She would let the cows out to graze and then round them up at night and lock them into the corral where they would be safer until morning. Grandpa taught her how to know the lateness of the hour by holding her hand up to the setting sun. He said, "Put your hand out from you and when you can see the sun just *over* your hand and the top of the mountain just *under* it, then gather up the cows." Just about the time she got home it would start to get dark.[27]

Later their family moved to a nice acreage with an artesian well near Caldwell, Idaho. They were hard-working and industrious. Grandma Bunt was a good homemaker and a fine, domesticated lady; they were God-fearing people and very hospitable. They went to several different churches at times but were never committed to any one in particular (imagine getting that many kids ready on Sunday morning!) Consequently, they were believers but had a limited understanding of the Word of God—like many pioneers with similar circumstances of the times. The next pattern of the Weaver's Hand, however, brought two lives together sovereignly to experience the presence and power of God in a way their ancestors had only longed for.

Destinies Come Together

There were large tent revivals in those days and one evangelist who came to Caldwell was Mattie Crawford. God was moving in a mighty way and many people were being saved from sin and healed of disease. Although Addie and LaVerne already knew of each other's families through their attendance at a little church on 11th and Blaine—where LaVerne played his cornet in the orchestra—they became better acquainted at this revival. The Bunts invited him home for dinner a couple of times, and on one of these days Addie and Verne lagged behind the group, walking home together. They began to get better acquainted and soon fell in love. With the arrival of winter, however, their relationship grew only by mail because the cold and snow prevented LaVerne from coming to town.

As a note of special interest, my father graduated from Greenleaf Friends Academy which was founded in 1908 by the Friends Church as an institution of Christian education in the remote area of Greenleaf, Idaho. An early catalog is quoted as saying:

> No education is complete without a personal knowledge of and acquaintance with God. The highest intellectual attainment is of little value unless that attainment is controlled by Him, who is the source of all knowledge.[28]

I don't know what it cost in those days, but this speaks to my grandfather's staunch dedication to his faith in providing a Christian education for his son in the days when many young people received very little education of any kind. LaVerne rode his horse to school and, years later in the 1990s, two of my grandchildren, Angie and Ben, attended Greenleaf Academy and testified to the fact that the hitching posts still stood in front of the school!

Verne and Addie wrote letters and sent cards to each other that winter of 1926-27, and the following March he came to town to see Addie and to ask her Papa for her hand in marriage. Her Papa was in favor, but when Verne asked Addie to marry him, it took her a week to say, "Yes"!

Mama says it is because she was taken by complete surprise! Although she was very taken with Verne, she thought for sure that he would choose one of her sisters, May or Sadie, who she thought were much more attractive than she. That week must have been a little tense for my dad as he awaited her reply; but when she finally consented he lost no time in catching up with her! That Friday, as she walked to school, Verne met her on the road and escorted her back home! Evidently, he had another plan for the day that was more important than anything else, and those who mattered in their lives apparently agreed. For Addie's parents called Pastor Hammond and some close friends to come to their house that evening, while Verne and Addie went to the courthouse to get the marriage license. That night, in front of about twenty people, they said their marriage vows.[29]

Addie married her "knight in shining armor" on March 18, 1927. They had been doused by a fresh wave of God's spirit and saved and filled with the Holy Ghost. Only He knew what great adventures were ahead for these newlyweds who loved Him so deeply.

CHAPTER TWO

Verne and Addie

In those days, newly married couples did not often have a home of their very own waiting for them. Verne and Addie lived with a variety of relatives, moving six times during the first year of their marriage! In the next four years they moved several more times, and even spent one month in a tent somewhere in Nampa—with four small children in tow! This was in September of 1931 while waiting for a new house that was being built by LaVerne and his father, my Grandpa Jacob Mussell. They moved into the new house in October of 1931 and stayed until my dad, with the help of a good friend, finished building a house on an acre of land on Grandpa Mussell's old homestead. They moved into this one the last week of December, 1932 with their growing family, which had multiplied to parents with five children in only five and a half years![1]

Our Special Blend

Like gourmet coffees and teas, every family begins with a special blend of unique elements and is enriched over time as these individual components mix and meld. Our "family flavor" was the best I ever tasted; and the sweet aroma began with Addie Catherine. I can't imagine a more wonderful mama than mine! She was very shy; I remember her as being humble and obedient. She loved God, her husband and her children, serving them all with sacrificial devotion. Always aiming to have three good meals on time, keep the laundry done and maintain a clean house, Mama worked from sunup to sundown; *singing*, always singing. Mama never worked outside the home or got involved in things that took her away from the family. In fact, she never drove a car; so she was always at home unless we went somewhere together. She lived for others, rarely thinking of herself. Among the many hats she wore, Emergency Nurse was a frequent one; and she was the best around! If anyone was sick or ailing, she flew into action and gave them her full attention. Following heart-felt prayers, every home remedy, comfort, and bit of care or nourishment she could find was lovingly administered to the one in need until they were completely recovered. I remember how she toiled to sterilize all the dishes in a big pot of boiling water to keep sickness and germs from spreading. Moreover, she took the same meticulous care over our spiritual health as well.

Mama talked a lot about the early days of revival and quoted lots of scripture, always taking the time to answer our questions and teach us about God, the Bible and Heaven. Mama was an exhorter and encourager. She often told us as children that we could do anything that God wanted us to do, and that we should have confidence to achieve good grades, individual skills, and the talents to become significant Christians in our world. Considering the fact that her own self-assurance was lacking, the level of confidence she built in me was amazing! I always felt that God and I could do whatever needed to be done!

I remember that Mama lost her two front teeth somehow when she was a young mother and didn't get false teeth until she was in her forties. I guess they couldn't afford to buy them; but something like that would definitely chip away at a young woman's self image! They say pregnancy is hard on the teeth, and she had seven children by the time she was twenty-eight! Regardless of the inferiority she always felt about her appearance, education, and personal ability, however, she was a champion at home preparing her little brood for life in the world.

I was so proud of my little mother. Always plain and simple, but impeccably neat and clean, Mama was very modest in her apparel, and without makeup or jewelry. She was extremely conscientious about how her appearance represented the Lord Jesus. Teaching us contentment by her own example, she never asked for things and could always "make-do" with whatever she had. Sweet, cotton-print dresses were what she wore at home, with an apron, of course. For church she dressed in a tidy, conservative suit—neat as a pin. She sewed and mended, keeping everything in good repair. She never had expensive clothes but, when I was fourteen and she was forty, Daddy bought her a two-piece, black taffeta suit. It had shoulder pads and it buttoned in front. She had some matching pump heels and a cute, white hat that paired perfectly. Weighing no more than about a hundred and ten pounds, she looked adorable! Mama never cut her hair, but kept it long and combed it back into a bun; or braided it and wrapped it around her head or pinned it up in a roll. I never saw her in a pair of slacks while I was growing up—except overalls for field work.

Mama said so many things I will never forget. She would often say, "You can do it if you try! *I-can't* never did anything! *I-can* gets the job done!" She taught us the value of hard work, and showed us by example how to put our whole heart into our duties, as unto the Lord.

She always said, "Make your work fun!"

"Never be lazy!"

"Never be indifferent and careless!"

"Be resourceful!"

"A penny saved is a penny earned!"

"Don't cry over spilt milk"

"Learn from your mistakes, and go on with confidence!"

"Where there's a will, there's a way!"

"Be yourself; don't try to be like someone else. Even the snowflakes are all different from each other, and God planned it that way!"

"Just love the Lord and love one another; that's how you can best love me."

"Be like Jesus."

My dad, Jules LaVerne, brought the warm, authentic flavor to our family blend. He came to Christ as a boy and was baptized in the Holy Spirit when he was eighteen at a big tent revival meeting. He felt a call to the ministry when he was a young, single man but life has its delays. He was married at age twenty and, when seven children came along within eight years, it took all his time to feed and clothe his family!

My father was one of the hardest workers I have ever seen. When he was a very young man, he had a shoe shop. He was very good at half-soling shoes or putting on new heels; so he always fixed our shoes for us. Daddy was born on a farm and was knowledgeable about livestock and crop-farming. Three times he pioneered large plots of virgin sagebrush land into thriving farms. He loved all of his farm animals because they were our livelihood. As busy and hard-working as he was, my dad was also in the ministry while we were growing up. He was ordained with the Assemblies of God —a full gospel Christian denomination— and pastored several churches. Other times he held the office of a deacon, and was often engaged in street preaching and evangelism.

After the Great Depression, he went to Mechanic's Trade School for General Motors in Los Angeles and got a job as an auto electrician/mechanic. Several times throughout his life he opened his own mechanics shop where he worked on auto-electronics, alternators, carburetors and tune-ups. He had all his own tools and did excellent work. One of his shops was called, *Verne's Auto Electric*. Another time he owned a service station.

He believed that women should stay at home rather than seek higher education, and Mama gladly complied. One of her great delights was to keep him in dazzling, clean clothes. She starched and ironed all his shirts, whether for dress or work. When he worked as a mechanic he wore uniforms that always looked sharp and were durable and practical. When he farmed in the country he wore jeans, long-sleeved shirts and a brimmed hat for sun protection; gloves, work shoes, and galoshes in wet weather. When he pastored, or worked in churches, he wore suits, crisply-starched white shirts with ties, dark stockings and well-shined dress shoes. He always looked good, stayed clean, and was trim and tidy. People used to comment about what a nice-looking man my dad was; and with his thick, dark, black hair and twinkling gray-green eyes, I certainly agreed!

Although my father contributed the strong, firm, and capable tones to our family mix, he was sweet and kind; a gentle man who never raised his voice in anger. He was the "calm and steady" type who seemed to maintain ample control of every situation. His love for his family was absolutely unquestionable; I always felt that I had his approval. He often spoke tender words to me like, "too cute" when he patted me or pinched my nose.

Daddy loved God supremely and always put Him first. He was a true spiritual leader; loving and serving the Lord, honoring God's Word and teaching all of us to do the same. He prayed and read the Bible each evening to the family, a memorable tradition that we called "Family Altar". I loved to hear him tell stories of famous Christians. He would tell of their faith ventures, miracles of healing, and experiences of financial provision with such enthusiasm that it inspired our faith as well! Looking back over his life with all its challenges—and now that I have lived a full life of my own—I see why it was so important for him to recount stories of faith that demonstrated God's faithfulness to his people in times of need. Ephesians 3 tells us that God, from the riches of His glory, will grant us the power of His Spirit so we will be strengthened with might in our inner man. So, while building the faith of his eager listeners, Daddy was encouraged as well, strengthening his own spirit for the journey!

Although I learned a few common childhood prayers, they were more like devotional poetry to me. Real prayer was learned by my parents' example. They taught us that prayer was about faith and expectancy. We had a lot of prayer in our household: morning prayer; prayer over meals; prayer any time of the day over needs that arose such as sickness, finances, business, or for friends; as well as prayer every evening during family devotions.

Our father also demonstrated to us, by his own life, the importance of loving the church and all of God's people. He was a soul-winner, always handing out gospel tracts and witnessing. His philosophy of life was to live for God and to "win the lost at any cost." He gave to the church, was generous to anyone in need, and was highly respected by many. I saw eye-to-eye with my father most of the time and I think I inherited many of his strong personality traits. I always revered him for the great example that he was in my life; we were blessed with such a wonderful dad!

Both of my parents gave us treasures for life in the words they spoke to us; like the truth of Proverbs 25:11 (NIV) they were *"words fitly spoken...like apples of gold in settings of silver."* I not only remember so many things he often said to us, but I cherish them, and passed them along to my children as well. Nuggets like: *"Be content with such things as ye have,"* from Hebrews 13:5 (KJV).

"Never get in debt!"

"Stay close to Jesus!"

"Love one another;"

"Praise the Lord!"

"If you can live without it, you don't need it."

"Things like that don't matter," one that I heard so many times in so many circumstances, always reminded us that our security was not in material possessions.

Verne and Addie had seven children, of which I was sixth. My two brothers, David LaVerne and Paul Joseph, were the "first" and the "last", respectively, with five sisters in between them: Nancy Jewel, Dorcas Faith, Juanita Rosemary, Lois Catherine, and me—Eunice Christina. Although my birth certificate says, "Huston, Idaho", I was born at home; in the house my dad had built on Grandpa Mussell's old farm near Homedale in Canyon County. My father brought me into the world. Mama said that we were all born at home except my eldest sister, Jewel. She didn't always have a midwife around to help, as in the case of my arrival, but sometimes she did—a benefit that her own dear mother could never have dreamed of!

Loaves and Fishes

There were seven of us; Mama called us her *five loaves and two fishes*! The children in our family brought such a variety of texture and delight to the Mussell blend that my senses still burst with delicious mementos from my childhood! Each one of my brothers and sisters enriched my life by special impartations of their own unique gifts.

My older brother, David, was my hero; a stabilizing force in my life. He brought the stalwart effect of a forest of evergreens, pungent and over-arching; capable of anything from a playful poke to a cover of protection. He was an "in-charge" person who looked after his five sisters and little brother, Paul. He told me real-life stories, shared meaningful philosophies of life, and gave me detailed explanations of how things worked. He was ambitious, trustworthy and fair. I thought he could do anything, and he *would do* about anything I asked of him. When I was seven years old I begged him to make a doll buggy for me.

He said, "I can't do that, Eunie!" but soon he gave in because I was so sure that my big brother could do *anything* he wanted to do! First he cut four wheels out of wood with a coping saw and filed them into shape. After sanding them, he drilled holes in the centers for the axles. Then he made the carriage out of a cardboard box and fastened it to the axles. I will never forget my sheer delight! In fact, the older I grew, the more it amazed me that he would take on the challenge and spend the time to do something for me that must have been so trivial to him! David was a super star to his littlest sister!

Jewel was the eldest of the five girls and very dear to me. The first "flower" in our brood, she added the sweetness and beauty of song to our nest, our melodious rose. She loved to sing and often had a chorus on her lips. Jewel always called me by endearing names like *"honey"*, *"sweetie"* and *"darling"*; and she read me Bible stories. As the eldest daughter, she was the first to learn household skills so she naturally filled the role of helping the younger girls learn. I remember when she stood me up on a chair in front of the sink and said, "I'm going to teach my baby sister how to wash dishes!" She showed me how to fill the wash pan with soapy water, how to wash each piece carefully and then dunk it in the rinse water pan before putting it up onto a towel to dry. I was so amazed by all those bubbles that I would become fascinated by filling cups and bowls with soapy water and pouring them out again and again.

She would say, "Now, honey, you're not washing dishes; your just playing in the soapy water!" Then she would take my hands in hers and exclaim, "Look at these cute little, dimpled hands!" and would get me back on track to finish the job. She would then dry my hands and take off my apron, showing me every aspect of doing this chore well whenever it was my turn to help. Jewel also taught me to set the table for meals, as well as other domestic chores. I don't remember her playing with the rest of us. I think that she was so busy helping Mama with things that she never had the time to be outside; and being four years older than me she may not have had as much interest in our activities.

Jewel was close to David's age and didn't want him bossing her around. While the younger ones looked at him as more of an authority figure, she undoubtedly endured a few things that resulted in the needed reminder that "even roses have their thorns". I remember one time when our folks were gone and she locked him out of the house. We lived at Lynwood so I must have been about six, making her ten and David eleven-plus. She was cleaning house, probably sweeping or mopping the floors, and didn't want him in her way. David, however, was not so easily put off! He went out to the shop and made himself a skeleton key which worked like a charm! When Jewel heard him open that door she hollered at him to "Get out!" and somehow grabbed his miracle key and locked him out again! He made another one, though, so I guess he was not duly deterred from his mission! I don't remember how the story ended, but after raising two boys of my own it was easy to see how anxious David must have been to take on such an irresistible challenge!

Jewel was saved and filled with the Holy Spirit as a young girl, and was always very close to the Lord. She loved spiritual things and was drawn to Christian people. I remember her praying fervently and speaking in tongues at church. She loved singing and music, and reading the Bible. Although we were not playmates my image of her was endearing, my "big" sister who invited me to sit on her lap.

Dorcas was the next daughter in the Mussell family assortment, and brought the strong scents of inspiration and encouragement to our family blend. Like a full lilac whose blossoms exude constant fragrance she was a treasure trove of beautiful values and wonderful disciplines to me! She loved thought-provoking gospel tracts and stimulating missionary stories, which she read to me often. She inspired me to memorize scripture verses and encouraged me immensely in my own devotional and prayer life. She had a binder full of beautiful poems that she had collected. I loved to read through it, and was inspired to start my own collection later in life. Sometimes I would awaken to her voice, reading from her poem book as she knelt at her bedside during her morning prayer. This remarkable visual memory had a lasting impact on my life. When I started my own collection, I chose a variety of meaningful poetry and prose which ministered to me at different times and seasons throughout my life, and still does! I also collected old hymnals and books of choruses or scriptural songs that wafted through the church congregations I attended during the different stages of my life. I perused these poems and sang these songs often, memorizing many of them through the years, which planted their priceless values deep in my heart.

I'm sure Dorcas, like Jewel, was a good helper to Mama as well; because the only vivid memory I have of her playing with the rest of us was when we were jumping rope. Both of my eldest sisters loved me with care and devotion, however, and inspired me continuously. They were irreplaceable role models of Christian grace and femininity in my small, impressionable place of youngest sister.

My middle sisters, Lois and Rosemary, the two closest to me in age, were my favorite playmates and best childhood friends. Rosemary was our third sister, the fizz and sparkle in our blend! She was a vivacious and effervescent personality who constantly bubbled with creative energy! She was a spirited poet and amazing artist who amused me with stories of exciting adventures and fairy tales that she invented from her own imagination. She was full of fun and always ready to play a game. She could draw pictures and fashion adorable paper dolls with an assortment of clothes for me to color and cut out. She was also the one that pondered the words and meanings of songs in ways I never forgot. Out of the blue she might say, "Eunice, did you know that song we sang in church today is a funeral song?" After my expression of utter surprise, she would proceed to tell me why: "*Safe in the arms of Jesus; Safe on His gentle breast; There, by His love o'er shadowed, sweetly my soul shall rest*" describes a soul that has left the earth and is now in Heaven with Jesus." Of course, I would continually be amazed at her remarkable ability to decipher things that I would never have recognized by myself.

"Let's pretend that we're living in The Millennium!" she would say suddenly, and then proceed to imagine the greatest of miraculous adventures. "If I was in The Millennium right now, I'd ride on the back of a giraffe way up high; and hold onto its big neck!" she would continue, sparking the imaginations of the rest of us. "Oh! I'd ride on the lion and hang onto his mane! Wouldn't he be soft?" The Ball of Pretend would roll on for a long time as we all chimed in with our imaginative ideas of horses we would ride and places we would see. This was a favorite game for talking about all the things we didn't have, but could vicariously enjoy!

Lois was just one year above me, my lifetime friend and confidante. She was our faithful and loyal-to-a-fault flavor. Early on, she read me lots of children's stories and, as we grew up, she and I did everything together. She could do almost everything better than I could and she was very good to me; I thought my closest sister was "just it"! Lois was always a very generous person, giving to everyone all the time. She was devoted to Mama and Daddy first, then David and Paul, our brothers; but I came next! Being the youngest of five girls, I was often pampered by my sisters' doting. They helped me with everything imaginable; combed my hair, tied my ribbons, helped me dress, held me on their laps, and told me how cute I was. What last-born girl would not revel in that kind of daily affirmation!

We never got into mischief, as so many kids do these days. I think it's because we were taught so strongly that all of life was full of purpose and not to be wasted on thoughtless activities. Frivolity and jesting were actually

considered bad behavior in our household, and we were often quoted scriptures that mandated sober and earnest lifestyles such as Proverbs 24:9 (KJV) - *"The thought of foolishness is sin;"* or I Thessalonians 5:6 - *"...let us watch and be sober;"* or Proverbs 22:15 (KJV)- *"Foolishness is bound in the heart of a child, but the rod of correction shall drive it far from him;"* or Ephesians 5:4 which tells us that we will one day give account for every idle word. Therefore, we were usually very well-behaved and respectful; yet we never lacked for fun and laughter. David tells stories on himself that smack of orneriness (and the spankings that resulted!) but from my view, a ways down the line, I never thought of my big brother that way.

One time he went down to the river with a neighbor boy who was his age. He knew it was off limits, but there was a huge wash—completely dry until the rainy season—where they could cut bamboo to make things with. When Mama found out where he had been, he was in bad trouble and endured a sound scolding. She sent him back to the riverbank to fetch a willow switch for his own spanking. Knowing that the small, flexible ones hurt the worst, David cut a big tall one that little Mama could hardly manipulate in the house. But when she saw the big switch that her obedient son had chosen for his well-deserved punishment, she supposed he was truly humble and appropriately penitent; and her tender heart was overcome with compassion! I can't remember whether he actually got the swats or not!

Another time, because of his ingenuity, he figured out how to add an electric shock to a small chair that he had built. He had tested it on himself and found it to be tolerable, so he wanted to try it on the girls. The minute they sat down and touched the arm of the chair, a low voltage shock would be felt. Rosemary was so observant, however, that she saw the wire before she sat down, and ran for the house to expose his mischief. Mama came out, a little bundle of motherly wrath, and spanked him soundly with a soft leather strap that she used only for loving discipline. He always took it bravely with no crying, and with ultimate respect and repentance.

Rosemary had a slight bent toward playful teasing as well, along with an amazing ability to make a fantastical specialty from a little bit of nothing. One day when we were up in the apricot tree the neighbor boy came outside and Rosemary whispered, "Let's pretend like we're speaking a different language," and she proceeded to cause poor Elmer a great deal of confusion by making him wonder what in the world we were saying to each other. Her imaginary "foreign language" was simply saying the letters of the alphabet as whole words and stringing a bunch of them together into a sentence, such as A through M, "Aa Buh Cuh! Deh Eh-Fuh Guh! Huh i-jah Kuh uL eM."

Another time when Daddy was sick and couldn't work, we were almost out of food—basically down to the last handful of pinto beans. Elmer, the boy next door, always seemed to have tantalizing snacks and goodies that he would bring into the yard to eat in front of us. On top of that, he was a bit spoiled and seemed to enjoy flaunting his shiny toys and tasty cookies. This particular day, Rosemary and I had climbed up into our apricot tree and were chewing on chunks of Paraffin wax—for lack of anything more substantial to chew on—when she suddenly got the notion that this was a perfect opportunity to tease Elmer a bit. So she began to loudly express tasty pleasure with, "Mmmmm! Mmmmm!" accompanied by a look of utmost satisfaction on her face until his curiosity got the better of him and he asked, "What do you have?"

"White Goblin Gum!" she exclaimed with exaggerated relish. "Have you ever tasted it?"

Of course, he hadn't because this was Rosie's inventive imagination at work; and we really had him duped! She winked at me through the apricot branches as poor Elmer longed for a piece of this delectable delight that had somehow escaped his over-indulgent parents. As delicious as we made it look, however, he would surely have been very disappointed in its stiff and flavorless reality! I must admit that we took great delight in keeping this wily secret to ourselves as he visibly dripped with longing for a taste of the newest thing out, "White Goblin Gum".

Little Paul, last, but not least, was the dark-eyed darling of the patch! The only one to qualify me as an elder sibling, my little brother was my pride and joy! He was born sweet and agreeable; loving, affectionate and cuddly. Mama says that Paul and I were the two that loved most to be held. Of course, we *were* the babies of the bunch! I was two and a half when he was born. Mama used to say that if anything ever happened to Paul, she didn't see how she could live. He was peaceful and content, able to play by himself for hours, and never bothering anyone for attention. I, on the other hand, was a people-person who always wanted to be in the middle of the action!

One of the proudest times of my whole life was when Paul was probably a sophomore in high school. I was married, but had come back to the farm house for a visit. Our folks were on a trip to California, so David and Paul were home alone. Paul said he had to go sing in the Christmas program at his school and asked me if I would like to come along. When we got there, it turned out that my little brother had a major part as the main soloist! He was under the spotlight for the whole production! He was so humble about it that he had not even spread the word; but he sang like an angel and looked like a movie star! I wished so much that the whole family could have been there to hear him. One of his solos was, "Mine Eyes have seen the King in All His Beauty"; a song that, unfortunately, could never be sung in the public schools of today. The lyrics stridently extol the character and divinity of Christ as the righteous and Holy One of God.

Paul always had a beautiful, clear voice, and perfect pitch. Although he learned to play the trumpet and trombone in the band at Middleton High School, he also taught himself to play the guitar, violin and piano. Paul was a natural musician; filled to the brim with beautiful music to share with the world.

As for me, sixth in line, yet "baby sister" and "big sister" all wrapped up into one vivacious little person, my perspective on life with the Mussell clan was like no other —I guarantee you!

"A seven pound *purple* baby with black hair" is how Mama describes me at birth. Daddy chose my name from the Bible, and Mama agreed. When I was old enough to read, he showed me the passage of scripture from which my name was taken, and Mama told me that it meant "pleasant" or "happily victorious" and, as it turned out, it was prophetic—an accurate description throughout my entire life—because that's how I was. I have never had a day when I was not fully aware that God loved me, and that I was indeed His child. I always felt God's favor and blessing upon me, and knew beyond a shadow of doubt that he was guarding me with angelic protection and that his Holy Spirit was guiding my every step. My confidence in these spiritual truths was always very strong.

I was very much like my father in my love for Christian songs, music, and poetry. I loved reading, memorizing and writing them. I also followed him in his relish of evangelism, soul-winning and the study of God's Word. I easily identified with his strong work ethic and his life-long, solemn pursuit of spiritual things. He was also a Bible teacher, which I was privileged to do as well throughout my adult lifetime. From my dear mother, though, I was endowed with a bright enthusiasm for the smallest pleasures of life, from a butterfly or a bright blue sky to the line of a simple poem or the notes of a favorite song. So, I think it's accurate to surmise that my contribution to the Mussell blend was the flavor of confident zeal and eager anticipation, for the present and for the future.

My siblings and I shared a close bond of companionship and were very affectionate to one another. Mama taught us to love and appreciate our family;

to be honest and kind, practicing the Golden Rule. Matthew 7:12 tells us to do unto others as we would have them do unto us. This scriptural instruction indicates forethought; and can set a pattern in children's behavior from a young age that encourages response, rather than reaction, in communication with others! We were not only taught the importance of loving each other, but of showing love to others outside our family. We knew that we were each responsible for our own actions. We all played well together, and were eager to share and help each other however we could.

As the youngest sister I was a sponge, and loved being taught and nurtured by all of my older siblings; and Paul, my little brother, was sweet and adorable, never a tease or a bother. I was grateful for all of them and always felt loved. They were all special to me and I knew that I was special to them. This kind of love builds a deep inner confidence that is important for a fulfilling and happy life. I nurtured my own children with these same scriptural concepts. In John 13:34-35 (KJV), Jesus said, *"A new commandment I give unto you, that ye love one another. As I have loved you, that ye also love one another. By this shall all men know that ye are my disciples, if ye have love one to another."* God's love is the only reliable type; the only love that really lasts is *agape* (Greek), the unselfish and sacrificial kind. The sooner we can learn to practice it and teach it to our children, the better off we will all be; and the more peace and contentment we will enjoy in our homes and relationships.

My parents were very good to us and we loved them for the wonderful parents that they were! They nurtured us in scripture memorization, singing of hymns, including group harmony, and learning to play multiple instruments by ear. I was encouraged, by their example, to be resourceful and to make the most of what I had. They were diligent, hospitable, people of integrity whose individual strengths included strong faith in God and His plan for marriage and family living. Home was always a place of joy and comfort to me; a protective abode from the sharp edges of the world outside.

My relationship with my mother and father was always harmonious; I don't remember feeling any rebellion toward them. Instead, I wanted to please them; obedience came easy for me. My siblings and I saw their gracious, sacrificial living and respected it. We were taught to do what they asked and to honor them; we had the greatest confidence in their judgements. I don't remember disagreements about things. We wanted to follow their lead, and mirror their spiritual convictions. To me they were always "wise" and "right"! One time when we were getting ready for a street meeting, I tied a little scarf around the neck of my sweater. Daddy told me not to wear it because it looked worldly. It saddened me that he thought of me this way, because my motives were pure and innocent; but I took it off anyway and never wore it again. Honoring my father was much more important to me than the scarf.

Our parents were not only dedicated to providing the physical comforts of home, but they guarded our affections and emotional well-being even more.

Their protective leadership, paired with loving instruction, made for a happy and peaceable family life while preparing my heart to respond positively to truth and guidance. I was never unhappy at home; and I never saw anything selfish or crafty that would give me cause to question their motives. They wanted us to discover the great rewards of loving God and learning His ways, pure and simple. These principled ideals infused seven young personalities with the strength of our parents' resilient and experienced characters; and their proven life patterns soon became my own. As a teenager I felt totally responsible for my behavior, as well as my words and my thoughts. I loved the Lord, the Bible, the church, my family, and my life. I grew up with a very grateful heart, and a purposeful outlook.

Our world is not an easy place in which to live, and we all experience hardships, challenges, and events that take us by storm and cause hurt and heartache. God's will and plan for families, however, is to utilize all the tools He has provided for us and the guidelines He has given us to follow from His Word. When we are willing and determined to live by His plan, then we are surrounded by His protection and blessing. We are able to weather the ups and downs of life with strength and success, rather than being scattered or destroyed by them—which is the outcome that Satan would choose for us. Satan is a thief! He comes to steal, to kill, and to destroy; but Jesus came so we could have life... and have it more abundantly! (John 10:10)

Even with the obstacles along Life's way, some of which I will relay in this story, I can say that my mother and father lived life abundantly, and with great joy. Roots are important for a strong beginning, and mine were planted in the soil of hard work, devotion to family, and a deep love for God and His Word. As I grew to adulthood and experienced for myself the trials and challenges that life can bring, the admiration I had for Mama and Daddy became greater than ever! On the report card of raising a family well, they both get an A+ from me!

CHAPTER THREE

Life According to Me

On December 23, 1933 the little plant that grew to be *me* popped onto the scene of a busy Mussell household, and my life began to take shape. All the colorful strands of my ancestral history had now come to a place where some new colors would be woven into the tapestry of my God-ordained heritage—my colors. What direction would my branch of the Family Tree take? Would it be straight and monotonous? Would it grow with a twist or curve? What kind of blossoms would spring forth as I traveled my pathway; and what fruit would my branches bear? God held the secrets from which my story would spring, but the rest of the world could only look at this dark-eyed, dark-haired, fifth baby girl and wonder, "Who will she grow up to be?"

Abundance of Abodes: the Houses we made "Home"

Homedale, where my family lived when I was born, was a small settlement in a rural farming area of Idaho. My life began in this tiny community that my grandparents had named in the late 1800s, where only a small sign marked the spot on the road. I don't remember the house that my dad built here on the lower forty acres of my Grandpa Jacob Mussell's old farm, because I was just a baby when we moved; but when my older siblings talked about it they always called it "the square house."

We moved a lot, and lived in many different places—colorful bits and pieces of which I still remember well. Life was hard for most people back then, but seemed quite adventurous to my young mind as I gathered the sights, sounds and memories that were building the foundation for my future. As the littlest sister, I had a lot to keep track of and we were always busy...and often moving!

Early in 1935, Mama said we moved to Caldwell, "house and all!"[1] I was not old enough to take in the entire adventure, but the story goes that they cut the house in half and hauled it—one half at a time—on Grandpa's hay wagon! Mama's brothers, Jim and Joe, helped him. Apparently my dad had taken a Diesel Mechanics correspondence course and had gone to California to work as an apprentice for three months, because times were hard and he couldn't make a living on the farm during the Depression. He moved us to Caldwell to live close to Mama's parents while he was away. His plan was to save money and find a house before sending for us to come and join him in California. My little brother, Paul, was born on Easter Sunday, April 12, 1936—which was also Jewel's birthday—while we lived in the house at Caldwell. I was only two and a half years old so I don't remember that, nor our next move to another place we rented while Grandpa helped Mama sell her house and prepare to travel by train to California.

Preschool Perspectives

This train ride, at three and a half years old, was my first vivid memory and childhood recollection of any kind of trip; or more accurately, my first memory of anything. Daddy was already in California, so the rest of us packed up as much as we could into trunks for our move by rail, and Mama took her seven little ones on the train to Los Angeles by herself in May of 1937. It was great fun for me! I remember sitting on those big, leather bench seats that faced each other—half of us on one side and half on the other. The clickety-clickety-clack of the train wheels on the track was exciting; and when the older kids would hold me up, I could see the countryside passing by in the windows. I remember walking down the aisle to the restrooms and trying to keep my balance while the train was moving! Mama had a brown paper bag packed with sandwiches, bananas and graham crackers for our lunch. I remember the Porter bringing us pillows. I slept along the way, but I woke up as we were arriving at the depot. We got off the train into a crowd of people and many bystanders were noticing the charming spectacle of Mama with her brood of seven. As if it wasn't enough for a three-year-old to absorb, a man from the crowd pointed directly at me and said, "I'll take the brown-eyed one!"

Assuming he was serious, I was momentarily petrified until I looked up into Mama's smiling face and realized that I was safe. Soon we were united with Daddy and Uncle Ed, who were waiting for us at the depot. It was so exciting! We all loaded up in the car and drove to our new home!

Willowbrook Wringer

This house that Daddy rented in Willowbrook, a community in Los Angeles, California, is the first home I can remember. Even though I was just a little tyke, it seemed like new. As we ran through the house exploring our new territory I can remember shiny, clean, hardwood floors. There was a table with chairs in the dining room, and some kind of shallow pit by the back fence where we had to bury the garbage. I don't remember much more about this place, except for the old-fashioned Maytag wringer washing machine! It rings a bell in my memory because I caught my arm in it one day! I was watching Mama do the laundry and was fascinated with the moving rollers that could wring the water out of the clothes. She went in the other room to answer the door and told me not to touch the wringer, but the temptation was too great for my young, curious mind. I tried to use the stick to get an item of clothing started through the wringer, but it wouldn't catch so I reached in with my tiny hand to give it a poke. The wringer grabbed my fingers and I screamed for Mama as my arm went between the rollers. It was up to my elbow before she could hit the Emergency Release to turn it off and get me out. She had to run to the neighbor's house to call Daddy from work. His brother, Uncle Ed, brought him home so they could take me to the hospital.

I came home wearing a sling, and with a row of stitches under my arm, which generated lots of love and attention from the rest of the family for "poor little Eunie". The injury must have been minor, however, because I was swinging around in circles showing off my new sling when David, my brother, exclaimed, "Look at her! She's going to fall down and hurt it again! Stop spinning!" Later when Mama was telling the story to someone, she said, "When I heard that high-pitched squealing I thought it was the tea kettle whistling on the stove!"

Daddy's older brother, Ed, lived in Compton, California with his wife, Ina, and their boys, Donny and Jimmy. Uncle Ed was a car salesman and they had a nice home. They had beautiful furniture, and Ina was very domesticated. We only saw them occasionally, but I enjoyed these visits. Uncle Ed came to visit at Christmas-time wearing a Santa Claus suit with all the trimmings. We heard the bells ringing outside, but Rosemary saw him taking off the costume and ran in saying, "Guess what! I found out that Santa Claus is really Uncle Ed!" Later, Daddy put on the suit and we all got to sit on his knee and tell him what we wanted for Christmas. He asked me if I wanted a ragdoll, so I said, "Yes!" But I remember that I was disappointed with it because the neck was not stuffed firmly and the doll's head kept flopping forward. I wanted her to look at me like a "real" doll! I didn't want Daddy to know that I was sad about that, so I never said anything; but my sisters all got rubber dolls—the kind you can only find in antique stores these days—and I played with them whenever I could.

As young as I was, there were life-lessons at this house that I learned from and always remembered, even though they didn't happen to me; like when Jewel laid a rake in the grass, tines up, and then got hit in the head with the handle when she stepped on it later. At four, I learned how "not" to lay a rake in the grass!

Rosemary had a pair of skates at Willowbrook. I remember that while she was skating on the sidewalk outside our fence a mean dog ran after her and bit her so hard that it left a big scar on the back of her leg. To add insult to injury, she crashed into a concrete wall and knocked out several baby teeth! I remember Mama cleaning up her wound and warning us that we could contract hydrophobia from dog bites. It's no wonder that I was never too keen on dogs as pets for the rest of my life!

All the kids went to school in Willowbrook except me and my little brother, Paul, who was still a baby. Lois cried so hard in kindergarten that they let her quit and stay at home with us. This house was also the place where a neighbor boy who was playing in our yard burned Paul's face with a cap gun—point blank. The outcome, of course, was that none of us would be playing with the neighbor kids again!

Living out in the country most of the time we didn't have many neighbors but, when we did, some of them were family. This was the case when we moved to another place after less than a year at Willowbrook.

Our Lot at Lynwood

In April of 1938, we moved to a place called Lynwood where Daddy had purchased a large lot at 11073 Right Road on which to build us a new home. I have lots of memories of this place, even though I would not be five years old until December of that year! I remember lumber sitting around and Daddy working on things all over the place, even inside the house because it wasn't finished yet. I remember that he built an outhouse first—custom-made for a family with large, medium and small toilet holes and fitted lids! In the unfinished room where our bathroom was supposed to be he kept grain bins for feeding the goat and chickens he had purchased. But there was still ample space for our tin wash tub where we all got our baths each week.

The kitchen is still very clear to me; and I remember a couch—or divan as they were called in those days—in our living room on some kind of smooth, red floor that must have been colored concrete. Daddy built a nice fence around the back yard, and I remember watering a tree that he had planted in the front.

Two of Daddy's sisters, Aunt Lillian and Aunt Maimie, lived next door to us where they, too, had purchased a lot. The homes they had, however, were two old railroad cars that they converted into living spaces! In those days, the railroad would sell used boxcars to individuals very cheap. My aunts planted their yards with grass, flowers and trees. Another of my dad's sisters, Aunt Cora, bought us a big slide just like the ones in the park. Daddy got it set up solidly in our back yard and then proceeded to make a full playground! We had a swing, monkey bars, a teeter-totter, and even a sand box for little Paul. I thought we were rich with our big yard; a beautiful lawn in front and a regular playground out back!

Mama seldom allowed us to go to other people's houses, so everyone came to our house to play; and my, oh, my! How this home-grown paradise attracted the neighbors! Kitty-corner from us and across the alley were the Finleys. Next door were the Jacobson kids, Nate, Kenny and Ada Grace, who were always more than anxious to join us, calling over the fence, "Mrs. Mussell, can we come over and play?"

Mama had her rules, however, and after asking and receiving permission they could come over to play in the yard but were not allowed into the house. We played fast and furious for thirty to forty minutes and then Mama sent them all home with a smile. Besides fighting, the only thing that might send them home earlier was their use of slang: one byword like "gosh" or "golly" and they would be sent quickly on their way! So they promptly learned to mind their mouths!

The older kids helped with a nice garden that Daddy planted at Lynwood. I remember them talking about the tomatoes and Rosemary being so delighted to find a big, ripe one. Anyone who found one would take the salt-shaker and eat their tomato on the spot! So one day I decided to get in on the bounty and find one of my own. I went creeping through the tangle of vines in my little bare feet, only to come face to face with a big, fat tomato worm wielding its ugly horn! It scared me so bad that I ran lickety-split across the yard, spitting and spluttering and shaking my hands as if I had been slimed! That creature was so disgusting that I never entered the garden again!

Daddy had built a pen and a stanchion for our milk goat. I was always curious and interested in those things so he would show me how he led the goat up onto the small platform and locked its head in between the boards so it would stand still while he milked it. When he brought in the warm milk Mama would strain it through cheesecloth and refrigerate it. Daddy enjoyed drinking the milk warm but I remember that it had a very unique taste that Mama didn't like at all—even though she told us that it was very healthy for us to drink. I probably would have liked it since I was so young and impressionable, but when my older siblings expressed their distaste for it I assumed that I shouldn't like it either. When Mama made cocoa with it, however, I remember thinking it was quite tasty after all!

Daddy planted a lawn inside our new picket fence and I remember sprinklers watering the grass, which was a new concept since we were used to irrigation on our farmland. We also had a dog named Bowdger; and I remember that we raised some baby chicks. Some of them provided fresh eggs upon reaching full-grown status; but eventually they were all invited to dinner one by one. They got to sit "on the menu" while the rest of us thanked the Lord for his provision, and enjoyed them very much!

I reached school age while living at Lynwood and, although I later walked to school with my brother and sisters, my mother went with me on the first day of kindergarten. I was frightened, so she walked to school with me and sat in the back of my classroom for a while. I kept looking to see if she was still there as I participated in the activities. When I realized she was gone, the tears began to flow. She had pinned a pretty handkerchief to my dress yoke, which I thought was just for looks; but when she got up and left the room, I realized the true reason. I could not hold back the tears; they gushed like a river and soaked my hankie, although I never made a sound.

Lois was having the same problem in her first grade classroom, so they finally walked her down the hall and let her join me in kindergarten! When I saw her I was comforted, and actually dried my own tears so that I could console my sister. She got to be there for a few days until she got used to things. I remember sweet, Miss Butterfield, and the play stations with all the housekeeping amenities that we had at home—including a tiny ironing board and iron. It was not long until I decided that I liked school very much! I even remember some of the songs we sang:

> *Sailing, sailing, red and purple and yellow!*
> *Each balloon, will be soon, out of sight in the sky!*

Or...

> *Little Ducky Duddle, went swimming in a puddle;*
> *Went swimming in a puddle quite small. "Quack! Quack!"*
> *Said he, "It doesn't matter how much I splash and splatter!*
> *"I'm only a duckie, after all! "Quack! Quack!"*[2]

Another favorite was:

Toodle-umma-lumma; toodle-umma-lumma, toodle-aye-ay!
Any um-berellas? Any um-berellas to mend today?
I'll mend up your troubles and go on my way,
Singing, Toodle-umma-lumma, toodle-umma-lumma;
Toodle-aye-ay![3]

For some reason it was easy for me to remember songs and I sang them over and over again at home after learning them in kindergarten. Singing was something I always loved, so the fact that it was a regular classroom activity back then most likely enhanced my overall school experience.

One day, however, it seems I was a little *too* eager to get there! I was out the door and on my way to school as usual; but, as I climbed over the back fence, I felt an exceptionally cold breeze under my dress and realized that I had jumped out of the tin tub that morning and into my school dress, forgetting my underpants. I quickly ran back to the house and told my mother, to which she exclaimed with mortification, "Oh, my child; my child!" and straightway remedied the matter before sending me on my way again!

We moved so often that we never could keep our school friends for very long, but I do remember some of them fondly, and Edna was my first. She was in my class and had decided that she liked me best of all, so we became fast friends! Her cousin, Dickie, said he liked me, too; so they called me his girlfriend, and my school-day adventures began.

One day Edna begged me to walk home with her so I could see where she lived. I kept saying, "No!" but she pursued me until I finally gave in. I was afraid that I would be unable to find my way home, but with her pleading I decided that maybe it would be a harmless detour. On the contrary, as I turned around to go home everything looked different from that direction and, to my horror, I got lost! I walked up and down the sidewalk trying to find my path but to no avail, and soon I began to cry. Finally, a lady came walking by and asked why I was crying but I couldn't answer her without crying harder so I just kept wiping my tears.

"Well," she snapped, "has the cat got your tongue?"

Being scolded by a stranger did not help at all and as I cried even harder and retraced my steps, I decided to pray with all my might. "Please, Jesus! Help me find my way home!"

Suddenly I saw a dirt road that I recognized, which we called "the brown road", and with a sob of relief I gladly turned toward home. I was so thankful and happy that I was soon skipping along swinging my lunch pail. I came running into the house with such great joy that when Mama asked me why I was late, it took me completely off guard and I burst into tears and lied, repeating something I had heard my older siblings say. "The teacher kept us after school because someone was talking!"

My five-year-old heart smote me to the core for telling my mother a lie; but I was afraid that if I told her about going to Edna's I would get a spanking. The sobbing drew pity from both my parents as they sat at the kitchen table so, to comfort me, Mama gave me a whole banana that was leftover in Daddy's lunch pail. I am quite sure that this incident went a long way in making the banana my favorite fruit for life. I didn't reveal my lie to Mama until much later after I became a Christian; but when I finally did, I still got a good scolding!

This spot on my little road of life is where I became fully engaged with another branch that sprouted on my tree—the branch of my Journey of Faith—fully-budded with the beautiful people in The Body of Christ! While growing up, most of our extracurricular activities growing up were centered around the church. The first special 'group' I remember being a part of was our Children's Church.

We began attending *Jesus Name Pentecostal Church* in Los Angeles at the corner of 87th and Avalon. I loved the singing most of all, and still know many of the songs I learned there at such a young age. My favorite things were special numbers when individuals or small groups would sing solos, duets, or other group songs in harmony.

I was still too young to read the hymnals proficiently, yet I memorized everything I heard and sang the words with all my might! One song included these lines:

> *"…In that land there'll be no sorrow and no tears will dim the eye;*
> *But it'll be a bright tomorrow in that golden by and by."*

To my little ears, however, the second phrase sounded like, *"But it'll be alright to borrow…"* Imagine my embarrassment when I got old enough to read the actual lyrics and realized that I had been bellowing out the wrong words all along with utmost confidence and enthusiastic delight!

At this tender stage of life, I learned to love the saints and to consider them my extended family. Here at 87th and Avalon, I gained a strong foundation of the biblical teaching about the Family of God; the understanding that they were my brothers and sisters in Christ. We had wonderful fellowship with many kind and loving Christian people who became friends for life. Sadly, I believe that today's busy parents do not realize the valuable impact of Christ-centered activities and fellowship in constructing a strong foundation from which their children can build successful lives. Even at six years old, seeing my parents' dedication to what they believed had a profound influence on my life and future.

We always loved going to church, and I never remember a time when it was not a highlight of our lives. I've never gotten over that feeling, and it's still the delight of my life to be in the House of the Lord worshipping with the saints and hearing the Word of God. I miss a lot of those good old songs, and I'd like to hear those spontaneous testimony services again where everyone participated; but the love that I developed over seventy-five years ago is still going strong. Church is still my favorite place to be!

Elementary Era

In October of 1940 when we moved again I was six and a half, and I well remember giving our nice big slide to our neighbors, the Finleys! It seems that this move must have had something to do with my father's health because he was struggling with bouts of asthma. Daddy gave away everything that would not fit in a small utility trailer. I was nearly seven, and that trip back to Idaho is still vivid in my mind. We sang most of the way and on this trip we girls all learned how to harmonize! Rosemary had an excellent ear for music and picked out the alto parts. Jewel joined her while Dorcas, Lois and I sang soprano.

I still remember the songs, one of which was:

> *Following Jesus, every passing day;*
> *Nothing can harm you when He leads the way!*
> *Sunshine or shadow, on your pathway fall;*
> *Jesus, my Savior, is my all in all!*[4]

Daddy, Mama, Paul and David rode in the front seat, with us five girls in the back. Mama had packed food for the journey so we either stopped beside the road to eat, or ate while traveling. In those days, people carried a big canteen on their car and when the radiator would heat up on the mountain roads we

would stop and pour water from the canteen into the radiator. Mama always had us praying to get over the summits without over-heating the car. There were no Rest Areas with facilities in those days, so when it was time for a bathroom break, we jumped out of the car and scattered in several directions in search of bushes to hide behind!

Caldwell: Misfortune to Miracles

When we got to Caldwell, we stayed at my grandparents' house for a week or so and I remember the excitement of being there. They had a gushing artesian well on their property and Grandpa Bunt explained to us what that meant: that the water source never ran dry and the well continually bubbled forth with clear, clean water from under the ground to water his crops and stock. He was a hard-working farmer, and Grandma was a picture of domestic perfection! I remember her crowded china cabinet, and all the pretty jelly jars and pickle dishes she would use on her table!

When Daddy found a little green house to rent, we settled in; but, in my young memory, it seemed like a very, very old house with worn linoleums and odd, stuffy smells. No sooner had we unpacked than my sister, Dorcas, became very ill. She was ten years old and almost died. I remember that we were placed in isolation and our house was branded by the County with an orange sign that hung outside on our garage saying, "QUARANTINED".

My mother's journal account says:

> We were Christian people who believed in divine healing. The people around us told us if we didn't get a doctor, the law would get after us. Daddy wasn't feeling well at all, but he walked uptown Caldwell and talked to a doctor about Dorcas. The doctor said, 'I won't take her case because the last typhoid patient I had died.' He told Daddy that we would have to be quarantined because all the rest of our family would get the disease, and we would have to put Dorcas in the hospital.
>
> Daddy came home and said, 'I have seen a doctor so they can't get after me now. I will take care of Dorcas myself.' He put a bed in the front room for her, and a cot on one side of the room for himself to sleep on. He said, 'I will take care of Dorcas, and you can take care of the other kids and yourself.' We had two bedrooms and a kitchen for the kids and myself; we kept completely away from where Dorcas and Daddy were. He put a chart on the wall to keep track of her fever temperature every day.
>
> Dorcas went through six weeks very sick. When she began to get well, she craved for food, but Daddy was very careful to only give her very small helpings. Her teeth rattled so badly that the rest of us could hear it from the kitchen. While she was sick those six weeks, all the other kids went to school except Paul, who was only four years old. The kids and I were all healthy the whole time. No one else took the typhoid fever as the doctor had said we would.
>
> Dorcas got well, and was up and dressed in her clothes, walking around, when Daddy decided to go back into town and see the doctor. He took the fever chart with him and talked to the doctor about Dorcas. The doctor said, 'Well, don't let her walk for a few days.' Daddy told him that she had been up and walking around for three days already! Then the doctor said, 'Well, I want to come down and take some blood from her to send to Boise for testing.' So he came to the house and took Dorcas' blood to send for testing. The answer came back that it was the regular, old-time Typhoid Fever—two strains![5]

It was a big event, and I remember scenes such as my parents wearing cloth over their mouths to protect them from germs while caring for my sister; and Mama boiling all the dishes Dorcas used and sterilizing all of her clothes. I remember the smell of Clorox that she used to keep surfaces clean. There were some pleasant scents and sounds, too: like the smell of wood fires as residents in our neighborhood began to counter the cool Fall temperatures with cozy, wood fires burning in their homes; the sound of the lonely train horn on a nearby track, or the mill whistle blowing in the distance, signaling shift changes or lunch breaks for all the workers on the job.

I remember that when Dorcas was almost well, Mama opened the door to the living room and let us look in at our sister. She was very skinny, sitting on the edge of the bed, and had a scarf tied around her little bald head because the fever had caused her to lose all of her hair. Mama was singing the victory all over the house! It was a miracle; because in those days Typhoid Fever was a fatal disease and many victims died. For us, it was an unforgettable experience and a family faith-builder!

As soon as she recovered, we moved back to California, packed in the car like sardines and pulling a small utility trailer behind filled with all our meager belongings. In my mind, it seems like we sang all the way! I remember singing "Friendship with Jesus":

A friend of Jesus; O what bliss!
That one so weak as I
Should ever have a friend like this,
To lead me to the sky.

Chorus: Friendship with Jesus; fellowship divine!
O what blessed sweet communion;
Jesus is a friend of mine!

A friend to lead me in the dark
A friend who knows the way;
A friend to steer my weak, frail bark;
A friend, my debts to pay.

A friend when Life's rough voyage is o'er;
A friend when Death is past;
A friend to meet on Heaven's shore;
A friend, when home at last! [6]

Sometimes Mama, Daddy, and the boys would join in, but it was mostly us girls. Rosemary and Jewel would always sing the alto; Dorcas, Lois and I would sing the melody.

As we were driving and singing along, one wheel came off our utility trailer and went whizzing by the car, bouncing over the gullies and desert terrain beside the road! Mama saw it first and Daddy heard the axle dragging and stopped as quickly as possible. David jumped out and ran after the runaway wheel and found that it was in good shape. Daddy fixed it and we continued our trip with no further problems. In fact, we actually had a nice surprise in store! David spotted a large box alongside the road and exclaimed about his find. So, Daddy pulled over and allowed him to jump out of the car to investigate. Low and behold, David discovered it to be filled with individual-sized boxes of dry cereal—all different varieties! Daddy tied the box on our trailer and we enjoyed eating them for snacks throughout the trip.

Lifelong Impressions from Ivy Street

So, by December we were on our way back to California. Mama's account defines a difficult transition.[7] She remembers that we stayed in a motel at Bliss, Idaho and then slept in our car at Baker, California (imagine that night for a family of nine!) It is not surprising that they found a dealership in Los Angeles the next day where they promptly traded their utility trailer and bought a house trailer! This new mode of accommodation was pulled first to Indio and then back to Redlands, California where we ended up in a trailer court. Due to unknown details that only parents need struggle with, we returned to Los Angeles where Daddy rented another small trailer house to add to our own. We lived a little more comfortably until he found a house near the Firestone Plant where he had landed a job, once again with General Motors! To a nearly-seven-year-old, this was simply more high adventure on the Road of Life! Yet this arrangement was not to last; for on New Year's Day of 1941 we moved into a house on Ivy Street in a Hispanic neighborhood in East Los Angeles. Daddy immediately called the health department and had a nurse come out and give all of us shots! He didn't want anyone else getting sick like Dorcas did. The nurse administered vaccinations to all of us for diphtheria, tetanus, and whooping cough. I remember cute, little Paul sitting with his bottom lip protruding in a desperate pucker and wiggling his little toes as fast as he could to keep from crying while getting his shots.

I was now seven years old and in the second grade. I remember that our house number was "8735" and we had a white picket fence. I remember the bathtub at Ivy Street because we didn't have a bathtub at many of the places we lived. We were taught to conserve everything: no more than two inches of water in the tub; never drop the bar of soap into the water because it melts away and soap is expensive; hurry along and use your time wisely because others are waiting to bathe.

There was a sidewalk going up to a front porch where a swing was hanging from chains. I remember that we had a fireplace in the living room and a built-in china hutch. We were not allowed to go outside the fence without permission but it was never a temptation. Ivy Street is where I learned to play oodles of wonderful childhood games with my siblings. Mama taught us games for rainy days like *Button, Button; Who's got the Button?* and *Guess What I'm Hiding In?* Some of our ongoing favorite games were *Pick-Up Sticks*, *Checkers* or *Chinese Checkers*, *Jacks*, *Hopscotch* and *Marbles*. Mama allowed neighborhood children to come into our yard to play for half an hour at a time and they always wanted to because, with our big family, we could play any game imaginable! There was always a line of kids playing *Jump-rope*, plenty for *Hide and Go Seek* and a big enough group to choose teams for all kinds of ball games or *Kick the Can*.

I don't know why, but there seems to have been a lot of flies around the area—which Mama and Daddy both hated. So Daddy would give us a penny for every 100 flies we killed! We could walk around the corner to a tiny mom and pop grocery store and buy bubble gum or BB Bats, which were small taffy suckers flavored with chocolate, strawberry, vanilla, or banana.

There was a large apricot tree in the yard that we used to climb. We would sit up high in the branches to talk and tell stories. There was also a large vacant lot where Daddy had made a place to go and pray. The grass and weeds were taller than I was; but there was a beaten path that led to his solitary place. It was like a small room surrounded by walls of tall grass. I guess they didn't realize in those days that asthma could be aggravated by grass and weeds because our father went here frequently. We called it "Daddy's Secret Prayer Fort". I was afraid to be there alone but with a sister or two it was fun and exciting, although Mama didn't let us go very often.

Our father was always interested in witnessing to all the neighbors so we were also active in our neighborhood with door-to-door evangelism. We handed out gospel tracts, held weekly street meetings, and invited neighbors over for meetings in our home. My brother, David, made a pulpit and benches and set up a Children's Church in our garage. We always seemed to have hymnbooks around so we invited neighborhood children to come and learn all of our church songs and to hear Bible stories. David preached salvation messages and we led some of them to the Lord.

Once again, we attended the Pentecostal church on the corner of 87th and Avalon that we had grown to love when we lived in California the first time. Our family attended this church faithfully under three different pastors; and when we returned this time, the Wyricks were there. I remember Brother Wyrick most because he was a good preacher and I enjoyed listening to him speak. Our previous pastor had gone into evangelistic work and was holding tent meetings in East Los Angeles. Daddy took us to some of those meetings, and I remember my folks calling him a "fiery preacher". One story had him climbing the tent poles while illustrating his sermon!

The orchestra was also thrilling to me; and I still remember the man who played the drums. His son played a saxophone and another man played both the Hawaiian guitar and a harmonica. Brother Jack played some black rhythm "bones"; and Brother Thurman played the guitar. Later, when Buddy and Billy Hume took the pastorate, Sister Billy played the piano—Evangelistic style! Those Pentecostal pianists were always the best; such as those who played for the great quartets and southern gospel singers later in my life. Their fingers flew all over the piano, enriching the main melody. It was beautiful and inspiring!

In this particular church, the sanctuary was upstairs and the Children's

Church was downstairs; how I loved it! There were tiny benches all in a row that the men of the church had made kid-sized just for us. Daddy taught the Adult Sunday School class and also filled positions as a deacon, usher and the Secretary-Treasurer, who counted the offerings. My memory is full to the brim of the many revival meetings, all night prayer meetings, street meetings, tent meetings, camp meetings, and fellowship dinners on Sundays after the services. Sometimes after dinner we even had afternoon services with foot-washings, communion, singing and prayer. We had so many happy times, often staying through the afternoon until the evening service. The preaching was always anointed and powerful; the singing, victorious and happy. The atmosphere was vibrant with shouting, hand-shaking and clapping—a wonderful place to be! Following every service was a call to prayer at the altar, which was a sacred and holy place to me. I knew God was there with us and that He was happy to have us gathering in His presence.

Brother and Sister Wyrick were elderly people who loved to sing. They performed special numbers from time to time for the congregation. I remember Brother Wyrick playing his banjo and singing an old song that delighted all the children called "This Train". It was a catchy tune about the gospel train that was bound for heaven carrying all those who had put their trust in Christ. This popular song boldly described those who could *not* ride the gospel train as well, allowing the singers to insert a wide variety of societal vices! Many vocal artists sang their own versions through the years and I heard several different renditions. The churches of that time had more individual participation in the services. Many people sang special numbers or gave personal testimonies before the congregation. Anything to do with music was a highlight for me. We sat up close on the second or third row, with Mama, Lois and Paul in the next row behind us. We all got baptized in the Holy Spirit at this church, except for my little brother, Paul.

I loved the people and still remember many of them; we gained many friends who were with us through thick and thin. Daddy had an emergency appendectomy, and also became very ill with asthma at the same time. Our church family surrounded us with love and support, and was a great blessing to us.

When the Wyricks moved away and the Humes came to pastor, they had a tiny little girl named Carol Ann—I thought she was the cutest thing that ever was! They were all little people; Sister Billy was probably less than five feet tall. Carol Ann could sing like a bird when she was only two years old, and with the greatest confidence!

Another family I remember had come from somewhere in the Ozarks, as revealed by their thick southern drawl! They had a little girl named Betty who was close to my age and invited me over. This was never a practice in our family, but Mama allowed me to go home with them one time between the morning and evening Sunday services. My mother made a learning experience out of everything, and there was a lesson attached to this experience that I never forgot.

The next day, she gently scolded me for whining. She said, "You have always been a happy little girl; but ever since you got home from your friend's house you have been whining about things! If that is going to happen I will never let you go there again!"

"I named you 'Eunice' because that means 'pleasant'!" she continued. "Your name means 'happily victorious'; and I won't have my little happy girl whining like this!" What a memorable lesson that was for me! From then on I recognized how easy it was to be influenced by others and how important it was for me to always guard my character and live up to my name!

Well, life is full of learning, and one day I decided it was my turn to skate! I was the little sister and rarely got a turn to use the roller skates—not to mention that I really didn't know how to attach them to my shoes like my sisters did! But on this day, I got them tightened properly and went sailing down the sidewalk with glee. Soon I heard my name being called and skated back to the house to discover that my Dad was waiting inside to talk to me. Off went the skates, as I wondered why he had called me back so soon.

"Eunice, you know that this is the Lord's Day, and you shouldn't be outside skating. This is not just like any other day; we keep this day holy unto the Lord. If you go out and skate you'll get all dirty before the evening service, and even show a bad example to our neighbors that we are trying to witness to! Now put your hands out for a swat to help you remember."

I stretched my hands in front of me, palms up; but he made me turn them over and proceeded to gently slap my knuckles several times with the handle of the fly swatter. Then he lovingly reminded me that on Sunday I was always free to rest, read my Sunday School papers, play games or sing songs in my room; but not to play outside. I remember many quiet Sunday afternoons like this with all of us engaging in quiet activities. Sometimes Dorcas would take me out to the front porch swing and read gospel tracts to me. There was one I remember very well that was a true story about a man named Cuff.

"*Cuff was a negro slave who lived in the South before the war. He was a joyful Christian and a faithful servant…*" the story begins. It goes on to describe how this humble man witnessed faithfully to his angry, abusive master about the Gospel of Christ. Finally the evil man became very ill and called for Cuff to come and pray for him. When he was healed of his illness he gave his life to the Lord, treated his servants kindly, and promoted Cuff to an important position on his estate. I loved this story with its happy ending!

During this time Daddy was having severe asthma attacks, which he had struggled with off and on for several years; so our family prayed and fasted a lot. Sometimes they had to put a bed in the living room, against the wall near the front porch, where Mama would prop him up with pillows at night. We learned to stand together in faith, believing that God would answer our prayers. Rosemary had a school friend from a family with seven children like ours; her father had asthma too, and one day we heard that he had died during the night.

As their family planned his funeral I realized, even as a small girl, how imminent death could be; I hoped and prayed that my daddy would not die.

Mama worried often as well, and would fret aloud, "Oh! I don't know what I would do if Daddy died! I can't work; I need to take care of my children! I can't drive a car and have never held an outside job! Daddy's the breadwinner! I'm going to fast and pray!" One time she fasted a whole week without even a drop of water. "Well, Moses fasted without food or water!" she reminded us, and thought she should do it that way, too!

She created our own Family Prayer Chain to petition God for Daddy's healing. Inside a walk-in closet, Mama set up a box with an alarm clock on top. We took turns praying for Daddy in fifteen-minute intervals. She said we were going to do this until Daddy was healed of asthma! An older sibling would set the clock for my fifteen minutes; but it sure seemed longer than that when I could hear the girls outside playing jump rope and chanting, *"Down by the river, down by the sea, Johnny broke a bottle and blamed it on me!..."* Yet I soon learned to focus my mind and pray fervently so that, before long, I was surprised at how fast the time passed.

We prayed more fervently than ever and the church people joined us. The elders came many times to anoint Daddy with oil and laid hands on him to pray for his healing. Sometimes he would get a little better, and at one of these times he invited a neighbor to come over and play his guitar for our family so he could share the gospel with him. This man had known the Lord at one time so when he came he began to sing some of the old gospel songs he remembered. We joined in, too, as he played his guitar with eyes full of tears. Daddy was an Evangelist through thick and thin—never too busy to share the "Wonderful Story of Love" with a lost soul.

Finally, our father became so ill that he could no longer perform his job at General Motors in Los Angeles and finally, after only four months of employment there, he had to quit because of his illness. With no employment, there was no money for food; and I remember Mama telling us that we had to fast, even as growing children. One time I was so hungry I opened the refrigerator to look inside and there was nothing but a lemon! Lois decided she was hungry enough to eat it—rind and all! It made her sick, however, and was promptly regurgitated!

I remember going outside to find other things that might be edible and coming upon a loquat tree which, although mostly bare, provided a few bite-sized fruits to eat. At that time people could buy bread for a penny per loaf; and a large bag—about the size of a plastic garbage bag—full of various day-old loaves such as white or rye bread for only a dollar. Though Mama didn't have a dollar to her name, she must have found a penny and sent David for a loaf of bread. We found a jar of mustard to spread on slices of bread—our food for the day. It must have seemed like manna to me because I still love mustard on my bread!

The next day there was a box of groceries on the porch. I remember Mama drying her eyes with the corner of her apron as she thanked God for the kind church people who brought the food when we needed it so badly.

During this time, Daddy took a trip to Idaho with a couple of his sisters and stayed for three weeks. I'm guessing he believed that Idaho's fresh air would improve his health and went to investigate the possibilities, leaving Mama alone with us kids. One time, when she sent David to Watts for bread, he was confronted and threatened with knives by a Mexican mob in the area called the "Zoot-suiters". A 'zoot suit' was a men's suit with high-waisted, wide-legged, tight-cuffed, pegged trousers and a long coat with wide lapels and wide padded shoulders, although these particular teens sported only the suit jacket with their blue jeans. This style of clothing became popular in the Mexican and Italian-American communities (among others) during the 1940s.[8] It was widely reported that this loose-fitted clothing was chosen by the mobsters because they could fit their weapons in the pockets—inside and out. Although these weapons were brandished with evil intent that day, God protected David and he was able to get away from them without injury.

Mama says we quit going to church because Daddy was too sick to drive the car and the pastor had told us to stay home. She says Daddy knelt beside the davenport four days and four nights, fully dressed in his clothes but unable to lie down and sleep because of his asthma. Mama continued to fast and pray and one day the Lord sent a man of God.

Elijah in Disguise

Daddy had gotten a little better and had taken the car to the church to take care of the offering, the books and his other duties as deacon and Secretary/ Treasurer at our church. Since he was an evangelist at heart, he always carried gospel tracts with him. That day when he came out of the church and locked it up, there was an elderly man on the bus bench in front of the church. Daddy went over to give him a tract and talk to him about the Lord; but just as he approached him, the man pulled a tract out of his own shirt pocket and gave it to Daddy! This prompted a great conversation which became a life-long friendship. The man was Brother John Sivak, a true prophet and evangelist. He told my father that he lived in New York but that, as he was praying, God had told him to go to Los Angeles, California. When he got off the bus, he said, "Lord, I am here. Where do you want me to go now?"

The Lord said, "Get on that streetcar and ride it as far as it goes," which he did. It ended at Firestone Boulevard. He wanted to cross the street where there were more houses so he could hand out gospel tracts; but the Lord told him to stay on this side of the street. After he had walked about a block, he came to the church and sat down on that bench to wait. After talking for a while Brother Sivak said, "I see you are a sick man," and Daddy told him about his asthma.

"I will pray for you, and God will heal you," Brother Sivak answered.

Daddy answered politely, "I have already been to everyone who prays for the sick; well-known preachers and evangelists."

"Well," Brother Sivak replied with assurance, "I will pray for you and you will be healed."[9]

So, Daddy brought him home for dinner and to meet our family. God had already prepared Mama because during her fasting she had prayed, "God, don't you have any more 'Elijahs'?" When Brother Sivak got out of the car and she saw his bushy, white eyebrows and his thick mustache and beard, she said that something leaped inside her spirit and she said aloud, "The Prophet Elijah!"

He prayed the prayer of faith that began the long-awaited process for the healing of Daddy's body. For five years he had suffered with this affliction, going down from a healthy weight of one hundred and seventy pounds to a weak one hundred and eleven pounds. Although it was not instantaneous, he got progressively better until he was completely well and was never bothered by asthma again!

Brother Sivak remained very close to our family through the years. He came often to stay with us. He was a Czechoslovakian Jew who walked close to God and could hear God's voice. He lived entirely by faith, just like an Old Testament prophet, and always carried a bottle of anointing oil with him. A godly widow had given him a room to live in rent-free so that he could do street evangelism and go wherever God directed him to go. He was a street preacher, and told stories of how people persecuted him and scoffed at his message, and how God used him in spite of it to lead many to faith in Christ. He loved my dad because they had the same heart and vision for the lost; they always had good fellowship together.

"Thank the good Lord for His mercy; glory, Hallelujah!" he would often proclaim in song. John Sivak told us that he prayed for our family every day, lifting each of the seven children by name to the Lord. God had raised his own little five-year-old girl from the dead in answer to his prayers when he had taken her in his arms and commanded life to come back into her body. After being dead for some time, she opened her eyes and came back to life! He was full of amazing stories of dreams, visions and revelations that God had given to him. We always listened with awe as he told of great healings and multiple miracles that God had performed as he went all over spreading the gospel and praying for the sick. We were greatly impressed by the power of God that flowed daily through this man's life, and how God supplied all of his personal needs. As a child, I didn't get all the details but I was greatly influenced by his life and experiences.

One time God told him to go to a certain place where he would meet a crippled woman that God wanted to heal. He was directed to Figueroa Street, one of the longer streets in the city that runs through Los Angeles neighborhoods for over thirty miles.[10] There he saw a lady walking down the street that was bent over at the waist. He asked her if she believed Jesus would heal her. She said she did, so he responded immediately with a very frank prayer of faith. "In the Name of Jesus, straighten yourself up!"

The woman immediately stood straight and began to walk normally. She thanked him and went on her way rejoicing!

Another time Brother Sivak told of seeing a vision where a huge snake stretched completely across the sky. He prayed against it and it disappeared, but he believed God was showing him the extent of the evil spreading across the world. Our family revered him as a great man of God—a holy man on par with the prophets of old.

Our father's miraculous healing made a life-long impression on all of us. We saw the suffering, the fasting, the crying out to God for help again and again; and we saw God answer prayer. We felt the grief and saw the pain; but we saw the victory, too, and rejoiced together in God's goodness and mercy. We endured the hardships of life, but learned how to "look to the hills" for help from above—as the Psalmist wrote—and to wait on God until the answer came. We learned faith, hope, persistence and resilience. Our cup of trembling became a dose of nourishment, sweetened with a supernatural grace and fortified with strength that has lasted our whole lives through. We learned the value of hardships that send us running to Jesus.

Arkansas Adventure

When Daddy came home from his trip to Idaho some church friends, the Edmonds, wanted him to go to Arkansas with them to start a church. They said the small community could not support a pastor so the little church had been closed and the windows boarded up. They explained that there would be a rent-free house for our family to live in if Daddy would take up the pastorate. So we packed up for another Mussell Family Adventure and hit the road for the Ozarks with old Mr. Edmonds, his son Clarence, and pregnant daughter-in-law. On the way, Mrs. Edmonds wanted to ride in the car and visit with Mama and Daddy, so she asked if we kids could ride in the back of her husband's truck. He had a bed back there and plenty of room so Daddy agreed. Their boxes and furniture were tied into the front part, with the bed in the back. We were all having so much fun riding in the back and watching the scenery whiz by through the wooden slats!

After a couple of hours, Daddy began to blow the horn and when we pulled over he said he wanted all of us back in the car. The desert sunset dominated the landscape as it began to get dark near San Simon, Arizona. Mama always brought blankets in the car because there was no heater; and I remember getting into a cozy spot and feeling sleepy. Before long, I woke up to someone saying, "Oh, no! That's Clarence!"

There he stood, all covered with blood and waving his hat. As Daddy pulled over to the side of the road and jumped out, Clarence cried, "I turned the truck over and I think I killed my dad!"

Daddy always protected us from seeing bad things so he ran back to the car and said, "Everybody stay in the car! Give me the flashlight; quick!"

Clarence had fallen asleep at the wheel and their truck had careened over an embankment, spreading their furniture and belongings all over the desert! No one was killed, but they were bruised and scraped. Mama turned the incident into another life-lesson and exhorted us later, "Daddy felt like all of you kids should get back in our own car; and if you hadn't willingly obeyed you could have been killed in this wreck. Praise the Lord for His protection!"

Mama's journal says that when we got going again, their truck was being pulled behind our car and small utility trailer. In the mountains near Lordsberg, New Mexico our car broke down and we discovered that the axle had broken from the stress of pulling the additional weight of their truck. So we took Mr. and Mrs. Edmonds with their baby into our car with our family of nine and sat there all night long waiting for morning. We cooked pancakes over a sagebrush fire and then the men went for help in town while the women and children stayed in the desert with the vehicles. It was February and the weather was cold and windy. We got the axle fixed and the Edmonds rented a motel room where we stayed overnight and took baths.

Our family started out alone for Arkansas then, because our friends had to wait for their own truck to be repaired before they could continue the trip. We broke down again near Pecos, Texas and had to look for another axle.[11] My brother, David, had been scolded for tormenting one of the girls and his punishment was to sit on the running board of the car and remain still. While he sat there, he watched Mama trying to get a fire started for cooking; but the desert wind kept blowing it out. So he came up with another one of his ingenious inventions.

"If you'll let me get up from this running board," he offered respectfully, "I will make you a fire that won't blow out." He carved out a place in the bank alongside the road that was sheltered from the wind.

We were there for three days, cooking anything we could find to eat. When the axle was fixed once more, we traveled on and finally reached Arkansas. The road into our destination was washed out and rocky, and we were very disappointed to discover that the house was totally unlivable! The windows were broken out and boarded up; the doors were off the hinges; and the spring was polluted and full of pollywogs! We found an old teeter-totter hidden in the tall weeds and ran out to play! Before long, however, we heard Mama's frantic voice calling us back. "You kids get in here quick! There are ticks and chiggers in Arkansas and you'll get bit if you don't get out of those weeds!"

It was getting dark and there was no electricity in the house; so she gave us a bite to eat and we made our beds on the floor for the night. In the middle of the night, we were awakened by Mama's frantic whispers, "Kids, get up! Quick! Daddy's dying; he can't breathe! We have to go back to California!" Daddy was having a severe asthma attack and, between the Arkansas climate and that old country shack, he was apparently getting worse by the minute. We had to leave that place.

"Pray!" Mama directed us in low, anxious tones. "Get your shoes on!"

She and David threw everything back in the car and the bedding in the trailer. Mama was so little; but I remember her and David struggling to get the mattress on top, cover it with the tarp and tie it on with ropes while Daddy sat gasping in the driver's seat. Mama sat beside him to help him drive and shift gears and David was up front, too. It was very traumatic as we headed out through the damp fog and tall weeds, but I was graced with the ability to sleep under almost any circumstances and soon drifted off. I awoke to a sunny, desert morning with a clear blue sky. Daddy was driving down a smooth highway and seemed to be breathing fine! We stopped alongside the road for a while and built a fire on the sand where Mama could cook a pot of beans in a cast iron pot. As we waited, a fat meadowlark flew into an overhead wire and fell right in front of us. Daddy plucked and roasted it and everybody but Mama got one bite.

After traveling a while longer, our car stalled next to an abandoned service station. We needed water, so Daddy hitch-hiked into the nearest town to get help. David now had the idea that he could kill birds for food. There were many of them nesting under the eaves of the old station, so he began pelting them with rocks. Mama was sad, as she sat with her little brood in the middle of the desert and as she watched David she said, "That poor child has tried all day to get a bird for food!"

As she walked and prayed, she found a tiny stickpin that said, *"PEACE"* and took it as a token of God's grace and help in our time of need. She kept that little pin all her life in a treasure box until she died. The same day, she found seven cents in the sand and exclaimed with praise that it would buy a can of milk for our cornmeal mush. So Daddy bought one the next time he hitched a ride into town.

We were out in the middle of nowhere and not one car came along to stop and help us. We just waited, and prayed. Rosemary and I were running barefoot in the sand, following David as he pointed out cactuses and other desert plants.

"Stop!" he shouted suddenly. "There are snakes everywhere!" They matched the color of the sand, and we were horrified to see them raising their heads to strike with their tongues slithering in and out! "Run!" David reacted quickly. "They could be poison!"

We heard no rattling that I can remember, but I was as happy to get back to Mama and our car as if I had narrowly escaped from a pit of diamond backs; and, of course, that was our last desert excursion because Mama wouldn't let us wander around after that.

Thankfully, the closest town was only about seven miles away and Daddy made enough trips to bring water for Mama to cook with, and to bathe the kids one at a time in our tin tub. Sometimes David went with him to help carry water back. Mama was always afraid for them to ride with strangers and, as they set off with the canteen and their thumbs out, she would pray fervently for their safety. Daddy sent telegrams to California to see if some of the people who owed him money for the furniture he sold them could send their payments by General Delivery. Also during this time, he went to a church and met a kind man who gave him a leg of lamb to feed his family and ten dollars which filled the gas tank. My folks had not planned on exiting Arkansas in such a hurry, so we were not prepared for the trip back; but we crept across the desert a tank of gas at a time. The next tank of fuel was obtained by selling mama's iron, which she wondered how in the world she could live without. Daddy explained convincingly that as soon as we got back home he could work and buy her another one.

Daddy's tools, or at least some of them, were the next to go and this time he stopped at a store and bought some groceries. For the first time in my life I tasted VanCamp's Pork and Beans, and have loved them ever since—cold, right out of the can. Neither had we ever had a Ritz cracker, and found these to be a tasty and satisfying treat!

The trip to Arkansas and back to Los Angeles, California took three weeks, and it was the longest three weeks of my life! I cannot imagine how my courageous little Mama endured such trouble, bravely following her husband through all of his ups and downs with seven children in tow! This was not the end of the Arkansas adventure, because the used axle Daddy had purchased in the desert had faulty gears which he had to file himself in order to fix it once more along the way.[12]

Bullied at Bonnie Brae: Supernatural Protection

Finally, however, we made it back to Los Angeles in April, 1942 after our traumatic trip. Daddy called our pastor who found a place in a warehouse to set up beds for some of us while the rest were sent out to stay with people in the church. During the war it was hard to find a house, period, let alone a landlord that would rent to a family with seven children. So when we finally found one it was a four-room house on the corner of Bonnie Brae and Temple Boulevard in the poor section of town.

Mama soon got all of us enrolled in the nearest school, which was predominantly Black. There was one other white girl in my second grade class, but she was absent often and I felt very conspicuous. On my second day at this school my classmates and I were standing in line to go out to our P.E. period where we would play outdoor games such as dodgeball, kickball, or baseball. As I stood on the stairway waiting, a girl turned around and looked at me with a mean glare and threatened, "I'm gonna beat you up after school for that!"

I turned around to see who she was talking to but there was no one else there. I was so small, and very afraid, supposing that she must have been talking to me! I decided I should get away from school and go home as soon as possible at the end of the day. Rushing out of class and down the outside stairs, I began to run. Alas! The older student on Safety Patrol brandished her authoritative armband and said, "You come back here and walk! You can't run in front of the school!"

As I slunk back to walk again, a big group of mean girls was right there waiting for me. They surrounded me so that I could not see outside the circle and no one else could see in. I kept walking as rapidly as possible toward Temple Boulevard with their tight circle pressing in on me from all sides. When we got out of sight of the school they began to taunt me, to pinch and hit me, kick me and pull my braids–*upwards!* If you don't know how that feels, it's much more painful than pulling hair downward!

"We're gonna beat you up! We oughta kill you," they threatened again and again with menacing looks and angry eyes.

They continued their abuse, assaulting me and saying horrible things. I was so frightened I couldn't cry; but I was praying silently with all my might for God's protection! They kept hitting me and slapping me until we came to an alley where there were barrels of scrap, tin and glass being collected for the war effort.

"Let's cut her to pieces!" they cackled threateningly as they picked up broken bottles and gathered bits of sharp tin. Crowding closely in front of me they began to torment me with these make-shift weapons. I was petrified! I didn't speak a word to them, but skirted around them whenever I could and kept moving as fast as I could toward home. They were calling me dirty names, kicking the backs of my legs, punching me and continually pulling my hair. It seemed like 'forever' as my little spirit cried out silently to God for help. Finally, glancing between two tall girls, I saw the "Bonnie Brae" street sign and darted between them, breaking out of their circle on a dead run for home. Across the street and through a vacant lot close to our house, I got away safely, bursting through the door to drown my mother in buckets of terrified tears. When I finally sobbed out the whole story she told me I would not be going back to school under those conditions.

The Social Services Department was gaining influence at that time, however, and had actually sent representatives to the homes of absentee students to investigate. Mama was afraid they would show up at the door since we had no telephone by which they could make contact; and sure enough, the next week someone came to see where I had been. Mama took me in to talk to the Principal and told her the story. She asked me if I could identify the girl who had threatened me, and said that she would take me to the class where I could point her out. I was terrified! But I did as I was asked and ended up in the office with three of the girls who had bullied me. The big one who first glared at me in the P.E. line told the principal that I had called her a dirty name, which was not true and I promptly denied this accusation. The issue was then resolved by the principal with threats of expulsion if these girls should ever bother me again.

I remained painfully shy, for it was very hard to be new and hated; but as time went by I made a friend—a large black girl who liked me and always chose me to be on her team for sports.

Tujunga: Galoshes and Angels

After our school-scare, we moved to a different area in East Los Angeles to attend a different school for the last month of the term. In April, May, and June, of that year, we had lived in three different places, finally settling into a house on Foothill Boulevard in Tujunga, California. Brother Sivak had encouraged Daddy to move out of the smoggy city to an area where he could breathe better. Tujunga was a higher elevation with cleaner air, and yucca growing everywhere! I remember David making plaques out of the yucca stems for gifts. He wrote verses and formed flowers with a wood-burner and then painted them with a protective shellac coating. Happily, we were able to stay long enough for me to finish third and fourth grades, and begin the fifth grade in the same school.

Most of my life, I was just "one of the group"! We had a large family and our parents worked very hard; so there was no extra time to focus on just one of us, though we were always together. One exception was when we first moved to Tujunga and my mother had to go to Glendale on a special errand for Daddy. She took me and my five-year-old little brother with her on that thirty-five minute bus ride. While we were in Glendale, we went into a Woolworth's 5 and 10-cent Store. It was fun looking through the store and shopping. There was a soda fountain with a counter and swivel bar stools up on a raised platform. The large colored pictures displayed the ice cream sundaes, milkshakes, banana splits and other treats. They all looked scrumptious, with whipped cream and cherries on top. I spotted the banana split and Mama saw my eyes light up!

"Would you like one?" she smiled. My eyes were wide with surprise at this unexpected opportunity! She had a cup of coffee, and ordered banana splits for Paul and me. Of course, I could hardly wait to tell my sisters!

World War II was happening at the time and I remember my Uncle Joe, Mama's little brother, coming to visit us. He looked so nice in his military dress uniform and we were very proud of him! Mama had lost another brother whom she was very close to—Uncle John—to a ruptured appendix and couldn't bear the thought of losing Uncle Joe, too. She cried and prayed for him often while he was in the army. I remember convoys of Jeeps, tanks and equipment filing past our house, sometimes all day long! We would make sandwiches for the soldiers and go out to talk with them when the convoy would stop. They were always friendly and allowed me to sit on their Jeep—which was very exciting and memorable for a small girl like me!

I don't remember my maternal grandparents before we moved to California, although I had learned of them through the prayers of my parents at Family Altar. I remember Mama crying, "O God, please bless dear little Mama and Papa. Keep them safe and well." Daddy's prayers also included petitions for his "Pa". In Tujunga, however, we saw Grandma and Grandpa Bunt fairly often because they lived about an hour away in Fullerton. Daddy would sometimes drive us down for a visit on a Sunday afternoon. Our grandparents often asked us to sing for them, which we loved to do; and it came easy because it was a regular part of our home life to sing songs of the faith together in harmony. Grandpa and Grandma Bunt were always very complimentary; in our teenage years he called us his "million dollar family".

Daddy had rented a store-front building so that he could start a little church. He immediately hung a sign on the door that said "Jesus Faith Pentecostal Mission—Salvation and Healing for all by our Lord Jesus Christ". Inside, he set up benches and a pulpit from which to preach. We had no instruments but we were all so full of music that we sang acapella whole-heartedly, and I am very sure that the angels joined our chorus! I learned so many wonderful hymns there! Daddy never passed an offering basket, but simply put a Tithe Box on the back wall of the church where people could place contributions. He would never take a salary, however, and since he didn't emphasize it almost no one gave to the ministry. Once in a while someone would drop a quarter or dime in the box. Things were already tight, due to the war, so we lived very frugally in an apartment that was located in the back of the building.

One day, we heard a knock at the door and Mama went to answer it. I was with her to see a large woman with a very pale complexion standing in the opening.

"Ma'am," the woman asked politely, "could you please loan me the money for my bus fare?"

"Well...how much do you need?" Mama inquired haltingly.

"Only twenty cents," came her quiet reply.

So Mama found two dimes and gave them to the stranger at the door. "Our church sign says, *Mission*," she whispered pensively after closing the door, "because we want to share the gospel with people; but this isn't a food or assistance mission at all! I hope they don't keep coming for handouts because we really don't have anything extra to give!"

Sometime later, the same woman showed up again at the door to ask for bus fare. Even as a child, the look of this woman was so unusual that I remembered her well and Mama did, too. This time the woman only asked for a dime and Mama gave it gladly, as before, but added, "I'm happy to help you this time, but this is not a mission that offers food or financial assistance. We just have a Mission for sharing the gospel of Christ."

The woman thanked her and turned to go; but when Mama closed the door she said, "Quick! I want you to follow that lady and see if she goes to the bus stop!"

So I ran out after her, practically on her heels, but she was gone. I ran quickly around to the front, but she was nowhere to be seen. The bus stop was right across the street, and though I looked up and down and all around, the mystery woman had disappeared. When I ran back inside to tell Mama, she was astonished. "What?" she gasped, knowing there had not been time for a large woman to get out of sight so quickly. "Oh, my!" she began to cry. "I think it was an angel! The Lord said to be kind to strangers because we might be *'entertaining angels unawares'*! I shouldn't have told her that! She only wanted a dime!" Until the day she died, Mama always thought that lady was an angel sent by God to test our kindness and generosity toward strangers.

Daddy had to go to work early each morning at his Mechanic Shop downtown and Mama didn't drive; so if she needed any groceries we had to walk about ten to twelve blocks to a Safeway store. Daddy had bought us a wagon to pull back and forth since it was too far to carry heavy bags. One day Mama sent some of us girls to the store and on the way home Jewel pulled and Rosemary pushed, while I rode in the wagon with the food. The streets were very hilly, like Seattle or San Francisco, and this particular street was steeper than some but had less traffic, which was why Mama sent us that way. Soon the wagon got going too fast downhill and was running over Jewel's heels! She saw that she couldn't stop it so she jumped out of the way and dropped the wagon tongue. It was too heavy for Rosemary to hold from behind, so down the hill I went, lickety-split and out of control with the wagon tongue flopping up and down! Thankfully, no cars were coming yet as I swerved back and forth, gaining speed. My overwhelmed sisters were praying up a storm, and I remember wondering briefly what would happen to me. Suddenly the bouncing tongue caught a crack and turned the wagon over, dumping me out on the asphalt with all the groceries. As I skidded to a stop, my knees and elbows paid the price! The groceries kept on rolling and my sisters ran to catch them as they tumbled down the steep hill. When they finally came back they helped me into the wagon, mortified by their mishap and grieving for my wounds. Once I was safe and sound I began to laugh, and was in good spirits when we walked in the door to tell Mama. Of course that was the end of using the steep route, since it turned out to be just as dangerous as taking the busy route down the boulevard. This experience was a ride I never forgot, nor the "safety lessons" about steep hills and wagon tongues that followed when we got home! Neither did Mama neglect the opportunity to once again exhort us on the danger of riding bicycles, since a boy had recently lost control of his bike on the very street where our wagon had overturned. For him, unfortunately, that bike ride was his last chance to be safe; he did not survive the accident.

We always walked to school, up and down these hilly streets in Tujunga and, whenever it rained, the water would gush down both sides of the street in huge streams gathering speed from the surrounding hills. Because of these conditions the area was prone to flash floods; so, even though there were storm drains, the torrents of water were often too much volume for them to accommodate. In addition, these deep drains that opened up to underground aqueducts did not have protective grates over them in those days. We heard that a little girl got swept into a drain during one storm, and drowned before she could be rescued! I remember that Daddy bought all of us galoshes to wear over our shoes so we could wade whenever the water was too deep; but as a third grader, it seemed at times that the force of it would sweep me away!

My father had been taking my older brother, David, out of school to help him at work; but by this time educators were looking down on this old-time practice. In fact, they were creating policies to prevent children from being taken out of school by parents who believed that work was more important than education. Daddy didn't like this but was also thinking it would be good for our family to get in on the government's Homestead Act while it was still possible. Additionally, there had been some kidnappings reported in the area and he had decided that this area of southern California was a bad place to raise his family. So he took David to Idaho with him to check out other options.

Meanwhile, a letter came from the office of David's high school saying that he needed to return to his classes. Mama was frightened of school officials because even in those days they were beginning to take kids out of homes where they could prove some kind of neglect or civil disregard. Brother Sivak was visiting us when she got the letter and he said, "Sister Mussell, just write them back and say, 'David will go on Friday.' They don't have to know that you're moving to Idaho on Friday!"

So when Daddy and David came back we packed everything up, closed down our little church, and left for the Great Northwest. Mama had put two cases of canned milk aside to be put in the trailer and somehow they got left behind. Canned milk was like gold to us because, since we rarely had refrigerators, we used it exclusively in the place of milk that had to be kept cold. I'll never forget how Mama grieved over that canned milk, and since it was such a big trauma for her I picked it up and started grieving too! *'Oh! Our brand new canned milk! We needed it so badly and we have left it behind!'* I remember Daddy saying, "Now, Mama; don't grieve over that canned milk. Whoever lives there next will be glad to get it and it won't be wasted."

– CHAPTER FOUR –

Growing Up

Life had already been so full during my first nine years, but now a very distinct corner was being turned. I was growing out of the small child place and stepping up onto the platform of unique personhood, becoming my own character on the family stage. My little brain was alive with possibility, anticipation, and curiosity about my world; and I soaked in more details during this time of my life than any other. Our years on the homestead became a catalyst for perspective; a point of reference that made me strong and, in my adulthood, often drew me back for balance and tranquility. This powerful season of my life was a springboard for learning to reach past the basics and soar toward the heights, as I discovered that I could capture the smallest wonder and choose to make it the crowning moment of even the dreariest day. The poignant memories that I gathered during these years were so vibrant and so large in my mind that they seemed numerous enough to fill up a lifetime. Indeed, living on the homestead was a whole different life, and one that attracted my eager attention and held me happily captive.

Fruitland: Happy on the Homestead

My father often had dreams that he knew were from the Lord. Sometime before we left Tujunga Daddy had a dream in which he saw a piece of land where a basement house was built—an underground house with only the small windows showing above the surface. The message in the dream was that he was to take the gospel to the occupant of that house.

It was October of 1943[1] when we moved from California to take up a one hundred and sixty-acre homestead south of Fruitland, Idaho; and, low and behold, when Daddy found our land the adjoining plot had a basement house! Later, when we actually moved out to the homestead, he got acquainted with that neighbor and led him to the Lord, just as he was instructed to do in his dream.

I was nine and a half years old and in the fifth grade as our family set out on this grand adventure, and I have a comprehensive account of every unforgettable feature locked in my memory banks! When we first arrived we stayed with Daddy's sister, Aunt Pearl, and Uncle Frank Lynch (of Merrill and Lynch) in Homedale, Idaho while we got settled and obtained our permits and papers to work the land. It was fifty dollars for a homestead permit, with stipulations and required improvements that had to be completed within set time frames before the deed could be released to the homesteader. These requirements were projects such as digging a well, building a house, and planting a certain number of acres in crops within three years. It was very exciting to be out in the country and we were overjoyed!

Back at Aunt Pearl's house she found places for all of us to sleep, including one old mattress that was brought down from the attic. When Mama unrolled that mattress there was a nest inside with a mouse and her tiny batch of pink babies. Mama shrieked so loudly that Daddy assumed the worst and came running to see what horrible thing had produced such a scream.

"That won't hurt anything," he said when he saw the source of her panic. "Just sweep it off and put it down on the floor."

My cousin Helen and her husband, Cloyd, had purchased my grandfather's old farm where I was born and it was on the other side of the hill from Aunt Pearl's place. It was like a home-coming, yet filled with so many sights that were new to me; rows of apricot trees, apple orchards, and water flowing in canals for irrigation. I was taking in all the details of our new surroundings and it was so much fun to see everything on the farm! Cloyd would milk the cows and pour the milk into a separator that spun around, separating the cream from it. Then they made butter from the cream.

I remember being excited to walk to the little two-room country school with my cousin, Evie, and my siblings who were young enough, for only grades one through eight were taught there. Dorcas, Rosemary, Lois and I, and our cousin were all together in the same room for grades five through eight. The lower grades were in a classroom downstairs. The teacher would write the daily assignments for each grade on the board so we could do our lessons. At recess we would all go outside for fresh air and exercise. There was no outdoor equipment of any kind; just a big, bare yard. It seemed like it rained a lot; so we often had spelling bees or played indoor games. One that I remember was a word game called *Teakettle*. We had to think of words that sounded the same but had different meanings, then use them in a sentence substituting teakettle for the mystery words so that the others could guess. For instance, "I would *teakettle* on the couch waiting for my brother to tell mother his version of the story, which was usually a *teakettle*." Whoever guessed that the word was 'lie' got to have the next turn.

The teacher's daughter was the only other fifth grader besides Lois and me, and she was very smart. One day, we were learning about sentences and the teacher asked, "Lois, what is a sentence?"

Lois felt shy and on the spot as she answered, "Ummm...a sentence...is a sentence!"

Angrily, the teacher scolded, "Lois Mussell! When I ask you what a sentence is, don't you ever say, 'A sentence is a sentence!'"

Just then, the teacher's brilliant daughter raised her hand and answered, "A sentence is a group of words expressing a complete thought," which brought a wave of kudos from her mother and laughter from the older students, as Lois sat in total embarrassment. That was a bad experience for starting at a new school and Lois didn't like going after that; but before long we were moving to our own house and the adventures of homestead life took precedence.

Daddy was ready to leave Aunt Pearl's as soon as he got the outhouse built. She wanted him to wait, but he didn't want to be a burden to anyone with his large family. We thanked our relatives and said our 'goodbyes' and climbed into the car to head for our patch of land. We were excited about the idea of pioneering together and watching Daddy build our house. We had to drive down a gravel road and then follow the ditch bank to a steep hill beside a flume. This was a cement channel to carry water downhill from the big canal by the road to several smaller ditches used for irrigation. As Daddy began to creep down the steep hill beside the flume, Mama panicked.

"Oh, Daddy! Daddy! Daddy! This car's going to turn over!"

"Stay in," he assured her. "I am going slow, and it's not going to turn over."

If my memory serves me correctly, however, I remember that she was too afraid and got out of the car to walk down the hill on her own two feet! At the bottom of the hill she got back in the car, but Daddy was ashamed of her for letting her fears overtake her and for scaring the kids when he had been down the hill many times with no incident. The home site was across an irrigation ditch that had no access for vehicles, so he and my older brother, David, had built a sturdy little bridge —over which we now drove—and then rolled right out into the sage brush across our own land where Daddy stopped the car and said, "Well, this is where our house is going to be!"

We all piled out of the car to investigate and I remember the flat, high desert with sage brush as far as the eye could see. We could look out over the valley and see the flat plateaus toward New Plymouth and beyond.

"Praise the Lord! Here we are out in the country with our whole family!" Daddy exclaimed, as he took off his hat. "We got one hundred and sixty acres!"

He was cheerful and eager, smiling broadly. He told us enthusiastically about the coyotes that we would hear crying in the night; but that put a bit of a damper on the excitement of the moment for me. I would have to choose other things to focus on for my first impression to be positive! I spied the cute, white outhouse and Daddy showed us his handiwork. In the world of 'country outhouses' we had seen some shabby shacks; but ours was perfect. He attached little knobs on the doors, installed air vents up above, and cut three holes for various sizes of 'bottoms'! There was a Papa Seat, a Mama Seat, and a Baby Seat—all with perfectly fitted lids—and a special place for the Sears and Roebuck catalog which, of course, served as our toilet paper roll.

The next thing was to dig a dirt cellar, which David worked on while Daddy started on the house. He made several bins in the cellar for produce: one for potatoes—which could be gleaned free from many farms—one for apples, one for onions, and a sandbox for wintering carrots. I remember how rich the soil was; and that during the digging he never hit a rock.

Daddy had to sell all of his auto mechanic tools in order to buy building materials. He ordered the lumber and had it delivered to our home site. There was no electricity so every board was cut with a handsaw. They made two saw-horses right off the bat to accommodate all the woodworking they would have to do. The tools were the simplest in the trade: a measuring tape, a square, a level, a handsaw, a planer, and string. He had a box to mix his concrete in and any of us who were old enough helped with the stirring of the sand, cement, and water mixture. There was no foundation, but he squared off the area with corner stakes and string. David helped as the walls were raised one at a time; then the rafters; then a roof over our heads.

Before the roof was on, Daddy would always comment about the starry skies, often leading into the story of God's promise to Abraham when he told him that his descendants would be as numerous as the stars in the heavens. Mama had herded both sheep and cattle as a young girl and knew all of the constellations by heart. She would point out Orion's Belt, the Milky Way, the Big Dipper, and many other starry sites as we lay on our ground floor to sleep at night.

All along the way, Daddy would kneel each night to pray and thank the Lord for every bit of progress and every simple accomplishment of the day. He made the door by hand on the south side of our one-room pinewood cabin, and cut out each well-planned window, explaining to us that he would cut no windows on the north or west sides of the house because that was the direction from which the cold winds would come. He covered all the knotholes with tin can lids, tacking them in place so the mice couldn't get into our house.

The irrigation canals stopped running in October of each year and did not flow again until around April when the water was released to the farmlands again. So until our well was operational, which was not until the spring of 1946, we hauled water from town which was five miles away. Daddy cut out the back of our car and built an extension behind it so he could use it like a little pickup truck. He could fit several five-gallon milk cans in the back of it for hauling water.

That first winter, 1943-44, he got a job at the Amalgamated Sugar Refinery in Nyssa, Oregon. David helped Daddy with everything and did an excellent job at whatever he was assigned. He never finished school because there was too much work to do on the homestead. The rest of us rode the school bus to our little country school in Fruitland, Idaho. I remember walking to the bus stop in bitter winter weather with our faces toward the cold winds of Idaho's high-desert.

One thing our father always did right away when we moved was to look for a church close by. At the homestead, he found one in Payette, one in Ontario, Oregon, and a couple others in Fruitland and New Plymouth that were very small, like home group fellowships. We lived from five to eight miles from all of them so we visited each one and decided on the one in Payette as our home church. Our pastor was Brother Robison, a sincere man and a powerful preacher. The church was stable and we made good friends. Sister Slaughter was my Sunday School teacher and I still remember her demonstration of David feigning insanity to avoid capture by his enemies!

After my baptism in the Holy Spirit at our wonderful church in Los Angeles, I had never used my prayer language again and now I longed for a refilling experience. So I went to the altar, and still remember the congregation singing,

Pass me not, O gentle Savior; hear my humble cry!
While on others thou art calling, do not pass me by![2]

I felt almost as though I could see into Glory through my tears. Bright light seemed to envelope me as the Holy Spirit came upon me once again and tongues began to flow from my childhood lips. It lasted long enough that the church people asked me afterwards what was happening and what I had seen. They supposed that for a young girl to stay that long at the altar, something supernatural was surely taking place. I only remember light, and the presence of Jesus; but from this time on, my spiritual language came easily and was very fluent.

We were able to participate in an Easter program while attending this church. I was given a portion to memorize from the book of Mark about the resurrection, which I still recite. Scripture that is learned in childhood lasts a lifetime!

In early spring, all the farm chores began. In order to purchase farming implements, starting with one horse and a plow, my dad had to sell our car. During this time he had to walk to his job in Nyssa, five miles each way! The weather was still very cold and I remember Mama being worried and praying fervently for his safety each time he had to walk to work. On the homestead, he first began to work the ground with his horse and plow. The soil was rich and dark once the sagebrush was removed. He plowed a section right next to the house in order to get a few crops in right away. David dug very precise ditches to bring the irrigation water from the culvert to our farmland.

Mama often feared that the huge canal above our house would break and flood the homestead. It was wide, swift, and deeper than our house was tall! All the irrigation ditches in the valley came out of that major canal. One night there was a break in the smaller ditch that David had dug for irrigating our fields. The water had somehow broken through and cut a trench about ten feet deep! When we discovered it the next morning, we were so amazed that a small stream of water could do such damage. Then Daddy got grape vine starts from Aunt Pearl and we planted them all along the bank of our irrigation ditch to reinforce the soil. Some died, but many of them lived and grew into healthy vines. We also planted some trees eventually, but we were not there long enough to see them grow very tall.

At some point Daddy got a team of horses in order to clear the first forty acres of land, which was a requirement of the Homestead Act. I remember how he collected the necessary tools one by one to complete the process. He broke up the brush with a disc harrow first so we could pull it and haul it to the burn pile. It was quite a process, which I describe in more detail in a later chapter, and we all helped. After the brush was removed, he plowed the ground and then dragged a tooth harrow over the land that loosened the soil, followed by a homemade leveler −a framework of heavy lumber dragged behind a team. Finally, he used a corrugator that made neat furrows for irrigation. Then the prepared field was sowed with alfalfa seed.

The alfalfa field was so beautiful, and I remember what a pleasurable relief it was to have that beside our house instead of all that scrubby sagebrush! Then, at harvest time, we got to ride on the hay wagon a couple of times. Daddy had built a nice rack on the front of the hay wagon that we could hang onto as we sat high atop the hay on our way to town where he would sell it; such a happy memory!

A smaller patch that Daddy had planted in wheat brought double the crop that was expected, for which he ardently praised the Lord!

After planting, it was time to dig postholes so that we could fence things in. Daddy had purchased a cow for milking and we learned to separate the cream and shake it up and down in a jar until it turned into butter, as we had seen while staying with Aunt Pearl.

Our home was very simple, and we learned to live with the bare necessities. Daddy built two sets of bunk beds that were double. On the north end of the west wall in our one room cabin was the girls' bunk bed and on the south end was our parents' bed. The boys slept on a bunk above them. Between the two bed chambers there was a space big enough to house our barrels of beans, rice, and other food storage. The arrangement was very modest, with a curtain that hung across the northeast corner for privacy. This private corner housed

Mama's trunk, nails in a wall for hanging our Sunday dresses and other clothes, our bathing tub, and our "pot". Chamber pots were common in those days, and often made of porcelain-covered steel. These large containers had a bailing wire and wood handle, and a lid. We used it as a toilet when inclement weather prevented a trip to the outhouse! In that case, the pot would have to be emptied and sterilized the next morning, and this job always fell to one of the elder sisters—lucky for me.

There was a boiler that usually sat on the right side of our wood cook stove. It was a large pan, approximately a yard long and two feet deep, with handles and a lid. It was kept full most of the time so that warm water would always be available to dip out for washing dishes, taking baths, and such. When hot water was carried to the private corner for filling the tub, at least two of us had to use the bath water before filling the tub again. When baths were finished, two people would carry the tub outside and dump the water.

We used a coal-oil lamp and a kerosene lantern for light. The lamp sat in the center of our crude, homemade wooden table and the lantern was used for trips to the outhouse after dark, trips to the cellar, and to light the way before dawn as Daddy went out to the barn to milk the cow. Daddy built two benches for the long sides of the table and at each end was an orange crate for a chair. He also nailed these wooden crates one above another all along the wall of the southeast corner for Mama's cupboards. We had a large aluminum pan for washing dishes and a teakettle that was always simmering on the stove. Fires had to be built daily—summer and winter—in order to have hot water for cooking and cleaning. Our stove had burners that were actually round, lift-off lids through which the wood fires could be stoked to keep them going. There was also an aluminum kettle with a long handled double-boiler top that we would dip into the big boiler for hot water to fill up the dish pan. Two dish pans would be placed on the kitchen table: one held the soapy water for washing dishes and one was for scalding—a process of pouring boiling water from the teakettle onto the soapy dishes for rinsing. It took three of us to do the dishes after each meal: one to wash, one to scald, and one to dry and put away the clean dishes. The dirty dish water would be poured into the slop bucket to take out to the pigs. We also added grain and bits of food scraps like potato peelings or apple cores to this bucket for pig food.

The slop bucket was beside the door and next to it was an orange crate with a wash basin on top for washing our hands. Just above it was a little shelf Daddy had built to hold the single family mirror. A comb with a hole drilled into it dangled nearby on a string, where he had hung it for safe keeping since it had been misplaced a time or two. We all had to share it for combing our hair each day! There were also two nails, one with a wash cloth and one with a towel. If we used the washcloth, we were responsible to pour our soapy water into the slop pail and get clean water for rinsing out the cloth and rehanging it on the nail. We all used the same washcloth and towel several times before wash day, when these would be replaced with a clean set.

Daddy built a clothesline for Mama, and all the laundry was done by hand on a rub board in a tin tub or, in the event that we were coming in from field work, in the ditch where our overalls got a good dousing before coming into the house. Sometimes Mama would say, "They're just dusty, not very dirty; so rinse them out and hang them over the barbed wire fence to dry."

One day we were using a large bar of P&G soap to wash our jeans in the ditch. Focusing on our scrubbing, we didn't see what was coming. Before we knew it, the pig had snatched the soap and made a run for it, like he had gotten away with the prize! Dorcas and Jewel chased after him with sticks to try to make him drop the soap; but he gulped it down whole before they could catch him. It never ceased to amaze me how those pigs could eat such things and never get sick!

The roads were dirt in that area and we could only know a car was coming by the great cloud of dust that boiled up around it. Our legs would be covered from our ankle socks to our dress hems with that fine, powdery dust in the summer. One time, we had an old metal Maytag washer with no motor and Mama asked if there was a way to power it to help with her enormous laundry duties. So Daddy bought a small gas motor and hooked it up; but because of the fumes, we had to put it outside the house—besides the fact that there was not room enough in our small cabin. Mama was one happy little lady…for a few days; then the motor went out. I remember Mama holding her little apron up to her face, swabbing her tears of disappointment.

We didn't have a refrigerator so Daddy nailed an orange crate on the north side of our house and we kept food outside in cold weather. It was almost too high for me to reach because it had to be far enough above the ground so that coyotes could not raid our supplies. We poured milk in jars and kept it out here in winter, being sure to leave the lids loose enough to allow for expansion if the milk froze; but in summer we had to use it up every day to keep it from souring. We always had plenty to share with our dog, Tippy, the cat, and even the pigs!

Our only heat source was our wood cook stove. We burned sage brush, and in the coldest weather Daddy would buy a tow sack of coal for five dollars which made perfect hot coals for baking bread.

One time Daddy brought home a gas lantern, which was the newest thing out, and unfamiliar to all of us. He hung it on a nail by our bunk beds and it lit up the whole cabin. It was as bright as an electric light and we were so excited to be able to see and read so easily after struggling with our dim oil lamp for so long.

We had some Bantam chickens running free range to provide eggs. I remember the hawks circling on high, waiting for a chance to swoop down on one of the baby chicks that got separated from the brood. This scenario was a real-life example of how the Enemy of our souls prowls about, waiting for a weak moment when we slip out from the shadow of His wings, momentarily leaving the shelter of God's protection to step carelessly into the vulnerability of the world outside. It demonstrates so perfectly the safety of remaining within the sound of God's voice. Just like the chick that has wandered away from Mother Hen's warning call, we can stray from "the secret place of the Most High" into the danger zone where His voice becomes a distant echo.

One of the ways we best learned the spiritual truths for life was from the lyrics of the old hymns. I remember Daddy having an old pump organ off in one corner and the visual of him sitting there playing it is stamped forever in my memory banks! He could play music by note because of learning to play the cornet as a young person. I can still hear him singing as he pumped that organ:

If I gained the world, but lost the Savior,
Would my gain be worth the life-long strife?
Are all earthy treasures worth comparing,
For a moment, With the Christ-filled life?

Oh, what emptiness without the Savior,
'Mid the sins and sorrows here below;
And Eternity—how dark without Him!
Only Night, and Tears and Endless Woe.[3]

The songs that he sang always made a deep impact on me. Watching and listening as our father sang and played was important to all of us. We were always attentive, revering his abilities and his dedication to spiritual things. Mama could play a little by note as well, and taught us everything she knew so that we could play on our own. We all played some, but Jewel played the organ the most. I remember her singing out the notes as she played a tune: "B, C, B, G, E…" In this way, she was helping the rest of us to learn the names of the notes that made up a familiar melody. I remember my siblings learning to play songs such as "Jesus, Lover of my Soul" and "Oh, How I Love Jesus". I did not learn to play music at this time because I was younger, although I always enjoyed hearing it!

I remember how we all gathered around on our wood floor each night for singing, Bible reading, and prayer—our Family Altar time. Daddy had purchased a rocking chair from an auction and either he or Mama would sit in it with the rest of us scattered here and there around the center of the room. For prayer, Daddy would begin and Mama was next, then David and so on down the line to the youngest, Paul. But by the time it was little Paul's turn, he was often asleep! In fact, as second to the youngest, I remember falling asleep myself, and being awakened when it was my turn to pray!

I remember a place below Canyon Hill in Caldwell, Idaho where Grandma and Grandpa Bunt lived. They had livestock on this acreage and it had an artesian well. Grandpa was a hard worker and made everything he could from scratch. He even made a tin cup with a smooth handle to hang on a hook by the big water pipe that came out of his well. He could make latches, gate locks, and anything that would help make life more convenient and efficient. I thought he was a regular genius!

Grandma Bunt was very domesticated and loved cooking. They invited us for dinner a few times, one of which must have been Thanksgiving because I remember a gorgeous table with fancy dishes and lots of food. I was always impressed with Grandma's great variety of jams, pickles, relishes and spiced crab apples in pretty little glass dishes. We were all overwhelmed by Grandma's glass curio cabinet. It was packed as full as she could get it with knick-knacks and keepsakes. We would stand in front of it straining our eyes to take in what seemed like hundreds of ceramic, wooden, and silver objects on the shelves. One item I remember well was a miniature, intricately-carved covered wagon with the cloth bonnet over the frame. My brother, David, had made it for grandma, and she displayed it proudly with all her other treasures.

On my dad's side, my grandfather, Jacob Mussell, was very old by the time I got to know him. He seemed so tall to me as a child, but he was only 5'10" with fine features and thick glasses, as I remember, in his later years. I was with Daddy one day when he stopped by Grandpa's house in Caldwell on Dearborn Street. He was married to his second wife, Emma, by this time but she was gone that day and Grandpa greeted us with a cheery smile. He wanted to sing us the tune of a song he had written. He had the music on a music stand in front of him and he tapped out the rhythm as he sang us the song. I remember seeing a desk and lots of book cases with many books, dictionaries and Bibles sitting around his small living room.

I especially remember a time when he decided to visit us on the homestead. He had devised a plan to ride the bus from Caldwell to Fruitland and get off at our school; then he rode the school bus home with us! We wondered how he could ever walk all the way from the bus, down the ditch bank, and to our home site. He surprised us, however, and—as old as he appeared—he made it! I remember him stopping on the ditch bank to survey our house and the layout of our land below. He seemed very pleased, and we felt very happy about it.

After that first summer on the homestead, we all started back to school except my eldest sister, Jewel, and my elder brother, David. Living in Idaho in the 1940s, eighth grade was the highest grade requirement to be completed because High School was often thought of as people today would consider a college education. Since Jewel had finished the eighth grade, Daddy wanted her to stay home and help Mama.

One of my teachers, Mrs. Heinrich, was extremely strict. She kept a yard-long piece of rubber hose to spank the boys with (because, of course, none of the girls were about to misbehave with odds such as those!) She was an excellent teacher, however, and quite obviously kept perfect order in the classroom! I was behind that year because the Idaho schools were so much farther ahead than the California schools we had come from that I couldn't keep up. My classmates were standing in front of the class for oral reading assignment from history books with small print and no pictures. I was accustomed to younger versions of historical facts with fewer words and more illustrations! This was intimidating for me and made me somewhat uncomfortable.

Also at this time, Lois fell and sprained her arm. She didn't want to go back to school and, in the absence of a doctor's professional care, Mama guessed that her arm might be broken. So, rather than take a chance on hurting it again, she allowed Lois to stay home for the remainder of the semester while it healed. One day, Dorcas and I were the only ones going to school; Rosemary must have had a sore throat, which was fairly common for her. As we walked along with our faces into the wind, Dorcas suddenly exclaimed with fright, "Oh! There's a band of coyotes!"

I looked up and saw, through the fog, a large group barreling toward us at a rapid pace! We turned and fled, running back toward home and praying with all our might that we would make it safely. After what seemed like a long time running, Dorcas finally got the courage to turn around and see how close they were. Imagine our great relief to breathlessly discover that the huge pack chasing us home was nothing but a giant bundle of tumble weeds stuck together and rolling across the plain! When I see coyotes today, they seem skinny and non-threatening; but the ones on the homestead seemed huge and menacing, like fierce police dogs! Their constant yipping that surrounded our farm in the dark of night sent a chill down our small spines, and left an eerie image of a beast on the prowl that might see us as their supper! I was definitely afraid of them, and the trauma of running for my life from what I thought was a pack of hungry ones still touches a nerve in my soul.

One thing that was hard for us was the muddy roads. After Mama became so frightened on her first visit to our land by Daddy driving down the steep hill beside the flume, he made a road that bypassed the high ditch bank. The only problem was that, in order to do that, the road had to be quite long between our home site and the closest gravel road into town. Therefore, whenever it rained, the mud and ruts would make it partially impassable and we kept getting our car stuck! I remember heading down our road—dressed up in our clean, tidy church clothes and shoes, only to have to get out and walk back home in the mud! We had to take off our shoes and socks and walk back home in our bare feet. We held up our dresses, too, because the mud was above our ankles. We had church at home that day.

Life on the homestead was harder for everyone else than it was for me, as the youngest girl. I remember all the good stuff, but after the first year, Brother Sivak came to visit and advised Daddy to go back to California and work. So in December of 1944 [4] Daddy and David made a trip to Los Angeles for work. He boarded up the windows of our homestead cabin and moved the rest of us into an extended stay motel in Fruitland, with a kitchenette. This place was very small, but close to our school; and it had electricity! Mama loved the electric range and laundry capabilities. I remember a parade that came through the streets while we were there. It had something to do with the war or our veterans and there was lots of shouting, blowing of horns and celebration.

The next month, January of 1945,[5] we were back at home and Daddy was working the farm again. David had worked so hard helping Daddy to get started on the homestead—and being unable to finish school because of it—that our father wanted him to be able to attend Bible College to pursue the call of God on his life. Unable to buy him clothing or supplies, they gave him my father's suit to wear and, with old shoes and a small suitcase and barely enough money for a down payment to get started in school, they put him on a bus to the Seattle, Washington area. Mama cried about sending him away with nothing; but he was confident and determined. In order to enroll, he was required to make up all the classes he had missed the first semester. He was smart and very inspired so he did very well for himself, getting jobs to pay his way and making excellent grades. He would sometimes send charts of his studies, or a picture of himself, which made us all so proud of him.

The first summer that he came home from Bible College, he dug the telephone postholes for installing electrical power lines. It was two miles to the gravel road and the power company said they would not bring the power into our homestead site unless we dug the postholes ourselves. Now, we are not talking about postholes for a fence; but for 30-foot telephone poles! Daddy was able to get some equipment for it—possibly from the power company—and David worked industriously to complete the job. Mama grieved from the window, "That poor child has been out there all day and he's still digging those postholes." David finished the holes from the road to the home site before he returned to Bible College, although it was still some time before we actually got power to the house.

When we got electricity, Daddy purchased fifty to a hundred White

Leghorns that we raised to provide eggs, to eat and to sell. He built them a nice-sized chicken coop that was always stocked with fresh straw. Rosemary was in charge of feeding the chickens and gathering all the eggs in baskets. She also had to divide them carefully into flats so that we could sell them. She took such excellent care of the chickens that they never failed to provide one egg each day per hen in our brood. We held the eggs up to a light to analyze them. The double-yoked eggs were considered unacceptable for selling, so we would keep these for ourselves. We lost a few of our chickens to weasels or coyotes that would sneak in at night and dig under the fence.

The summer of 1945 we all worked in the surrounding fields to help make ends meet, which I describe in more detail in another chapter. Suffice it to say, times were hard for everyone in those days; it was expected that the entire family would help to bring in the funds necessary to live.

Another cherished memory of our move to the homestead was the summer that Daddy decided to build a little cabin on our land for Brother Sivak so that he could stay as long as he wished whenever he came to visit. He furnished it with a bed, a table and chair. It had no electricity, but only a kerosene lamp and pegs for hanging his clothes. We called it The Prophet's Chamber. He came on the bus from Los Angeles and stayed with us for a couple of months.

After a nice visit, he told my father, "This is a beautiful place to live, but I can stay here no longer; for when a man is called to minister to people he cannot isolate himself for his own comfort. I must return to Los Angeles where the people are."

Daddy was sad to see him go; and, although Brother Sivak never hinted that the homestead was the wrong place for a growing family, I don't think my father was able to shake the message that a man of God needed to go where the people were so that he could evangelize and preach the truth to those who needed to hear it. After that, Daddy had several discouragements that set him back as a homesteader. One of them was the death of Coalie.

Daddy had bought a shiny, black work horse that he named Coalie. We had longed for a horse, even though Daddy had always instructed us that they were a luxury we could not afford! We knew that every animal we had to feed would be designated for work! Daddy had no saddle, but would ride him bareback down to the mail box or hook him up to the plow. We had only seen him plod along, but one day Daddy mounted Coalie and went galloping down the ditch bank! The bank was up high, so he and his charger became a fascinating silhouette against the brighter skyline as they raced toward the far pasture. One day, Daddy came in the house and straightway knelt inside the door on our wood floor, laying his hat upside down beside him. Then, with the deepest grief and concern, he called us all to join him in prayer, saying, "Come children, we need to pray for Coalie; he's very sick. He has distemper."

Daddy had been plowing with him and Coalie had become hot and sweaty from the hard work. Daddy unharnessed him and turned him loose, since we didn't have a barn or corral yet. Coalie went straight up to the canal, which was supposedly dry but there were still puddles of water that had frozen. He broke the ice with his hoof and drank ice water to his fill—a deadly combination with heat exhaustion. Although this homestead memory of my father is most precious to me, his fervent prayers were to no avail this time, and Coalie died. Daddy was mournfully sad over losing his wonderful plow horse, and his grief was so deep that I never forgot how it felt.

The last year on the homestead Daddy also tried a venture with dairy cows. Others had encouraged him that money could be made by selling fresh milk, so he spent money on a few cows for milking. Although they were good producers, they developed mastitis and Daddy had to call the veterinarian to come and treat them, which was very expensive. The dairy would not take the infected milk so we lost our money. I remember him being very sad and discouraged about the outcome.

In the fall of 1945[6] our folks boarded up our little house while we traveled back to California for more work. On this trip, Daddy, Mama and Paul were in front and we five girls in the back. It was night and we had fallen asleep when I began to kick my feet again and again. Daddy reached his hand into the back seat and tapped gently, saying, "*Who* is kicking their feet? Stop that!"

Mama turned around to see what was happening and saw that I was passed out and had vomited all over my clothes. Knowing that I had a strong stomach and had never been prone to this reaction she was immediately alerted that something was bad wrong. Carbon monoxide had leaked into the car and all the girls had passed out from breathing the poisoned air. "Oh, Daddy! The girls are all sick! It must be gas fumes!" she cried, and he stopped the car and pulled us all out into the open air.

Stretched out by the side of the road in the cold desert air, they roused us one by one except for Dorcas. They worked and worked with her, moving her arms and talking to her, yet thinking she would never wake up. Finally they were able to revive her and get us all to a motel for the night where we could recover safely. Mama said later that, because of my strong stomach, I may not have vomited at all had I not eaten a large serving of canned cherries that she was trying to use up before our trip! This chance coincidence saved our lives. God works in mysterious ways!

I guess Daddy had the gas leak fixed somehow, because Mama says we worked the apricot harvest in Red Bluff, California after that, before driving back home through Reno, Nevada and the snowy Sierra Nevada Mountains.

The following spring, my father seeded a field with alfalfa and paid to have a well drilled; but the project was fraught with problems. The driller broke several shafts from hitting slate or granite and each time he would have to attach another one. Mama prayed him through, and we finally got a deep well that provided plenty of cool, fresh water. We had to pump it by hand, and we were very grateful to do so, but we never did get running water in the house.

Even with the progress we were able to make, Daddy decided to give up the homestead and, after a farm sale in April of 1946, he traded it straight across for a house belonging to a man in our Payette church who had always wanted a nice piece of land in the country. It had been a great adventure, but a very difficult time for my folks; and after the afore-mentioned series of discouragements, they were ready to move on.

We lived on the homestead in Fruitland for two and a half years, from October, 1943 to April, 1946 and I can still picture everything exactly as it was. The homestead was where I learned to work. I loved to do most anything that we were all doing together, and I loved to see the finished product. We helped dig ditches, plant trees and grape vines, put up fences, haul water, chop and stack wood, paint things, and every detail in between. We all helped to clear the land and we burned the brush. We also worked in the fields picking peas and potatoes on neighboring farms.

I saw some amazing things during our homestead years! There are sights, sounds and scents of the country that always take me back to this time of my life. I will never forget the clear blue skies, which we had most of the time—even in winter. I loved the fruit trees—the smell of the apple orchards; the fields and the clover; the poignant smell of sagebrush; the call of a meadowlark; ground squirrels peeping from their burrows, and lots of jack rabbits! I remember huge moons on the evening horizon, with the lonely call of a coyote in the distance. The crowing of a rooster and even the gentle buzz of a bee are still so nostalgic for me. I can still smell the aroma of Aunt Pearl's fried bacon, a memorable and tasty treat that did not frequent our own breakfast table. We loved watching the water run in the irrigation canals and ditches, with cattails and tules (tu'li: a large bulrush[7]) growing along the banks. Some of my keenest and most cherished memories are of our family sitting around the table with the kerosene lamp in the center; morning birds' song; gathering eggs; pitching hay; digging fence postholes; walking to school; and wading in the irrigation ditch.

I think fondly of the many times I sat on the canal bank meditating as I soaked up the peace and quiet of the surrounding sage landscape, the dusty roads and the spreading green fields of alfalfa hay. I loved the aloneness of the country, and this favorite spot on the canal bank overlooked the entire valley below, from Fruitland to New Plymouth. It was a perfect place to pray, or to sit and talk for long periods off the beaten path. One indelible and perfect memory that is etched on my mind forever is sitting on that ditch bank and singing:

My Jesus, I love thee; I know Thou art mine!
For Thee, all the follies of sin I resign;
My Precious Redeemer; my Savior art Thou;
If ever I loved thee, my Jesus, 'tis now! [8]

As young as I was, I still remember the thrill of singing that out across the valley with my whole heart; and every time I hear that song, it all comes flooding back with every thrilling sight and sound of that day.

I loved the flat bluff hills to the North and I would meditate on God and His creation as I sat there by myself singing and talking to Him. It was a great experience that left vivid and cherished memories on my heart. With my big, happy, always-together family, these walks to the ditch bank were probably my only solitary times to think or meditate; not that I longed for time alone. As the little sister, sixth in line, I thoroughly enjoyed my place in the midst of the action! I might miss something if I was away too long!

My father always liked having a watch dog whenever we could, and one of my homestead memories is our dog Tippy. He was black and brown with a white tip on his tail, the reason for his name. He sat dutifully by the front door, unless he was following Daddy around the farm, and after school we would see him running down the ditch bank to greet us.

I will never forget getting up early in the morning to work in the fields; being afraid of coyotes; our many happy times going to church together on Sunday mornings; our Family Altar times with Daddy playing the pump organ and singing; the stars and moon shining brightly above our home site; the new-fallen snow before any footprints were in it; chopping sage brush; Mama's homemade bread, baked fresh daily and spread with fresh butter—churned by shaking thick cream in a quart jar; my loving family that was always there together, with a mother and father who loved each other, loved us, and prayed together faithfully.

I also remember one terrible storm that came in the night with fierce, howling winds. Mama was afraid it would blow our house away because we didn't have a foundation underneath to secure it. Daddy kept saying, "Don't fear; God will protect us." But as the storm worsened through the night, Mama let her fears get the best of her and she woke us all up and hurried us out into the stormy winds and across the yard to the dirt cellar into which she had squeezed a mattress for us to sleep on. We all bedded down with cozy blankets and pillows to wait for morning. Daddy stayed in the house, and the next morning it was missing some shingles but still standing firm! We always wondered how in the world Mama got that mattress crammed into the cellar because it was so *hard* to get it out!

Payette Impostor

The house in Payette was on two acres of land. It was hard enough to leave all of our homestead memories and move into town; but to add insult to injury, the man we traded with had removed all the cupboards from the walls, all the linoleum and mop boards from the floors, and everything he could take with him. We were shocked beyond belief that a Christian brother would act so deceitfully and Mama wanted Daddy to confront him on the matter. Daddy, however, decided it was best to suffer wrongfully and make the best of it. Until we arrived, we didn't realize how run down and dirty the place was, nor how it was situated next to the noisy railroad tracks in one of the worst parts of town.

To top it off, I was in a Junior High School for the first time and hated it.

Thrust in at the end of the semester like this was very confusing to me. I had a hard time with the structure and struggled in many of my classes from being farther behind than those who had been at this school all year. For the first time in my life, school was difficult and far from fun. I never made a friend there. I was isolated and miserable. It was a bigger school so I didn't even see my sisters during the day.

Mama was very sad, and this experience did not help with Daddy's recent string of discouraging events. We were there long enough to clean up a very dirty house and sell our furniture. Then he sold the house and we moved back to California. First, Daddy wanted to go up to Pasco, Washington to get David from Bible School since he had graduated. He had bought a small travel trailer with some of the money from the sale of the Payette house, and Mama was delighted with all of its tidy compartments and comforting features. With no reliable communication available, we found out upon our arrival that David had made plans to help another pastor start a new church and would not be coming home that summer. So we turned around and headed for California once again.

Turning Into Teenagers

My wonderful older brother was away at Bible College, making his way in life. My older sisters were growing into beautiful young ladies. We had already moved more than seven times and I was only twelve. Time was passing by and the first half of my childhood was blowing around the bend. Yet, for me, life was still full of adventure and promise! I have heard it said that the years speed up after we reach adulthood; but I had not yet arrived! I eagerly observed everything around me, stacking up good memories in full detail wherever they could be found. My enthusiasm for life was strong; I felt blessed, secure in my place, and ready for whatever lay ahead.

Four Years at Fernglen

When we came to La Crescenta, California it was sunny and beautiful. Daddy pulled the trailer up onto a hillside road among the cactuses and yucca plants. He was always a spontaneous personality and had landed once again without a plan. He wanted to unhook the trailer and leave us all there while he drove the car into Tujunga to buy a piece of land! Mama was petrified that the police would come and tell her that she was on private property, but her worries changed nothing.

The searching was difficult because a small bare lot in California was listed for several hundred dollars, compared to his one hundred and sixty-acre homestead in Idaho that he got for fifty dollars, plus the promise to develop the land! Finally he found a piece that would suffice, and bought two tents to pitch on the lot until he could build a house. One tent was for the girls and one was for Paul and supplies; the trailer was for Mama and Daddy.

Always able to find a job because of his mechanical skills, Daddy went to work almost immediately, leaving us with the instruction to clear our very rocky lot of all debris. Our job was to pick up rocks all day long and throw them off to the far edges of the property. When we got the lot cleared, Daddy began to dig the foundation and drew his own idea of a house plan.

I was twelve and a half when we moved back to Tujunga, California and built the house on Fernglen Avenue. It was a very square house with two bedrooms, a living room, a kitchen and a bathroom that was nowhere close to the bedrooms! When Mama commented about that Daddy's extreme practicality reminded her that any bathroom was better than an outhouse and he went forward with his one-of-a-kind abode.

Daddy had barely constructed the framework and tacked tar paper on the outside when a terrible wind storm came and blew our tents away. From then on, we had to live in our unfinished house as it was being built, which was slow-going with Daddy working at another job all day. Eventually, David was able to come back and help. He worked very hard and finished the house for us. The girls' room had three bunk beds, a closet, and one dresser with a drawer for each of us. We used five of the bunks and left the extra available for friends. Later he added a concrete driveway and a garage with an extra room attached for the boys' bedroom, plus a half bathroom. David also created a beautiful rock wall about three feet high around the lot from all those stones that we threw to the sides of the property! One thing that happened later was that Daddy cut off all the beautiful eves around the house that David had built! At that time, it was a fad to have no eves; but it didn't last long because it was not only very unsightly, but provided no protection from the weather. Instead, it allowed rainwater to run down the outside walls of the house, staining the nice stucco finish.

The school grades were arranged differently back then, possibly due to so many families traveling from place to place for work and enrolling their students at all times of the year. So when we got there I skipped half a grade and enrolled in the same class with Lois. She was very happy about it because she hated doing anything by herself and was glad to be together. Our schedule included some very fun classes like Home Economics and Foods. We had History and English and all the regular subjects as well, but it was much easier for me and from then on I did well in school and had no struggles.

I remember my dad working very long hours driving from Tujunga to Los Angeles every day to work in his shop. He was always off on Sunday, in honor of the Lord's Day, but worked many Saturdays. Still, our family held Saturday night prayer meetings at our house. The fellowship and refreshments were always wonderful, and I always looked forward to the friends and conversations. George and Ione Eaton would bring their children to sing and pray with us. Ione always brought her guitar to accompany the singing and I really wanted to learn to play it; so she taught me the three main chords for the key of C. From there I was on my own, and how happy I was when Sister Durbin sold me an old Gibson guitar for ten dollars! Now I could join Ione in playing along with the group! I also began to play my guitar whenever my sisters and I sang together and before long I was playing at church on a regular basis. From there, we were asked to sing often at Youth for Christ or other special meetings in the area.

I was only fourteen when my Aunt Mary—Mama's younger sister who lived with Grandma and Grandpa Bunt—invited me to ride the bus down to Fullerton and stay for a few days so that she could give me a perm in her hair studio! It was all very exciting, but also a mite unsettling to ride the bus alone. Tujunga was north of Los Angeles and Fullerton was southeast, about forty-five miles away, so the bus route took me through the streets of Los Angeles to the place where she would pick me up. I was a little apprehensive, but it all worked out. I remember sitting in Aunt Mary's beauty parlor with the giant mirrors on all the walls; it was a brand new world for me!

I stayed for three days and thoroughly enjoyed the time with my grandparents. I slept in a guestroom all by myself, and was amazed to see something in the huge, framed mirror on the bathroom wall that I had never seen before: the back of me! Grandma Bunt's house was full of beautiful pictures and portraits on the walls and fine, plush furniture! She had a nice porch with big pillars; and a yard with beautiful trees! There were citrus trees hanging with large lemons and rosy grapefruit as well as big, swaying trees full of birds. I remember the songs of the birds in the morning sounding like a thousand-voice choir!

Aunt Mary did all the cooking, and the food was mostly familiar to me except that the potato soup had celery in it, which was a rarity at our house. I was surprised to see that Aunt Mary barely rinsed it off in preparing it for chopping. I mentioned to her that Mama always scrubbed it with a brush to get all the poison off; to which Aunt Mary offered a disapproving harrumph that silently said, *"Stuff and nonsense!"*

I sat at Grandma's feet and listened to story after story of her life on the wild frontier among the Indians. During this time I also received a special surprise gift from my grandpa! He was very resourceful, and often collected things that other people had discarded in the trash barrels along the alley. One day he had come across a pair of gray suede, three-inch heels with rounded toes and brought them home. While I was visiting them I went out in his garage to talk to him and soon spied those darling heels in a box with other stuff. He saw that I liked them and asked if I wanted to try them on. They fit perfectly and he let me take them home! I was always very fond of them; not just because they were my first special pair of heels, but because they were a gift from Grandpa Bunt.

The only camping trip we ever made was when we lived here in Tujunga. I was about fourteen and Daddy decided to take us all to the mountains. He was very excited! We packed our food, bedding and supplies to head for the hills of Charleston Flats. David was already gone and Dorcas had to work her drugstore job at the soda fountain, so she stayed home. My parents, younger brother, Paul, and we four girls enjoyed the drive and sang all the way. We arrived and set up our camp, had our picnic and enjoyed the evening. After we ate our meal and got bedded down, Daddy began to focus our attention on the beautiful stars in the sky above. We laid there looking up at the moon and the Big Dipper. Mama pointed out Orion's Belt and the Little Dipper too; and I remember the tops of the pine trees swishing in the breeze. Soon after we all got snuggled into our beds for the night, however, Daddy became worried about Dorcas. Mama had been reluctant to leave her alone anyway, so when he said that he felt a strong caution to get up and go home, we did so immediately! We were disappointed, but trusted our parents' discernment explicitly. We soon discovered that it was, indeed, a warning from the Lord because our sister was in grave danger! A man had tried to pick her up after she closed the drugstore and when she refused the ride he followed her in his car. The full account is described below with other similar incidents we experienced as teen girls in Los Angeles.

Tujunga, in those days, was also called "JewJunga" by people living in the area because it was a Jewish settlement. I remember when Israel became a nation in 1948 because all of our neighbors began selling out, packing up and moving back to Israel. I didn't realize the full significance of it back then; but Daddy explained that Bible prophecy was being fulfilled right before our eyes. Thousands of years ago, the Bible predicted the return of the Jewish people to their homeland; and now that Israel had become a nation, it was coming true!

We lived at the house on Fernglen for four years and attended the La Crescenta Assembly of God church while we were there. It was a wonderful, thriving church with a strong focus on evangelism and many outreach activities in which we participated. The Sunday evening services were filled with wonderful testimonies and many began joining our family for Sunday afternoon street meetings. Jewel could play the pump organ quite well by then, so Daddy would set it up on the corner and we would sing to draw a crowd so that Daddy could share the gospel message with them. My siblings and I shared as well, giving our personal testimonies often.

I had several church friends who went to our school. Helen Brewer was led to the Lord by my sister, Dorcas. Joy Lash, Ernestine Conrad and Lois Collins were school and church friends as well. I am still in touch (now in my eighties) with Helen Brewer-Stratton as well as Joy (Lash) and Dale Wilson. Charlotte Durbin was a friend who became family when she moved to Idaho and married my elder brother, David. She is a wonderful sister-in-law and I love her dearly. Rosemary fell in love with Charlotte's brother, Brice, who was the Youth Leader at that time. He had installed a large speaker system on his car so that he could play gospel music as well as announcing youth meetings as he drove around town.

Our parents were very careful to promote good influences. They were strict about friends who didn't have the same spiritual convictions or level of commitment to God that they wanted for us. Seeing role models of consistent Christian living and teaching, and knowing that they whole-heartedly believed it, made me have the greatest confidence in God and His Word. It was "time at home" that allowed me to see the dedication of my older siblings to prayer and scripture memorization; and I was profoundly influenced by my father's daily Bible readings at our Family Altar times. We read books about the great men and women of faith and we saw first-hand the Christian values at work in church friends that we spent time with. These associations were powerful examples like strong, golden threads of faith woven into the fabric of our lives that gave us substance and purpose for living. There was so much health and happiness around us that I never questioned whether a different life might be better or more interesting; and I never felt like I was missing out on something else. I loved our life and felt completely free! The only social "freedoms" I was concerned about were the freedom to have a Bible Club in our high school; or to observe public, united prayer times for certain things, which we went to our school principal about and appealed as a group for these permissions. My ideals were to be a virtuous Christian and have a good testimony; to witness to others by my words and my ways; to live my life in such a way as to have no regrets, but the confidence that I had pleased the Lord.

When I was at Verdugo Hills High School, I belonged to a Bible Club. There were about twenty teens who were members but only about half of them came regularly, four of which were my own sisters. We thoroughly enjoyed the Christian fellowship, sharing the Lord with one another and singing our favorite songs. In my junior year of high school, the president, Ralph Mahoney, did a wonderful job. He planned great assemblies, parties and outreach functions for evangelism. One activity was a Billy Graham film he arranged to show during the lunch hour. We sold tickets to pay for the film rental. It was well-attended by the student body. Another special event was a banquet with an African mission emphasis. It was a nice dress-up occasion at a local restaurant. He also contacted The Soul Clinic in Los Angeles and invited one of their dedicated soul winners to come and speak to our Bible Club. She gave her testimony and shared her experiences of aggressively witnessing on the streets and learning how to lead souls to Christ. She had made a commitment to share Christ every day and lead someone to faith in Jesus. She testified how the Lord had enabled her, every day since that commitment, to win a soul for God and pray the salvation prayer with them.

When our Youth Group heard about her visit to Bible Club, they made arrangements to visit The Soul Clinic. They had Bible verses on their walls like, "*...he that winneth souls is wise*" from Proverbs 11:30 (KJV). We made large signs that we carried on our shoulders. One side said, "I am a fool for Christ's sake..." and the other side said, "...whose fool are you?" We wanted the message to draw attention and serve as a segue for sharing the gospel. We were inspired to win souls for the Kingdom of God and, although my family only visited that one time, others went back later to witness on the streets of Los Angeles with The Soul Clinic.

The next year, as a senior, I became the president of Bible Club, which was a great experience for me. We met during lunch hour on Tuesdays. Someone always gave a devotional; we shared testimonies and had prayer together for any needs people wanted to share.

My siblings and I also helped in Billy Graham crusades and were altar workers, attended all the area-wide youth rallies, and loved to help out with summer Vacation Bible School programs. My brother, David, had returned home and had his own car so he took us girls on Saturday nights to Youth for Christ meetings at the Presbyterian Church in Montrose, a small community next to La Crescenta, as well as to every C.A. (Christ's Ambassadors) Rally. Daddy also took us to every great revival meeting that we heard about and could get to.

One of my most treasured memories from childhood is our family going to Camp Meeting together. We usually got to go to the meetings for a day or two but never camped overnight; just drove back and forth. We always learned new songs and sang them in the car on the way home. Then we continued singing them all year long until the next Camp Meeting. I loved hearing the Missionary reports, too, and browsing in the book store at the camp. Besides books and Bibles there were bookmarks, promise boxes, pictures and plaques; treasures of all kinds!

Then some bad things began to happen in our community and Daddy became concerned for us girls. There had been several kidnappings in the area and we actually witnessed one! We were sitting in our car and heard a woman screaming, "Kidnapper! Kidnapper!"

We were filling our car tank at a gas station and some witnesses tried to follow her, but lost her in the crowd. Later we heard it on the news and realized that we had been right there on the scene of the crime. We were working jobs downtown Los Angeles by then; my older sisters had full-time jobs and the rest of us had been hired for Christmas help. So we were riding the bus back and forth to work, and all of my sisters actually experienced some kind of frightening event with strangers. I was the only one who had no such encounter while living in this big city.

When Rosemary was about sixteen and still in high school, she was working part-time at the May Company in Los Angeles. She had to walk quite a distance to catch the bus for work. She rode downtown to the bus terminal where she got off and walked several more blocks to her place of employment. One day after work she had walked to the terminal and was standing in line at the ticket booth when the man behind her tapped her on the shoulder and said in a strange voice, "Hi, Rosemary."

Startled, and frightened, yet trying to appear brave, she answered, "Hello... how do you know me?"

"I have known you for a long time. I have seen you in seven states," he answered eerily. "You have four sisters and two brothers."

Horrified at such familiarity from a total stranger and very disturbed at his detailed knowledge of her personal life, she hurriedly purchased her ticket for Tujunga and stepped out of line. As she stepped away, however, she heard him ask the clerk for a ticket to Tujunga also! He was a young man in his early twenties and would have no way to accumulate the knowledge that he had about our family. Rosie quickly made her way through the terminal to her bus stop, waiting nervously to board. She saw the strange man enter the group of people waiting for the same bus and, although he didn't speak to her, he kept watching her. When she got onto the bus and sat down, he soon came and sat beside her on the same seat. He continued telling things about her that he had no way of knowing, as well as making it plain that he'd had his eye on her for a long time and was very fond of her.

Knowing that she had a real psycho on her hands, she began to worry about the ten blocks she would have to walk in the dark after getting off the bus! Sure enough, when she got off at her stop, he got off behind her. When the bus pulled away she was petrified but could not run because of the three and a half inch heels she was wearing. He stayed behind her until they got away from the street light at the bus stop but, a short distance farther down the dark sidewalk, he caught up with her, grabbed her and tried to snatch a kiss. Struggling fiercely, she got away and began to run, kicking off her heels and running in her nylon stockings.

When she finally got the courage to look behind her, she saw him heading back to the bus stop, a slinking silhouette in the dim light of the street lamp. Crying in sheer panic by now, she opted for the quickest way to get out of his sight, which was through a barbed wire fence and across a vacant lot. She got home safely and entered the house with her key, but was utterly traumatized. No one else was home because the rest of the family was gone to a Billy Graham Crusade where we were all enlisted as Personal Workers. Alone and afraid, she locked all the doors and prayed that the stalker had not discovered where she lived. She actually saw him a few times at the bus terminal after that; but each time she hid in the crowd and avoided him at all costs.

Around the same time Dorcas, who was seventeen, got a job in Tujunga at the Drug Store Fountain on the corner of Commerce and Tujunga Canyon Boulevard. This was her first public position and our parents were concerned because she often had to work until closing time. She was still in high school so her shift was from 6:00 pm until 10:00 pm.

One weekend her boss had to be gone and asked her, in his absence, to stay until everything was cleaned up and ready for the next day. He trusted her to lock up and take care of everything, but she would be all alone and she was uneasy. Earlier that evening a young man had come in to the counter and ordered a Coke. He was flirting with Dorcas and asked her if he could take her home after work. She declined; but he knew she usually got off around 10:00 pm and said he would be back, to which she declined again.

At closing time she finished all her duties as the other waitress, the clerk, and the boss left. She felt afraid because she had seen the young man's car parked outside on the street. She would lock the front and go out the back, onto Tujunga Canyon Boulevard which was a long, winding road that was very dark. She started quickly down the road but soon saw his car coming and ducked behind some bushes to hide behind the porch of a house along the street. Watching from her hiding place, she saw him drive down several blocks and turn around to come back, flashing his lights and driving very slowly as he looked for her along the road. When he passed her, she jumped out and ran as far as she could before he turned around to make another pass. This went on for a while, him driving back and forth while she gained a little distance closer to home each time she ran for a new hiding place. Finally, he gave up and she hurried home as fast as she could, fearful that he would come back and find her, or see where she lived.

Meanwhile, she knew she would be alone at the house because this was the time I mentioned before when Daddy had taken the rest of us on a camping trip to Charleston Flats. As previously described, our father's intuition had abruptly ended our camping trip and sent us home that night. When we arrived, we found Dorcas praying that very thing! She had been crying and didn't want to spend the night alone in the house after her frightening experience.

"Daddy is always right about these things," Mama confirmed. "God gives him warnings!"

"He that dwelleth in the secret place of the Most High shall abide under the shadow of the Almighty," from the 91st Psalm was probably the scripture that my parents quoted after that incident. They never missed an opportunity to turn our life experiences into a Bible lesson of some kind! They had scripture verses for every occasion and circumstance.

My eldest sister, Jewel, had a close call here as well. She took Mama's grocery list one gray day and walked to Safeway to buy the food. It was a long way to walk and she had some heavy things in the bag, such as half gallon milk cartons, which made it awkward to carry. In addition, the clouds above opened up again and began pouring rain. She was walking home on Tujunga Canyon Boulevard, the same long, winding road that Dorcas had traveled the night she was followed from the Drug Store. Jewel's grocery sack got wet and began to tear. She knew that if it got worse it would not hold her groceries and they would spill out on the sidewalk.

Just then, a pick-up truck pulled over beside the curb and the driver hollered, "Hop in! Looks like you need a lift!"

She was very reluctant, but felt her choices were limited as she struggled to hold the torn sack together with both arms. She was already half-way home, but took the offer to get out of the rain and got in the truck. "You can let me off at the next corner," she directed him; but he had other plans and drove past the corner without so much as a tap on the brake. Feeling uneasy, she stated with concern, "You passed my street. Please stop and let me out!" When the man ignored her and kept driving, her apprehension rose to another level and she raised her voice, threatening, "Stop right now or I'll jump out of this truck!" and she reached for the door handle to jerk it open.

"Don't do that!" the man shouted, as he slowed his driving. "If you're going to jump I'll stop and let you out."

She was relieved to get out of his vehicle, but now she had a soggy, torn grocery bag to carry several blocks farther than if she had never accepted the ride. She took the tail of her blouse and wrapped it around the bottom of the bag, holding it close to her chest. She was frightened as she made her way home, realizing that God had protected her from the kidnapper's questionable intentions.

As soon as she got to the door, we opened it and she stepped in and put the groceries down. The bag dissolved in a heap of wet scraps around the grocery items, and she was soaked to the skin.

Seeing the heap of brown paper, we were all amazed that she made it home without dropping everything. She told her story and it frightened all of us.

"I've told you never, never, *never* to get in the car with a stranger!" was Mama's pronounced emotional rejoinder.

"Well," Jewel defended feebly, "I never would have but because it was raining so hard I just thought he was being kind and trying to help me. Instead he took me farther away from our street." Whenever these things happened to one of us, we all learned from it and thanked the Lord again and again for His sovereign protection over us.

Lois' episode was during the Christmas holidays. She worked at the May Company and, like the rest of us, had to ride the city transit to Los Angeles and back to Tujunga each day. One day when she was waiting at the bus depot, she stepped into a phone booth to call home and heard a man's voice on her phone line before she even dialed a number. "There's a little blonde here at the depot that we want to pick up..." the voice continued describing her clothing, hair, size, and figure in detail. She froze in place as she realized that this allegedly covert conversation was about her! The men continued talking as she listened, offering explicit descriptions of what they wanted to do with her once they got her in the car. She was stunned and knew she would be kidnapped if she left the phone booth. So as soon as the men hung up, she put her money in the slot and called home. She told Daddy what was happening and what the men said. He told her to go back inside the depot and stand beside the information counter until he got there. He was coming to pick her up so she would not have to ride the bus under such vulnerable conditions. Before this time Lois had been exceptionally naïve; but from this point on she was very careful. She knew that God had worked a miracle on that phone line to warn her of imminent danger.

It was uncanny to have all these things happen to my sisters during the few short years that we lived at Fernglen, but because these dangers were a reality in this area, none of us were surprised at our Father's decision to leave. One day when we all got home from work Daddy told us that he was thinking of moving back to Idaho. He wanted us to graduate first so nothing happened right away. Before the end of the school year, however, the folks decided to make a trip to Idaho to look for land; they left us home to work, finish our schooling and attend our graduation ceremonies. Later, I was surprised that they didn't want to attend our ceremonies; since most families seemed to celebrate together in this way. But they also took Paul away from his ninth grade graduation ceremony to go with them on the trip. In their generation, there was never a big to-do over these things; in fact, many of them—including my parents—didn't have the opportunity to finish their own secondary education.

Sister Dudley, a dear church friend, insisted on picking us up and taking Lois and me to our graduation ceremony. She found out we were going to have to walk all that way and back in heels! She brought nice cards for each of us, attended the ceremony in our honor and took us home afterwards. It was held on the football field because we had no auditorium large enough to host the crowd. Ralph Mahoney graduated at the same time and asked if he could pick us up that night to go to a revival meeting, to which we agreed. Later in the week he took us to a Latter Rain meeting, where I first saw people worship the Lord in song instead of the loud volume of voices raised in fervent, corporate prayer that we were accustomed to! They never tired, but kept their hands raised for a very long time, each singing their own words of musical praise to God in unison with the others. It was fascinating and exhilarating to be in that atmosphere of free, harmonious worship!

We had lived here four years. Paul finished ninth grade, and Rosemary got married. My other sisters and I graduated from Verdugo Hills High School in Tujunga, California, including Jewel. Mama wanted her to be able to finish her education after sacrificing it while living on the homestead, so she was able to re-enroll and graduate high school. She did very well in her classes, especially thriving in Spanish language, which she so enjoyed. Rosemary had become engaged to Brice Durbin the summer before her junior year of high school. Our father disapproved of "long engagements" once a couple decided to marry, so when Brice Durbin expressed his hopes of marrying soon, Rosemary quit school in November to comply with his wishes. She was only seventeen but our father agreed because, after all, they had been engaged for several months already! True to cultural norms of the day—as well as his strong conviction that women should marry, have children, and keep homes— he felt that marriage was the highest calling and encouraged all of us in that direction. Consequently, by the time the rest of us had graduated, Brice and Rosie had a baby girl and we were all aunts! So, when the folks returned and announced that they had bought a forty-acre farm in Black Canyon, north of Caldwell, Idaho my only tearful regret was leaving my vivacious, creative sister behind. We packed up for Idaho, and we were on the road again!

Becoming Adults

Black Canyon

I was sixteen when we sold our little house in Tujunga, California and moved back to Idaho. We stayed with Aunt Pearl again while Daddy got started on the house. David was there to help again, but this time we had electricity! They poured a concrete slab for a foundation, so Mama would not have to worry about the house blowing away in a storm. Also, when the well was finished, they piped the water into the house, but not for a bathroom; we had an outhouse again. They built a main room, a bedroom on one end for the girls and one on the other end for the boys. Daddy had plans to add onto one end of the house, so it was not finished. Our walls were only chicken wire and tarpaper, which was freezing cold in the winter. When we washed out a blouse or sweater, and laid it flat on the trunk to dry, it would freeze solid before morning!

In the middle room, there was a table with chairs around it, a couch, and a small wood stove for heating the room. The refrigerator was in one corner and on the other side were a few cupboards and a counter for preparing food. We also had a wood cook stove. A single light bulb hung in the middle of the room and Daddy made doors to close off the bedrooms. Eventually, the concrete floor was covered with linoleum, too.

David got a good job right away through the Carpenter's Union. Jewel was employed by Caxton Printers; Dorcas got a job with Sears and Lois got hired by the BLM. None of them had cars, however, so Daddy would take them all to work each morning. I made lunches for everyone before they left, and Paul rode the bus each day to Middleton High School where he was a sophomore. I remember seeing kids my age on that bus and thinking, *"I'm only sixteen; why did I get out of school so young? It's lonely around here…"* Mama was very glad to have my help on the farm, though; and we worked around the place all day while the others were gone to town.

I was still getting letters from a young man I had worked with in our Bible Club in La Crescenta and one day Mama came in with one in her hand. "You got another letter," she said, with a look that told me instantly that she had read it!

So, I asked, "Mama, did you read it?" to which she answered, "I'm not saying…" but as I turned it over I could tell that it had been opened and glued back together! This particular letter was a bit "lovey" but it was the first one to include that kind of verbiage since we had been corresponding these past months; so I told Mama that.

"Well, it looks like he would be interested in one of the older girls." She thought he sounded too serious for a young one like me who was not ready for marriage. That connection was not to continue anyway, however, for my true soul mate would soon pop onto the scene!

The weather was warming up and Daddy wanted to buy Mama an electric range for her birthday, June 22. He was smiling and had a twinkle in his eye as he asked Lois and me if we wanted to ride to Caldwell with him to the Second Hand Appliance store. He had all the wiring ready for it and was so excited. We looked around and found the perfect stove for Mama. It was nice looking white enamel and sat up high on legs. The oven was higher, too, so she wouldn't have to bend over so far. He was so pleased as he doled out his twenty-five dollars in cash, which was hard to come by in those days. We loaded it into Daddy's little pickup and he mused, "Well, it's sitting pretty tight; I don't think it will go anywhere."

I was apprehensive because it was top-heavy, and balancing on four skinny legs. It sat very well most of the way home but, as we made the last turn onto our property, it flew out of the pickup and crashed in the field sending springs and doors and pieces in all directions. Daddy was so sad! He took off his hat and knelt to pray right there in the road. "Oh, God; I knew I missed your will somehow."

Lois and I felt the impact of the tragedy and could hardly keep from crying. When we got home Daddy walked in the house and put his arms around Mama. He told her what happened and she cried out in the shrill voice of distress that she often used at times like this. "Oh! Daddy! Daddy! I told you to always tie things down. Papa always said it was important to tie everything down!"

He assured her that he would get her another one but it wasn't right away. Several months later he found a smaller one and brought it home. This one was not as nice looking but she was very happy to have an electric range.

Lumping pieces of life into a story, out of sheer necessity, shortens the years. The richness and depth of experience must be summarized into a book. Yet these glimpses represent the fullness of a long and exciting—though often arduous—journey that I hold dear. All the places we lived while I was growing up were pleasantly engaging to me. I suppose I was young enough to define as "adventure" some experiences that my older siblings may have interpreted differently, yet all of them seemed as happy as I was! Each house held its own flavor of mystery and treasure and—like a child who delights to wriggle her toes in the sand and run along the beach to find pearly seashells and shiny stones—I gathered a surplus of special memories to cherish from every abode, tucking them into the pockets of my heart for keeps.

CHAPTER FIVE

Treasures from My Tapestry

There are not enough pages in this book to pour out my glad heart-full of treasured memories. All the places we lived, described in the last chapter, were like a brief "drive-by" of a gorgeous meadow on a road trip. This chapter will be more like going back to spend some time in that beautiful place and gather mementos for keepsakes. I have thought many times that I must have had the happiest childhood of anyone I ever knew. I will always remember my mother's love for all her children, and my father's guidance and spiritual impartation to us. My brothers were loving and kind, never teasing or making fun of me, and my sisters all nurtured and cherished me as the littlest sister. I always felt loved and accepted in my own family and, consequently, had a good foundation for experiencing the same thing from God's family—that's why church and Christian people are so dear to me. It's like coming to the Father's Table to share the good things that He has provided with all those who mean the most to me. We learned at home how to love God's people and have fellowship with one another; we had many close friendships through the years. All our relationships were rewarding and memorable because they were centered on the Lord and the biblical life patterns that produce the most wholesome and happy results.

Faith Highlights

Faith was the crux of my entire life, and was birthed in me at a very young age. So it is, without doubt, the most appropriate place to begin describing the wonderful highlights of my childhood that were woven by God's loving hands into the tapestry of my life.

My own parents and family were by far the greatest spiritual influence on my life. They were consistent, predictable Christians who lived what they believed and taught. As I grew up, my family had prayer and Bible reading daily, and teaching every evening. My father loved to sing and taught us hundreds of songs and hymns. We sang at family times, but I learned many of these treasured tunes just by hearing my parents sing them around home. My folks were humble and godly; very kind to everyone. I grew up always hearing about God and being deeply devoted to Him. We had a high regard for His Word as our rule of faith and conduct. Our parents emphasized the concept that the Christian was not to live like the world; that we were pilgrims and strangers on our way to a celestial city–Heaven–our eternal home. Consequently, our personal and family activities centered around spiritual things and our prominent relationships were always with the Family of God, whom we were taught to honor and cherish. I don't remember a secular book in our home, or a family activity that was not faith-oriented. Even carnivals, rodeos and other societal entertainments were not a part of regular family life.

Everyone I knew believed in God and talked about him; the reality of his presence seemed very natural. There was never a question or doubt about his existence. God *is*; that's all I ever knew! It made perfect sense to me that there had to be a Creator who made the universe and was in charge of everything. At the same time, it was very easy to believe that He created me, and that He would always love me and guide my way. My mother would verbally relate all of life to God, speaking to us at every opportunity that, "It is He who gives us our very breath, keeps us alive and makes our hearts beat. God supplies our food, gives us shelter, clothing, sunshine and rain!"

She had a scripture for every occasion, quoting them throughout the day. She used the Proverbs for correction and always gave thorough admonitions along with any necessary discipline for wrong-doing. Because of my family's Christian perspective which daily enriched every detail of our lives, I felt that God was very close to us. I could not imagine anyone thinking otherwise; or having doubts about God's love for them. The love that was daily expressed by my family sealed my trust in God's love as well.

I loved and looked forward to both Children's Church and Sunday School classes. Brother Dean was a wonderful teacher of our first Children's Church. He prayed for all the children in attendance to receive the Baptism of the Holy Spirit, and many of them did. We learned the books of the Bible, many Bible verses, and stories of all the biblical heroes of the faith. We also learned how to pray, and to develop our own personal relationship with God.

When I first heard the gospel story, about Jesus dying on the cross to save us from our sins, I wanted to be saved myself, and to live as a Christian girl. I was in kindergarten and first grade when we lived in Lynwood, California, and our family attended the Pentecostal church in Los Angeles. One Sunday night after the service during the prayer time around the altar—which was very common in those days—I was sitting about three rows back taking it all in. Suddenly, the Sunday School Superintendent, Brother Woodworth, looked at me and caught my eye. He came back to where I was sitting, put his arm around my shoulders and said, "Honey, wouldn't you like to pray?"

In the tenderness of this spiritual moment, I instantly began to cry and nodded, "Yes." I went to the altar where my sisters and mother were praying, among many other saints. I knelt down next to Rosemary and began to pray. The presence of the Lord was there and many were being filled with the baptism of the Holy Spirit, with the evidence of speaking in tongues.

An older lady said to me, "Lift your hands and praise the Lord!"

When I did I began to weep, as I spoke with stammering lips and a quivering chin. Then I experienced the miracle of speaking in tongues; and I heard someone say, "Eunice got the Baptism!" I continued praying and worshipping for some time and, when we got up to leave, I felt the joy of the Lord so deep in my little soul that I couldn't stop smiling! When I squeezed into our car with my sisters, I remember looking out the window and grinning from ear to ear; nobody could see me but God. When we rolled into the streets of Los Angeles and the bright lights shone on my face, I felt the excitement of something great—like winning a wonderful prize—and said to myself, *"God's Holy Spirit lives in me!"* The Bible says we are 'quickened' by the Holy Spirit and, when I woke up the next morning, I could still feel that quickening down inside. I remember walking to kindergarten that day and looking up at the sky with awe, realizing that the Creator himself now lived in my heart!

That wonderful night started a new chapter of my young life, for even as a very small child I felt holy, clean, and very near to God. From that day forward I always felt safe in God's care, close to Jesus, my savior, and secure in God's family. Although I remember being too young to participate in the communion ceremony before I gave my heart to Jesus, I now received communion right along with the rest of the saints, and I understood its meaning. We usually had communion services once or twice each month. It was always a solemn time of remembering what Jesus had done for us. The songs we sang were about the sacrifice that Jesus made on the cross, as the Lamb of God, for the price of our sin. We were always given time to pray; to examine our hearts, confess any known sin, and be sure that we were clean before God prior to partaking of the elements. It was a special, sacred time. I clearly recall many of the devotional hymns we sang during communion services: "O, The Blood of Jesus", "There is a Fountain Filled with Blood", "Jesus, Keep me Near the Cross", "Nothing but the Blood of Jesus", "Jesus Paid it All", "Under the Blood", "At the Cross", "Cleanse Me, O God", "Blessed be the Fountain of Blood", "He was Nailed to the Cross for Me", "When I Survey the Wondrous Cross".

After I gave my heart to Jesus, I began to pray on my own whenever I felt a need. I prayed when I was afraid, alone, or in any danger; I prayed over my food, at bedtime, and in church. We also took turns praying at our Family Altar times at home. Our family prayed faithfully for anyone who was sick. One time when my father was very ill with asthma, we had a family prayer chain where each of us prayed for 15 minutes at a time, continuing the rotation throughout the day. I learned a lot about prayer during those times. I also prayed for God's help before every spelling test or exams on other school subjects. Even as a small girl, prayer brought God ever closer to me, and made me realize how awesome and powerful He was.

Our Children's Church was very vibrant and exciting! Our director, Brother Dean, always had some sort of contest going to help us learn. He had a big box of prizes to give away to anyone who could answer the Bible questions or recite biblical facts. One of the prizes was a miniature "Bible" of select scripture verses; they had white ones for the girls and black ones for the boys. I wanted one so bad but I was too young to read, while my siblings were reciting the books of the Bible to earn their prizes. Daddy had given them a "Books of the Bible" game for Christmas which they played often. I was too young to participate but I watched and listened, soaking in the details. I learned the categories of the thirty-nine Old Testament books: *Five Books of the Law; Twelve Books of History; Five Books of Poetry; Five Major Prophets;* and *Twelve Minor Prophets,* as well as the sections for the twenty-seven New Testament books: the *Four Gospels, Acts of the Apostles,* the *Twenty-one Epistles,* and *The Revelation.*

Finally, my sisters helped me to learn all the names of the books of the Bible by saying them to me a few at a time while I repeated them back. They helped me learn the correct pronunciations as well, and soon I earned a tiny, white "Bible" of my own. For a 5-year-old who could not yet read, reciting the sixty-six books of the Bible in order from Genesis to The Revelation was an amazing feat! I was so pleased to receive my prize from Brother Dean. My parents gave me a complete Bible when I was about seven. At nine years old I decided to read through the scriptures and it took me three and a half years; so I was twelve by the time I finished. I loved running across familiar Bible narratives that I had read in my Bible story books, and reading the actual account from scripture. When I was thirteen or fourteen years of age my sister, Dorcas, offered to buy me a new, white zipper Bible with my name engraved on the front in gold if I would memorize all the chapters, passages, songs and poems that she assigned to me! She made the same offer to two other siblings, so we all took the challenge and earned our new Bibles! I remember memorizing ten Psalms, Isaiah 53, Romans 12, John 14, Ephesians 5, the Ten Commandments, the Beatitudes, and a song, "Take Time to be Holy", among other pieces.

I was baptized in water at the lagoon in Long Beach, California with my brother and sisters and a group from our church. We were asked to give testimonies of our confession of faith in the Lord Jesus Christ as our Savior. I remember that my sisters had all ended theirs with, "...and I want to go all the way with Him"; so I decided that would be a good ending for my testimony, too! I experienced water baptism twice, and when I asked my mother the reason for that she told me why. The first time I was only baptized in the Name of Jesus; but our father wanted us to be baptized "in the Name of the Father, Son, and Holy Spirit". Both events, however, were jubilant and glorious times of worship and celebration in my memory.

Saturdays were busy because we spent all day getting ready for Sunday. "The Lord's Day" was all about God and others. We worked diligently to get everything done around the house as well as preparing ourselves with baths, hair washing, shoe polishing and studying of Sunday School lessons. Sunday morning was always happy. At breakfast we listened to music on the radio from Angeles Temple, and then got ready for church quickly so we could get there early. We sang all the way to church. Sunday is still my favorite day and I always associate it with being clean, joyous, and restful—having the work all done in order to relax and enjoy the entire day in God's house. We always attended both Sunday School hour and the morning church service. Our mid-day family meal was kept simple; and the rest of the day we were expected to be quiet, to rest, read, or take a nap in preparation for the evening church service.

We had special Sunday dresses that we only wore for special occasions and had to change out of as soon as we got home. I loved them all, though we only had one at a time. Once I remember that all five of us girls had similar–almost matching–Sunday dresses that were made of flowered Batiste with ribbons for belts and matching ones for our hair. Mama would tie our long hair up in rags the night before and it would hang in long ringlets the next day. We got lots of compliments on how nice we looked. Once we were called "The Braid Family" because we had five girls who wore their hair in braids—except on Sundays.

Daddy often took us to the beautiful Echo Park after church. We were dressed up in our church clothes so there was no rowdy play but we walked down shady lanes and across little arched bridges. We watched the ducks in the ponds and were awed by the beautiful, stately swans. We sat on the benches and enjoyed the scenery, all the beautiful flowers and cultivated landscapes. This garden backdrop for a season of my life is etched deep in my memory, and I still enjoy bringing it back in full detail! Mama always said, "We don't have a yard where we can plant pretty flowers; but we can go to the park and enjoy all the beautiful scenery that God made especially for us to enjoy."

Later on, as a teenager in Tujunga, California, we attended the Assembly of God church in nearby La Crescenta. After the Sunday service, Daddy would often buy fresh lunch meat, cheese, and bread. After eating our own lunch at home, our family would form an assembly line and make deluxe sandwiches with pickles and the  works to wrap individually and pack in a large grocery bag to take to a street meeting. In those days, we often went down to Los Angeles to sing and testify on the corners at The Plaza or Pershing Square. Daddy taught us many songs to sing at the street meetings. He treasured "Jesus Loves Even Me" and many of the Christian choruses of the day that had a clear salvation message. As people began to gather, Daddy would give a short message and sometimes have one of us give our own testimony of faith in Christ. After sharing the gospel we would all sing together and he would close in prayer. We handed out the sandwiches, often with gospel tracts which Daddy always had plenty of, before going back to church for the evening service. The entire day was dedicated to the Lord, from morning until night.

This spiritual foundation carried us though all of our travels and adventures as a family with joy, and through our frightening experiences with peace and trust. Every crisis drew us closer together and to the Lord as we all cried out to Him for mercy and divine intervention. We saw many miracles and developed a great sense of confidence in God's protection and care over His people. As a younger child, these truths were most evident; but as I grew up I began to experience the more difficult challenges of the Christian walk. I learned about dying to self, identifying with the sufferings of Christ, and believing God in the face of circumstantial contradictions. It's not easy to brush away the tears, ignore your fears, walk through deep waters, go through the fire, smile when your heart is breaking, and do what you *need* to do instead of what you feel like doing! Only by dying to ourselves can we experience the almighty power of Resurrection Life. When we *fully* trust Jesus, rely on supernatural strength, defy the Devil who is trying to destroy us, obey God's Word and never give up, we can have ongoing victory! Jesus is more than enough for every fiery trial of life and, although there is no easy way to die, we are never alone in our battles.

My life verse is Romans 8:28 (KJV):

> "And we know that all things work together for good to them that love God; to them who are the called according to His purpose..." (35) "Who shall separate us from the love of Christ? Shall tribulation, or distress, or persecution, or famine, or nakedness, or peril, or sword? As it is written, 'For thy sake we are killed all the day long; we are accounted as sheep for the slaughter'; Nay, in all these things we are more than conquerors through Him that loved us. For I am persuaded, that neither death, nor life, nor angels, nor principalities, nor powers, nor things present, nor things to come, nor height, nor depth, nor any other creature shall be able to separate us from the love of God which is in Christ Jesus our Lord."

We had a plaque on our kitchen wall at Foothill Boulevard that I memorized when I was about eight years old. The poem was: "What God Hath Promised"[1]

> *God hath not promised skies always blue;*
> *Flower-strewn pathways all our lives through.*
> *God hath not promised sun without rain;*
> *Joy without sorrow; Peace without pain;*
> *But God hath promised strength for the day,*
> *Rest for the laborer, light for the way;*

> *Grace for each trial, help from above;*
> *Unfailing sympathy, undying love.*

One of my daughters now has the same poem on a wall in her home. The message is as true today as it was then. God is faithful to provide all that we need.

Daily Delights

Mama was a good cook, and I loved everything she ever made! Suppertime, which we called the evening meal, was probably my favorite time of day. We ate together at every meal, but supper was more special because it seemed like we had more time together. The girls helped to set the table and Mama did most of the meal preparation. Daddy liked to sing a song to call us to the table. Often he would choose "Revive Us Again" with all the verses; or a happy chorus. When all nine of us were seated he would offer thanks to the Lord for His bountiful provision, and then the food would be passed around the table. The conversation was always pleasant but we were not allowed to be noisy. If anything was brought up that was unpleasant, Daddy would say, "Don't talk about that at the table." When the meal was over everyone would pitch in to clean up and do dishes, according to whose turn it was to do each particular chore. Mama always orchestrated this schedule diligently to ensure that we were all duly exposed to the necessary responsibilities of home life. Being the youngest girl, however, I don't think my name came to the top of the list very often while my elder sisters were at home, except as a helper learning the ropes.

We always had meals at home; going out to eat was never even a thought in our minds! Mama cooked three good meals every day. Our main diet for breakfast was cereal—usually oatmeal—toast, and hot cocoa. We always had good jam, jelly or peanut butter for our toast. We had a lot of cornmeal mush, which I still love to this day! Sometimes we had scrambled eggs, Cream of Wheat or warm, white rice with milk, sugar, and cinnamon on it. Periodically, she soaked and cooked whole wheat for hours and served it as a cereal. Once in a while we had pancakes, or biscuits and gravy. She made muffins of all kinds.

Lunch was usually a soup—tomato or potato, and sometimes split-pea with ham—with crackers or sandwiches. Sometimes we had plain bread with gravy. I remember Mama's fried potatoes and her fluffy, homemade bread –baked daily on the homestead—that saturated our one-room house with savory aromas! She made meatloaf often, and sometimes lamb chops for Daddy. My favorite menu was probably roast beef and gravy but a close second would have been her homemade cornbread and beans seasoned with salt, pepper and onion. We had this a lot because we raised pinto beans on the homestead. A pot of beans is nostalgic to me! I still make this for myself and enjoy it! Mama cooked lots of rice and prepared potatoes in every way imaginable: baked, fried, mashed, boiled in chunks, or pressed from leftover mashed potatoes into patties to fry in a skillet.

Everyone loved Mama's stew. She always used the pressure cooker to tenderize the meat, and then added the vegetables and perfect seasonings. With carrots grown in our garden, she sometimes grated them for a salad mixed with mayonnaise and raisins.

Mama made lots of good desserts, too; cakes, pies and cookies. She brought apples up from our dirt cellar on the homestead and made fresh, warm applesauce or her wonderful apple pie. One of my favorites was baked apple slices with cinnamon and brown sugar. She poured fresh cream over them and served them in a bowl. She made taffy and chewy peanut butter candy by boiling honey, stirring in peanut butter and pouring it in greased pans to cool before cutting apart.

Nothing was wasted, so rice or oatmeal puddings with raisins were common creations from breakfast cereal leftovers. I loved her home-baked custard, which I make very often to this day, and share with my friends in the Senior Apartments where I live. It seems to be as much a treat for them as it was for me, and for my own children who all inherited the recipe! You can find this one and more of my favorites below under *Mama's Heirloom Recipes*.

When we lived in town, Mama had an electric range to cook on. I don't remember having refrigerators much, although there was one at the house on Ivy Street. We had iceboxes at times, but couldn't usually afford to have the ice delivered! We always managed somehow. Other people were beginning to have electric toasters then, but we toasted our bread in the oven.

I loved watching my mother cook. She was very good about explaining to us what she was doing, and why. She always allowed us in the kitchen and often asked spontaneously if we'd like to "crack the egg", "beat the batter", and such. Mama was a first-class homemaker and she taught us girls the ropes of cleaning, cooking, washing, mending and ironing. We all helped with chores around home. When we were teenagers living in Tujunga my jobs were things like scrubbing the bathroom sink and tub, emptying waste baskets and peeling potatoes. We all took turns washing dishes, setting the table, helping to fix meals, cutting up vegetables for salad, mixing and serving drinks, or whatever Mama needed. Daddy drove the family car to work in Los Angeles so Rosemary and I were usually the ones that took Mama's grocery list and walked to the store every day. We shopped for the groceries and carried the bags home. I remember that it always seemed like a very long walk!

There are many sounds and scents that are nostalgic to me, bringing back fond memories of my childhood: The smell of well-seasoned pinto beans cooking reminds me of winter days on the homestead. The smell of hamburger frying, homemade bread baking, fried or baked potatoes all remind me of Mama in the kitchen; along with the smell of Palmolive or Lifebuoy soap! A wood fire burning, a tea kettle steaming on the stove, the smell of a hot iron all remind me of Mama ironing our clothes, keeping the home fires burning and the lamps lit. I loved the buzz of activity on a summer morning as Mama handed out chore assignments before we could go out to play: laundry done, beds made, dishes washed and floors mopped. I loved the clean feeling of hanging freshly washed clothes outside on the clothesline, or the smell of a hot iron ready to press all the wrinkles out. Mama's clean house inspired me to love and appreciate the effort it took to keep my own house when I grew up. I always loved housekeeping, and felt privileged and fulfilled in making my own house a home for my cherished family, just like Mama did for us.

Our home life was well-ordered, as we were all required to obey and respect authority; to honor our parents and elders. We were always held accountable for our actions, our words, and our time. We were taught to be responsible with our money and possessions, knowing that we would someday give an account to God for our stewardship. We were never allowed to waste time, or anything of value, or to damage or destroy any property. We had to get permission before using anyone else's things. We were responsible to help with any family duties, as assigned, and to participate in any family work projects. We learned an excellent work ethic from our hard-working parents, as well as the importance of being prepared and punctual for scheduled activities and getting to the table on time for every meal.

Every Saturday was a work day to clean up after a busy week and prepare for the Lord's Day. Mama would gather cleaning supplies and put us all to work. As the youngest girl, I was always learning how to do everything. I remember Mama saying, "Don't keep scrubbing too long in the same spot! You'll wash the paint off the wall! Just wipe around the doorknobs and wherever you see fingerprints or smudges."

Our laundry chores included hanging the wet clothes out on the line to dry and then bringing them in to fold, iron, and put away. We had no special laundry detergent; in those days bar soaps were used for everything from dishes to bathing. Lux was for baths; but for laundry we grated slabs of P & G white laundry soap into our wringer washing machine and then agitated it until it dissolved. Then we put the first white load in, and after it was clean we rolled each piece of clothing through the wringer into a tub of rinse water. Then we put the next-lightest colored load into the same washer to clean, wring and rinse in the same way finally ending with the darkest colors, such as blue jeans.

We always enjoyed plain and simple furnishings, and our dwellings were never elaborate. Our family would have been considered very poor by worldly standards. We were, as the Bible says, "Poor in this world, but rich in faith." Everything in our lives was common and shared. I never had my own room, and never thought about wanting one. We shared dressers and closets—when we had them—and slept three in a bed on the homestead; I was usually in the middle. I always fell asleep instantly, so all I remember about bedtime is getting in and getting up! To this day I am a testimony to Psalm 127:2 that says, *"The Lord giveth his beloved sleep."* (KJV) When I was twelve and a half we moved to California again and actually slept on army cots in tents! Later, when °°Daddy got bunk beds for all of us with springs and mattresses we felt rich because we each had our own! I loved making my bed as soon as I got out of it. I remember the sun shining through the window on summer mornings; I would leap out of bed feeling that I must have overslept and was wasting precious time because my siblings were already up-and-at-'em!

Mama's Heirloom Recipes

Here are a few recipes our family enjoyed that have been passed down from Mama to at least three more generations of cooks!

— Mama's Home-Baked Custard —

3 eggs
¼ c. sugar
1 tsp. vanilla
2 c. milk, scalded
Dash of salt

Beat the eggs, then add all other ingredients. Pour into custard cups or a large Pyrex dish. Sprinkle with nutmeg and bake at 325° for 40 minutes (she doubled this recipe for our large family).

— Mama's Meatloaf —

2 lbs. ground beef
1 beaten egg
1 T. chopped onion
1½ tsp. sage
2 slices of dry bread, moistened & crumbled
¼ tsp. celery seed (optional)
Salt and Pepper to taste

Mix all ingredients well and form into a loaf. Place in center of baking dish with 1/8 inch water, unless using a loaf pan. Cover with foil and bake for 45 minutes at 350°. Uncover and top with a sauce made of ketchup, Worcestershire Sauce and tomato sauce. Bake uncovered for 10 minutes longer.

— Mama's Beef Stew —

Cut lean beef into 1-inch chunks and brown in skillet with 2 T. shortening. Place browned meat in large saucepan or Dutch oven with 6 cups water, salted. Add carrots chopped into 2-inch chunks. Cook the meat and carrots while preparing other vegetables, and adding them in the order of how fast they cook. Add potatoes after cooking carrots for 10 minutes; then add celery and onions. Season the stew with pepper and other desired spices, such as parsley and sweet basil. To the skillet used for browning the meat, add 2 T. flour and brown it in meat drippings; then add 1 cup water, whisking to blend. After the mixture thickens, add it to the stew and stir to thicken the broth.

— *Mama's Traditional Birthday Cake* —

½ c. shortening

1½ c. sugar

2 beaten eggs

1 tsp. vanilla

2½ c. flour

½ tsp. salt

3 tsp. baking powder

1 c. milk

Cream shortening and sugar together. Add eggs and vanilla, beat until fluffy. Add dry ingredients alternately with milk, mixing thoroughly after each addition. Pour into 2 waxed-paper lined 8-inch cake pans. Bake at 350° for 25-30 minutes. (This recipe also makes one dozen cupcakes). For a 3-layer cake, increase the recipe by half.

— *Seven-Minute Frosting* —

2 egg whites

1½ c. sugar

1½ tsp. light corn syrup or ¼ tsp. cream of tartar

1/3 c. cold water

Dash of salt

1 tsp. vanilla

Place all ingredients except vanilla in double boiler; mix well. Cook frosting mixture, beating with egg beater or electric mixer constantly until stiff peaks form (about 7 minutes). Remove from heat; stir in vanilla. Frost and stack cake layers, spreading strawberry jam, sliced bananas, or pudding between layers. Top frosted cake with shredded coconut.

Playtime Chronicles

We could invent more fun with almost nothing than any family of kids I ever knew. Indoors we played *Jacks* a lot and I became proficient at all the different levels–from "Onesies" to "Sweep the floor; move a chair; pick it up, and put it there". We told riddles and stories; played guessing games, *Checkers, Dominos, Pick-up-Sticks, My Ship Goes Sailing, Button-Button-Who's Got the Button?* and all kinds of "pretend". We loved many Bible games and quizzes, too.

Like most little girls, we loved "playing house" with dolls. We made play houses out of cardboard boxes with as many homemade accessories as we could come up with. We were "mothers" cooking, cleaning, caring for our "children" and taking them to church where we sang hymns, prayed, and "preached" about angels, miracles and all the Bible stories. When we played paper dolls we would cut people out of the Sears Catalog to make families of mothers, fathers, children and babies. We played Jacks, at which I was proficient, with all the levels and rhymes to go with it. We also had Amateur Hour talent shows when each one would share a song, poem, story or experience in turn. Of course, we all loved to sing any time!

Outside play usually included our brothers and sometimes a few neighbors. We played games like *Marbles, Tug-of-War,* and *Cars.* Since we had so many siblings we could always play any popular group games such as *Hide n' Seek, Mother May I, Red Rover,* and *Big Bad Wolf.* We had a game called *Statue.* Rosie would take our hands and go fast in circles; then she would let go and however we landed we had to stay in place. The funniest "statue" was chosen as the winner. I really enjoyed *Hopscotch* and *Jump Rope;* only Lois and Rosie could beat me! I learned all those fun, rhythmic verses that we chanted when we played. My favorite Jump Rope rhyme was:

> *Down by the river, down by the sea*
> *Johnny broke a bottle, and blamed it on me.*
> *I told Ma; Ma told Pa; and Johnny got a lickin' so Ha! Ha! Ha!*
> *How many lickin's did Johnny get: One, Two, Three...*

As we got older, David would find places where we could play ball. We loved *Three Flies Up,* baseball, dodgeball or soccer. We got so much practice at home that we all excelled in our P.E. classes. We had our own team to practice with all the time for almost any sport!

My older brother, David, could carve anything out of a block of wood with his pocket knife. He used a coping saw from time to time for cutting out larger items, such as a pair of stilts that he once made. For smaller, more intricate items, he whittled all the details and fine-tuned them with sandpaper. One of our favorite activities was playing *Cars.* He made each of us girls the wooden car of our choice and then helped us make miniature cities with block buildings on which he whittled roofs and chimneys and added drawn windows and doors. He even made a Post Office with a tiny American flag! We had a church, a gas station, and stores lining the little roads that we traced in the sand, where we poked in twigs for trees and bushes. We could play all day with our miniature city, driving our cars around our town.

I loved my childhood and could write volumes more of happy memories. We lived simply but had everything we needed and were very content. There were a few times that I wished for something else, like being able to ride a bike or learning to ride a horse; but there's not much of anything that I would want to change. When I was seven or eight, I had a neighbor that I barely knew who allowed me to coast down the sidewalk on her bicycle until I learned to balance. It happened so naturally that my rides were easy and smooth; I never crashed. It was exhilarating, a dream come true; but I never got another opportunity until I was grown. I never wanted things for my own children that I didn't have for myself growing up, like so many young parents do these days. The few things I thought I wanted then were not important as time went by. Now I always encourage young parents that teaching their children to "be content with such things as you have" will make them much happier in the long run than striving to give them everything they want as they are growing up!

I never had a pet of my own but we had lots of family pets and, being number six out of seven, I never had the chore of caring for them! There were no house pets, and no special privileges. They all stayed outside; the dogs ate table scraps and were plenty healthy without the expense of specialized pet foods. We had a cat when we lived on the farm and we gave her milk from our cows periodically; but the rest of the time she had to catch mice for her supper, at which she was very proficient! At Lynwood we had a dog named Bowdger. We were not overly sentimental about cats or dogs; they weren't companions for us—we already had plenty of quality companionship! We were very kind and caring toward all of our animals but they definitely had a particular purpose to fulfill, especially on the homestead.

We had a smart, little dog named Tippy that I liked very much. He was a short-haired dog but stayed outside through all kinds of weather with our other farm animals. He was a good watchdog, always barking at strangers, but never barking unnecessarily. He was well-fed on the pheasants and jack rabbits that he caught himself. He was also a pro at catching gophers and snakes, although I would not blame him if he didn't feast on those! Sometimes we gave him fresh milk from our cow, and if we threw him a biscuit or some table scrap he would always catch it in mid-air. He was self-taught! He obeyed our commands to sit or lay down, too. We had milk cows and, though I was allowed to experience the milking, that chore was reserved for Daddy and the boys. Daddy also had a goat that he milked.

Celebrations and Holidays

Every celebration as I grew up was Christian in nature because God was the center of our home, even on our birthdays. No outsiders were invited, but we had a family dinner together with Mama's famous and traditional family birthday cake! This three-layer, confection was piled high with fluffy, white frosting! She put candles on the top and the family always sang a cheerful "Happy Birthday" song to the member of honor. We gave homemade cards in which we had all written poems or loving accolades for the birthday person, plenty of hugs and kisses, and then we all contributed to the special prayer spoken over him or her. Although gifts were not the focus or the norm, we girls would occasionally get barrettes for our hair or a new box of crayons from Mama and Daddy; or ribbons from Grandma Bunt on occasion. I always felt loved and celebrated, surrounded by joy and security, blessed and happy! Birthdays were even celebrated at church! The birthday person was called forward to bring a birthday offering of loose change (usually corresponding to the number of years we were celebrating) as the church family sang the "Christian Birthday Song":

A Happy Birthday to you! A Happy Birthday to you!
May you feel Jesus near; every day of the year!
A Happy Birthday to you! A Happy Birthday to you!

And the best year you've ever had!

My most special birthday memory was in Tujunga when I turned fourteen. My sister, Rosemary, had a job at the May Company in Los Angeles so she had a little money to spend. She bought me a darling red jacket with gold buttons, which I adored, and a cute white blouse! I felt extra celebrated!

On Valentine's Day, we exchanged homemade cards that we had made for each other. Rosemary could write poems on hers, and draw pictures. Mama taught us how to weave heart-shaped paper baskets to fill with candy.

At Easter time we sometimes got new dresses and ribbons for our hair. We always dressed up in our Sunday best. I loved the wonderful Easter choirs, programs and performances of the resurrection that our church presented and considered it a great privilege to participate in them. To this day, I remember the memorized scriptures, recitation pieces, and songs that we learned. It was so exhilarating and unforgettable! Later, as a teenager, I remember an Easter drama directed by a young and gifted man in our church, Melvin Harold. He was very musical and also led the Easter choir. The drama of Jesus' life, the Garden of Gethsemane, Judas' betrayal, Jesus' trial and his death on the cross were all so impressive and real that I cried buckets of tears and pledged my love anew to Christ, my Savior, for life.

The church celebrated Mother's Day by giving every mother a carnation. I remember Mama quoting a poem that said, *"There is a day in sunny May throughout the whole creation, when every mother in the land should have a pink carnation"*.

On Father's Day the pastor always preached a challenge to the men about being godly dads and husbands, as well as living exemplary lives in their communities. After the message he had them stand so that he could pray over them; we always sang the hymn, "Faith of our Fathers", too.

Independence Day was celebrated with a church picnic, but I don't remember seeing any fireworks in the city.

We never celebrated Halloween as the world does because of its occult roots, and our parents were very careful about where we went and who we were with. Once I remember them allowing us girls to attend a Halloween Party at our church in La Crescenta when we were teenagers. I did enjoy some of the games, but a lot of it was insignificant to me. I would have rather enjoyed regular fellowship with lots of singing! Later, when Gail and I were married and pastoring churches, we sponsored activities like hayrides, bobbing for apples and other harvest events in the fall of the year for our youth groups. I always had mixed feeling about these things. Even as a very young pastor's wife, I felt responsible to exemplify to our youth the strong values and quality lifestyle taught in the Bible; yet so many celebrations that were "borrowed" from the world seemed like a pointless waste of precious time.

Thanksgiving was always a wonderful day! It was a time to thank the Lord for his many blessings and to take time to reflect on the past year with gratefulness. Sometimes we had a turkey dinner with dressing and all the trimmings; but other times we just had a simple family meal. Mama always made pumpkin or apple pies. The most special memory to me was that Daddy was off work and we were all home together. It seemed very much like a Sunday, quiet and peaceful. We slept a little later, and woke up to good things already cooking in the kitchen! Being home from school made it a fun time for us to play games, sing, read stories and recite Bible memory pieces. After every Thanksgiving dinner, Daddy read the Bible, sang songs and had each one of us share what we were most thankful for that year. I always had a happy, family feeling about Thanksgiving—contented, blessed, and hopeful for tomorrow.

In 1950, on our last pioneer farm in Black Canyon, my mother asked me if I would like to bake the turkey for Thanksgiving dinner. I had graduated from High School, but was only sixteen years old and had never done anything like that alone—not with all those elder sisters around! So I was reluctant, and hesitated at the opportunity; but she said she would show me how, and she did. Lois and I made the dressing, stuffed the turkey, greased and salted the breast and covered it with a greased tea towel. As it roasted, I had to baste it again and again to keep it from burning and drying out because it was so big we couldn't cover it with a lid! I am happy to report that it turned out great! The experience was enjoyable and resulted in a wonderful dinner, a happy day, and a life-long confidence that I would always be able to cook a great turkey! Mama's pumpkin and apple pies were the best; and she made an apple-nut salad with whipped cream and Maraschino cherries, which I loved and carried into my own family traditions later.

Christmas at our house was always quiet, peaceful and joyous. We always received mixed nuts in the shell, oranges and some candy; but it was never about Santa Claus, reindeer, or getting presents for ourselves. Daddy read the Christmas story from the Bible and we talked about how much God must have loved us to send Jesus to earth as our Savior to die for our sins. We sang Christmas carols and had a nice dinner together.

One Christmas at Ivy Street was a special memory because Daddy bought us Bible Story Books. There were four volumes in this series of the *Bible Story Reader*,[2] and each of my sisters got one. I couldn't read yet, but the books were full of beautiful pictures illustrating the stories, which my sisters would read to me regularly. I heard them so often that I memorized one of the volumes in its entirety and can still recite some of the stories and poems. Those beautiful stories played a big part in forming some of my earliest concepts of God and Jesus, for which I was always very grateful. I still remember some of the pieces such as this one, which was illustrated with a picture of squirrels with acorns up in an oak tree:

> *"God is Love!" the squirrels chatter, as they gather winter's food.*
> *And my heart is filled with gladness; God is great, and He is good!*
> *God is Love! I'm sure He's watching over squirrels and birdies, too.*
> *God is Love! I'm sure he's looking lovingly at me and you.*

The illustration for another one was a picture of a little girl planting a seed in the garden soil.

> *Into the earth, little seed, you must go!*
> *Else you will never grow up! Don't you know?*
> *I'll tuck you in snugly. The sun and the rain*
> *Will help you to come through the ground once again.*
>
> *So cuddle down, little seed, in your cozy bed.*
> *I'll watch for the day when you lift up your head.*
> *The birdies will sing a sweet lullaby,*
> *While under the ground you quietly lie*
>
> *When you wake, little seed, and peep to the light,*
> *You will hear the tap-tap of the raindrops bright;*
> *You will see the sun fairies playing about,*
> *And coaxing the rest of your family out.*
>
> *Down in your heart, little seed, don't you know?*
> *God put a wee germ to help you to grow.*
> *So hurry, dear seed, and come up right away!*
> *I'll be there to watch and to love you each day.*

Another favorite was a picture of a little girl and boy in their pajamas kneeling together on a window bench. The window had pull-back curtains and the children's faces were tipped upwards looking into the night sky. The poem read:

> *Little stars that twinkle in the heavens blue,*
> *I have often wondered if you ever knew*
> *How there shone one like you, leading wise, old men*

From the East, a long way, down to Bethlehem.
Did you see the presents they, in love, had brought?
Did you see the home which they in wonder sought?
Little stars that twinkled in the heavens blue,
All you know of Jesus, how I wish I knew!

One about the first Christmas Day reads:

In another land and time,
Long ago and far away,
Was a little baby born
On that first glad Christmas Day.

"Words of Truth and deeds of love
Filled his life from day to day;
So that all the world was blessed
On that first glad Christmas day.

"Little children did He love,
With a tender love always;
So should little children be
Always glad on Christmas Day.

I remember waking up one Christmas morning to see seven brown paper sacks sitting on our little wooden table. This is what we had instead of Christmas Stockings. Every bag had a large orange on top–the biggest I ever saw–and when my little brother, Paul, saw them he exclaimed, "Punkins!" which filled the cabin with hearty laughter. The little bags were filled with a variety of nuts, hard candy, chocolate bonbons, a candy cane and some gum drops. We were so excited and happy, delighting in every nibble of our edible treasures!

An important part of our Christmas holidays was participating in the activities at the churches we attended in the neighborhoods where we lived. I was often involved in a Christmas program, memorizing a short piece to recite, or taking part in a group song to be performed on stage. Although I never acted in a church drama production, I always loved watching them. When I was fourteen, our family had an opportunity to attend a professional musical drama in Los Angeles, California performed at Angeles Temple at Christmas time. The title of the drama was a very long word that I cannot recall; but it told the gospel story from The Creation through Christ's Ascension. There were two staircases on either side of the auditorium that arched from the balcony down to the stage. During the part about the birth of the Christ child, both of these staircases were lined with angels! As a young person, this awesome depiction of glory and might impressed me the most! I almost felt like I was among that poor group of shepherds, *"keeping watch over their flocks by night"*, who were so favored by God as to witness this glorious sight! It was a beautiful and inspiring production that I will never forget.

Aside from some outings like picnicking and Griffith Park Zoo, we didn't have vacations that I remember. One time when we lived on the homestead Daddy took us on a fishing trip. David was already gone to Bible College. I don't remember much about it except that we went to Payette Lake, rented a boat and Daddy only caught one fish! Although traditional American family vacations were not in my scope of reference, our many moves provided lots of road trips! It was always so exciting to pack up all our belongings, empty out the whole house and give away whatever we couldn't take with us. Mama was always very organized; laying out the clothes we would wear, packing up food for the trip and bedding to sleep on. We would get up before sunrise, have a good breakfast, comb and freshly braid our hair and get into the car in our designated spots. Daddy drove, David sat next to him, and Mama was on the passenger side with little Paul on her lap. We five girls were packed in the back seat. Mama always had a big lunch packed by her feet on the front floorboard. Traveling was always happy and exciting! We started out with a prayer for traveling safety and then we began to sing, and sang most of the way! Almost every song was in harmony, providing the greatest delight to my songbird heart!

We only stopped for gas; there were no rest areas like there are these days. Mama handed us sandwiches when we got hungry and we ate as we traveled. If we needed a potty break, we had to get out and find cover behind the bushes or in gullies alongside the road. On the desert roads we were sometimes allowed to get out and run awhile for some exercise. My older siblings would point out sites of special interest along the way. I felt like I was on a special tour, and I loved traveling! I'm sure that our many spontaneous, cross-country moves were at least as exciting and adventurous as many planned vacation outings could be!

Hobbies and Inclinations

To begin with, I think that a person's favorite subjects in school are very telling about their personality in general. In Kindergarten my favorites were Story Time and Recess! In First Grade it was Music; Second Grade, Reading; Third and Fourth, Math. Fifth Grade was a hard year for me because we had moved to Idaho and the schools were more advanced than California's, so I didn't like much of anything. In Sixth Grade I liked English and Geography; but Seventh Grade was another hard year because of moving again. Eighth Grade was a picnic! We had moved back to California where the studies were much easier, so everything was fun. I never did take to U.S. Government or History much; too many dates, names and places to remember in which I had no interest. The tests were always hard and I think I came out with a 'C' in those subjects.

Home Economics was my high school major, and my cooking and sewing classes were favorites. I got straight A's in those, and I still love to do all kinds of cooking, crafts, and sewing. Mama helped me make a handkerchief when I was young. She showed me how to cut it evenly and hem the edges, then to embroider some small daisies in the corner. Later, I made some doilies. I sewed quite a few things in my classes, but I can't remember them all. I made a cloth bag with a draw-string, an apron, a gathered skirt, and several blouses and dresses. It was very frustrating to sew at school because the teacher would not allow us to move to the next step without her inspection and approval of every cut and stitch! So we spent most of our time waiting in line!

My sister, Rosemary, bought a sewing machine when she got married and sewed a lot. She helped me make a couple of cute dresses, which I enjoyed much more than the tedious, supervised projects in Home Economics! I also learned to mend and alter clothing which I still love and spend time on. Resourcefulness is rewarding! I would rather repair or update something I already have than spend money on something new! Later in life, I made many baby quilts and craft items for others as gifts and found that, in addition to turning out as a better fit for my small budget, a homemade item from the heart was always valuable to the receiver as well.

My favorite toys were undoubtedly dolls, but I didn't have one of my own. The year that I turned four, Lois and Rosemary got rubber dolls with diapers and plastic bottles for Christmas. My rag doll didn't look like a "real baby" to me. I played with my sisters' baby dolls whenever I could get hold of one! I loved to cradle them in my arms and feed them by poking the tiny bottle tip into the little readymade holes of their puckered, rosy mouths.

The swing was my favorite playground toy, although I loved slides, teeter-totters, rings and the merry-go-round. At seven years old, I loved to roller skate. Our family had one pair that we all shared. I wasn't strong enough to tighten them up very well, so they fell off easily but I loved it anyway! My favorite sport was kickball. At eight, riding someone else's bicycle was close enough to having one of my own; and at ten, watching someone ride a horse was as close as I would ever get to having one! Never one to focus on what I didn't have, I simply enjoyed playing the sports that were accessible to me and pretending the rest!

School equipment in high school Physical Education classes provided great opportunities to experience sports we would not otherwise have been able to enjoy. At fourteen, I loved badminton, and at fifteen, basketball. I also enjoyed learning and playing volleyball, lane soccer, and field hockey.

Music was my perpetual, unrivaled love; playing instruments and singing. My favorite songs were the hymns of the church and themes about Heaven. My first exposure to musical instruments was at church where I became acquainted with piano, guitar, drums, saxophone, harmonica, and "bones"–which were rhythm instruments that clicked like tap shoes. I loved them all, but we didn't have instruments of our own until we moved to the homestead. I was eleven years old when Daddy got a little, old pump organ to play. I think it must have belonged to my Grandpa Mussell, as he was a fine musician and songwriter. Even though we never had the opportunity for formal music lessons, I was able to join the school orchestra during my ninth grade year to learn violin. My grandfather had also played the violin well as a young man but would not play it later because he associated it with the secular music provided by fiddlers in the dance halls, which preachers did not frequent. My dad had learned to play the cornet as a young man.

Daddy would always sit at the pump organ and pick out melodies of hymns and gospel songs. He usually played two-part harmony when he learned the song. Mama sometimes played hymns, too, and most of my sisters learned as well. Later on, after we moved back to California, Daddy bought a portable pump organ that we could fold and take with us to street meetings. By then, Jewel could play the hymns by note, adding chords to the base staff. My little brother, Paul, had learned to play the trumpet and the trombone in school and later got a trombone of his own. He was a natural, and could play anything he experimented with! He also learned to play the Baritone, piano, accordion and guitar! The violin lessons that I had in the school orchestra—with my sisters, Rosemary and Lois—never had a chance to blossom. Since there was no way for us to practice we never excelled at it.

I so loved singing, and hearing harmonious special numbers, accompanied by the guitar and accordion that I decided to learn to play both instruments. When I was almost fifteen, I bought a Gibson guitar from a church friend for ten dollars and practiced every day after school. I learned to play in three keys—C, F, and G—and with the capo I knew enough chords to play just about any song I wanted to sing. I played the guitar for our girls' quartet: Jewel, Dorcas, Lois and me! Later, I experimented with the piano and organ; first learning to play the C scale and a few chords. At seventeen, going on eighteen, I ordered an accordion out of the Sears and Roebuck catalog. It was delivered to our home in Black Canyon. I had no one to show me how to play it, and no opportunity for music lessons, so I learned on my own. An extra motivation was my acquaintance with Gail, who kept asking me if I was practicing my accordion because he wanted us to play our instruments together at church meetings! I gave my little guitar to my brother, Paul, when I married and left home.

Years later I discovered the Autoharp and Omni Chord, as well as electronic keyboards, and have enjoyed playing them all! The most popular tunes that I liked best were gospel songs by various quartets and ensemble groups like the Blackwood Brothers and the Stamps Quartet. Two popular soloists during my teen years were Jack Holcome and Ira Stanphill; I learned to play and sing most of his songs, which were a great inspiration to me.

I loved to read, and my favorite books included the Bible, Bible storybooks and *The Pilgrim's Progress*, by John Bunyan, which had the very greatest literary impact on me. It was a poignant analogy of our Christian walk, a pilgrimage through life. It demonstrated in detail how Satan opposes us and tries to set traps for us. At my Junior High age, it had a very positive influence on my own Christian experience. I was very careful to watch for snares and pitfalls, to choose carefully, and to walk circumspectly through life.

During my Junior High years I also read *The Call of the Wild*, by Jack London. Although I enjoyed it very much, I was never fonder of fiction than I was of true stories. Past the grand imaginations of childhood playtimes with my fun-loving sisters, I held a certain sober-mindedness that preferred true stories of bravery and heroic deeds, as told in many Christian biographies. My love of collecting poetry rounded out my reading experience with a touch of cadence and grace—like crystal raindrops splashing into a pond and sending myriads of bobbing ripples in every direction. I still love to read and quote many of the poems from my past collections.

My father loved to read biographies of great men and women of the faith, which is probably where my personal interest began to develop. He often relayed portions to the family which he had read about such greats as George Muller, Charles and John Wesley, Fanny Crosby, Frances Ridley Havergal, and Smith Wigglesworth. *Deeper Experiences of Famous Christians*, by James Gilchrist Lawson and *Foxe's Book of Martyrs*, by John Foxe were two of the great inspirational books that our family read together.

There were, and still are, so many things I love to do; mostly things that are somehow productive or helpful to others. Since my childhood was flocked about by people who practiced the conscientious use of their time, I have maintained this same value as my own. I am apt to more readily justify activities that are in service to the Lord, or a tool of blessing or edification to someone else. This practice produced a natural conviction against wasting precious time. Now it has become an auto-response that kicks in whenever I become involved in a hobby that is time-consuming, yet bears little fruit for the Kingdom. My happiest hobby times have been—and still are—when I choose for enjoyment things that can bless others, too. Sewing baby quilts for young mothers is not something I engage in as often these days; but writing letters, cooking meals for seniors (even though I am one), and singing in rest homes are current activities which I thoroughly enjoy and believe to be an encouragement to those who receive them.

Volunteer Services, as soon as I was old enough, consisted of anything and everything to do with spreading the gospel. I helped with Vacation Bible School when I was fourteen and enjoyed telling stories to the children, as well as assisting with crafts, singing, and tidying the classroom. It was a great experience during which I also learned the Christian Flag salute and the Pledge of Allegiance to the Bible.

Since our family frequented all nearby evangelistic efforts, we attended Billy Graham's very first tent meeting in Los Angeles. I also remember my experience as a Personal Worker in the first Billy Graham Rally at the Hollywood Bowl as a great affair! I had several of those experiences, since Daddy always took us to hear any great evangelist or speaker whose meetings were close enough to attend. We heard evangelists such as Clyde Henson, Oral Roberts, William Freeman and Katheryn Kuhlman. We saw several of the fabulous dramas performed at Angeles Temple, and heard Amy Semple-McPherson and Howard Rustoy preach there. We attended events at the Shrine Auditorium and the Old Pisgah Mission, a place where many of the old time revivalist preachers had ministered. All the "old timers" spoke of the wonderful preaching and singing there; so Daddy took us to one of their Sunday afternoon services. We did lots of street meetings and volunteered—or received invitations—to sing at nursing homes, Juvenile Hall, the jails, the Mission and the State Prison.

Slices of Society

The basic economy during my childhood years was very poor. We were growing up just after The Great Depression. Times were hard and people learned to be thrifty and extremely resourceful. Things were very cheap compared to modern prices, but we still bought only the bare necessities because money was very scarce. Life was simple and most Americans were not concerned about acquiring excessive material possessions. People lived frugally; there was no waste of food, water, electricity, paper, or clothing. Possessions and personal items lasted for years because everyone took care of whatever they had. In our household tools were always cleaned, oiled and hung in the shed or garage. We burned our paper trash in incinerators, buried the garbage, and saved all tin cans to recycle for National Defense. During World War II the scrap drives were promoted every day in school. We wrote rhymes such as, "If you want our troops to win, save your scrap metal and your tin!"

Everyone was willing to work and do their share; and we never expected to be paid for doing things around home. There was no such thing as an "allowance" for doing chores! We didn't get paid to work until we were old enough to find a job.

Commodities were scarce, so they cost less. We might pay eighteen cents for a gallon of gas and maybe only three cents apiece for postage stamps. As my sisters got old enough to work, they might pay ten cents for a bus fare into town. Although dinner at a restaurant was only about seventy-five cents or a dollar, those luxuries were not in the family budget. We grew a garden, baked our bread and shared clothing. Even forty-eight cents for a gallon of milk was plenty; or seventy-five cents for a pound of coffee. A pound of potatoes could be purchased for five cents, as well as a candy bar and, between the two, candy bars were not the option of choice! A new bicycle could be purchased for only twenty-four dollars; but on an average income of barely $2,500 per year—about forty-five dollars per week—this was a sacrifice, not a deal! A house could be purchased for a year's wages, around $2,500, and a new car for about $1,000.

Things were different then; of course there was no television at that time, or small appliances like blenders, cassette players or electric rollers. We curled our hair by tying it up in rags, and later used bobby pins for "pin curls". We were fascinated by new things that were invented, like plastic products and electric appliances. I remember talking on a telephone for the first time when I was fourteen; and I remember hearing records for the first time. As I grew into adulthood so many things began to come on the market that seemed like absolute luxuries–especially since we didn't have anything extra growing up. After washing so many clothes by hand or having old washing machines that were not dependable, I was so thankful to have an automatic washer. After all the hours it took to hang so many baby clothes on the line, every tiny sock and bib, and then having them feel so stiff when they were dry, I remember being thrilled with the electric clothes dryer! All those little clothes came out so warm and soft that I was filled with gratefulness every time I took a load out of the dryer. It saved me from a lot of ironing, too; but even when I did have items that were wrinkled I could use an electric iron instead of one that had to be heated up on a wood stove; so even ironing was a great privilege! Some of the other things that amazed me were electric mixers and skillets, heating pads, electric blankets, tape players. The list kept getting longer and more amazing as the industrial age came into full swing, making life fast and easy.

Anything that saved time was wonderful to me! The vacuum cleaner, dishwasher, and electric range are such gifts because I can remember doing all the work without them! I love everything that helps me keep things clean and tidy. The microwave oven is probably my favorite invention. I use it for almost every meal, and even for canning. It has saved me hours and hours of time and energy that I am able to use on other things that are important to me. I love to "redeem the time" (Ephesians 5:15-17)! Now we even have modern air travel; it not only saves time but prevents the extreme exhaustion that can result from a long road trip. Flying is very expensive, however. I suppose we have to choose these days whether we want to save time or save money. Convenience can be costly!

My personal conviction about conveniences of our modern age is that they are blessings from the Lord and we should show our gratefulness by giving more time to Him and to his work. So often we use our extra time on pleasures and leisure instead of investing it in the Kingdom of God. If you have never lived without these things, it is hard to imagine; but, because of our pioneering days and living on the homestead, I can't even fill a bathtub or take a hot shower without saying, "Thank you, Jesus, for this wonderful warm water." It seems when you have lived without things, you appreciate them more.

Society used to be much more respectful as a whole. People kept the law and honored the police officers, considering them friends, not foes. Children were taught to be law-abiding citizens, helping to build strong communities instead of tearing them down by selfish behavior with no thought for their fellow man. We were proud to be in a country that honored God and His Word, and most of our leaders knew that this foundation was the reason for America's success. We didn't have to worry about the future of our nation because most Americans were dedicated to keeping it strong and healthy for generations to come. When elections came around, they voted for the people who would maintain our strengths, not apologize for them and court our enemies.

We addressed adults by titles such as Mr. or Mrs., Aunt or Uncle, and addressed our elders at church as "Brother" or "Sister", followed by their surname like Smith or Baker. The children and young people were expected to obey adults and to show honor and respect. Children were to be "seen and not heard". We were taught to sit quietly and listen, not to speak in public when adults were present unless we were spoken to. It was common knowledge that things were done only with permission; getting food, getting up from the table, going outside to play. Rules were to be followed, whether at home, church or school; obedience was a way of life and no one felt abused by it!

There was a proper standard for attire in every circumstance, and dressing appropriately was part of showing respect to others in attendance. The fashion trend for girls when I was in grammar school was mainly cotton print dresses, and for boys it was cords or jeans with button and collar shirts.

In Junior High, full gathered skirts were in style, and white blouses with full, puffy sleeves. The skirts were about four inches above the ankles. We wore Bobbie socks with shoes that tied until I was about fourteen. Then the no-socks fad came in and we wore light-weight, slip-on flats.

In High School, the hair style was shoulder-length cuts curled with bobby-pins and combed out fluffy. The cotton print dresses were still trending, or shirt-sleeved pastels. Cap sleeves were fashionable and the dress length was mid-calf. Sack dresses with three-inch wide patent leather belts were very popular. We made them easily with a long piece of fabric doubled over, sides sewn to the armpits, hemmed at the bottom, a dip cut out for the neck, and shoulder pads sewn in; so simple, yet pretty. In winter, long straight skirts were worn with soft pastel sweaters. The skirts were predominately black, brown, beige or grey and cashmere or rabbit hair sweaters were the rage. We also wore little scarf ties with them and, for dressy occasions, we added our 3-inch spiked heels to our skirt ensembles or suits. Our coats back then were long and flared, usually plain colors; I had a long, gray gabardine coat that I loved. We also wore colorful silk scarves with these.

Clothing choice was not about personal preference alone. Everyone wore their best clothing for church, weddings, funerals, graduations, and celebrations of all kinds because it demonstrated honor toward the host and the occasion. I had a yellow taffeta dress for special occasions that drew lots of compliments.

Modesty was expected, required and enforced; if students were not properly dressed for school when they arrived, they were sent home. Ladies didn't wear jeans unless they were working in the fields and, in those days, there were no such things as dress slacks or a pant suit for women. People rarely wore shorts in public and sloppy jeans were considered "home clothes". In fact, when people travelled by plane, train, or bus they ordinarily wore suits and hats. The men got weekly haircuts to keep themselves tidy, and many women saved money by learning to cut hair for their boys and men—often by trial and error!

We frequently received clothes from other people. When I was thirteen a family friend gave us two large boxes of cute clothing from her adopted granddaughters with sizes that fit me. I remember a darling, pink checkered pinafore with a big bow-tie belt and ruffles, which I wore over a white dress. I was so proud of that, and it came just in time to wear to the Southern California Camp Meeting. I felt like the best-dressed girl there!

There were music trends back then just as there are now, but most people sang old war songs like "Rainbow at Midnight", "Blue Eyes Crying in the Rain", "I'll Hold You in my Heart", and "You're my Angel, Judy". Country songs like "Don't Fence me In" were popular, as well as music groups such as The Sons of the Pioneers. Gospel songs were the predominant choice of music in our family, and hymns of the faith.

The movie scene was plenty big in society at that time, but not a part of our life at home. The first movie I ever attended was *The Life of Martin Luther* after I was married and pastoring with my husband in Blackfoot, Idaho. We were previewing it with the Ministerial Association in Pocatello. It was a wonderful story that we really enjoyed.

Television was in the same category—after it was invented, that is, which I remember! Many years after I was grown and married, my dad finally purchased a television in order to watch the news broadcasts and keep up with world events. He posted a small sign on it that said, "No worldly programs, please!"

We felt no need for entertainment because we got such great enjoyment out of our own activities! We went with our church to sing for a Girls' Detention Home, and to street meetings. The Plaza, near the train station, and Pershing Square were literally teaming with sailors, soldiers, Marines and Airmen. The streets were where it all happened in those days; soap box speakers of all kinds, atheists and communists along with evangelists, found busy corners where they could draw a crowd. There were also bums, winos and many homeless people. These were prime locations to sing, give personal testimonies of our faith, pass out gospel tracts and pray for people.

We never had cars of our own as teenagers, and never dared assume that we could ask to use our father's vehicle. It was only his, and was considered a tool to support his livelihood. He took very good care of it and used it for the family only when we needed to travel together. My father was an auto mechanic when we lived in town and a farmer when we lived in the country. We had several cars while I was growing up, and Daddy always kept them in good running condition. The first one I remember was probably a Ford Model A. I remember a Buick that Daddy had to crank in order to start it up. He always insisted that the car be kept clean, and never allowed anything to be left inside when we got out. Many times on long or out-of-state trips I remember him carrying a canteen of water and stopping along the road to add some to the radiator. One time, when we lived on the homestead, we all worked hard to earn the down-payment on a new Ford. It was so clean and pretty, a light aqua-blue; but we enjoyed it for only a short time and then Daddy had to sell it.

I learned to drive when we lived out in Black Canyon on the farm; I was seventeen and my brother, David, offered to teach me so I could get my Driver's License. In those days we simply sent two dollars in the mail to request our license and they sent it to us without reading a book or taking a test of any kind. We used Daddy's Buick and drove down the country roads to a place where I could practice parking, and then drove back. It took about twenty-five minutes! Even though I got my license, I never really got to drive by myself until after I got married. Reliable transportation is a blessing for me, because for much of my married life I had no car available. At eighty-four, I still drive myself all over town to the places that are important to me; and I thank God every time I drive that I have the opportunity, the vehicle, and the ability.

School Days, School Days

School, in general, was different then. Chewing gum was not allowed in school and kids were not allowed to use the restrooms until recess or before and after classes. Spanking was a common and expected teaching tool for both parents and teachers, and was accepted as valuable and effective discipline at home and at school.

I was not quite five when I started kindergarten at Lynwood in 1938. I was afraid at first but the teacher, Miss. Butterfield, was very cheerful and wisely ignored my tears, which helped a lot because no one else seemed to notice. She was loving, sweet, and organized; because of her, my foundational experience was positive and I always loved school after that. When recess time came, another little girl named Edna came and took my hand and said cheerfully, "Do you want to play in the playhouse?" It was so cute and special that it ended my tears! That shows you what a gesture of kindness can do for a sad heart, even among the very young. I loved that playhouse, with its little toy iron and ironing board and tiny dishes. I didn't have toys like these of my own, and loved every minute of it. Maybe that's why I remember playing mostly indoors at Kindergarten. I remember large, soft, rubber balls, London Bridges, and taking rests at our little tables with our heads down on folded arms for a quiet time. Miss Butterfield was beautiful to me. She was young, always pleasant, and a very engaging reader of wonderful stories.

I went to that school through first grade and half of second. Then we moved back to Idaho very briefly and I went to school in Caldwell. This was a time of searching for our family and we were very unsettled, moving back to Los Angeles, across the country to Arkansas, and back to L.A. again. When we lived at Bonnie Bray, a Black community of Los Angeles, I was in second grade where I attended for barely a month because of the extreme racism, which I described earlier.

Then I entered Ivy Street Elementary where our school day was five and a half hours. We started at 9:00 am and went home at 2:30 pm. My second grade teacher was Mrs. Planting who was loving and pleasant. She had brown eyes, shoulder length brown hair and was very pretty. I loved all the subjects, but was especially fond of recess! I enjoyed kickball, the swings, maypoles, rings and merry-go-round, and any kind of organized games. My best friend was Violet. She kept inviting me over to her house but her family was somewhat dysfunctional. Therefore, Mama limited our time together, though finally allowing me to visit her one time for thirty minutes. Violet had a big trunk full of dolls! One of them had *"Magic Skin"*, which was a soft, tender rubber that felt like real skin. It was not rigid like the old rubber dolls and I loved it! However short-lived, it was a dream-come-true!

Next we moved to Tujunga, California where I attended third and fourth grades, and I remember some of my teachers, Mrs. Davis and Mrs. Black. I loved Reading and Spelling and excelled in both. I was assigned as Teacher's Helper in our reading circle. The teacher said to me, "You're a very good reader and you can help your classmates learn to read." So she put me in a circle of kids who could not read well to assist them in sounding out the words they struggled to pronounce while reading aloud. I also did very well in Math. I remember my teacher complimenting me for my aptitude in Arithmetic, and presenting me with an award for getting the best scores in the class.

She called me up to the front saying, "Eunice has earned 100% on all of her math papers so she is receiving this reward for her excellent work!" It was a hair comb with a green pipe cleaner design. Later that very day, another boy and I were called up to work arithmetic problems on the chalkboard for the rest of the class. When my turn came, I was so petrified that I couldn't think and had a total mental block so that all the concepts I had mastered suddenly escaped me!

As I stood there trembling, my teacher said, "Eunice, you know how to do this because you always get the right answer on all your papers. You have done this before so I know you can solve these problems."

With her encouragement I was finally able to get my wits together and perform my math functions, but I was very glad when it was over! I'm not sure what happened after that but, even though I don't remember struggling in school, I certainly did not retain my math prowess throughout the rest of my education. It just became another subject in which to complete my requirements. I was never fond of any kind of drama or speaking before a class; I was painfully shy. I never asked questions, which made me an excellent listener because I had to learn from everyone else's questions.

When we moved to the homestead in Idaho, I was in fifth grade. I attended the Fruitland School for three years. I seldom missed a day at school; our only problems arose from the frequency of our moves. We had to keep adjusting to new environments, teachers, friends and curriculums; but most of my school experience was very pleasurable. Our family moved back to Tujunga, CA in 1946 and I attended Verdugo Hills High School and graduated in June of 1950 at the ripe old age of sixteen. Since Lois and I both entered the same grade at Verdugo Hills we were in the same class from then until we graduated. We got along famously and were best friends–I never felt alone again. We were both skillful in sports and earned high marks in Physical Education class. We also played violins in the orchestra and joined a Bible Club.

We had lots of friends from church that also attended our school, so we enjoyed fun activities together such as revival meetings, Christmas plays, and Youth for Christ rallies. High School was a great experience for me. I was never interested in learning for the sake of knowledge alone. I preferred subjects that were useful for life, gathering information and skills that would be profitable for my future. Even so, I was always a good student, studied well for tests and worked to earn good grades because this was about responsibility, respecting the teachers and doing one's best at any task set forth. Being a person who wanted to do the right thing always served me well, and I always believed that developing a conscientious character was another way that I could please the Lord.

I was glad to be a Christian and to live for God. We testified to all our school friends and lived the Christian lifestyle before them. We didn't really date, nor even have boyfriends in school. I suppose if I had a "first crush" it would have been Lloyd. I was in ninth grade and he was a sophomore. We both walked home for lunch each day; sometimes he would be in front of me and sometimes behind, but we never walked together. Once in a while our eyes would meet, and his were soft and brown, but I never got to know him. He gave me one of his school pictures and he signed my annual; that was the extent of our friendship! We did not attend co-ed parties, even though we were invited periodically. We didn't participate in the dances, sports events or school assemblies, yet never felt that we were missing anything! We never questioned our family conviction that these activities were unsuitable for Christians because we were always very busy doing other things we loved! Since we spent all of our time and energy in Christian circles we were not "worldly wise". We didn't know the names of movie or sport stars, read the comics or use common slang in our communication. Never being exposed to "bad influence", I grew up as innocent and protected as any child ever could. We were modest teenagers accustomed to appropriate Christian behavior and not interested in finding out what might be going on in the neighborhood or the social scene, despite the rumors that always make the circuit at this stage of life. We were separate from the world around us, but considered being "separated unto God" as the highest calling and felt privileged to be on "higher ground" free from the dangers and risks of our fallen society. Aside from our ninth grade health class film about boy/girl anatomy and the reproductive process, the only sexual content we were familiar with was Mama's exhortation that "Nakedness is an abomination to God" and the Bible accounts demonstrating dire consequences of wrong choices! We identified with the blessings of right choices, and God's desire to warn us of pitfalls and to keep us clean and pure. It all made perfect sense to me and I was very comfortable with who I was and what I knew.

Work-a-day World

Until I was about seven years old, I don't remember helping very much around the house. My first chores were things like setting the table for a meal, or clearing it afterwards. On cleaning days, Mama would give us rags and let us wash the woodwork, or clean sinks or tubs. Even though we had few heavy responsibilities, we were all Mama's helpers at her beck and call. We swept walks and ironed handkerchiefs. She would often say things like, "Take this out to the chickens" or "Bring in a bucket of water" and we followed her directives.

Helping with family chores was part of life and we were happy to do it.

When we moved to the homestead in Idaho, every hand was needed and this is where I really learned to work hard! We all had to "grub brush" and load it on the "slip". Grubbing brush was a process of loosening the brush from the soil in order to clear the land. The first step was to break up the brush with a disc harrow pulled behind a team of horses. This was frightening at first because the men at the stock auction had lied to Daddy about the training and ability of the team he was looking to buy. After getting them home, it became obvious that only one horse was well-trained, while the other was not at all familiar with the process. This one got spooked while pulling the disc harrow and began to run wildly and jump sideways. When they got out of control, Daddy lost his footing and was clinging to the reins shouting, "Whoa! Whoa!" as he stumbled along behind them with those sharp discs bouncing along too close for comfort! He finally got them stopped and the vision of their big, sweaty bodies flinching and shaking all over was traumatic to me. Another time, the same unruly horse got spooked while pulling a plow and went leaping and bucking until he broke the halter and all the straps and kicked himself free from the other team horse, which stood there dutifully and staring at the bronc as if to say, "What in the world is wrong with you! It's just a farmer and a plow!"

Daddy would keep all of his farming implements clean and tidy in their own place while not in use. Once in a while he would let us climb up carefully into the seat of one of them and pretend. The danger surrounding this heavy equipment, however, was severe and we stayed at a safe distance whenever they were in use—especially with that skittish work horse! If both horses in the team had been as wild, someone could have easily been killed or badly injured. I look back and thank God for His mercy and protection during those years of hard work on the homestead.

After the disc harrow, Daddy and David would use a tool called a "mattock", like an axe with two heads. On one side was a blade for hoeing or digging in hard ground. On the other side was either a cutter for chopping the root of the sagebrush, or a pick—like a Pulaski—for breaking or prying small rocks. After they loosened the brush with these tools, the rest of us had to grab hold of it and pull it out of the ground with our hands. Most of the trunks were about the size of an upper arm; but some bushes had grown so big that the trunks were as big as a person's neck! I was too young to do this, but I would run along behind the others and get the small pieces that were left. The slip was made of large, heavy planks with boards nailed across them to form a sort of homemade sled on which we piled the brush. It was hooked up behind a team of horses so they could pull it along for us and haul our "grubbed sagebrush" to the burn pile. David chopped it all into cord wood that he stacked up against the house for stoking our fires. These sagebrush logs were the only wood we had available for warmth and cooking in our wood stove. David set aside the larger wood trunks for wood-working crafts. He could cut them in thin slices and engrave messages in the centers with a wood-burner for gift plaques. Sometimes he painted flowers or other delicate designs on them as well.

I was nine years old the first summer on the homestead when our family went to work together in the fields. There were farms in Fruitland, Idaho that hired laborers to work their lands. We could weed onions, pick up potatoes, or pick the fruit, peas, hops or other crops at harvest time. Daddy found field jobs where our whole family could work together to help make a living.

Mama had been taught—as many in her generation—that "pants" were "pertaining to a man" and should, therefore, never be worn by women. Brother Sivik, our prophet friend, was visiting one time as she worried over this. "Now, Sister Mussell," he interjected, "if that's what is worrying you, let the decision fall on me. You don't want to be climbing a ladder or something with your dress on, do you?" This was something she could live with. If the Prophet was in favor she would not feel guilty! So we put our dresses on and tucked the skirts down inside our overalls. With our girlish sleeves sticking out for all to see and our long, braided hair swinging to and fro, we were recognizably feminine! Mama was even comfortable enough to do the same.

Our first job was working in the onions. Early in the morning we would arrive at the field and spread out between the rows to cut weeds with small knives. The soil seemed hard, like clay, as we slashed away at the weeds growing between the crops. We wore knee pads strapped onto our legs because we had to crawl down the rows all day long. I remember hearing my father's welcome voice calling cheerfully, "It's lunchtime!" Mama would hand out our sandwiches and start one single carton of milk or juice around the family circle so everyone could have a drink. I never knew anything about the pay because each was working for the livelihood of all.

Picking peas was also a job we did as a family. No morning fires were built because we didn't have time; but Mama wanted us to have the closest thing possible to a hot breakfast and somehow found a way to poor warm milk on our corn flakes. It was very soggy, but apparently better for us; and at 4:00 am I was thinking more about the warm bed I had to leave than the breakfast set before me! Then we were all loaded into our makeshift pick-up bed that Daddy had built on the back of our car for hauling things. Mama let us lie down and cover up with blankets for the drive to the pea fields, which seemed about an hour away. We got there just before sunrise and were literally picking peas at the crack of dawn! Our fingers would fly to snap off as many peas as possible before the sun got hot enough to make the stems leathery. After that, they were hard to pick and the Pea Boss would shout that work was over for the day. She wouldn't let anyone keep picking when the vines would begin to pull because if any of them broke off it could hinder the harvest. We were finished by 10:00-11:00 am and on our way home.

We picked apples, peaches, cherries, and prunes and Mama did a lot of canning on our wood cook stove so we would have plenty of food stocked up for winter. You name it, we did it; and I always enjoyed the work. Our folks were careful to make sure we did not overdo, and we always got lots of encouragement, compliments and good, hearty lunches for our break time. After a full day's work, Daddy would sometimes stop on the way home for a treat such as soda pop or ice cream as a reward for our diligence.

Another job I remember was digging postholes for fencing our property on the homestead. After school, Daddy would say, "Okay, girls. I want you to dig three postholes before supper!" We would walk down to the "back forty" and work together on the job. Daddy had taught all of us the process in detail, so with our shovels, hammers, posts and wire we could dig the holes and set the posts as straight as arrows in their places. I remember all of his instructions and I can still describe it in detail. Jewel, Dorcas, and sometimes Rosemary, would do the digging and Lois and I would help with the rest. We were so pleased to go back and tell Daddy that we had accomplished our goal, and according to his specifications! His fences were always straight and strong.

Back in Tujunga, California, at twelve and a half I babysat for neighbors at fifty cents per hour, as well as inheriting other babysitting jobs from my older sisters when they moved on to something else. Almost daily, Rosemary and I did grocery shopping for our mother. At fourteen, after Rosie got a job in Los Angeles at the May Company, I took her ironing job for a neighbor lady. I got fifty cents per hour for that, and for weeding and watering her yard. She had only two sons and it was unusual to me that she even had me ironing their jeans! She had been in an auto accident and her settlement from the perpetrator's insurance company included money to have all of her house and yard work hired out, which may be why her own sons didn't help. She held a full-time job and seemed to be able to do whatever she wanted to. As a kid, I remember thinking it seemed very unnecessary to give extra money to help someone who appeared to be as healthy as a horse! On the other hand, I was glad for the job.

My first public job was in 1949 at age fifteen. Our school had a program that would recommend students who had good grades for jobs at the department stores that needed holiday help. I was hired as a sales clerk at the May Company in Los Angeles, California where two of my sisters worked; which is probably the only reason I was brave enough to do it. Rosie and Lois worked in different departments and we had different shifts so we never saw each other. Since I was "holiday help" I was placed in the Notions Department and got stuck at the button counter selling buttons, buckles, and sewing supplies. It was the quiet, "out-of-season" section of the store; nothing very interesting and not a busy place. Even at Christmas, while other departments were buzzing with excitement, mine was dull. The other girls talked about the crowds in the Toy, Clothing, and Christmas Decor departments and I felt that I was missing all the fun! I was able to work for a couple of months, however, and was glad for the money. We had to use public transportation but were glad to have a bus to ride back and forth. It took thirty minutes or more from our home in Tujunga to Los Angeles where we worked. I liked working and felt very privileged to have a job at my age. Since it was the Christmas season, I was able to buy gifts for my family and some new clothes and shoes for myself. It felt good to have money to spend on the things we needed, and had previously learned to get along without.

In 1950, after I graduated from High School, we moved back to Idaho once again to pioneer a farm. I stayed home the first year because I was still too young to get jobs in most public places. I helped Mama around the house, and I worked in the fields on our neighbor's farm.

I had applied for work at the phone company but I was still too young to be hired. So I found a job at the Crookham Seed Company to do field jobs. It was a crew of workers that were transported daily by vans out to the fields. We never knew for sure what job we would get until we got there. Some days we wore knee pads and crawled on our knees all day in the muddy irrigation furrows, planting onions. Other days we had to weed and hoe, cut onion seed, or whatever they needed most.

At seventeen, I finally got a job at the Telephone Company in Caldwell. I was an operator and I loved it! My sisters had all been hired in town as well: Dorcas was at the Sears Switchboard Office, Lois worked at the BLM and Jewel had a job at Caxton Printers. Daddy could not continue to drive all of us back and forth to town so our folks made arrangements with the Rowens, their long-time friends and pastors, for us girls to rent their downstairs apartment. We all shared the rent and other expenses and walked to work each day. Sometimes we went home on weekends, or in between if we had a ride, to see our family and attend church together. Later we rented one of the bedrooms to Gail Bryan's sister, Bernice, who also worked at Caxton Printers. Other friends roomed with us from time to time. There were up to six girls at once living together in that small, basement apartment; those were fun times.

I worked for a year as a Switchboard Operator, but then the dial system went in and I got laid off with the other operators. The last job I held before I got married was at the Fish Fly Company in Caldwell; but by this time I was engaged so it didn't last very long!

Hopes and Dreams

As a child, I always dreamed of being exactly what my mother was to me. I wanted to be a mother like her, to raise happy children, keep a tidy home, cook and sew. I wanted to learn to play the piano, too. Sometimes I thought I might like to be a missionary and take the gospel to people who had never heard of Jesus; but I never worried about my future because I anticipated finding God's will for my life and knew that if it was His idea it would lead me to the best place. I fully expected Him to lead me, to guide my steps and to be my provision. I had worked in Vacation Bible School and enjoyed telling Bible stories and teaching songs to the children. Consequently I thought I might like to teach, or be in pastoral work and the Ministry of Helps. I wanted to live a life of Christian service.

In eleventh grade, my English teacher asked us to write a paragraph stating what we wanted to be when we grew up. I wrote: *"I am planning to marry a Christian man and raise a Christian family. I want to be a pastor's wife and work for the Lord.*" I felt very strongly that this life would be my future; I just knew this was what I would be doing! When our family moved back to Idaho after my graduation from High School, I wanted to save money for tuition to attend Bible College as my older brother, David, had done. There I could meet other young people with the same interests. However, my plan to attend Northwest Bible College in Seattle, Washington never happened. I started writing to Gail Bryan, who was already in the ministry and holding evangelistic meetings around the country. After our engagement, he didn't want me to make plans for college, but to marry him and travel in evangelism together instead, which we did.

I finally got to attend Bible college classes when I was in my early forties. My husband and I started our own *Rhema Bible College* through the church we pioneered in Hoquiam, Washington, using a curriculum accredited through Portland Bible College. Only then was I finally able to enroll, and earn my two-year certificate.

My family had lots of variety and adventure wrapped up in our diverse experiences and life challenges, the many places we lived, all the schools we attended and the church friends we made. God used every life circumstance to mold my character and teach me valuable spiritual lessons. I was happy about our large family, and enjoyed going through life with all my siblings. I was glad about our good churches and wonderful friendships. I loved our moves and trips across the country from place to place, and relished our pioneer homestead experiences. I will always cherish our musical family, and all our singing and story-telling times. We were blessed, and had so much to be thankful for!

As far as "hopes and dreams" I could not imagine hardly anything better than I had already experienced growing up! I was contented, happy, and fulfilled; blooming with purpose and enthusiasm about the life ahead of me that would surely be as wonderful as the life I was leaving behind! I have learned since then that our view of life is very small compared to the big picture of God's great plan. He loves his children and wants them to be happy yet, all along Life's Pathway, he will turn us, change our circumstances, and allow challenges that we would never choose. Only he knows the things that will better prepare us for accomplishing his greater purpose in us and in the world.

"What? Know ye not that your body is the temple of the Holy Ghost which is in you, which ye have of God, and ye are not your own?" The scripture exhorts us in 1 Corinthians 6: 19-20 (KJV), *"For ye are bought with a price: therefore glorify God in your body, and in your spirit, which are God's."*

I believe that we often become so consumed with "life on earth" that we forget, despite the freedom God has given us, that we are not here to accomplish our personal goals or pursue a vision of our own imagination. Instead, Almighty God has set in motion a Plan of the Ages, from Genesis through The Revelation and beyond, which we—His creation—are privileged to be a part of. In this light, it is imperative to remember that He is in ultimate control; and will help us choose—or very often, stumble onto—the paths that best accomplish *His* goals, and *His* vision for the lives we have each been given.

We should, of course, take the initiative in using our time and talents as wisely and as responsibly as we are able, while holding loosely to our independence. We will have an easier time of it if we will, with grace and humility provided through the Holy Spirit, align our will to God's will along Life's way. He is, after all, the *"Author and Finisher of our faith"* (Hebrews 12:2, KJV), and will finish the work that he started in each of us, constantly working behind the scenes to bring *"all things together for good to them that love God, to them who are the called according to his purpose."* (Romans 8:28, KJV)

Our human, limited, and very emotional perspectives can keep us on a level of struggle when, in fact, God wants us to live on a plain of victory; trusting Him with every bend in the road instead of allowing doubt to reign. God is faithful, meantime, to nudge us toward faith and away from fear when life takes turns we do not expect, takes us to places we do not want to go, or shrouds us in a fog that prevents us from seeing the road ahead.

While I look back on my life, and as you look forward to yours, I will tell you now: the sooner you learn to *"endure hardship as a good soldier of Jesus Christ,"* (2 Timothy 2:3, KJV) the faster you will overcome despair, disappointment, and discouragement—enemies of your soul that seek to smother your faith and malign your trust in the goodness and love of God, from which He guarantees that *nothing* can tear you away (Romans 8:37)!

Never forget that Jesus has promised to never leave you, to never fail you, and to always go ahead of you (Deuteronomy 31:8) into all of your unknowns and uncertainties. You can be strong and courageous, knowing that everywhere life takes you He has already been, lovingly preparing the way ahead for your safe passage. I knew this truth, but had no idea of the extent to which I would experience its value. How could I have understood the depth of meaning it would hold for me as I entered a life of my own; one I had never imagined?

CHAPTER SIX

Life with Gail

Simultaneous Settings: Old South

When a young girl thinks of marriage she may imagine possibilities from the most familiar places of her growing up years, or from adventurous childhood fantasies; but when she grows up and meets the man of her destiny her reality is often much more fantastic than any fiction she could have written on her own. The pieces of my marriage mosaic began to take shape in the Old South, far from the Great Northwest farmlands where my own destiny sprouted.

Four years before my own mother was born, the world was graced with another sweet girl who would become an integral part of my lifetime collage... the dear mother of the man I was to marry.

Sally Hazel Newton was born on February 23, 1904 in Dover, Arkansas. She grew up near Russellville where her parents, Frank and Minnie Newton, lived on a farm in a large country home. They had a big family, in which Hazel was second-born. Marzo was an older brother and they were followed by seven more siblings. Ruby, Helen (sometimes called Opal), Olive, and one sister who died from medical complications as a young adult. Paul and Raymond were younger brothers, and Fern was the youngest of the Newton children. (She was actually born two months after Hazel's first daughter, Bernice).

The Newtons were not Christian people, but were respectful and kind to preachers who dedicated themselves to Christian service. Frank Newton was greatly affected by his daughter, Hazel's, conversion and baptism in the Holy Spirit as a young girl of eleven. He attended church after that and cooperated with Revival Meetings by hosting the visiting ministers in his home. Frank was known as an honest and reputable man who paid his bills, was charitable to others, and exhibited great concern for his children and for his community. His wife, Minnie, was a small and beautiful dark-eyed lady who was part French. She and Frank were both converted before they died. Frank died at age fifty-seven of bone cancer while Minnie still had young children at home.

Charles Ulis Bryan, was born on August 18, 1903 in Hagarville, Arkansas. His parents were Charles and Laudra Bryan. They were not Christian people, and died when "Doc" was young. I did not know much about them, but I heard from Hazel that Charles senior was an atheist who had no use for Christians. Yet, thinking back on the tender-hearted responses that his son, "Doc"—later my father-in-law—so often demonstrated toward God and His Word, I thank the Lord for His great and merciful plan to save the world. For it is not His will that any should perish, from the most innocent child to the most biased atheist. Instead, He desires that all who are willing should come to repentance and be saved to spend eternity with Him. (2 Peter 3:9)

Hazel and Charles were seventeen and eighteen years of age, respectively, when they married on Christmas Day of 1921 in Tag, Arkansas. They settled in Dover and had six children: Laudra Bernice, Wayne Ulis—who died of diphtheria at eighteen months old—Paul Bailey, Lelus Gail, Grace Louise, and Hazel Medora. Lelus Gail Bryan was born at home in Mentone, California on May 12, 1932. He also lived in Redlands and La Crescenta, both in California, and spent a few summers at his Grandma Minnie's farm in Dover, Arkansas. He graduated from Glendale High School in a class of five hundred students.

Meetings and Greetings

I met Gail when I was only fifteen because we always saw his family at church. He sometimes played his trumpet in the church orchestra. The Bryans lived in La Crescenta, California and our family live in Tujunga, so we were not closely acquainted. Gail stopped coming to church for a while and we heard that he was not serving the Lord. When he was a senior in High School, however, he committed his life to the Lord during a revival meeting at our church. Kenneth Schmidt was the evangelist for these special meetings and Gail's mother had persuaded him to come with her because the Schmidts were friends of their family. When the altar call was given, a friend of the family spotted him and started down the aisle toward him. Afraid that they would try to drag him to the front for prayers of repentance, he fled the scene, jumping over a bannister and running out the door to his car before they could get close enough to talk to him!

Drawn by the power of the Holy Spirt in spite of himself, he came again the next night; and at that meeting a special song was rendered called, "Will the Circle be Unbroken". Later he told me that he was so troubled about the possibility of his family circle being broken because of him that he finally became utterly convicted of his sin and dedicated his life to Christ. He said that his heart was always stirred just as much by music and song as it ever was by a good sermon.

Soon after his conversion, he was baptized in water and gave a powerful testimony at church. Gail immediately felt the call of God on his life and took his conversion very seriously. He began taking his Bible to school with him every day and soon classmates were calling him "Reverend" and "The Preacher". He became a very bold witness for the Lord and testified to many of his friends about how God had changed his life, and could also change theirs.

At this time, I was attending Verdugo Hills High School and was president of the Bible Club that met during our lunch hour. Gail was preparing for the ministry by studying the Bible and spending time in fasting and prayer. He was only seventeen, but was already receiving invitations to preach. He spoke for our C.A. group, and I remember him preaching one Wednesday evening for the church service. At this time I had no particular attraction to him at all. He was just another young man in the church, but with a very inspirational testimony.

After I graduated from high school and our family decided to move back to Idaho, our church in La Crescenta gave us a going away service. Sister Bryan came up to us during the celebration and told us that her son, Gail, was in Emmett, Idaho preaching a revival meeting. "If that's anywhere close to the town you are moving to," she continued, "it would be wonderful if you could go to the meeting and hear him preach."

In July of 1950, we arrived in Caldwell, Idaho where we would live on a farm at Black Canyon. My older brother, David, told us that the revival meeting Sister Bryan had told us about at the Assembly of God church in Emmett was only about twenty-five miles away. He said he would drive over there if we would like to go. So three of my sisters and I went with him to the Emmett meeting. As we turned into town from the highway, we saw Gail Bryan driving a pickup toward us and he swerved to the side of the road and hopped out. We pulled over as he strode across the street to our car. "The Mussells!" he exclaimed. "I saw your California license plate! What are you doing up here?"

David answered, "Well, we just moved up here and your mother told us about your revival meetings so we decided to come."

"That's wonderful!" Gail said. "I'm just going to change my clothes; I've been at the church all day praying and studying for the service. I'll see you there!" Then, poking his head in a little farther, he looked at me and asked, "Did you bring your guitar?" Of course, I had it with me because, in those days, anyone who could sing was often asked on the spur of the moment to share a song with the congregation. We were accustomed to being asked to sing and were always prepared to do so, since we grew up hearing that God's people should *"be ready in season and out of season."* (2 Timothy 4:2) Upon confirming this, he said, "Good! Have a song ready!" and went his way.

It was a small church with about sixty people packed in like sardines. Gail had only been saved for about six months but he was fervently seeking God and had been fasting and praying for these meetings. He introduced our family and we sang our song. Then he preached a powerful sermon that blessed and inspired all who were there. After the meeting, Gail showed special interest in us and talked with my brother at length. He loved our singing and requested that we sing every night for the duration of the meetings. Since David had a car, he drove us each night from Caldwell to the meetings so we could sing and attend the services. Later, after Gail returned to California, he sent a post card to my brother, David, thanking him for attending the services and asking him to "tell the family, *Hello.*"

During this time, I had been hired by the neighboring farm to help plant onions for a seed crop. It was October and very cold; I remember my lips being chapped and dry from the wind. I had knee pads strapped to my overalls because I had to crawl on my hands and knees all day; so I was very dirty by the time my work day ended. This farmer had an adopted son named Buddy who was about my age and took a liking to me, but rode the bus to school every day. He was very cute and I saw that he was a hard worker. I would see him out in the fields driving the tractor and working the land, but we never really got to know each other. One day as I was working in the onions and Buddy was driving the tractor close by, I looked up to see my little brother, Paul, skipping across the field from our house. I wondered what he was doing and watched him run all the way to where I was working. Grinning and breathless, he said, "Guess who came to our house?"

"I don't know; who?" I asked.

"Gail Bryan; and he's asking to see you!" Paul exclaimed.

Taken by surprise, I retorted, "He is not!" With a bandana around my hair, I was soiled from head to toe and in no condition to see anybody! I had dirt in my eyes, and even up my nose from the wind that had been blowing around me all day. I looked like a regular hard-working farmhand! "I don't want to see anybody; and I'm not coming home until he's gone!" I finalized.

"Well, he's gone already," Paul confessed, slightly amused by my dread. "He asked twice about you and I told him where you were. He kept acting like he was going to come across the field and find you, but he didn't. They came with their relatives from Emmett so they had to leave; but they invited us to their house for Thanksgiving."

I was so surprised to hear this because I didn't even think he knew me, let alone that he would be asking about me! I went on home and heard the whole story again from the family, and that Gail had said to tell me to bring my guitar to Thanksgiving dinner.

When Thanksgiving rolled around we drove to Emmett, looking forward to the holiday dinner and fellowship. Gail's Aunt Ruby and Uncle William Freeman hosted the dinner. They were very hospitable and we enjoyed a wonderful meal with their family. Then Gail said, "Well, I'm ready to hear these girls sing!" As they all sat around the table, we sang a number of songs at their request and had a great time. Our families got better acquainted that day, as the Bryan's were there visiting from California.

In December, on my seventeenth birthday, I received a card from Gail that said, *"It's the folks we like, we think about at all times of the year; And send the best of wishes when a Happy Birthday's here! It's the folks we like, we wish the best a day and year can send; and because you're liked SO MUCH this brings Good Wishes without end!"* He signed the card, Love, Gail; and I was completely taken by surprise! I was still corresponding with another young man in California who had been sending me letters for almost a year. I would have to think on this turn of events; I wasn't going to change anything just yet.

I wrote back to Gail and thanked him for the pretty card. He continued to write and his letters became more interesting and more personal. Over the next year and one half he wrote me fifty-three letters and sent several cards, all of which I saved for keepsakes. We hardly ever saw each other during that time, because his family still lived in California, so we had to get acquainted through the mail! He was getting invitations for quite a few preaching engagements from various places around southern California such as North Hollywood, San Jacinto, and Hemet. He was also preaching in different types of churches like the Church of God, Pentecostal Church of God, and various Assemblies of God churches; barely receiving enough in offerings to buy his gasoline. Yet he always wrote with enthusiasm about each opportunity and about what God was doing in these communities.

Soon he received another invitation to preach a C.A. Rally in Horseshoe Bend, Idaho. He was so excited and expressed his wishes that my sisters and I attend the meeting with him and sing again. At this time, his elder sister, Bernice, was traveling with him and playing piano for his meetings. So when they got to town, he came with his sister to pick us up and the four of us piled into the back seat. When we came out of the meeting to drive home, Gail stopped me from climbing into the back seat and chided playfully, "Oh, no you don't! You are sitting in the front seat with me this time." I slid in beside him and, with a giggle, Bernice slid in beside me. The next night he had another speaking engagement and called to see if we would come again, but suddenly my sisters were not on board! "We don't want to go because we know he's only coming to see you!"

After this meeting, Gail went back home to California and it was 'life as usual' for the Mussells, except that I soon got a job at the telephone company in Caldwell. My sisters were already working in town so we moved into an apartment in the basement of Calvary Temple, a United Pentecostal Church. Daddy and Mama had known the pastors for years and felt that we would be safe there. They offered to rent it to us for about forty-five dollars per month, so the four of us were suddenly out of the nest and on our own!

The next time Gail came to Idaho, he was preaching a revival meeting in Emmett and he called to see if we were going. I told him my sisters couldn't go and he said, "Good! What about you?" I said that I could and he responded promptly, "I'll be there to pick you up at six o'clock." We talked some on the way but I was very shy and quiet, as this was my first time to go with him alone. After we got to the church, his mind was totally on the service and his sermon. He knelt at a church bench for a time of prayer and then stayed in another room until the service began.

Afterwards we stayed to pray with someone at the altar so it was late before we started the drive home. He had borrowed his father's car because he didn't have one of his own, and it had no heater. The winter temperatures were icy cold as we began to climb out of the valley on Little Freeze Out Road, which was extremely rough. Soon I was so cold I was shivering. Just past Purple Sage, way out on a pitch-dark, country road, we had a blow-out and Gail had to get out in his church clothes and change the flat tire. When we were finally on our way again, he reached over and took my hand and said, "I'm sorry it took so long. You really got cold, didn't you?"

Having recently moved north from sunny California, I had no warm clothes to wear! He apologized that his dad's car didn't have a heater, and he held my icy hand for a while squeezing it several times. When he got me home he walked me to the back door, which was our entry to the basement apartment, and surprised me with a kiss!

On Gail's next visit to Idaho to preach, he asked if I would go with him to the meetings and I went several times; but we never had a formal "date". It was always a Youth Rally, Revival Meeting, or Camp Meeting service, and usually where he was preaching, since his visits from California were always for speaking engagements.

He never had any money, so we didn't go out to eat after church like a lot of others did. He would just pick me up, spend time together in church, and then take me home again. He would hold my hand on the way home and we would talk about the services, the preaching, and the people who responded to the altar call; Gail always prayed with people at the altar.

One day, after I had gone on several occasions with Gail to church meetings, I heard the doorbell ring and ran upstairs to answer it. There he stood on the back porch. He had come by my apartment to tell me that he would soon be going to Arkansas to preach some revival meetings. He didn't come inside, but we talked, and he asked me to pray for him and for the meetings while he was gone. When he told me "Goodbye", he put his arms around me and held me and kissed me. I suppose I should have expected it by now, but it took me totally by surprise again, and I told all the girls about it after he left.

Jewel's job was temporary and soon ended. When she decided to move back home, we contacted Bernice Bryan and said she could live with the rest of us in the apartment. So when she came, we gave her one bedroom to herself and the three of us shared the other one. This connection strengthened our relationship with the Bryan family and we were always in the loop with what was going on, especially with Gail and his meeting schedule.

Gail and I began to correspond regularly and, before long, he expressed how much he cared for me, and it seemed his intentions were long term. I was never aggressive in any way, nor outspoken about any boy I liked; so even if I had special feelings for someone nobody ever knew about it. In my heart, though, from this time on, I never wanted to pursue a relationship with anyone else. Even though several other boys asked me out on dates, I always declined. Gail was my first and only love and I knew that he was the one for me. I wrote to the other young man to let him know that I'd been corresponding with Gail regularly and thought it was best for us not to continue writing to each other. He was very disappointed but kind and understanding.

Meanwhile, my father had convinced my brother, David, to build a little country church out at Purple Sage on Highway 30 about two miles from where we lived. He wanted the farming families to have a place of worship closer to home. Daddy and David had finished the church and set it up with benches and a pulpit; then we started services with David as pastor. David had made a huge canvas sign to hang on the building that said, "Revival Meetings, Nightly." When he was in town, Gail sometimes worked with my brother in making preparations for special meetings at Faith Assembly in Purple Sage. Gail looked forward to all the Revival Meetings and when he was invited to speak he always asked me to pray that the Holy Spirit would give him an anointing, that souls would be saved, and that hearts would be opened to the truth of God's Word. He was very sincere in his ministry, and dedicated to the work of the Kingdom of God.

Popping the Question

Gail had come up from California again to preach in Emmett for another Revival Meeting. We had known each other for several months by this time and had been corresponding regularly. I planned to attend the meetings with him and I put on my yellow taffeta dress. He was at the apartment to pick me up right on time, and we drove about an hour to get to the meeting in Emmett at the Assembly of God church. On the way there, he whistled and sang sweet love songs like "The Tennessee Waltz", "Upon a Summer Night", "I'll Hold You in my Heart", "Up on the Mountain" and "The Whippoorwill Call". He held my hand and told me how beautiful I was in my yellow dress. The Idaho sunset was gorgeous and, to my surprise, he pulled over to the side of the road at a convenient place to stop and took my hand.

"Eunice, honey," he began; "before we go any farther there's something I want to ask you. I'm getting ready to leave for Arkansas again to hold some revival meetings in the Ozarks and I'll be gone all summer. I hate to leave you for so long. You know I love you very much. I don't deserve a precious girl like you because I haven't always lived a godly life. I've sowed some wild oats and done some things that I'm ashamed of; but if you are willing to forgive me, I know that God has. I'd love to take you for my wife. *Will you marry me?*"

He had already brought tears to my eyes, and seeing them now he said, "Why are you crying? Is there a reason you don't want to?"

"No; I'm just happy;" I replied. "I love you too, and I will marry you."

"I don't have anything to offer you except myself and my love," he continued. "This won't be our formal engagement since I don't have the money yet to buy you a ring; but I just wanted you to know my intent and where my heart is, and to find out how you felt about it. If you agree, we'll just keep it in our hearts and pray about the future and work towards it." That night after proposing, he had a great liberty and anointing in his preaching. It was as though a great concern had been lifted from his shoulders, and he felt free and happy. My dad and brother had also attended the meeting that night and they commented later about the strong anointing and freedom in his preaching. They said he had a "divine unction".

I still didn't know Gail especially well because of our long distance courtship, although I knew he was a very good preacher who was called by God to be an Evangelist. I thought he was an eloquent speaker and he seemed to love and respect his parents. I believed that he would love me and be a good husband. I can't say that it was "love at first sight", but I found out that love grows. He carried himself too proudly at times, and seemed desirous of approval from others. He was very romantic, however, and showed lots of affection; so I loved him more and more as we became better acquainted. I also came to realize that, deep down, he had a certain insecurity and lack of confidence that made him more self-conscious than he needed to be, and caused him to appear more arrogant than he really was. I was very attracted to his unmistakable zeal for God; and his fervent faith in the power of God was something that remained constant through the years. All of his family, my family, and mutual friends said that he and I were the "ideal couple" and fit each other perfectly because we both came from Christian homes with Pentecostal backgrounds. We had known the Bryans for quite a few years since we attended the same church in California. Brother Bryan used to shout accolades such as, "Amen!" "That's right!" and "Preach it!" during the sermon. My parents approved of Gail and liked his family. My father and older brother loved to hear him preach and went to his meetings every chance they got. Everybody I knew really liked him and thought he was the right choice for me. Gail later said that he loved me because I was humble and of few words, loved God, and came from a stable Christian background. He thought I was the right partner for him in marriage and would be a loving companion, suitable for the ministry. He knew that I would fit into God's call for his life; that we could be a team to work together for the Lord. We both believed that God had arranged our relationship for His glory.

The Ring

After revealing his future intentions and finding that I was agreeable, Gail went to Arkansas to preach a revival meeting and was gone for three months. Upon his return he brought his sister, Bernice, back to the apartment because they had used her car for the trip. Then he saw his relatives for a couple of days and returned to California. He wanted to save some money to buy a car because everywhere he went he had to ride the train, the bus, or borrow someone else's vehicle. Consequently, he was very glad to be offered an opportunity to work with his Uncle Gray laying stone for fireplaces.

About this time we girls heard from our Aunt Mary, my mother's younger sister, who said that Grandma Bunt was not well enough to stay alone anymore. She was calling to find out if one of us could come down to Fullerton, California and stay with Grandma. Interestingly enough, this was when the telephone company where I worked had decided to lay off a group of operators. The company was making the transition from the old fashioned switchboard system to the new dial system. I had been a switchboard operator and thoroughly loved my job, but I was laid off along with several other girls. Because of this change in my circumstances, I was free and decided to go to Fullerton and help care for Grandma. Lois decided to go with me and we thought we could both live with Grandma and possibly get part-time jobs down there as well. So we rode the bus to Fullerton.

Gail was glad I was coming and was anxious to see me. He was holding some meetings in nearby towns and wanted me to go with him to one of them.

When he arrived to pick me up, however, Aunt Mary was quite perturbed. "I don't know you!" she said to Gail, as he stood harmlessly before her critical glare. "You're just an immature young man who doesn't know about responsibility!"

"Oh, yes," he answered calmly; "a lot more than you'd ever dream of."

Aunt Mary proceeded to tell Lois and I that she was responsible for us and we were not allowed to go anywhere. I was utterly stunned by her attitude since we had been living on our own for over a year in Caldwell! After talking to her and explaining that Gail's family would be with us as we traveled to the meeting and back, she finally relented but was still unhappy about it.

Lois was disgusted with Aunt Mary's attitude; but I was just glad she allowed us to go.

The meeting was in Hemet, California and all of Gail's family came out to hear him preach. He had purchased a ring and after we picked it up he slipped it on my finger—a beautiful .25 carat solitaire diamond—with his family there to share in the occasion. On February 28, 1952 we announced our engagement. My parents, his parents, and everybody we knew felt good about it. His dad told me later that he had said to Gail, "If I was choosing one of those Mussell girls, I'd pick that black-headed one."

Unbeknown to Lois and me, Aunt Mary had apparently promised our mother that she would watch over us and supervise our activities carefully; so when I came back with a diamond on my finger she was beside herself. Lois was disgusted about her reaction again, more than I, and decided she did not want to live with Aunt Mary if she was going to be so bossy. "Let's get on the bus and go visit Sister Dudley!" she deliberated, who was a good friend of our family from the church in La Crescenta. I was unsure about it and said 'No' at first; but Lois persisted, pointing out that we were not really needed anyway since Aunt Mary seemed to be there all the time and Grandma was doing fine. So after a few days we revealed our plans and told Aunt Mary that we had decided to go work in La Crescenta. She was upset, but we said our goodbyes and rode the bus to La Crescenta.

Sister Dudley was delighted to have us and assured us both that we could easily get jobs at the Glendale Telephone Company. We filled out applications and talked to the supervisor who felt sure we could get hired right away; but it was not to be. When we got back to Sister Dudley's house there was a telegram waiting for us from Daddy:

"Come home immediately"

After having dinner with the Bryan's and saying our goodbyes to them, we rode the bus back to Idaho, having accomplished nothing but spending some of our savings and having a brief adventure in independence. When we got back we found out that Aunt Mary had called Mama and Daddy as soon as we left her house. I don't know what she said, but it was enough to motivate our father to send for us. We moved back into the basement apartment in Caldwell and started looking for jobs again.

The Months Between

I got a job at the Fish Fly Company and also worked a variety of other temporary positions until I got married. I was able to save enough money to pay all my wedding costs. My folks had no money and Mama apologized for not being able to help me with my wedding. She was proud of me for having good jobs and saving the money to pay for everything myself. I only worked at the Fish Fly Company a short while, and quit a couple weeks before my wedding to finish my plans, make all the final arrangements, and buy the supplies. We also had a big job to complete before the ceremony because of a turn of events that I had not counted on. My family had attended the Caldwell Assembly of God Church for years under Pastor John Shaw. He had recently resigned and I didn't know the new pastors, but I still wanted to be married in my home church. So I called to reserve it for the night of our wedding and they were happy to accommodate us; but when the pastor's wife found out that I wanted Brother Shaw to officiate, she changed her mind!

"We don't think it would be good for the people to have John Shaw come back here and do your ceremony after resigning the pastorate. Since your brother has a church out at Purple Sage maybe you should just have your wedding there."

I was shocked, and didn't understand their perspective. In addition, I already knew that the little church at Purple Sage would not be large enough to house the number of wedding guests we had invited. So two weeks before the wedding I was back to square one on my venue! In talking about it with my sisters and wondering what to do, we decided to ask the Rowens –our landlords and longtime family friends—if we could use their church for the wedding. It was the right size and our apartment was on the grounds. When we asked Brother Rowen, he said he would be glad for us to use the church. "But the floors are old and worn," he apologized. I was ready to exclaim gratefully that his generosity was a welcome relief and the floors would not matter when, to our amazement, he added, "Would you girls be willing to wax them in exchange for using the sanctuary?"

I was temporarily speechless, but we agreed to do it. The week before the wedding my sisters and I got on our hands and knees and waxed the hardwood floors throughout the entire sanctuary! After I had thus earned my keep, I spent my last few days at home with my family before Gail arrived from California. The night before the wedding, I went back to the Caldwell apartment with my sisters since Calvary Temple was next door and it would be easier for all of us to get dressed there.

Gail and his family came up about a week before the wedding to arrange tuxedos and other details for his groomsmen. I didn't know this at the time, but he had come up on the bus and then gone into Boise to purchase a new car with the money that he had earned in California. It was a 1952 Chevy; white with gray interior, and had an automatic transmission. It was an expensive wedding present, at a cost of $2,600! Gail made a down-payment of seven hundred and fifty dollars in cash, and our monthly loan payment would be seventy-four dollars and forty-eight cents, which was a lot back then! We always struggled to make those payments and I wished again and again that he had bought a nice, used car for cash instead.

The Perfect Wedding

We were married on June 29, 1952 at Calvary Temple in Caldwell, Idaho. The annual Southern Assembly of God Camp Meeting was in session at this time and it was always the highlight of the year. People came from miles around, and the meetings lasted for a week and were held both morning and night. So we planned to be married on a Sunday afternoon, after the morning service and before the evening one! I woke up excited. Everything was planned and ready. My bridal trousseau was laid out in detail and ready to put on; my sister's gowns were pressed and prepared. We did not go to Sunday School or church that morning, as tradition said that the groom was not to see the bride until she came down the aisle! After breakfast, I showered and fixed my nails and hair. I checked my list of everything that needed to be done and everyone who was to do it, and all items were completed. The apartment next door to the church made everything so convenient and easy; no cramming into cars or dragging everything to a church dressing room!

I wore a beautiful, antique white satin gown with a long, full train. It had tiny buttons from the high, scalloped neckline to the fitted, drop-waist. The long sleeves were puffed at the shoulders, and came to a V-shaped point overlapping my wrists to my hands. I wore Rosemary's veil, which lay very nicely and had a sparkling, beaded crown on top. I had a shiny string of pearls and I wore flat slippers of white satin. My bouquet was made of red rosebuds. I was able to have a beautiful wedding inexpensively because I borrowed the gown from Gail's eldest sister, Bernice. My bridesmaids wore the same dresses that they had worn in my sister Rosemary's wedding in California three years before—rainbow pastels. I chose my sister, Lois, as my Maid of Honor because she was closest to me all through school. I made her a pink satin formal to wear and she looked adorable. My other bridesmaids were my sister Dorcas, Charlotte Durbin (who later married my brother, David), and Grace Bryan, Gail's sister. I wanted to have all my sisters in my wedding, but Rosemary lived in Sunland, California and was due to have her second baby that week. He was actually born early so she was able to attend the wedding after all, with her new baby in tow. In fact, her daughter, Elaine, was one of my flower girls, even though she was only two and a half. She had an older girl to walk with and did fine. I made her a pink satin dress, too. Our ring-bearer was the son of some pastor friends, the Shakleys. My candle-lighters were Medora, Gail's little sister, and his cousin, Marilyn Freeman.

Gail, his groomsmen, and my Dad wore sharp, black tuxedos with crisp, white shirts and black bow ties, dress shoes and socks. Gail had a boutonniere on his lapel. He looked like a very young Prince Charming! His Best Man was his only brother, Paul, and his other groomsmen were his cousin, Bill Freeman, and my brothers, David and Paul. When I came down the aisle and stood with my father, Gail sang a special song to me, "God Gave Me You". It was beautiful, and such a sweet surprise! Then Gail took my hand as Daddy gave me away, and we linked arms to face Brother Shaw. The ceremony was very traditional and conservative; we wanted it to be biblical in every way. He gave a beautiful picture of marriage from God's point of view, and we repeated our vows to each other promising to love, cherish, and honor our spouse until parted by death. The wedding vows were very sacred to me, and I took them very seriously. After the presentation and exchange of the rings, Bill Freeman sang a solo, "I Love You Truly". This was one of my favorite songs, and he had a beautiful, soft baritone voice. When we started to kneel for the prayer and blessing, I realized that I had forgotten the "kneeling pillow" so we just knelt down on the wooden floor and no one knew that something was missing. Gail's sister, Bernice, played the piano and sang with a girls' trio, "Savior, Like a Shepherd Lead Us" and then the prayer was given, fervently and with great anointing. My father was so impressed that he said later, "There was such an anointing there! We could have given an altar call! There wasn't a dry eye in the building!" Many people commented on how sacred and blessed our wedding was. Everything went smoothly, just as we had planned.

We had two hundred and fifty guests in attendance. Gail's mother, Hazel, had been significantly instrumental in decorating the Reception Hall. The flowers were all white; the cake and all the accessories had arrived when expected, and it was beautiful! We had bouquets of white gladiolas and snapdragons and a beautiful archway where pictures were taken. Our wedding day was peaceful and I remember a feeling of happiness and harmony; it was all very lovely. We got many compliments on how beautiful everything was.

We opened our gifts at the reception and one that was prominent in my mind was the gift my mother gave me. It was an iron; and when I opened it scenes from my childhood flashed through my mind. I will never forget the many hours my dear Mama stood and ironed all our clothes! I think that memory was the reason that the toy iron at my preschool had quickly calmed all of my first-day-of-school anxiety; because suddenly I felt right at home! Daddy presented us with a money gift, which was much needed for a honeymoon since Gail's money had gone for our new car. He was very grateful that my dad had the foresight to give us some cash!

After the reception my cousin, Billy Bunt, and others gathered around to "shivaree" us. This was a modern form of the original French "Charivari" which was "a noisy mock serenade to a newly married couple made by banging pans and kettles".[1] For ours, Gail was made to roll up one pant leg of his tuxedo and wheel me around the streets of Caldwell in a wheelbarrow, in my wedding gown. A gang of young people chased us, dragging a bunch of tin cans down the road. Billy grabbed Gail's arm as he ran past which caused him to dump me part way out on the sidewalk! No damage was done but Gail was embarrassed and aggravated with my cousin.

After the chase, Gail presented me with the new Chevy he had just purchased, while everyone cheered. Paul Bryan and Bill Freeman had decorated it with streamers, balloons and tin cans, and a "Just Married" sign. We took off in our new car and they followed us for a few blocks; then Gail ditched them and we drove to nearby Nampa where we stayed in a small, modest motel along Nampa-Caldwell Boulevard. The next morning when I first opened my eyes, Gail said, "Good morning, Mrs. Bryan;" and I suddenly realized that I was not a Mussell girl anymore!

A Harried Honeymoon

The next day we took a beautiful drive up to the mountains. We didn't talk much, but sat close and enjoyed just being together amidst such gorgeous scenery. It had been quite a long time since we had seen one another, since Gail had returned immediately to California after his Ozarks revival. He had barely arrived in Idaho long enough to buy the car and make last minute wedding preparations. We stopped at a small restaurant in Cascade and had a hamburger for lunch. Then we went to Cascade Dam and walked around, taking in the lovely sights. It was a beautiful day, restful and relaxing, and a lovely trip in our brand new 1952 Chevy.

Gail was anxious to get back to Emmett to see his brother, Paul, before we left for our honeymoon in California. So we drove back to the valley and they wanted us to spend the night. They offered us a place to sleep on their back porch. When we got into bed, Gail rolled over and it crashed to the ground! We didn't know what had happened but soon discovered that they had set the box spring on top of four apple boxes! Needless to say, it did not hold up and the whole contraption caved in with us in it! My new relatives ran out to see what had happened and helped us set it up again; I was mortified, but this was only the beginning!

They had two little boys and were expecting another one. Our plans were to head back to California immediately because Gail was scheduled to be the Master of Ceremonies and song leader at a tent meeting in Riverside, California. Since his brother was taking a temporary job in Montana where he could not accommodate his family, Caroline asked if she and the boys could ride down with us to her parent's place. Gail's mother and sisters were staying in Idaho to spend time with Aunt Ruby but Doc was taking the train home since he had to go back to work. When Gail agreed to drive Caroline his dad also got a bright idea; "Well, so long as you are taking passengers, maybe I could ride back to California with you, too!" to which my husband naturally agreed. I can't pretend I wasn't disappointed. It made for a hot, crowded trip with fussy babies, diapers, and spilled milk bottles in our new car! Despite all of these unexpected events, we made it just fine and with a lasting souvenir to boot: the spilled milk soured and we could never get the smell out of our car—a fitting initiation into family life, I suppose!

After spending one night and day with Gail's dad at their La Crescenta home, we headed for Mill Creek Canyon, near Forest Home, where we stayed for a full month at Gail's relatives' place. Uncle Gray and Aunt Helen Bright had a lovely log home in the mountains and had invited us to stay there while they were gone to Arkansas on vacation. We stopped at a little grocery store to buy some food and supplies and I asked Gail what he wanted to eat. He grinned with his irresistible smile and beamed, "Macaroni and Cheese; I love it!" I was actually relieved and happy, because that was something I knew how to make: quick, easy, and fail-proof! He raved about it, and from that day forward was always complimentary and thankful for any meal I ever made. The Bright's mountain home was a beautiful place to spend our honeymoon.

Newlyweds 101

I had worked quite steadily at various jobs from the time I graduated High School in 1950 until I got married in June of 1952. After marriage, however, I considered it a full-time job being a wife and co-worker in the ministry with Gail. There was plenty to do! He was a traveling evangelist and preacher for the first six months of our marriage, and I immediately became his companion in the field. Before we even got married, Gail was scheduled to participate in a big tent meeting so, while on our "honeymoon", we were attending nightly services nearby. The First Assembly of God church in Riverside, pastored by Brother Carl Goad, was sponsoring the Revival Tent Meeting with a popular healing evangelist. We drove back and forth to these meetings every night for four weeks, probably thirty to forty miles each way, down a winding mountain road.

The meeting tent was always packed out, from seven hundred and fifty to a thousand people each time. Gail did a wonderful job as the Master of Ceremonies. He opened every meeting, led an inspiring and anointed song service followed by announcements and a prayer before introducing the speaker. This evangelist always came out like a celebrity, with his white suit and white shoes, to preach and then pray for the sick. After the meeting was over we had to straighten all the chairs for the next night, tidy the song books, and pick up any papers or trash so the tent area would remain clean and orderly. These meetings were a good spiritual time that we really enjoyed together. I don't remember a lot of miracles, although we saw a few healings. Each week, Gail and I were given the Friday night offering for our assistance. Thankfully, the total was enough to make our car payment for that month, which was seventy-four dollars and forty-eight cents.

At the close of that revival, the Goads asked us to stay at their parsonage in Riverside and fill in for them while they went on vacation for three weeks. We were delighted to do it! Gail preached two times each Sunday, as well as every Wednesday night. We earned enough money to make our car payment for the second month, and to buy the food we needed. Several times during this stay, I would look for Gail and he would be gone. One minute he would be on the front porch while I was making breakfast, and the next minute he was nowhere to be found! When he finally returned he would say that he went for a walk which, at first, just seemed odd to me. After the third or fourth time, however, the mystery became concern. I felt so uneasy and wondered what would cause him to leave so suddenly without telling me. I was shaky inside, but didn't know why. I sensed that something was wrong, but didn't know what it could be. I had no reference point for these inner cautions, so I would just pray. It didn't make sense to me that he would disappear at such inconvenient or inappropriate times. There were unanswered questions, and when he finally got back and I asked him where he went, he just shrugged it off with vague answers. His manner was distant, and there was never an open explanation; it was always veiled and incomplete. What was this?

Although I was newly married and had a lifetime of learning ahead of me, I had lived with a father and two brothers who were always open-faced and genuine. I was also surrounded by the constant example of warm communication from good Christian men in the Body of Christ. A closed relationship was something strange to me and the only way I saw to navigate this unfamiliar territory was to keep doing what I knew to do. My sisters and I understood that we were responsible to serve our families. Our mother taught us by her own example to be devoted wives and mothers. She believed in the biblical mandate that a husband should be the head of the wife and the leader of the family. She demonstrated obedience and submission to her husband's authority, always showing sacrificial love and deference to him. As strong as she was, Mama struggled with fearful thoughts and worried too much about the safety of her husband and her children. Although she always turned to prayer with her concerns, I saw the anxiety that she went through about things that often never came close to happening! I had decided that in my own life I would cast my care upon the Lord and not allow worry to dominate my thoughts; especially when speculating about things that may never happen. I began to practice this on a daily basis; praying and focusing on things that would keep me busy and faith-filled.

After this, Gail was invited to speak for the Southern California Bible College students and I wanted to go with him. His mother had asked me to stay with them and enjoy some shopping while he was gone. She wanted to get better acquainted with me and thought this would be a good time to do it. I didn't want to be separated from my husband but was too shy to decline, so I stayed and Gail went alone.

Next we were invited to take part in another tent revival outside Bakersfield. This pastor owned a vineyard in the area and made a little extra money on the grape harvest. Whenever he visited his vineyard, he made a point to always attended one of the small churches in this country area, becoming acquainted with several of the pastors. He eventually rallied them to participate in a tent revival and had rented a big tent that would hold around three hundred and fifty people.

This time Gail drove a big truck, heavily loaded with the tent, chairs, and equipment to set up for the meetings. He didn't do any of the preaching but just assisted with the tent set up and tear down. We stayed with one of the sponsoring pastors in the area and they gave us a guest room and provided meals while we were there. This revival lasted about one month. Although there seemed to be a lot of evangelistic zeal and the meetings were well attended, this pastor sought to operate in the Gift of Knowledge and kept making mistakes! He would tell someone they had a stomach problem and they would say, "Not that I know of; but I'd appreciate prayer for my back." This was awkward and disconcerting to us, although the tent was always packed to the gills and we were glad for those who were hearing the gospel and coming to Christ. These apparent blunders were embarrassing; and we discussed these things every time we left a meeting. Gail knew that the Gift of Knowledge was not truly operating here, and wished the evangelist would simply preach the Word and pray sincerely for the people's spoken needs. We prayed for the meetings and for our pastor friend, always honoring him and his ministry, and did our job dutifully and with gladness. We had confidence in the faithfulness of God toward those who seek Him, for we understood Jeremiah 29:11-13, *"For I know the thoughts that I think toward you, saith the LORD, thoughts of peace, and not of evil, to give you an expected end. Then shall ye call upon me, and ye shall go and pray unto me, and I will hearken unto you. And ye shall seek me, and find me, when ye shall search for me with all your heart."* (KJV) We were glad that people were being encouraged in their pursuit of God and that new converts were added to the Body of Christ.

When these meetings ended we loaded the truck and headed back to La Crescenta for revival meetings in San Jacinto, California with Brother and Sister Claude Thurman. Gail had preached for them the year before and they invited him back. They were wonderful pastors and we ministered there for two weeks. They had prepared a nice guest room for us to use. The Thurmans were so welcoming and accommodating to us that we felt like family! They called us, "you kids" and showed the love and care that parents would give to their own children. Sister Thurman was very domestic, spreading pretty tables and serving wonderful meals while we were there, as well as snacks after church which was the common practice in those days. Due to early meeting times, most families opted out of the dinner hour in order to attend evening services.

Next we were invited to hold a revival in Hemet, where some major learning experiences awaited us. We had barely made enough money from the last meeting to make our car payment, buy a few groceries, and get to Hemet. The people who pastored the Assembly of God church there, put us up in a trailer house that was empty—no food, no utensils, nothing to accommodate our stay. We were usually hosted by the pastors when we were invited for meetings and had no supplies of our own that we traveled with, which we explained to them.

"Oh, that's no problem!" the pastor replied nonchalantly. "I'll bring over a skillet and some eggs."

With no salt or pepper and nothing else to eat, no curtains on the windows, no bath towels, or any kind of soap for dishes or for bathing we sat there in temporary shock wondering how this assignment was going to work! The next day was Sunday and after the service we were invited to their house for dinner. We were surprised to see that their home seemed large and spacious; they only had one child and seemed to have plenty of extra room! We went back to our empty trailer and only after sleeping on the three-quarter cot in the corner for two more nights did we discover the reason for this barren accommodation: they had put the trailer up for sale, and it sold! They were moving us to another place. We packed our few clothes and instruments into the car and were told that they would take us there after the service. That night we followed them quite a ways out in the country to a farm house where a large family lived. Some of the kids moved out of their room to give us their bed, but the house was so full of clutter there was hardly a place to step—let alone place our belongings! So, after receiving the refreshments they offered and visiting briefly, we left all of our things in our car and went to bed.

"We have farm duties in the morning, so we will be up early," our hosts explained. In the middle of the night, however, we heard someone fall and Gail ventured out to see if everyone was alright. The man of the house was dragging his wife to a couch saying that she had passed out and needed to go to the hospital. Upon inquiring how we might be able to help, he answered, "If you could just pray, and stay here with the children."

We all went back to bed after he left and when we got up in the morning the children had gotten themselves off to school and we were there alone. Gail decided he would get dressed and drive into town where he could prepare for the meetings at the church. He thought that I should stay there and try to help around the house. I started in the kitchen but there were so many dishes to wash that I filled the sink several times, scrubbing what seemed like a mountain of dirty plates and pans. It seemed overwhelming to me, as a young eighteen year old coming from a home that had always been sparkling clean and well-organized. I had compassion on this woman in spite of the mess, however, because she had to work in the field all day with her husband to get the farm work done! They were very nice to us, and had accommodated us to the best of their limited ability, which we felt was generous and commendable. The man had returned from the hospital that morning and had gone straight to work on his farm; but he came in at noon to get something to eat and I asked him if there was something else I could do. He seemed embarrassed that I was doing their housework, but mentioned that the laundry needed to be done. So I went back to the laundry room to see how I could help and it was waist-deep with soiled clothing! Laundry, however, was something I was accustomed to; so I washed load after load and hung them on the clothesline outside. That afternoon when he drove in to the hospital to see his wife, Gail came back from the church and I shared my utter amazement with him. "This is really something! I don't know what to do next! It's so cluttered in this place I can hardly move!"

The pastor came out to see how we were doing and was horrified with the conditions; as I described everything that I had tried to do to remedy the situation he felt worse! He decided that, despite their invitation for us to stay, he would rather take us back to town to find another place. My first thought was that this place at least had a bed to sleep in, which was more than the trailer offered. I remembered the scripture in Matthew 10:11-13 that says, *"And into whatsoever city or town ye shall enter, inquire who in it is worthy; AND THERE ABIDE till ye go thence. And when ye come into an house, salute it. And if the house be worthy, let your peace come upon it: but if it be not worthy, let your peace return to you."* (KJV) I didn't want to spurn a worthy invitation, yet I will have to admit that my peace did return to me knowing that I did not have to stay longer!

The pastor said there was a lady in the church who lived in a small trailer (oh, the thought!) but was gone on vacation and would allow us to use it for temporary accommodations. We followed him to the site and it was another country setting where the trailer stood under a tree. We had to leave all of our belongings in the car again, since the trailer was crowded and full; but we were able to use the bed and bath. Of course, there was still nothing to eat, as she had cleaned out her cupboards and fridge for the summer. The pastor said that the people of the church would bring food, and he made an announcement encouraging all of them to do so. The first night there was a cardboard box in the lobby of the church containing two jars of prune jam, a jar of pickles and a watermelon! We ate watermelon for every meal and by the second night Gail had to run for the door right after the altar call in order to make it outside and retch over the rail! He loved preaching, and never said anything to the pastor; and we scraped up a few cents somewhere to buy a loaf of bread on which to spread the prune jam. The next Sunday they took an offering for us, and the pastors invited us for dinner again—our second meal in a week's time. We were young, and none the worse for wear, although I think we may have been better fed by ravens!

After finishing the Hemet meetings, we drove back to Doc and Hazel Bryan's for a few days of rest and reprieve. We were met with a draft notice that had come for Gail while we were away. Like other young men of that era, he was being inducted into the armed services, and I was devastated. Firstly, we were barely married and, secondly, I had discovered that I was pregnant! Gail decided that we should go back to Idaho so I could live with my parents while he was gone. When we got there, however, we were told that a small Assembly of God church in southern Idaho was looking for a pastor and that if we were pastoring a church the government would not require Gail to go into the army. In light of this new information, and the fact that I was expecting our first baby, he decided to audition at this church and see if they would accept him. We traveled to Blackfoot, Idaho where Gail preached for the congregation, and heard soon afterwards that they had reached a unanimous vote to bring him on as their new pastor. He was then formally deferred to a "Class IV-D" exemption from military service under its definition: "Ministers and full time students preparing for the ministry under the direction of a recognized church or religious organization."

First Pastorate

So finally, in late November of 1952, we headed for Southeast Idaho to resume our first pastorate with everything we owned packed in our '52 Chevy. Navigating very icy roads about twenty-five miles north of Shoshone, Idaho we crested a hill and the car began to slide off the road. This area is covered with lava rock, close to Craters of the Moon National Monument, and this treacherous landscape was the worst place for a car accident. Gail struggled, but could not regain control and we crashed in the lava rock past the shoulder of the highway, smashing in the front of our new car and breaking off one front wheel. We were both safe and our belongings survived the crash. Out in the middle of nowhere, staring at our instruments and the pumpkins that my mother had given us from their garden to make pies for our first Christmas, we began to pray and ask God for help. God works in mysterious ways and this time he brought a carload of heavily intoxicated folks to our rescue who, albeit more smashed than our car (in a manner of speaking), were kind enough to give us a ride back to Shoshone where we called for a wrecker. The car was repaired but it took a month; so we were grateful that some folks from our new church could drive to Shoshone and pick us up with some of our bare necessities to take us to our little parsonage at Blackfoot.

Our first home was a basement apartment in the church that was furnished with a wood cook stove, a couch, a table and four chairs, a bed, a dresser and one lamp. We moved our things in and made it cozy, happy to have a place of our own after being on the road for the first five months of our newlywed life! I was comforted to settle into these new surroundings, especially knowing that our family would be growing and it would be hard to tote a baby around to evangelistic meetings.

Blackfoot was very cold in the winter, with frigid temperatures from October through April. The wind blew continually as well. The ground was frozen and there was about two inches of frozen snow when we arrived. We had to build a fire in the wood cook stove to fix meals and, without a refrigerator, had no way to preserve left-overs or perishable foods. The heater burned coal, which we had to retrieve from the stoker room in the church basement. The floor was asphalt tile, and very cold; but the living room had a rug by the couch and chair. We dressed warm and kept two bedrooms closed off from the rest of the apartment in order to stay warmer. Gail read the Bible aloud to me every evening, a practice he loved and continued throughout our lives. Our home was very quiet; the phone hardly rang and we had no television or radio. We played our instruments and sang together; Gail read books and I wrote letters.

The first service was a Wednesday night and there were only six people in attendance. We met in a small room of the church and built a fire in the pot-bellied stove to keep warm. One man told us that because they had been without a pastor for six months the numbers had diminished quite a bit. He said not to expect any more than twenty people on Sunday morning, and there were twenty-six. We dived wholeheartedly into our new assignment with church meetings, prayer meetings and visitation. We were also "initiated" almost immediately into the ministry of service to the needy. We had a constant stream of people at our door asking for help. From residents on the nearby Fort Hall Reservation, to desperate families, to traveling hobos, we got it all. We had so many scary characters stay with us! Gail would give them everything from food or gas money, to lodging; or even his own coat! One man who had gone through a divorce stayed with us for two months; then he went to California and got his estranged wife and three little boys. They all came back and lived with us for two more months in our tiny, crowded basement apartment. We were happy to help with counsel and support until our relatives came to visit and we ran out of room. The wife left him and the little boys, so he stayed with another family from the church until he got a job. Life is tough; and part of the gospel is helping people get through the rough spots, even if you have a few rough spots of your own!

Gail went hunting that winter and got a deer so we would have meat; but we had to keep it in a meat locker in town. The outdoor temperatures were cold enough; but to walk into that meat locker and go down the row to our freezer, retrieve our meat, and go back home was enough to cause frostbite! Our menu that first winter was venison… or venison and potatoes! It was potato country and the farmers left gleanings along the edges and in the corners of their fields that anyone could gather freely. There was also a lady in the church who lived on a dairy farm that supplied local dairies. If the milk did not make the acceptable grade for the dairy, a pale pink dye was added to separate it from the rest. This lady would bring me 5-gallon containers of pink milk. She said it was not contaminated; just below dairy grade. So I used it for whatever I could. I made ice cream with Rennet Tablets. The process was to pour the mixture into ice cube trays and freeze it. Later, we popped the frozen cubes into a bowl and worked it with an electric mixer until it became soft like ice cream. After the baby came I would also boil the pink milk and use it in the baby's bottle when I got in a bind. The milk lady would also bring cheese periodically, which was a real treat because we couldn't afford to buy it in the store. Since we had a refrigerator by this time, I could keep more food on hand, but we lived quite meagerly during this first winter. Our basement apartment was fairly well-insulated against the cold temperatures and winter winds. Once we built a crackling fire we could stay quite warm. We felt very blessed to have rugs in the bedroom and in part of the living room—something I had never had before. I also had a rocking chair, and enjoyed my little home with its simple comforts.

As newlyweds, we were always invited to someone else's home for holidays. Our church deacons were like parents to us because our own folks were 1,000 miles away and we couldn't travel to spend the holidays with them. I played my accordion for every service since we did not have a pianist. Gail preached faithfully and served the congregation there and because he was so gifted and outgoing he became well-known in the area. He was soon elected CA Representative for our section, Christ Ambassadors being the youth program for the Assemblies of God in those days. Gail was also the Assistant Secretary and Treasurer for the Southern Idaho District of the Assemblies of God. Due to difficult family circumstances for the man he was assisting, however, Gail had a plethora of additional duties which kept him very busy. He also started a radio broadcast right away, which our little church somehow funded, and he hosted a weekly program in the local Blackfoot area.

Our small congregation in Blackfoot was interested in coming to church and enjoyed the meetings, but they were not much inspired to engage in church ministry or helps. There was a severely crippled girl that Gail transported, along with her single mother, to almost every service and outlying meeting. He had to carry her to and from the car and in and out of the buildings. I hosted the WMC (Women's Missionary Council) meetings in our small, basement apartment. It was only a short devotion and prayer before the women began working on their sewing projects for missions; but no one wanted to help with arrangements or preparations. We did everything ourselves and learned a lot in the process, about service and about human nature!

Soon after we arrived, we met a wonderful man named Dwight Richey who had dealt with Mormons all his life and had pioneered a church in Salt Lake City, Utah. He was a very prophetic and godly man who gave us many insights and enriched our lives. He loved us like a father and stopped to see us whenever he came through on business. He lived in Missoula, Montana, but traveled several states and we set up a room in our apartment for him to use whenever he came to Blackfoot. Gail had a deep hunger for the things of God; he loved godly people and always gravitated to them. Brother Richey was a man of prayer ad we had the greatest respect and honor toward him. Gail wanted his advice on how to break through the thick veil of Mormonism that dominated our area of the state.

"Place an ad in the paper," he instructed, "that reads as follows: '*Have I Been Mistaken in Rejecting Mormonism?* Come join us to hear Dwight Richey discuss Mormonism."

Our church was too small for the crowds that we expected, so we held the meetings in an old Baptist Church in Firth—which was later an Assembly of God—about eight miles away. It was packed out for three nights in a row.

Brother Richey spoke first and then took questions at the end. He simply compared the truth of the Bible, including detailed references, to the doctrines of the Mormon religion. For instance, he countered the Mormon belief that says, "As man is, God once was and as God is, man may become," with scriptures such as Isaiah 45:5 that says, *"I am the LORD, and there is none else, there is no God beside me..."* During the question and answer period, one lady stood up to utilize the audience as a place to "bear her testimony about the joys of living in a polygamist family with a father who had three wives"; but Brother Richey kindly met her delusions with truths from God's Word. There were several young people who were interested in the differences that he pointed out, but said they were motivated to study their own religion more carefully. Mormonism, however, is a deep, dark cult holding many prisoners captive and we knew that further study of their own religion would only draw them deeper in. Gail always counseled people, "Do not study error; study the Truth. Then, when error appears, you will recognize it for what it is." We prayed for the supernatural revelation of the Holy Spirit to touch their hungry hearts with the truth that would set them free.

Gail was also nominated as the President of the Ministerial Association. As soon as we took the position in Blackfoot there was a large piece in the newspaper about the "new pastor at the Assembly of God Church." So he was invited to participate in the Ministerial Association right away. The first time he was asked to pray at one of the meetings, they saw the value in his leadership and nominated him as president. This was an interesting experience and a real eye-opener for us. We found that ministers of other denominations in our community were often involved in worldly lifestyles and spoke as the general unsaved public! The first time we attended one of their dinners we discovered that the Episcopal minister was in the State Hospital undergoing treatment for alcohol abuse. His wife sat among us blowing smoke and using curse words, defending her bad language with comments such as, "I think there's a place for a good, healthy *'damn it'* in everybody's vocabulary!"

Gail conversed with a Methodist minister there who declared that Charles Wesley wouldn't be welcome in any of their churches these days because they had become so modernistic. He went on to say that they didn't believe in the supernatural, or any of the miracles of the Bible. We were so overwhelmed to discover so many leaders pastoring churches in our area that didn't really know the God of the Bible and were openly opposed to His Truth! Nevertheless, Gail continued in that position for a while, hoping to do some good. When the National Day of Prayer came around they asked him to preach. They were handing out topics to every minister who would be participating in the program. His assigned topic was "There is no Geography in the Realm of the Spirit". He thought it might be a trap, but did a masterful job anyway; to God be the glory!

During this time Gail was working very hard in multiple outreaches, always involved in some branch of the Lord's work. The Assemblies of God asked him to operate the Bible Book Store for the district out of our church since we didn't have as many family responsibilities as the other pastors in the area. Gail loved books and was very interested in building a library so he took on the responsibility with gusto and arranged an upstairs room to house all the book stock collected by the district. At the Fellowship Meetings, which we attended every month, Camp Meetings and any other district gathering where a book table would be, Gail was responsible to set things up and oversee the sales of all books and Bibles. The book inventory was purchased by the district and all pastors could order their study books through the organization; so Gail was responsible to fill all orders that came in. We were busy with many healthy activities and we were learning a lot about pastoral leadership with all its joys and challenges.

Many young ministers in those days were assigned pastorates without completing years of seminary education. As a young evangelist in California, Gail had earned his "Christian Workers" papers identifying him as part of the ministries of the Assemblies of God. He completed the expected study requirements in Blackfoot in order to receive his ministerial license and later, in Twin Falls, he was finally ordained with the denomination after further approval by the district. Although we entered our first post with less book-learning than some, we cut our teeth on the hard knocks of on-the-job training. Along with many of our young pastoral colleagues in those early days we took the accelerated education route, which taught us more in a few months about pastoring God's flock then we could have possibly gleaned through several years of college instruction. Ordered by the Lord, we found that he supported this method as well, and lovingly filled in all the gaps as we followed him step by step.

– CHAPTER SEVEN –

Feathering the Nest

A Brood of our Own

Psalm 127:3-5[a] says, *"Behold, children are a heritage from the LORD, the fruit of the womb a reward. Like arrows in the hand of a warrior are the children of one's youth. Blessed is the man who fills his quiver with them!"*(ESV) We believed that children were a blessing and we planned on raising a family together; but I remember Gail saying, "Honey, we should wait for at least a year before we plan to have children since we are traveling around in ministry."

When I found out I was pregnant, the very next month, we were both surprised, and realized that the contraceptives we were using so faithfully were not very effective! There were no birth control pills in those days, so it was expected that all marriages would be blessed with children right away, and regularly thereafter! It was always considered a blessing and a privilege to bear a child and everyone responded joyfully to the news of a new baby on the way. I had four good pregnancies and never experienced morning sickness, though I had a headache off and on during my first and third pregnancies. Other than that, I felt as normal as if I were not expecting a baby at all. I never gained a lot of weight, so I did not experience the misery that many other women speak of. I enjoyed carrying all my babies and felt blessed and honored to be given another child. I only wish I had some pictures of those precious months!

By the most common tell-tale signs, I assumed that I was pregnant and my doctor's visit confirmed the fact. He said that I was losing too much weight and I knew that was true. I had gone down from a healthy one hundred and twenty-five pounds at marriage to one hundred and nine at this time. I didn't want to tell my doctor that our life of Pentecostal evangelists kept us on the go and often wondering where our next meal was coming from! I knew nothing about pregnancy because I had never heard anybody talk much about it and there were no books in those days for pregnant mothers. God had it covered, though, for our pastoral friends from Firth came to our aid. Clara Caldwell took me under her wing. "No worries!" she chirped. "Everybody in the world has been born!"

I found the scripture in I Timothy 2:15, *"Notwithstanding she shall be saved in childbearing, if they continue in faith and charity and holiness with sobriety."*(KJV) God's Word was a comfort to me because I knew that I could trust Him, even though my only knowledge about this marvelous condition was that it happened all the time: women got pregnant and had babies!

After taking the Blackfoot post we found out the reason it was so hard to fill: the church was too small to support a family. Gail stated confidently that since we lived by faith anyway this shouldn't be a problem. He added that we needn't look for work because we were provided with a place to live and could trust the Lord for everything else. I was not afraid because my mom seemed fine with all of her childbearing experiences, even with my father delivering most of their babies. Since we were not planning for Gail to follow in his footsteps, I figured my experience would undoubtedly be more composed than hers. We could do this!

I was about six months along when we attended a sectional Fellowship Meeting. I knew very few people well enough to talk about my pregnancy; so you can imagine my shock when, after the meeting, an announcement was made. "We would like to honor one of our pastor's wives who is expecting a baby, and we have prepared a baby shower to bless her with while we are all gathered together." They brought out a huge umbrella that was full of gifts and placed it in front of me! I didn't even think they knew me, let alone the fact that I was pregnant! I was so taken off guard, and so nervous, that my lip developed an immediate twitch that wouldn't stop! I was trying to smile and be gracious but it was also embarrassing! After we returned home from the Fellowship Meeting, our church people put money together to purchase a baby buggy for us. Although it was too hard to carry up and down the stairs from our basement apartment, I was thrilled to have it for the baby to sleep in beside our bed since I had no bassinette for her when she arrived. She slept in the buggy until she was at least eight months old!

At another Fellowship Meeting just before our baby came, we met a couple who had heard Gail and I sing and play our instruments together at all the district meetings and rallies. We loved to sing, and learned to accompany ourselves with my accordion and his guitar just by practicing all the time. We weren't professionals but we could carry our own and they wanted to do the same. We didn't know what they were really after when they came to us with an offer. "There is a maternity home in Shelley that is very nice. They will keep you nine days with full care for you and the baby. If you will go there for the birth and use our wonderful doctor, we will pay the bill of five hundred dollars. We believe the Lord wants us to do it." We were both reluctant because the doctor at the Blackfoot hospital did not charge a fee for ministers and the hospital costs were only fifty dollars. We saw no reason for them to pay five hundred dollars when it was so much less in our own town. They kept after us, however, coaxing that we would be exceptionally pleased with the place where their own baby was born. They seemed so anxious to bless us in this way that we finally relented.

Dorcas Christina, our first baby girl, was born on April 18, 1953 in Shelley, Idaho. While in the maternity home after our daughter's birth, Gail came up to visit me. "Guess what happened," he said gravely; and proceeded to describe how this couple had showed up to our apartment with the story that they had come for the instruments that we had agreed to trade for their coverage of the hospital costs! I was stunned!

"What do you mean?" I exclaimed. "They didn't say anything to me about that! Did they say anything to you?"

"No; they never said a word to me about it," he answered.

"Well, did you tell them that? We would never have agreed to this if we had known! We need those instruments for our church; and we could have had a fifty dollar bill instead of a five hundred dollar one!"

"Well, it's too late; I didn't know what to say and they already took them." This was robbery, and I wanted to call them on the phone and confront them reasonably; but Gail said that we should suffer wrongfully and leave it in the Lord's hands. I felt sick inside; our beautiful instruments stolen right before our eyes.

Our daughter, Dorcas, was named after my precious sister, who was always such a saint. I also liked the name because of the wonderful woman of the Bible by the same name that sewed garments for the poor. We had discussed the name and Gail liked it as well, so it was decided. I haven't heard of many others with this name, but we always knew it was fitting for our little girl. Dorcas means "gazelle" and our baby had large, soft eyes. She also became very light on her feet as she grew, and loved to run outside and be free like a deer bounding across the landscape. Dorcas had the colic, and cried very hard for the first two and a half months, but after that she was quite easy to care for. She ate baby food very well at five months old; but she never learned to crawl because the concrete floors in our basement apartment were cold and abrasive to her soft baby skin. Instead she learned to sit up quite early, and was walking well by nine months old.

That first summer, Gail wanted to plant a garden. He tilled some ground in the lot next to the church building and planted his crops. We had lots of corn, green beans, potatoes, tomatoes and various other garden vegetables. I had never canned vegetables in a pressure cooker because my mother had canned only fruit. Our neighboring pastor friends, Ed and Clara Caldwell, had been at our house for dinner and we talked about harvesting our garden and canning some vegetables. Clara said she would come down and show me how to do it. So I got all the beans ready to process: picked, washed, strung and snapped. She came and showed me what to do and I canned fifty-three quarts of green beans that year! I learned from the women in our church how to pickle beets and how to make sauerkraut. It was very fulfilling to be so resourceful with the Lord's bounty.

When Gail's family came to visit later they helped us can about fifty quarts of peaches. That second year of our marriage my canning projects produced many jars of tomatoes, corn, and beets also, which started a long and successful canning career that benefited our family for years to come!

Gail also went with other ministers that summer as a work party to help out on the Nampa Camp Meeting grounds. Dorcas was only two months old, and I was alone for the first time in my life! I felt so lonely and my baby girl was a great comfort to me. "You are Mommy's little company; and I will never be alone again!" I whispered in her little ears. She would never know how I cherished her presence; having her to love, to hold and to keep me busy making pleasant memories. I also made a trip by myself with my new baby at this time. I didn't like going alone, but Gail had bought me a bus ticket from Blackfoot to Caldwell, where my parents still lived on the farm. He wanted me to see my family and, of course, I wanted them to see the baby; but inside I really didn't want to go. Everything had changed so much; it wasn't the same with all of my brothers and sisters gone. I had a good time but I was anxious to get back home. My brother David and his wife Charlotte offered to drive me the three hundred miles back to Blackfoot and I was happy to take them up on it! I had a different life now; a new role with big responsibilities. I was a pastor's wife and a new mother; and there was no other place that I would rather be.

Gail and I were both so sad about losing our instruments that we decided right away to start looking for possible replacements in the *Evangelical Foreign Missions Society* catalog, which offered various equipment and supplies for ministers at discount prices. We found a nice accordion that I could get for one hundred and seventy-nine dollars and a nice Gibson guitar that Gail wanted to buy, and we began saving money to purchase them. Meanwhile, I struggled along learning to play the church piano, a few chords at a time, with little Dorcas in her bassinette beside the piano bench! She was as good as gold, rarely making a sound while I played the songs for our worship services. A wonderful man in our church, Albert Sundquist, who loved to hear me play the accordion, asked why I wasn't playing anymore, so I told him what had happened. He felt so bad about it that he offered to pay half the price of the new accordion so that I could get it sooner, which we did. I loved my new accordion; a beautiful Scandalli with a leather case, smaller and easier to play than my first one.

When winter came again, everything was frozen solid. From our kitchen window we could see the flag flying in front of the Post Office. The wind never stopped blowing in Blackfoot, and that flag never stopped whipping and snapping in its wake. I stayed inside with the baby unless we had meetings, which kept us plenty busy, and we faithfully visited the people in our congregation. We didn't telephone our families because they were far away, and long distance phone calls were expensive back then. We kept in touch through the US Mail, sending letters back and forth, or postcards which cost only two or three cents apiece. My sister, Lois, worked at a bank and had to wear business attire every day. She could not even have one runner in her nylon stockings; so she sent her used ones to me through the mail and I was thrilled to get them! I couldn't afford to buy my own very often, and with my long dresses, the runners hardly ever showed beneath my hems.

Big Sister Baby

Dorcas was still a baby herself, barely a year old, when her little sister came along. Our second darling was no better planned than the first. In those days, most pregnancies were a surprise, an automatic part of the marriage landscape!

This pregnancy was actually easier than my first because there was not even the occasional headache as before; but because there was such a short time between the two, my normal cycles had not yet resumed and I wasn't sure how far along I was. The doctor said I would have to watch for the first signs of life, and as soon as I felt the baby move I could judge from that. By this casual method, which felt very much like chance, I presumed my baby's due date to be the first of April. When I experienced some noteworthy pains mid-month, therefore, I felt it was definitely time, if not overdue! Gail's mother, Hazel Bryan, had come to help with the new baby so she was there to stay with Dorcas while I went to the doctor. We were without a vehicle, though, because Gail was gone; so I bundled up and walked to the doctor's office bearing my pains! Thankfully, it was not far, and upon examination he told me that it was not time and there was nothing wrong. So, I walked back home, freezing all the way!

"If you don't have that baby soon I'm going to go home!" my mother-in-law quipped in teasing tones when I told her the outcome.

In those days, getting the umbilical cord wrapped around the baby's neck inside the womb was a fearful probability. All expectant mothers were continually exhorted to refrain from reaching or stretching lest they cause the death of their child. Consequently, Gail and his mother helped with all the household chores these last weeks. I washed and rinsed the clothes in the tin tub and they hung them on the outdoor clothesline. Hazel was always busy doing anything she saw around the house that she could help with, and enjoying little Dorcas in the meantime. Being the end of April, it was springtime in Idaho—however chilly the weather—and time to plant potatoes. So Gail, his mom, and I decided to get our spuds in the ground. She was very experienced with gardening and showed us exactly what to do. We cut them apart, leaving an "eye" in each piece. She showed us how deep to plant them and we finished several rows. Then Hazel mentioned that there was a cooking school going on downtown and that she and I should go while Gail stayed home with Dorcas.

At the cooking class, we learned how to make an angel food cake layered with whipped cream and banana wheels, then drizzled with a beautiful orange glaze. I continued making this special but easy dessert for the rest of my life, drawing compliments from all who tasted! There was also a drawing after the class and I won two bags of groceries! When we got home and started to unpack them, my pains began for real and Gail rushed me to the hospital. He checked me in and raced back home to get a shower since he was still in his dirty garden clothes from our tater-planting project. Alas, Baby Girl #2 popped out only 45 minutes later and her Daddy did not make it back in time to see her grand entrance! He went down to the nursery and stood at the window to see his second child and heard two ladies exclaiming over her.

"Oh, my!" they marveled as they noticed Becca's thick, black hair. "Look at the cute little Indian baby!" Fort Hall Indian Reservation was close by and their little ones were regular residents in the maternity ward.

Rebecca Faith was born in the Blackfoot Hospital on April 27, 1954; so now we had two April babies. When Rebecca came, the church people gave me a baby shower and I got various little gowns and cute booties, onesies and receiving blankets. My most favored gift of all, however, was cloth diapers. There was no such thing as disposables in those days, so the more cloth diapers a mother could have, the easier it was to keep her babies clean and dry. Becca was a perfect baby in every way. She slept well and ate well; she was always happy and rarely cried. Dorcas loved to be the big sister of Becca, studying her constantly and wanting to feed her the bottle. The girls were never noisy, but a mother's ears are tuned to silence as well, especially when it becomes deeper than normal. One day the house became so quiet I decided I should investigate. As I walked into the room I saw that Dorcas had made the executive decision to try out the baby's bottle for herself and sat happily by her little sister's side, slurping away! When she saw me she gave the bottle back, touching the baby softly and saying, "Here, Babe."

Rebecca chided me about her name after she was grown. She was a young mother researching baby names for her own children when she discovered in a book of baby names that "Rebecca" meant *hangman's noose*! She telephoned me and said, "Mom! Why did you name me something that means *hangman's noose*?"

"What?" I exclaimed in reply. "Where did you get that idea? When I chose your name, it meant *beautiful*!" Later, we laughed about it together when she found out that it was depicted as "hangman's noose" because beauty can be a snare! Her middle name, Faith, was after my sister, Dorcas, although we had also considered Grace, after one of Gail's sisters. Ever since Becca discovered that the full meaning of her name was 'Beautiful Faith' she has loved it and thanked me for choosing it ever since.

Gail had been asked to come to Arkansas to preach another revival meeting. My brother, David, and his wife, Charlotte, were currently pastoring the little church in Purple Sage that David had built while I was still at home. They wanted to make a trip to Georgia to visit her folks. As we talked by telephone back and forth about traveling together, Gail decided that he also wanted to go pick up a new car in Detroit, Michigan. Some of his preacher friends had convinced him that he should never keep a car too long because an older car would not have enough value to be a good investment and that he should buy a new car every few years! It turned out to be the biggest mistake of our lives, however, because we had our first car nearly paid for and would have been better off staying content with that. Instead, we sold it to get money for a down payment and drove David and Charlotte's old Ford back to Michigan to pick up our new car. The plan was for them to go on to Georgia and for Gail and I to travel down to Arkansas to hold our scheduled meetings after picking up our vehicle. I was very unsettled about the whole trip. For one thing, I didn't want to leave my two and a half month-old baby with other people so soon. Gail explained that the extreme heat in Arkansas this time of year would be dangerous for a new baby.

"Then I'm not going," I firmly replied. "I don't want to leave her; she's too little."

"I need you there, Eunice," my husband coaxed with conviction. "You are part of the team and we need to sing together for all the meetings."

"No!" I cried with motherly concern. "I will not leave her!"

He wisely suggested, "Let's ask Albert and Flossie to keep her. They probably will." This was an older couple in our church that we both loved and trusted; so I finally relented. The Sundquists were more than willing to keep Rebecca; they were utterly delighted with the opportunity. This did not make it easier, however; it was very hard for me to leave my tiny, new baby girl behind and I secretly grieved about doing it, although I cooperated with Gail's plan.

David and Charlotte had a baby boy, whom they brought with them so that his grandparents could see and enjoy him; and I brought Dorcas, our one-year-old. Charlotte and I loaded up our babies and belongings in the back seat and David and Gail rode in the front. Way out in the middle of Nebraska, my sister-in-law became deathly sick and we realized that we were both suffering from carbon monoxide poisoning! The babies were both asleep, we hoped, and panicked to think that they could easily die from this! We stopped at a service station as soon as we came to one and I took Charlotte into the restroom, where she promptly fainted inside the stall! I ran to get David and Gail to carry her out onto the lawn where she could get fresh air. Both of the babies had been easy to wake up and seemed fine; but Charlotte was laid out on the ground for some time before we were able to revive her.

We didn't want to go any farther without fixing the problem that had caused the exhaust leak. Unfortunately, the temperatures were triple digits that July and the proprietor was uncooperative with our plight. David asked the man if he could borrow a certain tool from his garage and he exploded with anger. "Get off of my property!" he screamed. "We run a business here! We don't loan tools to anyone! Leave right now or I will call the police!"

"I will leave as soon as I am able;" my brother calmly replied; but before we could do so the hot-headed man had called the police department for assistance. We told them what happened and they were very accommodating, taking our side of the issue. "Don't worry;" the officers assured us. "These incidents are a common occurrence here. This fellow has a raging temper and is always in a fix because of it. Take your time and we will consider the matter resolved. He will get over it; the heat waves have just gotten the best of him."

We were able to drive down the road a ways, but stayed there for what seemed like a very long time before David and Gail could get the car in safe running condition. Then we had to travel with the windows down to make sure it didn't happen again, but we finally made it to Detroit. Gail and I were dropped off to pick up our new car and David and Charlotte were to head for Georgia. Gail gave them some gas money because he was afraid they didn't have enough to make the trip. Then we discovered that we did not have enough to make ours! With no money for motels, we drove all night and all day for several days. Gail wouldn't stop along the road to sleep because we had a baby and a new car. He was afraid that we might be accosted as we slept so he decided to power through instead. He got so exhausted that he began to talk in his sleep with his eyes open.

"Gail! Pull over!" I pleaded. "You're not operating with a sound mind!"

"No! I'm fine!" he assured me confidently. "Look at all those young people out there! I have a burden for their souls! All these young people need the Lord!"

I saw nothing but cows and countryside, however, so I knew we were in serious trouble! Finally I succeeded in convincing him to stop and sleep for a while; but it was not long before we were on the road again. About seventy-five miles from our destination, we ran out of gas. We hawked both of our watches at a local pawn shop and bought enough gas to get to Dover, Arkansas.

Once we arrived, the meetings went wonderfully. Many of Gail's relatives lived in the area and we enjoyed seeing and visiting with all of the aunts, uncles and cousins between services. The people of the area were all friendly and we received multiple invitations for accommodations, dinners and other elements of southern hospitality. Some of them had been at Gail's meetings before we were married, and had fond memories and many stories to tell. One very happy event for Gail was that he had arranged for his new Gibson guitar to be shipped to Arkansas since he knew we would be there for the revival meetings. When it arrived we were back in the saddle again, singing to our hearts' content and delighting the country crowds!

I learned something at that revival meeting; something about the importance of being *"instant in season and out of season."* The elderly pastor asked me if I would teach the young people's Sunday School class. I hesitated, having taught only children's classes before this.

"Of course; she would be happy to!" Gail stepped in to answer in my stead. I had previously determined to be the kind of servant that would be willing to step out in faith for anything that God wanted me to do. I had already been brave enough to lead the high school Bible Club, witness on the streets, and sing in front of large crowds. So, the pump was primed! I timidly agreed to do it if he could give me a lesson to teach. He gave me the Sunday School Quarterly and I studied the material that night in preparation for the morning class. When we got there, however, the class was in the main sanctuary and it was all adults! I guess the group seemed young to an elderly pastor, but I was only 20 years old so they were not young to me! I was nervous, wondering if I could do it; but the Lord helped me and everything went well. Gail got compliments later such as, "Looks like you married a preacher, Brother Bryan!" I learned the truth of Philippians 4:13(KJV), *"I can do all things through Christ which strengtheneth me."* I discovered that we can do much more than we think possible when we are willing to rely on the Lord for strength and wisdom, and to step out in faith.

We stayed in Dover for a month of meetings and the experiences were as rich as they were exhausting. Gail's grandmother, Minnie Newton, hosted us and had said with the sweetest of smiles when we arrived, "Now you kids just make yerselves at home and sleep as long as you want to!" She, however, was up the minute the rooster began to crow and would soon be saying, "Aren't you kids getting' up?" One time she opened the door to our room at 7:30 am and scolded, "Well...are you gonna sleep all day?" Since she was cooking, and breakfast for her was over by 8:00, we figured our mornings of "sleeping in" would have to wait until we got back home! The humidity was so bad that a sweat-soaked image of Dorcas' entire little body was left on the bed whenever I picked her up from nap time. All the relatives adored her and there were family gatherings a-plenty with the women standing over wood cook stoves to make wonderful food in one hundred degree weather!

Our new car was soon covered with layers of fine Arkansas dust, inside and out. There was no air conditioning to make the stifling summer weather more bearable, so we drove the dry, dirt roads with our windows down. With no such thing as a car wash to pull into for a rinse and vacuum, we would inevitably be taking this dust home with us to Idaho! On the way home I was introduced to one of Charles Bryan's sisters, Opal Gray. We stopped by Opal and Reggie's home so I could meet them. She was a very pretty, petite lady with bright blue eyes and the most lovely "aunt" image! Although we did not stay long, she seemed very happy to meet me and to see her nephew, Gail, again. It was a great experience to visit the people and places of my husband's heritage. He had shown me the creeks where he had baptized people who were converted in his previous meetings; the old home place where his mother grew up, and the favorite scenes he remembered as a boy spending summers at Grandma Newton's. Although our trip was wonderful and exciting, I was dying to see my baby! So I was glad when the day came for us to hit the road for home.

During our first years together we enjoyed a feeling of closeness and bonding as husband and wife, as companions, and as a team for service to the Lord in ministry. We were only eighteen and twenty years old when we took our first pastorate. Our congregation loved us and we had friends in the ministry that we shared good times with. We had worked hard to make our little basement apartment a cozy home for our growing family. Gail and I were both very conscientious about raising our little girls and training them in the ways of the Lord. Our major focus was the ministry, so we were always at the church or with church people.

The adventures we had in Blackfoot provided an amazing capacity for growth and experience. We were so young, yet given so much responsibility. We had many obligations with the district and in our community, including travel and heavy meeting schedules. Gail was invited often to preach camp meetings and also held some revival meetings while we lived there. We pastored in Blackfoot for two and a half years and I never missed a service during that time except when I birthed my babies. Our congregation grew by one hundred percent until we had close to sixty people regularly attending. Still, we couldn't seem to penetrate the heavy Mormon saturation in that area of the state and Gail came to a place where he felt his ministry was not productive enough. We packed as much as we could on a small trailer and left the rest of our furniture in the apartment for the next pastor. I remember wondering how I could live without my big tin tub. I used it for laundry and other things important to housekeeping. Neither could I bear to part with my rocking chair in which I had rocked my baby girls to sleep. Tub, rocker, and buggy all took second to Gail's books in the end and off we went with clothing and other bare necessities, traveling west toward home.

We reached my old family homestead at Black Canyon which was now occupied by my sister, Dorcas, and her husband, Rupert. Mama and Daddy had rented the farm out to them and moved back to California…again, where Daddy had a good job.

While we were staying with Dorcas and Rupert, Gail received another invitation to preach a revival meeting in Grangeville. My sister offered to keep Rebecca with them, knowing that it would be hard to stay at other people's homes with two babies. So we left her in Black Canyon and took Dorcas with us to Grangeville.

I still marvel at the many comical experiences we had, and the unique characters that crossed our paths while in the ministry! The pastor's wife at Grangeville was extremely moody, but we were doing our best to be kind and gracious during our stay. Gail had bought a watermelon to enjoy after the service and had placed it in the refrigerator to chill. When we came in after the meeting he said with great expectation, "Well, let's have some watermelon!" We took it out of the fridge and began slicing it up when this woman walked in and said saucily, "Danny wets the bed, and if he can't have watermelon nobody else gets it either!" after which she turned on her heel and stomped out. Her husband was in the other room and didn't see her display; but I quickly put away the watermelon to keep the peace. Gail, however, was not going to give up his refreshment so easily, figuring that he had earned it, after all! "Why, that's ridiculous!" he frowned in low tones. "I bought that watermelon. I've preached long and hard; I'm hot, tired and thirsty and I'm having my watermelon no matter what she says!"

Just then, the pastor came into the kitchen and apologized, "I'm sorry about that; let's all have some watermelon!" We sat around the table enjoying our cold, sliced watermelon but the pastor's wife would not join us. I was so nervous and uncomfortable that the watermelon was hardly worth the trouble. After a while, the pastor went out to talk to his wife and she came back in to apologize. "I'm sorry," she said grudgingly. "I just didn't think it was fair for the rest of us to sit around and have watermelon when Danny couldn't have any."

The pastor was still embarrassed and interjecting comments to lighten up the atmosphere. "Well, honey. We don't all have to be on the same program as Danny, do we?"

After that uncomfortable start, I was uneasy and trying to do all I could to smooth things over. The next day I wanted to help with the dishes but there was hardly any soap left in the bottle. I squirted it in the sink deciding to go ahead with what I had to work with. I got them all done; washed, rinsed, and dried before she came in.

"You didn't have to do my dishes," she said condescendingly. "I went to the store for dish soap. How did you do them without any soap?"

"Well, there was a little left and I thought it would be enough to get them done." I felt awkward.

"It probably wasn't," she returned in snooty tones.

The rest of that revival meeting we had to use a lot of grace and deference, tip-toeing around the pastor's wife and her moods. These days, I think there is a popular acronym for people like this: EGR: "Extra Grace Required"! I believe these attitudes left unchecked can seriously hinder the moving of the Holy Spirit; but her husband was an upbeat kind of guy. He worked hard at the lumber mill all day and came home from work each night with a cheerful countenance, ready to support and enjoy the evening meetings. In those days, most pastors worked a regular job all week long. Their pastoral duties were extra, and mostly voluntary, with very little pay. They went into their callings with a true understanding of Colossians 3:23(KJV), *"And whatsoever ye do, do it heartily, as to the Lord, and not unto men; since you know that you will receive an inheritance from the Lord as a reward. It is the Lord Christ you are serving."* Much later in life, Gail and I had a plaque on our wall that read, "Working for the Lord doesn't pay much; but the Retirement Plan is out of this world!"

After Grangeville, we went back to the home place at Black Canyon to get little Rebecca from her Aunt Dorcas and Uncle Rupert. Soon we heard that the Assembly of God church in Twin Falls was looking for a pastor and had requested that Gail and I come and hold a meeting there. When he preached in Twin Falls, the people voted us in unanimously to fill their pastorate. We returned to Black Canyon to pick up our few belongings, still packed in our tarp-covered utility trailer. The church in Twin Falls was the second largest in the district; a healthy church running over two hundred in regular attendance. There was a vibrant, enthusiastic youth group, too, and a healthy body of believers, including many stable middle-aged couples. They were all solid Christians who were dedicated to the Kingdom of God, and whom we knew would be supportive of our vision for the work of the ministry. One couple we became very close to was the Christophersons. Violet and Leander were strong and dependable, heavily involved in the ministries of the church. Violet was the youth leader, a small, bubbly lady who played both the piano and accordion. Her husband was on the Board of Deacons; a stable business man in the community and a mature mentor for a young pastor still learning the ropes. We both honored their life experience and appreciated their insight. Our first parsonage was partly furnished but the few pieces we had acquired were left in Blackfoot, leaving us with no furniture of our own. So we set about to acquire a refrigerator, a washing machine and a clothes dryer. People in the church loaned us some beds and a couch, and we settled into our new home. Like most young people, there were times we would have been better off by following the advice of our new mentors more closely. Christophersons were trying to help us secure a used washer and dryer, which would have adequately suited our needs. Instead, my young husband was convinced by another source to buy new ones on time! Unfortunately, on pastor's wages in those days, payment plans were never a good idea. Buying only what we had cash for was always the wisest option. We did not get to keep the new appliances for very long.

Here in Twin Falls we started the Sunday traditions of afternoon naps and company after evening services, carrying it through most of our lives! Sundays were always busy, but they were for us; a day of worship, rest, and quiet. After morning services we came home, changed our clothes and had lunch. Then *everybody* took a nap. We usually had a little snack before the evening service, but never a meal. Then afterwards we often had company over for fellowship and refreshments of some kind. It was always a happy day that everyone looked forward to.

Gail was still very involved with the district. He was Secretary/Treasurer for the Christ Ambassadors statewide and had to travel from time to time with those duties. We got acquainted with our people over time and enjoyed the fellowship. Gail went on hunting and fishing trips with the men of the church and had a great time. We always had plenty of deer, elk, and fresh fish for dinner.

One time Gail decided we could be doubly blessed if I would go hunting with him so that we could bring home twice as much meat. So he got two game tags and off we went to hunt for antelope! I had no idea what a hilarious adventure I was in for! The country was flat for miles around and the strategy for antelope hunting was to chase them across the desert in vehicles! Gail had sold our nice car so that he could spend more money on books and Bible commentaries for his pastoral library. Rather than have the high payments, he decided we could get along just fine with a used Plymouth Coupe. This was our "hunting rig" as well. Whenever he saw a group of antelope he would drive off the road into the desert landscape and the chase was on! The first day we found a spot to throw our sleeping bags out on the ground and slept under the stars. As soon as Gail awoke the next morning, he lifted his head and spotted a large buck grazing very close to us. "Eunice!" he whispered. "Look!" He picked up his rifle and got his target in the crosshairs, but did nothing.

"Shoot," I whispered, "before he runs away!"

"No," Gail said with resolve. "If we shoot him now we won't have anything to do all day." I thought he was crazy; but he reasoned that if this one was so close we were sure to see plenty more throughout the day. Wrong…and away he ran. We drove over bumps and down into gullies; chasing antelope out through the brush in a cloud of dust all day long. They had a strategy for losing us: they would race beside the car and then begin to leap and bound as if they were flying. As soon as they got far enough ahead of the car to pass in front of us they would bound across the highway and leave us in the dust on the other side of the road. We couldn't get close no matter how hard we tried. We had lunch and tried again; and finally had supper out on the shadowy plains. At dusk, we headed home with no trophies; but as we rounded a bend in the highway, a small buck popped into view and Gail couldn't resist. This time our chase was successful and I held the flashlight while he dressed out our game for the trip home. He strapped his antelope on top of the car. We had a very flat tire, which we changed before hitting the road; but on the way we blew out another one! Both wheels were badly damaged but, thankfully, they were on the passenger side. The noise of riding on the rims was unbearable, so we eked our way with the two good tires on the pavement and the two bad ones on the shoulder of the road. The trip was painfully slow and it seemed like forever until we found a place where we could buy tires and a couple of good, used rims. It may have been an adventure I wouldn't want to repeat, but it was certainly one I will never forget; and Gail, like most men, was probably in hog heaven despite the damages!

Our First Son

The best event of our short tenure in Twin Falls was the birth of our son, Mark Timothy, on February 1, 1956 at Magic Valley Memorial Hospital. As before, there was no family planning. I got pregnant with Mark while we were on a short vacation trip to Southern California to visit our parents. Gail was helping his brother, Paul, do some tree-trimming for the Assembly of God campground near Big Bear, California. While we were there, we went to the Indio Fair one day. Thousands of people flocked to this event every year and somehow Dorcas, not yet three years old, wandered out of our sight and slipped away in the crowd. I panicked when I couldn't find her and began to pray. We looked frantically through the crowds of people and suddenly spied her some distance away, walking along as peaceful and happy as could be. When she saw us, she ran to us and said, "Mommy and Daddy, you were lost!"

During my third pregnancy I had more headaches, but I think most of it was due to stress. I was worried about Gail. We were almost four years into our marriage and, although there were many bright spots through our ministry as well as family joys with our little girls, my husband had some grave inconsistencies that kept popping up. These random incidents filled my head with questions about the stability of our relationship. He was non-communicative during these times of obvious inner turmoil; preoccupied with something that kept him distant from me and the children. I could see that he was side-tracked and disengaged from his ministry and it was happening more and more. So while carrying our third child, I was often fraught with insecurities about our future together, both as a family and in the ministry.

My mother came on the bus to stay for a week when Mark was born because I had albumin poisoning and was on bed rest just before the birth. Our two little girls were not quite two and three years old so I was happy to have some help to care for them. While I was in the hospital, she cooked meals, cleaned house and did laundry. When I came home after only two days she was ready to leave, saying that Gail could probably do everything that she had been helping with. She had enjoyed the girls and told a story about Dorcas running through the house with a doll bottle while Becca was close behind with her mouth open as if she would take a chunk out of her big sister at the soonest opportunity! Dorcas ran into a corner and whirled around with her hands up, pleading, "Be kind! Be kind!" Mama called Dorcas "that little one" and Becca "the tiny one". I felt happy to have my mother with me and was sad for her to leave so soon, but it was not my decision to make. Mama assumed that Gail would do all that my dad used to do when their babies came. Daddy and my grandfather had lived like bachelors when he was a teenager and he had learned to cook, clean and do all the household chores along with farm duties. This was not likely to be my experience, though; I knew I would be on my own after my mother left.

Gail was totally overjoyed and could not wait to tell everyone that he had a son. He called the church immediately, then his parents and his brother, Paul. My first words were "He's a chip off the old block!" because his forehead was identical to his father's and I knew right away that he would look like his dad. Even though many thought he looked like me too, most people commented throughout his life about how much he resembled Gail, and some—seeing Mark for the first time—knew that he was Gail Bryan's son even before they were told! The name Mark seemed to fit, and although we considered Paul as his middle name, we chose Timothy because that was the son of Eunice in the Bible. One pet name for him was "Marker" because his Aunt Rosemary had called him that, and it stuck. Grandpa Bryan called him "Markie Boy", and his big sisters called him "Markie". Almost from day one, Gail called him, "Daddy's big, fine boy;" so often, in fact, that when Mark began to talk he used the phrase regularly to describe himself, making sure everyone knew just who he was!

Shortly after Mark was born, I had an attack of Acute Pyelonephritis, a severe bacterial infection of the kidneys. This bout was the first of many in my lifetime, three of which nearly ended my life beginning with this one. Many years later I learned that this disease is directly related to trauma of the soul. I was oblivious to this at the time but, looking back, I am positively sure that emotional stress caused this very severe attack. We had a registered nurse in our congregation who came to see how she could help. When I told her that my urine looked like dark coffee grounds, she was worried. "Oh, honey!" she said with concern. "That's blood in your urine and we need to get a sample of it and take it to the doctor."

I was deathly ill and could go nowhere. I had a high fever, chills and headaches, muscle aches, pain in my joints and all over my entire body. Sister Inman took the specimen to the doctor for testing and brought home a prescription for me. The doctors treated this condition with sulfa drugs in the early years. Sulfonamide was the first synthetic antibiotic used to treat and prevent bacterial infections in humans.[1] We had no medical insurance so we just stayed home and prayed fervently. I got better, but the Nephritis continued to flare up about once or twice a year with acute attacks.

Meanwhile, back at the parsonage, our family had grown to five and the parenting phase was in full swing! After having two little girls, Gail was so proud of his boy! Having a son was a high point for him. Mark, being the first born son, brought great pride to his young father. He had dark eyes and dark hair, though not much of it at first. He was such a winsome child with big brown eyes and abundant energy. He was a happy, healthy, and very lively baby who could never be still. As I held him he always squirmed and tossed, often bouncing up and down while standing in my lap. I nursed him for two and a half months, but then lost my milk after hearing some devastating news about one of my sisters. He thrived on the bottle, however, and became quite chunky with very rosy cheeks. Gail used to pinch his cheeks and sing, *"Rolly-poley, Daddy's little fattie; Bet he's gonna be a man some day!"* Everyone thought he was a beautiful boy and raved over him; but his response was always very sober and thoughtful, studying everyone most thoroughly! He sat up at five and a half months and learned to crawl about the same time. He stood alone at eight months and began taking steps two weeks later. By the time he was nine months old, he was walking like a champ and he learned to whistle at ten months! Soon after, he began saying lots of words which he enunciated very well, and these graduated directly into short sentences spoken with amazing clarity. Mark was able to do about anything he set his mind to, and do it well. From climbing ladders at a frighteningly young age to riding bicycles at precarious speeds, Mark was masterful for his age and experience. Once while still in diapers he got away from me and climbed a very tall ladder up to the highest peak of the church roof! I heard his baby talk coming from somewhere and couldn't find him. When I finally spotted him at the top of the ladder, a nearby utility worker noticed it at the same time and said, "Stay calm, ma'am. I think I can get him." He did, but my heart was pounding and I was shaking all over by the time he placed him in my arms. Mark was not afraid of anything; he was bold and adventurous from the beginning. He also loved all things mechanical, and would often hear Gail's car pull up to the curb. He was so overjoyed when his dad came home that I always played along by exclaiming, "Here comes Daddy!" Mark would get so excited that he would nearly spin in circles as he ran to the window to watch Gail park the car and get out. Then he would run to the door and, as soon as Gail opened it, Mark would reach up for his hug.

When our children were young we didn't have money for planning vacations, or interest in leaving our ministerial duties. Unless Gail insisted, I didn't like to travel without taking the kids. A time or two, we went to Sunday School Conventions or other conferences and left the kids for a few days, but it was worrisome for me and my preference was always to stay together. It didn't help that the few times we *did* leave them I came back to bumps and scrapes on Mark from tumbling down the concrete steps into the basement; diaper pins stuck clear through his skin and out again (that diaper was not going anywhere!), or haircuts done by the sitters without my permission! The church was our life and we were completely dedicated to the work of the Lord. We always felt that Camp Meeting should be our first choice for a "family vacation". We went every year and stayed all ten days on the campgrounds in Nampa, Idaho. We rented a tent and camped out, cooked on a small burner, and enjoyed the warm weather. It was always a happy time of good preaching and singing together with godly people, friends and relatives. The "Tabernacle" was the big cinderblock building with a fresh sawdust floor where the meetings were held. We had rows of church benches to sit in and the altar in the front was a few plain benches with no backs. They built a makeshift platform with several steps going up from the sawdust floor so that everyone in the audience had a clear view. We had the pulpit, microphones, and a piano brought in and placed on the platform.

Musicians who were proficient on their instruments were always invited to take part in the volunteer orchestra. The Tabernacle had very large windows along both sides that could be opened upwards on hinges when the building got too stuffy during the hot Idaho summers. There were long poles that were used to prop them open and several rows of folding chairs were placed on the ground outside for overflow seating. The extra seating was slanted for a good view of the platform through the big windows and was greatly appreciated by latecomers, mothers with small children, or the ample saints among us who needed elbow room or more fresh air! Everyone loved the smell of the fresh sawdust floors, something that registered in our memory banks for years to come and brought back visions of all these happy times.

From Progress to Pitfalls

We pastored in Twin Falls for two years. The church services were always good and we had a nice group of musicians that provided wonderful music for worship. We enjoyed a lot of things that we had never had before and we felt happy and blessed. These were good times for us and it was easier for me here being surrounded by such dear and dedicated people. Gail's family still lived in California and mine in Nampa, so our church congregation became our family. One of my sisters moved close to us with her husband and first baby while she was recovering from illness and we were able to spend some good times of fellowship with them, praying together often.

I have fond memories of a Christmas Cantata where Gail and I both sang in the choir. The joyful enthusiasm of all the young people involved in the concert was a beautiful sight to behold! Those wonderful songs stayed with me for years, and when I thought of them later I could still hear the group harmony in my mind's ears. It was a memorable and positive experience that I needed during a season when I began to feel a lot of inner turmoil and aching in my soul that stemmed from the severe personal struggles that Gail began to have at this time. I didn't really understand everything, but I had realized by now that these deep soul battles were ongoing for him. This was a time that he needed to be fully engaged and on board with the life of the church. Our youth group alone was forty-strong and the church building had no Sunday School rooms. Consequently, I not only had to get my three little ones fed and dressed, I had to make sure every room in our house was clean and tidy so that classes could be held all over the parsonage! We had classes in the living room, the bedrooms and all the available rooms in our basement. I had a big challenge trying to accommodate this scenario every weekend. One Sunday, the baby had one of those nightmare diaper explosions that every mother dreads. He had to be bathed, changed and re-dressed. I couldn't get the dishes done in time so, completely against my nature, I crammed them all in the oven to hide them until after church. Through the years, I have heard of other mothers doing the same, but at that time of my life it was nearly disgraceful!

During our last year in Twin Falls, we met another couple who was pastoring at Wendell. We enjoyed getting acquainted with other young pastors who had small children and were in the same stage of life as we were, and we became very good friends. They had a smaller congregation with no midweek service so he often asked Gail to go fishing with him during the week. They enjoyed these times immensely but Gail began to go more often than his schedule could afford and it became a major distraction for him. I was happy to have him developing good relationships with brothers in the faith, but his personality worked against his better judgement. Gail was a fervent person, very passionate about anything that was important to him. A person can only focus intently on so many things at a time, and when he got involved in hobbies or activities that he enjoyed they very often became a bigger priority than anything else in his life, causing stress for both of us.

This is a good place to say that when we as God's people—at any stage of Christian development—get distracted by secular activities that begin to dominate our thoughts and take too much of our time, our spirit man goes into a state of starvation. The voice of the flesh becomes more dominant. Since we are not walking in the Spirit, or renewing our minds with fresh insight from God's Word, we are slow-slipping toward disaster. "Slow-Slipping" is actually a geological idea that has to do with swarms of small earth tremors up and down the boundaries between the earth's tectonic plates. These clusters of tiny tremors, only detectable by sensitive seismometers, occur again and again over weeks, months and years gradually increasing the stress on the fault line. They are evidence that pressure is building beneath the plates and they can eventually trigger larger earthquakes and even culminate in catastrophic events.[2] This natural phenomenon is a perfect example of what can happen to us, physically with our health or spiritually within our souls. A tell-tale side effect of a spiritual slow-slip is bad decision-making. We do well to remember that wisdom comes from God, and our finite, earthly brains are not reliable without it. God promises to give us all the wisdom we ask for. Yet, when we are in a dull spiritual state, we are not asking for, or receiving, the godly input we need for good, strong choices. James 1:5-8 explains this well. *"If any of you lack wisdom, let him ask of God, that giveth to all men liberally, and upbraideth not; and it shall be given him. But let him ask in faith, nothing wavering. For he that wavereth is like a wave of the sea driven with the wind and tossed. For let not that man think that he shall receive any thing of the Lord. A double minded man is unstable in all his ways."* (KJV)

In such a state, Gail was drawn into another "brotherhood scheme". A prominent pastor in Boise was collecting interest among southern Idaho pastors to buy new Mercuries. The deal was that anyone who could find ten others to purchase a car would get theirs free. Unfortunately, most of those who got on board didn't think through the effort it would take to find ten eager friends— especially in the same area where others were trying to accomplish the same! Thus, only the first guy got his Mercury free and all the rest got stuck in nice, new cars with payments they could not afford! We were still driving the Plymouth Coupe that had survived the antelope hunt, and Gail sold it to a young couple in the church. I drove Gail and several men in our church who were participating in the deal to Salt Lake City where they would all catch a plane to Detroit and drive home in their new cars. "Smiling for the camera" I cooperated; but I felt sick about it. Also during this time, another pastor from the Ministerial Association convinced Gail to take a part-time job driving school bus. "It will be a good diversion for you," the man said; "and you will make some extra money on the side to help with expenses."

For Gail, however, this was a bad idea that Satan took full advantage of, and it started a downward spiral that ended terribly. I began to notice that he was often gone much longer than he needed to be for his bus route responsibilities. I asked questions but got no answers. Out of the blue, he decided to send me to visit my parents in Los Angeles. I told him I didn't want to go on a trip, but he said that I needed a break and it would be good for me. He gave me a one-way ticket on the train and said he would send money later for my return trip. When I got there it was very crowded because they lived in a small apartment and there was no room for me and my kids. My father was troubled in his spirit. "What are you doing here without your husband?" he asked. I told him how the trip came about and what Gail had said to me. "When will he send the money?" He queried further. I knew my father was suspicious and I was upset, but without answers. I didn't know what was going on any more than he did. We waited for word from Gail but it never came. So after a month went by, Daddy said that I should go home and he bought me a bus ticket. During the first part of the trip I had the long back seat of the bus to myself and there was room for all the kids beside me. When we got to Las Vegas, though, we took on more passengers and the bus became crowded. "How many bus tickets did you buy, ma'am?" the exasperated driver scowled at me in his rearview mirror.

"One," I answered timidly.

"Then you can only have one seat!" he practically shouted. My chin quivered as I looked around in despair with my baby on my lap and my two little girls huddled at my knees. I struggled to keep the tears from bursting forth as I pulled my things as close to me as I could.

"Here, ma'am;" offered a compassionate voice nearby. "I'd be happy to hold your little boy for a while if that would help." I looked up to see a kind man reaching toward me. I didn't know what else to do. I had no money for another ticket. Aside from a few crackers that my mother had sent for the kids, we had nothing to eat during the trip and no money to buy food. I was sad; I was weary; I felt abandoned and I cried most of the way, hiding my tears from my little ones who looked at me with innocent dependency. I was glad they were so trusting and naïve; but how could I protect them when I felt so vulnerable myself? *"Lord Jesus...help me! Please give me strength and wisdom."* I prayed silent prayers and wondered what I would find at home.

I had notified Gail that Daddy was sending me home so he met us at the bus station. When we arrived at the house, it appeared that he had been absent as long as I was. All the mail from the last four weeks was stacked on the counter; not one piece had been opened. I looked in the refrigerator and saw that all the meals I had prepared for him to eat while I was away were still there, spoiled and molding. I confronted him about his behavior and about having his mind somewhere else, neglecting his ministry and his family. This time, however, instead of completely ignoring the issue, he finally produced a confession. I didn't really want to know that what I feared was true; but the time had come. Apparently, just before I came home, another pastor had seen Gail in a questionable situation and had confronted him about it later. He told me some of the details, and said he was sorry. He was ashamed of himself, but unable to stay and face the music. He decided that the best thing to do was to leave the ministry and get another job. Struggling with what to do and where to go, he borrowed $1,000 from a dear man in our church and decided to drive to Pendleton, Oregon to see if he could find a job and a house for our family. He wanted me to go on this trip with him because he knew that his bouts of unfaithfulness had chipped away at my confidence. I think he was afraid that I might be gone when he got back. He knew that he had caused me plenty of grief already, which made him insecure about my desire to stay with him; especially under these latest circumstances. In an effort to keep his family together, he wanted to take me far away from familiar territory where we could start over in a new place. My thinking was much different; I didn't want to be isolated from my family in a place where I didn't know a soul and had little trust for what my future would hold.

We left the girls with Dorcas and Rupert again and took little Mark with us. It was a nice, smooth ride in our big, fancy Mercury—sad, but smooth. I had laid Mark down on the back seat for a nap and the last time I looked at him he was sleeping peacefully. There were not so many State Troopers in those days and it was common to travel at higher speeds on long stretches of country landscape where there was no traffic. Gail was sailing along at ninety miles per hour and the thought crossed my mind that, at this frightening speed, I should ensure the safety of my child. Good thought, but too late. These cars had a back window that rolled down and Gail had it wide open for fresh air. When I looked back, Mark had not only awakened and stood up on the back seat; he had crawled over it and scooted himself out the window and onto the trunk of the car! I was beside myself with fright but Gail, always calm under pressure, gradually came to a smooth stop and I retrieved our little one without incident. I knew the angels of God had hovered over our car and held him in their hands that day. It scared both of us so bad that we never rolled that back window down again. I have heard it said that it is fortunate God does not show us the future, or none of us would want to go there. An experience like this with a child is inconceivable to any mother's protective mind. The thought of it, in fact, could cause one to lose her mind! I don't know how I got over the trauma, and maybe I didn't. I do know that the anxiety surrounding this incident did not help with my already tempestuous state of being. I could feel the darkness pressing around us and, though I never struggled with depression, I felt it smothering my soul that day. The ache in the core of my grief-stricken heart burrowed deeper by the mile as we drove toward nothing, going nowhere. I think Gail was running from life without realizing that he could never get away from it.

When we finally arrived in Pendleton we drove around aimlessly with no plan. Frustrated and desperate, Gail finally turned back and drove all the way to Weiser where we wandered with no direction, just as before. This time, he found a house with eight acres where he could keep his horse, which he still owned and had been boarding outside the city near Twin Falls. The house was a two-story structure with all the bedrooms upstairs; the worst possible choice for three small children. I saw it only as a beautiful pasture for Gail's horse and an unsafe shelter for his children. I was numb and disengaged; he would do whatever he wanted to do. Gail put the borrowed $1,000 down on the acreage and was supposed to pay that much more in three months. We never saw that property again, and I was glad. Although we couldn't afford another expensive mistake, it seemed like the lesser of two evils.

Once we were back in Twin Falls, I discovered that I was pregnant with our fourth child. Gail decided to move to Boise and go to work with his brother who loaned him an old tree-service truck to transport our things across the state. Without explanation, he resigned his position with the Twin Falls church; our loving congregation was shocked and sad to see us go. Gail made a strong exit and put on a confident face, but I wonder if anyone saw the sorrow on mine. I did not see him turn his back like a whipped puppy, in shame and disgrace. It may have been easier for me to bear had I seen genuine remorse, but his apology to me was shallow and inconvenient. I wanted to come alongside my husband with hope, strength, and encouragement; but I had no more to give. Our troubled waters had only deepened.

CHAPTER EIGHT

Troubled Waters Deepen

Navigating the Unknown

When we got to Boise where Gail's brother and sister-in-law lived the only place to store our appliances and Gail's library was in an open shed, where we covered everything with a tarp the best we could. We stayed with them in their tiny house while Gail was deciding what to do. It was crowded and difficult. They had three little boys and we had our three children and all of us were sleeping on the floor. My three-year old Becca kept saying, "Mama, I want to go home." I explained to her, "Honey, that's not our house anymore; it belongs to the church. Someone else is living there now." She didn't understand, of course, and kept pleading, "Please, Mommy, can we go home? I want my home." Gail and his brother seemed to have their own agenda, and I didn't know what it was. After several weeks of floundering, I discovered that my husband had been unfaithful to me again and was in a backslidden state, apparently with no plans to find a job and no intentions of repairing the damage.

I don't remember how I was able to contact my sister, Rosemary, but she drove to Boise to get us. She took my children and I to Ontario, Oregon where she and her husband were operating a restaurant. My parents and my sister, Lois, had come up from California to visit them and I wondered what Daddy would say this time. It seemed there was no end to my humiliation, but after I explained to my father what was happening he made two phone calls. One was to contact Gail and tell him that he must take the initiative to inform the district Assemblies of God office immediately of his disqualification and resignation. The other was to make an appointment for me with a divorce attorney. Daddy was ready to set a few things straight. I was grateful that he was there to take charge, but what dreadful choices to be faced with! These scenarios were things I never dreamed I would have to face, and yet it was bitter-sweet. I was deeply grieved about my marriage, my little family, and Gail's ministry and wanted with all my heart to see all of them succeed; but I couldn't imagine going back again, choosing that life for my little ones. Would I be a single mom now, whose parents helped raise my children? Would my next baby be born in California? Would he ever know his Daddy?

My folks were currently pastoring a small church in Ridgecrest, California; a small town out in the desert between Sequoia National Forest and Death Valley. They invited me to come home with them, and Lois wanted me to sing in her wedding. I was to be her Matron of Honor so it sounded like a good plan for the time being. Daddy contacted Gail and offered to go with him to the district to relinquish his credentials. He didn't want to, but he did. My father took me to see the attorney who said I had a good case for divorce, which I knew but it still sounded awful to my ears. I wished there was more hope on the horizon. Life was feeling very sad and gloomy. I called Gail to tell him that I was going to California, and the next day he came roaring up in his big Mercury. "Why are you doing this?" he asked, as if my decision was astonishing under the circumstances!

"Why?" I asked in amazement. "Look what *you* are doing! You just leave me stranded all day when you know there is no room for us over there! I can't even go find work so I can feed our children!"

"Well, I want to see my kids," he said with feeble conviction, for he could see that his argument was weak and my mind was made up.

"There is nothing else for me to do, Gail. I'm going." That was the extent of it. He had no apologies, no remorse, nothing about responsibility...only whys, and complaints of what "I was doing to him."

I thought my life was over, especially my marriage, even though Gail sounded like he didn't want us to go and was angry at my father for "taking us away". I felt lost; I had three small children to care for and no place to live. The girls were three and four years old, Mark was eighteen months and another baby was on the way. Being safe with my family and taking part in my sister's wedding would be happy and healing for me; so I went with them.

Gail's mother came to Lois' wedding and had a lot of questions. I was honest with her and explained Gail's ongoing infidelity. She was ashamed of him but didn't want him to lose his family so she asked me to come and stay with her and Doc for a while after the wedding. My parents thought this was a good idea because they didn't want my family to be broken either, and figured that living with the Bryan's might help to mend things. It was all very confusing! Everyone around me was in a state of consternation and I was stuck in the middle with no options of my own.

My in-laws were kind and accommodating, but living with them was awkward. Hazel was a nanny and worked outside the home all day. I was expected to cook and was happy to do it but insecure about whether they would like the foods that I prepared, just as any young daughter-in-law would be. The children were very good, but it was hard because I still felt like we were in their way all the time. Mr. Bryan seemed very sad, even tearful at times. "I know Gail has problems, but don't divorce him," he said earnestly. "You have four little ones and how will you support them?" I sensed his genuine concern but thought to myself, *Living with your son will not help me take care of my children; it will only make life harder for them.*

Hazel said often, "Well, it's just the ol' Devil! Gail really wants to serve the Lord." In this way they often verbalized their desire to keep their son's family together. Everyone was working on his marriage except him. Since Gail had not come after us or attempted to stay in touch I didn't know what he was doing, or where he was spending his time. The children and I had been with the Bryans for over a month and, unbeknown to me, his mother had written him a letter but heard nothing in return. One day they informed me that they were going to Idaho to find Gail and determine what was really happening. The children and I were to stay at their house and make ourselves at home until they returned with the news. Sister Bryan was a good, conscientious woman but very outspoken and, apparently, gave her wayward son a piece of her mind. My father-in-law was a kind man, but he was also firm with Gail about abandoning his family and plainly told him that he needed to come to his senses and do his duty. They didn't reveal these things to me, but I found out later how strongly they shamed his behavior and staunchly defended my plight.

Reunited…Really?

Gail returned to California with his parents, or shortly thereafter, and said he had come to take us home. He said that he wanted to get back on track and promised he would do better. My heart was numb. What did "better" mean to him? I still felt abandoned and completely unsure of our future. I didn't trust him at all and I questioned his motives. I knew that he respected his parents and probably felt guilty that they had made a special trip to find and save him from his gutter. After all, he was not the one who had initiated all of this; they had done it for him. How long would it last once they were out of sight and out of mind? Even if he wanted me back I did not believe that he would change. On the other hand, I didn't have much choice. I could not continue living with my in-laws although they had been very kind. Under the circumstances, with no other possibilities, I concluded that giving him another chance was the only existing option for taking care of our children. He packed us up and headed out across the desert, and it was not long until my deep dread was undeniably confirmed.

My thoughts were swirling on the way home, wherever home was. I wanted to have faith but all the evidence was on the side of disappointment. I didn't understand spiritual strongholds back then. The teaching in the church at that time was that evil spirits could not cohabitate with the Holy Spirit and that if someone was truly born again Satan could have no power over them. I believed that if a person really wanted to serve God, they could! We were half way home before the conversation began. "Gail, how do you know that you will do right?" I asked with weary frustration.

"It will all work out," was his reckless and arrogant response. This thoughtless quip was not good enough for me.

"You know that you can serve the Lord!" I challenged him. "You are doing these things because you *want* to!"

"I guess I do," he obnoxiously agreed, then continued in the most denigrating tones. "You can't change me, Eunice. Lots of women have unfaithful husbands but they stay with them and go on being good wives."

This may have been my first time experiencing the full force of righteous indignation. "You are justifying your behavior!" He had no further comment.

He had made himself clear and all of my suspicions were justly confirmed; I felt hopeless all the way home. He still had no job and no place to live; so "home" was back to his brother's house in Boise. I realized we would simply be repeating what we had been through before, two families living together in a three-room house with most of us sleeping on the living room floor. The women would stay there with all the kids while the men were out and about doing who-knew-what all day.

As soon as we got back I started looking for apartments to rent. I saw that nothing had changed and that it would be better to be on my own than to depend on Gail. He had sold our refrigerator, and our appliances were repossessed while I was in California. After only a few days I realized that with three small children and no telephone, I needed help to make any kind of transition. I found a way to contact my sister, Lois, who had moved to Nampa where Andy, her new husband, was teaching school. They drove to Boise to get me and the children and took us to a little apartment in Nampa that they had generously secured for us to live in. Gail was nowhere around when they came, so Andy loaded up my household items in the little trailer he had brought and away we went! Andy and Lois convinced me that with three children and another one on the way I could not keep a job, and that I should sign up for Welfare until I was able to work. I was so humiliated, but saw no way around it. When I got to the Health and Welfare office and told them my story, I discovered that the benefits were monitored much more efficiently than they are today! If an applicant had any skill at all that could be used to earn money, the benefits were very minimal. Since I knew how to sew and cook I would receive the bare minimum, which was one hundred and thirty-three dollars per month. Amazingly, I was able to scrape by with my low rent and no vehicle to maintain.

Home Alone with My Littles

"*I can do this,*" I coached myself often. I thought about babysitting, taking in ironing, or finding other small jobs that I could do for extra money when I needed it. I was healthy, and all the kids were doing well. My biggest worry was trying to explain to them where their father was, and I grieved to think of little Mark standing at the window in Twin Falls waiting for Gail's car to pull up in front. Becca was still begging to "go home". No matter how hard I tried to keep their little minds busy with the childhood pleasures that small children should be free to enjoy, one of them would invariably ask about their daddy every day. "He's working; he's working far away," I always answered, relieved that they were too young to press for more.

During this hard time I cried many tears; but usually in church, and never in front of the kids. I wanted them to have the happiest, most secure surroundings that I could possibly create for them. Lois and Andy were very kind and helpful. They took us to buy groceries and took us to church where they attended, Nampa Assembly of God pastored by Warren D. and Marjorie Combs. With no telephone, and freezing temperatures outside by this time, I didn't venture far and had no adult conversation except with my sister and brother-in-law. I had one loyal Christian friend at church that was going through much of the same trouble as I was. We had a special comradery because of our similar situations but much of it was unspoken because most people didn't discuss details in those days. Life was hard and everybody had one thing or another to deal with. She and I enjoyed the fellowship, prayed together and trusted the Lord for peace and provision, looking forward to the next time we could be together in God's presence. We were in church Sunday morning and Sunday night, as well as Wednesday evenings. These were the sunny days of the week for me that fed my soul and fostered hope.

Mothers with babies can always take joy in the laughter and innocence of their little ones, and they were my lifeline. Mark was just over a year and a half when we went with Lois and Andy to a PTA meeting at Andy's school. The man sitting in front of us was bald, and Mark noticed that there was something missing. "Mama! Hair all gone!" he announced loudly, which brought a chorus of laughter from the folks around us.

All I could do was stay in my little apartment and cuddle my kids. I read to them; I played with them; I rocked my baby boy and we were safe, warm, and happy. Yes, we were living on a shoestring, and glad to have it! If I absolutely had to go somewhere, I used an old fashioned, bulky stroller that was big enough for both Mark and Becca to sit in. With little Dorcas beside me we would walk to our destination, which had to be close by because it was the middle of the winter and freezing cold outside. I was grateful, and doing my best, but my heart was sad most of the time. I had heard that the Salvation Army would give clothing to the poor, and all the kids needed coats badly. I had no money to buy them so one day I decided to brave the storm and walk down there. It was so cold that we were all looking quite blue when we finally arrived. I told the clerk what I needed, and she could see that we were standing there shivering. "Oh, no;" the lady disputed. "We don't just give things away! You have to buy them."

Looking at my little blue-lipped babies I asked again, timidly, "So, you don't have anything to give toward a need?" I was ready to burst into tears.

"Well," she said with a toss of her head, "there's a pile of stuff back there that we're throwing away. You can look through that if you want to." By God's amazing grace, I found three little discards that would do, plus a warm little cap for Mark. Becca's coat was too thin, but at least it would be one more layer. I was so surprised to find out that the Salvation Army had nothing to give to those in desperate need; but I was glad to find something useable in their trash pile. I had been in my apartment for over two months and it was time for the baby to come. I suppose other young mothers would have felt very insecure; but all of my pregnancies had been surrounded by elements of doubt and worry for the future. The only thing different with this one was that I actually felt quite secure on Welfare. I knew that I could be thrifty and I had canned foods left from my food preservation adventures in other places we had lived. I thanked God for them! I was in a place of peace and safety even though it was hard. God had taken care of us.

One day, out of the blue, Gail drove up to my apartment. He had not contacted me since Lois and Andy moved us to Nampa. He explained that he had been to a meeting at the Meridian Assembly of God church where Brother and Sister Charles Slaughter pastored. He said he had gone to the altar and repented of his life style. He told how he had recommitted his life to the Lord and now wanted to get back together. He wanted to be with me when the baby was born. We had a long conversation, as much as possible with the kids jumping up and down. "Daddy! Daddy!" They screamed with delight. They knew nothing; and their level of exuberance at having him walk through that door did not hold a candle to my level of dread for the next time he might walk out again, piling more disappointment into their little lives. It gave my heart a sad kind of joy to see how much they loved him, and I wanted him to love them back. I just worried about them growing up and finding out what he was really like; and feeling abandoned and betrayed all over again. I always wanted to hope for the best; but who could tell? Even if I agreed to cooperate for his and the children's' sakes, I didn't believe that I could ever trust him again. He spoke sincerely as though he meant what he said, but I wondered what was behind it all. What motivated his actions *this* time? Much later, when Gail was in a better place, he told me what happened.

Not long after I had moved to Nampa, I had spoken to another couple that had been friends of ours in the ministry, Linfield and Nellie, and they had asked about my husband. Linfield Crowder was a man of God and anointed preacher himself, but he loved Gail and greatly admired his preaching and teaching. I had to tell them I was not sure where my husband was, but that the last I had heard he was living with his brother in Boise. Shortly thereafter, this dear brother in Christ had gone to look for Gail of his own accord. He had located the three-room house on State Street and found Gail out at the corral with his horse. Brother Crowder walked up behind him. "Well, Gail," he greeted him soberly. "I don't know whether to put my arm around you or kick you in the teeth." Gail was resentful and defensive. He didn't want to talk to this man and resented being tracked down. Gail was cold, unfriendly, and cynical but Linfield persisted and challenged him about abandoning his wife and children. He talked to him about Philippians 2:12 where the Apostle Paul challenges believers to work out their own salvation with fear and trembling, allowing God to work His will into them and obeying His word with reverence. After the initial reaction of a man caught red-handed in the midst of wrong-doing, Gail softened and listened to this faithful friend. He highly respected Linfield for his courage and determination in seeking him out. He knew that what Linfield said was the truth, and as they talked about life, responsibility, and the future Gail came to his senses and thought, *'What a fool I am!'*

He Loves Me…He Loves Me Not

Our second son, David Gail was born on December 14, 1957 in Nampa,

Idaho at the Good Samaritan Hospital. David later changed his middle name to Elkanah because it meant *"God's Property"* instead of *"tempest"* or *"gale-force winds"*. I never thought about the meaning of the name 'Gail'; I only thought to name David after his father. But in his adulthood, David made the decision that he didn't want to be named after stormy weather, no matter how much he loved his dad! He felt that God was directing him to make this change.

Gail came to the hospital in Nampa bringing what he thought was good news. "My brother moved his family back to California and they want us to rent their house for thirty-five dollars a month!" I knew this should sound sweet, like a timely provision for our faltering family; but to me it was a bitter dread, and not my idea of comfort. I loved my cozy little apartment by this time. It was homey and cute; my safe place; my shelter in a time of storm. It was my peaceful dwelling away from the chaos and cruelty of life's dark valleys and I didn't want to leave, especially to return to the uncertainty that I had escaped from. I finally had a washer and clothes dryer again, and would certainly need them even more with the baby. Understandably, I was hesitant and expressed all of these feelings and worries to Gail, but to no avail. His mind was made up and he had already made arrangements; it was a "done deal". "Well, we can't pay for them both," he rejoined logically. "We have to choose one or the other. They left their hound dog in my care, and they have a pasture for my horse."

Your horse! I thought in disbelief without speaking my mind. *Why is a pasture for your horse more important than a secure dwelling for your family!* I was never one to argue, but this was not the first time my husband had demonstrated that his priorities were skewed. I was deeply saddened that other things were more important to him than the kids and me. The clincher was probably that my apartment rent was forty-five dollars per month and we could use that extra ten dollars for so many other necessary items back then. I was practical and resourceful by nature so I saw the value of this decision. Money went a lot farther in those days and every penny would count for us; so I relented, hoping he would not spend it all on the horse. While I was in the hospital Gail emptied my apartment and hauled all of my things back to Boise to the open shed where they had been hastily crammed before Lois and Andy rescued me! It was very hard to go back there because I had a new baby and no place to hook up my washer and dryer. The space was inadequate and always cold. There was a tiny, wood stove, but it didn't heat the house, however small, and we had no wood for the winter.

Gail had offered to help with everything while I was recuperating but straightway went off to find insurance clients, since he apparently had landed a job selling insurance. Consequently, my recuperation came to a swift halt and I got up and got busy. Dishes were stacked high in the sink so the kitchen was the first job I tackled. Up to my elbows in soapy water, I heard a strange grunting sound behind me and turned to see two-year-old Mark bringing me the baby! He had dragged David off the bed and carried him by the head into the kitchen! "Here! Mum! Here! Babe!" he panted as baby David began to turn blue. I grabbed him in time to keep him from passing out and carried him back to the safety of the bed.

Slim Pickings

I had only received welfare benefits for three months. Now I reported to the Welfare Office that I was no longer eligible for assistance because I was back with my husband; but there was no salary for his insurance job. It was based on commission only and he never made a sale, though he would travel here and there looking for customers. These weeks were slow and painful. The night of my birthday, December 23, Gail was gone and the house was so cold I put everyone to bed before 8:00 pm. As I lay there alone, nursing my new baby boy and feeling blue, I heard soft music wafting in from outside. I sat up in bed and saw that there was a group of Christmas carolers standing at our large picture window. "Kids; sit up and look out the front window!" I whispered excitedly. "There are carolers singing to us outside!" They sang several carols that warmed my heart and took the edge off that lonely winter night.

Christmas arrived two weeks after David was born and Gail was home because he had quit the job since there was no money to be made. We gave Mark a tiny metal car and each of the girls a package of gum and some hair barrettes. Dorcas was four years old. She looked up and chirped, "Is this all?" It was so cute and cheerful that it made me laugh, even though I wanted to cry.

"Yes, because Daddy doesn't have a job;" I answered. "And, anyway, it's Jesus' birthday!" To which she smilingly agreed and added sweetly, "…and we don't need any presents."

Everything was sad. The house was so cold in Idaho's zero-temperature winter that I had to dress all my babies in layers and coats indoors! I did what I could to bundle them up but, to accentuate these dire conditions, we had no groceries. Sister York, Lois' mother-in-law, found out where we lived and stopped by with two cases of canned milk, which was a life-saver. I diluted it for the baby's bottle and poured tiny streams of it on hot cereal for the others. We barely scraped by that winter. Gail decided to try selling NutraBio vitamins but he needed a small projector to start the business. There was a promotional program he was to show potential customers to draw them in. So, he hocked my beautiful Scandalli accordion at a Pawn Shop to get the money for this machine. Attempt after attempt, however, resulted in not enough sales to live on, let alone to recover my beloved instrumental companion. Gail was still driving his new Mercury from the seemingly innocent Twin Falls scheme and there was no way we could afford the two hundred and fifty dollar per month payment. So, out of money and out of options, Gail had to stand by while his "free Mercury" got repossessed! Thus, not only did we have no provisions and no job, now we had no transportation. Periodically, we would receive ten dollars in the mail from my sister or from Gail's mom; but we were scraping by on a little bit of nothing. I washed cloth diapers in the bathtub and hung them around the house to dry. There was an old Jeep sitting out behind the house that we drove to a laundromat once in a while. Back then you could rent an old agitating wringer washing machine for seventy-five cents. I couldn't afford the dryer so I would pack my wet clothes into my laundry basket and bring them back home to hang around the frigid house until they were dry. It would take days to dry them because there was no wood to build a fire and the house wasn't warm enough. Gail finally came to a point of feeling very sheepish about having a horse to feed when he couldn't feed his kids, but he had already purchased the feed and couldn't return an opened bag. At least we had a healthy horse to our name!

After several months of struggle, Gail realized that the vitamin business was never going to be enough to make a living for our family of six—seven, counting the horse. So in early spring he finally sold Scooter the horse and decided to hitch-hike to Brownlee Dam where he had heard they were hiring men. He took all of his clothes in a bag and said, "As soon as I get a check, I'll send you some money."

Please....Not Again

I remember watching him walk down State Street in Boise, heading West with his thumb out, as I stood there and cried at the window. There I was in a little, old house that wasn't even mine; no heat, no money, no car and no way to keep in touch with my husband or call anyone for help. I was all alone and flat-broke, in the dead of winter, with four little kids between six months and five years, and somebody else's hungry dog. God's grace is sufficient, and somehow we managed by staying bundled up and eating beans and oatmeal.

Meanwhile, Gail had been hired at Brownlee Dam and had written a letter to his brother to let him know that he could get a job there as well. So they moved back and there we all were once again, crowded together in the three-room house. Gail's brother drove the old Jeep to Brownlee for work and my dear sister-in-law decided to get a job since she had transportation this time. She was hired at the soda fountain in Albertson's grocery store on State Street. Her two older boys were in school, and I watched the kids all day while she was at work. Then I decided it would be good for me to take a night job while she was home with the kids in the evenings. My brother-in-law, Andy York, had an old car with only one low gear and no reverse; it also leaked brake fluid! He said that if I thought I could drive it he would loan it to me to get back and forth from work. My parents, who now lived in Nampa about thirty-five miles away, agreed to come and get baby David and keep him while I held this job for a while. I got hired at the In-N-Out Drive In on Vista Avenue and worked from 5:00 pm until the wee hours of the morning, praying all the way across town that my brake fluid would last. When it didn't, I had to depend on angelic protection at each intersection and thank the Lord that most people were home in bed! I was supposed to get home and get a few hours of sleep while my sister-in-law got her two older boys off to school. Of course, your kids don't sleep in just because you need rest, so all the little ones were usually awake, too. There was never enough time in the mornings to get everyone taken care of, and Mark was still in diapers. So by the time I got up he had worn a soggy one much too long! Every evening when I left for work, he puckered up and cried big tears. We had to have a neighbor girl keep the kids for a couple of hours from the time I left for my job around 4:00 pm until Caroline got home from hers. We were both burning the candle at both ends and doing the best we could with our circumstances. One night I had a close call as I careened down a hill with no brakes. I was nearly killed when my car entered the intersection and zipped narrowly between two others going in opposite directions in front of me. I was so frightened that I pulled over to the side of the road as soon as the car would stop and sat there crying and shaking until I could calm myself. Consequently, after only three weeks I quit my night job and my folks brought the baby back. Gail's brother had quit the job at Brownlee because he was worried about his family and didn't want to be gone any longer. He came home and the tiny house seemed even smaller. I had been sleeping on the living room floor with my children and I remember laying there thinking, *"There is no place for me and my babies; there's not a place in the world that I can go…"*

My father had very strong family standards and felt that the family unit should remain together at all costs; so I couldn't live with them. I knew that he would be completely adverse to my leaving this place, or calling anyone else to help me leave. He was not merciless; he just wanted things to work out God's way. In the midst of my quandary, some long-time ministry friends heard about my predicament and were appalled. They were pastoring in New Plymouth and drove to Boise to see me. "You can't do this!" they exhorted. "We will put a small trailer in the driveway where you and your kids can stay while Gail is away at Brownlee. You need your own place to live."

I didn't want them to because I didn't want to be obligated to anyone else; but I didn't want to stay in the house any longer either. My brother-in-law, Paul Bryan, had heard me crying in my pillow one night. "Don't cry Eunice; everything will be alright," he had said.

He gave our friends permission to bring the trailer and they parked it in his driveway beside the house. This would have added a little comfort since the kids and I would have our own space and separate sleeping quarters. Right away, however, I had another acute attack of Pyelonephritis and came close to death a second time. Life was so hard that I sometimes wished I could die and go to Heaven when these severe bouts occurred; but I fought for my life because I could not bear to think of leaving my kids alone in such a world. I felt very sick, but didn't know what was wrong. I sent five-year-old Dorcas to the neighbor's house to tell them that I was deathly ill and needed to get a message to my family. My sister, Lois, drove from Nampa to pick me up and take me to my parents' house. Andy went to the doctor for sulfa pills because they assumed I had a bladder infection. My sister, Rosemary, came for the girls, Dorcas and Rebecca, and took them to Ontario to keep them while I recovered. She thoroughly enjoyed them and sewed new dresses for each of them. Mama kept me and my little boys for several days until I began to recover. Then our pastor friend who had brought the trailer agreed to move me to Fruitland where I could rent a little house for thirty five dollars per month and live near some of my family. He came to Boise with a trailer to retrieve my meager possessions from the mice-ridden shed and move them to a cozy little two-bedroom house in Fruitland. Brice and Rosy offered to hire me to work as a waitress in their restaurant so that I could pay my rent.

I had not had any regular contact with Gail because he was working in a remote area and staying in a tent on the construction site; but I wrote him a letter to update him on our circumstances. He wrote back and said that he would come home and work at Durbin's restaurant as well! So he quit his job at Brownlee and drove back in a big, old Buick that he had purchased with some of his wages. Unfortunately, Gail was not doing well spiritually and had some very disheartening things surface again during this time. Even though the Lighthouse Restaurant was busy and could keep us both employed full-time, several scenarios came together causing him to become discontent. He said he couldn't work at the restaurant anymore so he went to Boise to look for a job. He obtained work in a meat-packing plant, and we found a house in Meridian that was closer to his employment. What was I to do? He was back now, so I felt that I had no alternative but to follow along and hope for the best.

My family wanted my marriage to work out but hated to see me go back to anxiety and uncertainty, especially after helping me several times to get away. I was discouraged but had mixed feelings; work at the restaurant was hard. The only babysitter I had was my young niece, grade school age. The house was down the hill from the restaurant so we were close by if she needed help, but I was nervous all the time. I think all of us were in a state of emotional spin. Gail said he wanted to go back to the church in Meridian because this pastor knew his history. When my dad had pressed him about going to the district, this pastor was the one that Gail had relinquished his papers to; yet he was still compassionate toward him. I felt good about being under Pastor Slaughter's covering and Gail's desire to be under his leadership was a positive sign. Maybe things could finally start turning around for our good. I decided to hope for the best.

Sweet Relief…Short, but Sweet

It was summer of 1958 when we moved to the two-bedroom house on E. Ada Street in Meridian, Idaho for fifty dollars per month. As we were moving in, the landlady offered to let us buy it for zero down and fifty dollars per month, rent-to-own. The total cost would be $4,000 and we were delighted! I felt as though things were finally looking up. This opportunity would allow us to put down roots and be a family again. Even though the second bedroom was very small, we made it work for Dorcas, Becca, and Mark. We put baby David in our room in his little bed. The house was old and the cupboards were hard to open; but we loved it because it was our own. It meant so much to have something we could afford and to begin building a little equity. It had a large back yard with a cinderblock building in back that could be a small shop or an extra room, although it was not heated. "Potential" was a good word to add to our somewhat ragged history! There had been plenty of black threads woven into my tapestry at this point. I was ready for some life experience that didn't look so dark. Gail worked night shift at the meat-packing plant in Boise and we attended church at Meridian Assembly of God. Charles Slaughter was a wonderful preacher and the church was vibrant. Gail was on an up-swing now, attending church regularly, working steadily and even inspired to witness to his co-workers on the job. The environment was rough and rowdy, with pornographic pin-ups in the lunchroom. The men didn't appreciate his "religion" and tricked him by sneaking alcohol into his thermos, mocking his standards. Thankfully, this was a strong time in his life. He was reading the Bible a lot and leading family prayer with the kids before bedtime. Consequently, it also became a very happy time of sweet relief for the children and I. I could breathe and smile at the same time! Hope reigned. We enjoyed our little home so much; I painted all the rooms! There was an open field behind us that no one was using, so we got permission to plant a garden there. We canned lots of tomatoes and green beans that year, although the neighbor boys often stole our cucumbers and someone helped themselves to all of our beautiful, ripe corn just as we were ready to harvest! Gail bought two calves to raise for meat and had them in pens in the back yard. He had also acquired a black hound dog named Ebony that scared the kids to death, and once bit Becca's hand, causing a "barking dog" trauma that lasted into her adult life.

There was an old man who lived across the street from us who was constantly ribbing the kids. He would sit in a chair on his front porch and holler at them with provoking words, trying to antagonize them or get them to react. He wasn't friendly, and didn't seem a bit pleasant or neighborly, so I didn't know what his intentions were and would not allow the kids to go over there. Mark ventured close enough, a time or two, to be threatened by Mr. Beaver's cane! He eyed the old man warily, but was never amused. Mark reminded me of myself with his ultra-sober countenance. He was a serious-minded child and never appreciated nonsense. As a little tyke, he would never even crack a smile if someone was cutting up or acting silly. Photographers could never make him smile unless they used something genuinely funny or enjoyable to him. He was pleasant of his own accord, but did not laugh easily at others. Instead, he would study them intently as if to examine the reason for their behavior. He would always respond to me if I said, "Mark, smile for Mama!" but other people had to earn his smiles, something Mr. Beaver never achieved, if indeed that was his purpose! The old man got no smiles from me, either; although he had offered to let me use his clothesline since we didn't have one. I dreaded his suggestive remarks every time I passed by with my basket of clothes, and avoided him as much as possible.

Since I had gathered wonderful memories during my own childhood, I subconsciously sought out every fun, joyful, and positive event to tuck away for safe keeping. Every butterfly, rainbow, comical individual, or interesting sight was magnified for my children's enjoyment so that they could learn how to focus on the good things of life. During these challenging years I often remembered my little mother making the best of everything life dealt to her and teaching her "loaves and fishes" how to look for the miracles and count their blessings. We enjoyed our home, our family, and our church; but this happy family interval was short-lived. Gail was laid off from the meat-packing plant before spring arrived and went to stay with his folks in California where he could get a job selling cars. I stayed in Meridian at our little house with my four kids and he said he would send money. I was relieved when I finally got a card telling me when to go to Western Union in Boise to get the money that he would wire to me. I packed the kids in the car, even though Dorcas had the measles and was very, very ill! When I got there I waited for hours but the money never came, and I finally went home crying.

I was so happy to have a place to care for my little ones, but this was a hard summer for other reasons. Once I went to Ontario to pick up my niece and nephew, Elaine and Danny, to attend our Vacation Bible School at Meridian Assembly. On the way home I stopped at a fruit stand and told all the kids to stay in the car. Mark was in the front seat and had tried to get out, unbeknown to me, leaving the door partly open. There were no seatbelts in those days, so when I drove away and made a quick turn to get onto the highway, the passenger door flew open causing little Mark to tumble out onto the gravel! I was petrified that the back tire had run over him because of the angle of the car, and ran frantically toward him. He was badly skinned up and his eyes were full of sand, but he was in one piece and nothing was broken. The people in the car behind me witnessed the episode and ran to my aid. I told the man that I could not go to the hospital because I had no money. He told me not to worry, that they would help me because my baby needed emergency care. Seeing that I was badly shaken, the man offered to drive my car so I could hold my son, while his wife followed behind us. They took us to the Good Samaritan Hospital in Nampa where the emergency staff cleansed Mark's wounds, put salve in his eyes, and bandaged his arms and ankles. The same compassionate people drove us home and offered to pay the hospital bill—I think they assumed that all six kids were mine! I considered it the provision of the Lord in a time of great need and, with many tears, thanked them for their generous kindness.

Money did not come often but when I would finally get some it would be just enough to make the house payment and buy a little food. I was well-versed in "doing what you have to do" so we made things work with what we had that summer. There was a drive-in on the corner called The Hungry Onion where I had walked with the kids a time or two for nickel ice cream cones. The owner begged me to work the noon rush hour for him because he could find no one else to take that shift. I courageously decided to try it, since I could see my house from the service window and watch my kids! I put them on a blanket on the front lawn with strict instructions to stay put until I got back. They were little champs! Each time I came to the window to service a customer, I could see the four of them playing on that blanket in the sunshine. Although a bit nerve-racking, the hour went by quickly and I was soon home again. I did this for a couple of weeks to earn a little money and then quit much to my employer's dismay. For me, however, it had been a precarious venture and I felt fortunate that my little ones had safely navigated the challenge.

As summer ended, Gail showed up with one of his brothers-in-law who said, "Guess what? You're moving to Tehachapi! Gail has a good job at the logging mill and everything is going to be great!" I was holding baby David and Gail looked at him quizzically, saying, "Who's that?" His smart remark would seem witty in other circumstances, but it hit a sour note in my mind from a song too often played. The wounds of having an absentee husband and father were still too fresh on my soul; and I wondered what wild goose chase he was following this time. They had come back from California to pack us up. Gail's brother—who had since moved from Boise back to California again—had talked him into renting out our darling house in Meridian and moving to Tehachapi, California to work at a logging mill with a friend of his. I was devastated! After all we had been through to get here, now he wanted to leave it all behind and chase another pipe dream that was not even his own. "Just think!" the brother-in-law exclaimed. "You'll have a nice job and you won't have to live with all this old stuff!" *Old stuff...*I thought to myself; *this 'old stuff' is all we have to our name and it didn't come easy!*

On the Road Again...Ready or Not

Dorcas had just started first grade in Meridian and I didn't want to move, for this and many other reasons. Ready or not, however, we were on the road again, and somehow I was not expecting a smooth ride. I was grateful that we were able to find a nice Christian family with seven children to rent our house. They were wonderful tenants who kept everything in great shape, even the garden. Down in California, the path we had taken proved to be as bumpy and uncomfortable as I had imagined. We lived in three different houses in Tehachapi. The first one was completely infested with cockroaches and, even if we had been willing to live with them, the owners decided to move back in, so they must have been fairly desperate! The second house had a few cockroaches, but it wasn't quite so bad. I dreaded moving all over again so soon. At least Dorcas could go to the same school; but she had to ride the bus, which frightened her. If she wasn't standing at the bus stop when the bus rounded the corner, she thought it was too late and would not run to catch it. I had to work with her to encourage her to be brave enough to do this, but I understood that it was a bit traumatic for her along with everything else that was happening. Unfortunately, the owners of the second house also found reason to suddenly make it unavailable and gave us thirty days to move out! Finally, we found a little house in town but it was more expensive to rent at sixty-five dollars per month and not in very good shape.

Meanwhile, the "good job" at the logging camp was revealing its true nature. The man who had made all the big promises would never give a whole paycheck, but only a few dollars at a time for necessities. I was grieved about this and exclaimed to Gail that he was not being treated fairly; but he kept vouching for his brother's friend. Soon the landlord came knocking because we hadn't paid the rent and when I told him we had not received a paycheck yet he flew into a rage. "I don't care if you have a paycheck or not! I have a mortgage to pay on this place and if you don't have the money by Friday you can just get out!"

Gail was apprehensive when I told him about it. "Well," he answered slowly, "if this guy doesn't pay what he owes me, we might *have* to move out on Friday." I was beginning to see this idea as a lost cause anyway, and Tehachapi was a miserable place to live. The wind blew constantly. The clothes on the line were always wrapped around so tightly that I had to iron almost everything when I brought them in. Every morning there was a pile of tumbleweeds at the front door where the wind blew them into a corner, blocking their escape. So I was the one who came to their rescue and set them free again.

When Christmas came, our pastors in Tehachapi gave us a two-wheel, twenty inch bicycle for Dorcas. We had very little to give during this lean time and at six and a half she was old enough to notice, although very content. Gail and I wanted so much to give her this nice gift, but it was Christmas Eve and Gail was determined to keep it a secret until morning. After the kids went to sleep we went to work to rebuild it and make it look new. We took the wheels off so we could sand and shine the chrome. Gail painted it shiny red and we had new pedals and handle grips to put on it. It turned out beautiful, and Dorcas loved it; but Mark was the one who was most ecstatic—at four years old! After Christmas, Gail found out that he was not the only one missing paychecks; his employer wasn't paying anyone else either. He had lost his logging contract and could barely support himself. So after only a few months it was—you guessed it—time to move again! A freak storm came through at this time and the weather dipped to freezing temperatures. While Gail was living with his folks earlier that year, his father had helped him to find an affordable green Chevy that he had been driving, and had used for our moves. Being from Idaho and accustomed to cold weather, we must have assumed that this car had antifreeze in the radiator. We were mistaken; the frigid cold cracked the engine block! We left the car in Tehachapi and packed our belongings and ourselves into a U-Haul truck that we drove to La Crescenta.

In La Crescenta we found a house for eighty-five dollars per month, which we thought was very expensive. Aside from our third house in Tehachapi, the highest we had ever paid was $50 per month, which was actually a mortgage payment since we were renting to own the house in Meridian. We moved into this house on a busy avenue and hoped for the best. Paul went into the tree business and Gail went to work for him, of course. They bought a winch truck and a dump truck and other equipment to do the job, all requiring high monthly payments. They were very skilled at this trade and did excellent work, although some of it was very dangerous. They enjoyed it and stayed fairly busy, but with so much money going back into the business our wages weren't nearly enough. Once again, the landlord was always after us for being behind on our rent payments; and Gail was always gone so I got the brunt of it! "I would give anything in the world to give you the rent money," I said once; "but I'm stuck in the middle and I don't know what to do!"

About that time, Gail's younger sister inherited some nice furniture from her mother-in-law who had passed away. Medora was tender-hearted and felt sorry for all we were going through; so she gave me a cute couch and chair, end tables and a coffee table. Never in my life had I owned enough furniture to speak of, let alone a matching set and I felt like a queen! My parents had moved as well and left some furniture behind in Beaumont. They told us that if we could go down and pick it up we could keep it. Now I had a kitchen table with four chairs, among other items. I fixed up the house the best I could, and felt happier and more settled once again.

My sister-in-law, Caroline, and I also attended a ladies' group together that we loved. The women called it Sister Burt's Prayer Meeting and we looked forward to it every week. I had no car, so Caroline picked me up on Tuesdays. David and Mark went into the nursery, my first experience with church child care, while we ladies enjoyed our Bible study and prayer. One Tuesday a lady came up to me with a twinkle in her dark eyes. "Honey, the Lord told me to give you ten dollars;" she said, handing me the money. I was stunned and very grateful since my cupboards were bare at home! I couldn't even make biscuits or cornbread; we were out of everything. On the way home, I found out that she had said the same thing to Caroline and had given her some money, too! We were both so thrilled, as ten dollars could actually buy quite a few groceries in those days. It was a reminder for two young mothers that God sees our struggles and lights our way with blessings; a great faith-builder during a difficult time of life. Just before this happened I was standing over the kitchen sink one day washing the dishes when I inadvertently let out a big, tired sigh. Mark, who was four and a half, immediately stopped his nearby play and ran over to me, looking up into my face with his serious brown eyes. "Mommy is it hard to be a house-mother?" he asked with great concern in his little voice. *Out of the mouths of babes.* God will use the smallest things to comfort a mother's heart!

Dorcas was still in the first grade in La Crescenta, her fourth school in one year. I don't know if her little heart was deeply relieved by the blessed security of remaining in one classroom, or if this particular teacher was extra kind and comforting. Whatever the reason, Dorcas loved her so much that she wrote her a note one day to express her devotion. *"Dear Mrs. Kimball,"* she scribbled; *"I love you more than anyone else in the world, except my mother."*

We had our school blue days as well, however. I decided to give Rebecca a permanent one morning since she had kindergarten in the afternoon. Of course I had two little boys at home as well, and the process took longer than I thought. I was unable to get her hair dry and combed before her class started so I sent her to school in rollers with a scarf tied around her head. Unbeknown to me, her tiny dignity was apparently shredded because of her head gear and she tottered on the verge of tears for most of the afternoon! A mother's experiences are wide and varied, and another day I had the chance to walk in the shoes of an Old Testament prophet! Dorcas got on a bicycle and innocently peddled down the driveway and onto the sidewalk without knowing how to use the brakes. La Crescenta Avenue was a steep hill and down she went! God must have seen my plight and imparted to me the anointing of Elijah who ran ahead of King Ahab's chariot! In my bare feet, and with the wind of the Holy Spirit at my back, I went running after her faster than I ever thought my legs could carry me. By God's grace I caught up with her and stopped the bike, saving her from a serious crash or a deadly collision with on-coming traffic. God was faithful in every circumstance, surrounding us with His great care for every situation.

The house was peaceful, as the boys got along famously during the day while the girls were off to school. They played together happily and all seemed right, or at least much better, with the world. Mark was completely fascinated with the big trucks that his dad drove in the tree business, which were always in the driveway since this was also Gail's transportation to and from the job. We have priceless photos from this house and our experiences there, as our little brood began to grow to school age and discover more about life. Some of Gail's cousins gifted our family with a sweet, blonde cocker spaniel named Tammy. The children adored her and she soon birthed a large batch of fluffy, cuddly puppies that brought hours of childish delight. We had a big front yard where they could run around, sprinklers on the lawn to run through on hot summer days, and even a kiddie pool that they could splash in. Someone gave us a lawn swing, and Gail also hung a swing from the tree in the front yard for the kids. This was a happy place to be.

The next year, when Dorcas was in second grade, our church was having special meetings with Evangelist Gladys Pearson. Dorcas was always very tender toward spiritual things and had been influenced by the prayer meetings during this revival. I walked into her room and she was kneeling beside her bed with her hands in the air, having her own little prayer meeting! This was also the place where Becca met the Lord. I walked to the library every two weeks to check out books for the girls to read, and books to read to the boys. Becca had a reading contest going on in her class and we would sit on the couch together as she read her books. Somehow the conversation turned to the Lord and I asked her if she wanted to invite Jesus into her own heart to stay. She did, and we knelt together in the living room and prayed the Sinner's Prayer. It was very real to her and she always remembered that event with the details of time and place whenever she was asked about her personal salvation and relationship with the Lord. Becca won that contest, reading over one hundred books in the first grade. It is always a joy for a mother to see the work of God in her children, and to see their tiny spirits growing in the knowledge of the Lord. I was thrilled every time I saw right attitudes and responses from the kids as their small consciences became aware of the differences between God's ways and the ways of the world around them. I remember walking into Dorcas' room one day to find that she had unraveled an entire roll of film with pictures of Gail's tree removal equipment. "Dorcas!" I exclaimed in horror. "What are you doing?" A second grader by this time, she was old enough to see the writing on the wall and knew immediately that I was upset. "Mommy," she defended fearfully; "I wanted to see how the pictures got inside."

"You should have asked me first!" I admonished. "Now see what you've done? You have exposed all the negatives and ruined Daddy's pictures!" She put her face in her little hands and began to cry, deeply repentant for her

careless mistake. "Oh, Mommy!" she wailed. "I am so ashamed of myself. I'll give you all the money in my piggy-bank!" Her remorse was so touching that, of course, she was instantly forgiven and duly commended.

While living at La Crescenta Avenue, my father had helped us find a cute little black Ford for two hundred dollars. We were able to attend our old home church, the La Crescenta Assembly of God, and this encouraged us greatly. This was the church where Gail had been saved as a youth at age seventeen, so many of the people knew him personally. It was a place of strong accountability because they trusted his ministry. Consequently, his passion for the things of God grew and thrived in this fertile soil with the Family of God. We both taught classes as time went on and Gail's young adult Sunday School class grew to about forty-five in attendance under his teaching. I saw firsthand the powerful truth of Romans 11:29, (KJV) *"The gifts and calling of God are without repentance;"* and this was only the beginning. For again and again I would see this play out in my husband's life, the tangible proof that God does not change his mind about what he calls

us to do. Papers can be revoked, and should be when necessary, but with God all things are possible; and I would see that His gifts were irrevocable because He is a God of many chances, amazing grace and unfathomable forgiveness. We loved being in La Crescenta and lived there for two happy years, but by this time Gail's heart was turning back toward the ministry. Some friends of ours up in Idaho wanted him to take their pastorate at the Homedale Assembly of God for five weeks during the summer while they took a short leave. So he left the tree business to his brother and we moved back to Idaho.

Money Don't Grow on Trees After All

Our friends were already gone by the time we arrived and we were to stay in their home while filling in for them. It was a comfortable home with a nice, big yard. All the bedrooms were upstairs. They had planted a nice-sized garden and left it for us to care for and harvest. It was another summer of canning dozens of quarts of tomatoes! When our friends returned we moved to a house on John's Street in Emmett, where we enrolled the girls in school. Gail and I took the boys with us to pick apples in the abundant orchards of that area to make some money to live on. It was hard work, and the weather was already getting cold, but we did it and were happy for the income. There was not enough of it, though, to carry us through the winter so we found out about a low-income housing project in Nampa and we applied. We had never heard of anything like this, but we were grateful and, actually, found it to be one of the nicest places we had ever lived! It was quite new and roomy, with freshly painted walls and sturdy doors that locked securely. Our rent was forty-five dollars per month which included utilities! We didn't have a stitch of furniture because we had sold it all when we'd left La Crescenta. As before, the utility trailer only had room for the bare necessities, Gail's library, and the boards and bricks that he always set up for a bookcase. We didn't even have window coverings; but we were glad to have a roof over our heads. We attended the Nampa Assembly of God church, pastored by Brother and Sister Combs, where I had previously attended with Andy and Lois. Gail started accepting invitations as soon as possible and was often out of town in evangelistic meetings. I remember a lot of quiet, cozy nights reading many Bible stories to my kids as they sat on their little bed mats on the bedroom floor. We walked to church together and I reconnected with my wonderful friend, Inez.

Mark started the first grade in Nampa at Lakeview Elementary School and was terribly shy. I had no car so Dorcas, Becca and Mark walked to school together every day, even in the cold weather. One day at lunchtime Mark showed up at home! "What are you doing, Mark? You're not supposed to come home at lunchtime; that's why I made you a lunch to take to school!" I exhorted him.

"I wanted to come home and be with you and David," he said haltingly, on the verge of tears. Then they began to flow abundantly as he continued, "Please, Mama! Please! I just wanted to see what it was like but I didn't want to stay. I don't wanna go back to school; I wanna stay home with you!"

Of course, I had to make him go; but with his reluctance I wasn't sure he would. So I decided to make a run for it while David was taking his nap. I got on Mark's tiny, little bicycle—the same one that took Dorcas down La Crescenta Avenue—and sat him in front of me on the bar. We rode lickety-split down the sidewalk as I peddled frantically to get him back to his class before the bell rang! We made it on time but he was about to cry and didn't want to stay, so I sat in the back of the classroom for a short while. I was praying for the angels of God to keep little David safe and asleep until I could get back home. When Mark looked at me again, he smiled and I saw my chance to smile back and wave. I got out that door and onto that tiny bike as fast as I could and rode like the wind back to our house. Bursting through the door, breathless, I was relieved to find that my little boy was still fast asleep and apparently in the best of hands while I was gone. God was always right by my side in those hard, alone times—making things work, giving me peace, surrounding us with protection, and providing the grace and wisdom to keep my home happy and comfortable for my four babies. I thought of my own Mama often, and how she prayed fervently about everything, protecting her own as I now protected mine. They never knew how many times they were close to danger, close to having no place to call home, or eating the last bowl of oatmeal as I prayed for God to provide another meal. Beans and oatmeal were our main food supply but I also had green beans and lots of tomatoes that we had canned from the garden in Homedale. I made tomato soup sometimes and we had lots and lots of popcorn because it was very cheap! As far as the kids were concerned, we had everything we needed.

Nightmares in Nampa

This period of time was a great learning experience because we had never been exposed to the welfare mentality of entitlement and lazy living. Most of our neighbors in the housing project were welfare recipients and the children were often ill-mannered and used bad language. I didn't want my children spending a lot of time outdoors because I didn't approve of the company! The woman next door lived a blatant immoral life-style with many male visitors. She did babysitting for extra money and would put the children who were under her care outside to play, locking the doors so they would stay out as long as she needed them to! They would come to my house to use the bathroom and they were always hungry. I'm sure they told us many things that she thought were her hidden secrets; but kids will reveal a multitude of sins in simple, innocent conversation! I do remember reaching out to these people with Christian kindness, and teaching the kids to do the same with as many safe boundaries as I could draw around them.

Since our income was dependent on any meetings that Gail could arrange there were many times in between that we had nothing. One time he scheduled a revival meeting in central Oregon that kept him away for almost four weeks. While he was gone on this trip, I had another attack of Pyelonephritis and became very ill. This time, alone with my children, no telephone and no transportation, I exhorted them to pray for my healing because I knew this was a dangerous disease and I believed that I was close to death. I did not express these fears to them and they were not afraid. They anointed me with oil as they had seen Gail and I do, and our pastors do, for many others. They prayed fervently for my healing and rebuked the Devil who was making me sick! They were excellent junior prayer warriors, but I was concerned about their needs and unable to get out of bed. So I told Dorcas, Becca and Mark to walk to church one Sunday and tell Brother and Sister Combs that their mommy was very sick at home. They did so, and the Combs' came as soon as they were able to anoint me with oil and pray for my healing.

The next day I was too sick to get up so I was telling the kids how to make their own breakfast. Dorcas was the oldest so I told her to plug in the electric skillet and break the eggs into it for cooking. Becca and Mark wanted to crack their own eggs and I was hearing all this from my mattress on the floor. Suddenly there was a knock on the door and it was Brother Combs coming by to check on us. He helped them finish the eggs and got them seated around the table. Then I heard him say, "Ok. Now it's time to pray." My heart was comforted by his voice, knowing that we were not forgotten and that my children would be fed and everything would be better. I was not alone after all. Sister Combs came by another day and changed my bed sheets because the illness made me sweat profusely. The kids bravely held the fort for about a week. I improved day by day, however, and before Gail returned I was functioning normally again.

On the way home from his meetings, Gail got caught in a terrible blizzard in the mountains near Sisters, Oregon. He had to stop again and again to scrape the snow from his windshield with his bare hands because the wipers were not fast enough to handle the pile-up. He was freezing because there was no heater in our little black Ford, so he lit a single gas burner that he had with him and set it on the floor of the passenger seat. He couldn't leave it on long because it would fill the car with fumes, but it was the only way he could endure the frigid temperatures. He began to feel ill and finally found a small motel where he spent the night. The next day he drove home, but it was a long journey and by the time he got to Nampa he had a high fever and was weak with illness. He had pneumonia and I nursed him back to health little by little over the next few weeks, thanking God for my own strength which had been so fleeting only a short time before. Soon after his recovery, Gail was invited to hold revival meetings in Shelley and Idaho Falls. We had not been back since leaving there in disgrace years before and Gail wanted me to go with him so that we could minister together and renew old friendships. I didn't want to leave the kids and felt that I should stay since they were all in school and needed me to keep things on schedule. A widow woman from our church found out about it and volunteered to stay with our children so that we could go and minister together. The kids remember her as being tall and somber; but she was a dear saint who wanted to do this as unto the Lord. She took care of them for two weeks while we were gone for these meetings. When we got back, Gail decided to go deer hunting to put some meat on our table and took our little black Ford far up into the Owyhee Mountains. Determined to get as deep into the wild as possible to find the best game, he soon encountered rough terrain that defied the frame of our smallish car. Suffice it to say, the axle broke deep in the back country and he had to leave our car in the woods and pack out with all of his gear on his back. He came across an empty cabin where he built a fire and cooked some food. Then, leaving some money and a note, he thanked the absent owners for their hospitality and hitch-hiked back to town. It made an adventurous story; but now we had no meat *and* no transportation!

Gail had, of course, been reinstated with the Assemblies of God by this time after his leave of absence in California. He wanted to attend a ministerial convention in southeast Idaho with our pastor friends from Homedale. They said that if I could take care of their three children they would drive to the convention and take Gail along with them. So I stayed behind with seven children while they all went to the convention. One night when all the kids were snug in their makeshift beds, I was putting my hair up in rollers when a sharp rap came on the bathroom window beside me, followed by a raspy voice! "Hey…how about going into the bedroom?"

"Gail! There's somebody out here by the bathroom window!" I hollered instinctively, even though my husband was away and this peeping Tom probably knew it! I turned off the light quickly and tiptoed down the hall and into the kitchen to turn on the back porch light, but to no avail. The bulb had been screwed out of the socket so that the porch could not be lit. I was very frightened, and slept in my clothes that night. The next day I told my neighbor about it and used her telephone to call the police. They said there had been several reports of peeping Toms around the projects with similar incidents.

Other times this house was full of strange noises that came out of nowhere;

or we would feel a strange eeriness in the atmosphere. Sometimes we would hear loud pops like an over-inflated balloon that was poked with a sharp object. Pots and pans would crash to the floor and, when I would run in to see what happened, everything would be undisturbed and sitting neatly in place. Gail stayed up one night to spend some time in prayer while the rest of us went to bed. Someone had given us an old, blue, overstuffed chair with broken springs that sat in our living room. He knelt there to pray. "Oh, God; reveal yourself to me. Lord, reveal yourself to me;" he prayed sincerely. Suddenly, the room was engulfed in a dark, satanic presence. Gail was frightened nearly out of his wits. He was always a brave man, and never afraid of anything; but that night I thought he was having a nervous breakdown. I had just fallen asleep and he came in and woke me up and turned on the light. He told me that something was in our house and his eyes darted around the room at the door, the windows and the closet. Then he described the presence of evil and how it had overwhelmed him in the living room. I tried to calm him, but he remained tense and afraid. Little Dorcas was disturbed in her sleep and got up to come into our room. As she came through the door he saw the white of her nightgown and thought it was a ghost. I kept praying and encouraging him in the Lord, but he wouldn't let me turn off the light. The next morning he woke up with an excruciating migraine headache that made him writhe and groan with pain. I ran to the pastor's house to borrow some aspirin—because we still didn't have a car—and to get their prayer and support. The Combs' were always very good to us. During these trying times, I felt comforted and safe having good pastors close by who cared about our family and showed us kindness. Later, Gail revealed that he had not fully come clean from his vices and was still toying with sin at that time. He had punctured the covering of spiritual protection by careless activities that left him vulnerable to attack—and his innocent family along with him. Thus, when Gail asked for revelation, Satan took advantage of the opportunity as if to gloat, "Yes, I am the lord of your life; while wearing these chains, you still belong to me!" I always wondered if some of the weird things that happened at that house were related to doors of evil that Gail had opened by his careless choices along the way. It was a bit spooky but we dealt with it the best we could and trusted the Lord to keep us safe.

When Gail returned from the convention he got an invitation to preach a revival at the Garden City Assembly of God. Our Nampa church was walking distance, about four blocks, and we had been walking to services as often as we could with our little ones ever since we'd lost our car in the mountains. When our pastor found out about our predicament he took an offering for our benefit and the church bought us an old Cadillac for one hundred dollars so that Gail could continue in meetings, which was our only livelihood at the time. The Garden City revival lasted for several weeks and it was a refreshing time for all of us. The people were very encouraged and gave us a grocery shower at the end. We drove home and I got the children to bed so that I could unpack our blessings in the kitchen. I was standing at the table in my under-slip, thinking only of the goodness of the Lord—and not about my bare windows in the living room. Later, after we had retired for the evening, we heard a sharp rap on the door and it was a neighbor lady from across the common area behind our house. She had seen a large man staring in our window earlier as I stood in the kitchen unpacking those groceries. She had watched his peeping until I had turned off the light, and then she had come to tell us as soon as she could. I was horrified; but when you have nothing you get used to living that way! We had moved so much, leaving everything behind nearly every time; we were sleeping on mats on the floor and had made do. Gail decided we would have to find a few extra sheets to cover the windows at least; but everything was hard and life was a plethora of challenges. A few other opportunities rolled in, including some meetings at my father's church in Nyssa, Oregon so we were getting by a week at a time. Then our friends from Homedale decided to move away and called to ask if we would take the pastorate there. By that time, however, Gail had already received an offer to come back to southern California and pioneer a new church in Redlands, but we didn't have the money to move! We had been praying for God's provision because we needed at least two hundred dollars to make the move. One more revival meeting in Nampa added a meager sum of forty-five dollars to our savings, the total offerings in two weeks! Our only alternative at this point was to sell everything that would fetch a price at the local auction, which we did. There were some fraudulent dealings happening there and we did not receive the payment that was due to us; but we were ready to move on and we knew that God had better ways to provide for his children. Our philosophy was simple: "Where God guides, he provides!"

CHAPTER NINE

Regrouping for Growth

We had already weathered a number of critical storms during our first ten years together. I felt like we were coming out on the other side of danger with better things ahead, yet I was reluctant about the circumstances into which we were moving. I would have rather accepted the position at Homedale and remained closer to my family, yet I was hopeful. I was wholehearted in my support for this transition because Gail was fasting and praying during this time. I always hoped and prayed that he would be able to walk in victory, because that seemed to be his deepest heart's desire most of the time. Apprehension always raised its head due to past experience but I wanted to be faithful to God's call on our lives. I wanted God's will for our marriage and for our family. To give myself to the ministry opportunity that God set before us seemed good and right, and I wanted to support my husband in doing the same. He seemed enthused about the opportunity in Redlands, and the district was involved in the planning, so I took on this new faith venture whole-heartedly. I wanted to be content, and I took courage from the scriptures, Philippians 4:12-13 (KJV): *"I know both how to be abased, and I know how to abound: everywhere and in all things I am instructed both to be full and to be hungry, both to abound and to suffer need. I can do all things through Christ who strengtheneth me."*

Redlands: a Time to Rejoice

Gail's folks were living in Redlands, California along with other friends and family who had been talking to their local Assembly of God leadership about the need for another church in this growing community, which the district had approved. We were anxious to get there and get started so we packed up the old Cadillac provided to our family by the Nampa church and headed for the border. It was roomy and comfortable, although leaking oil all the way. Behind us we pulled a small utility trailer packed mainly with Gail's library. We had taken everything else to the auction, which was not much, and we felt robbed by the little bit of money that we received from the things we sold. It was barely enough to get us to our new destination. When we pulled up to Gail's folks' house on Grant Street in Redlands, we had two silver dollars and four pennies to our name. "We've a dollar for you, a dollar for me and a penny for each of the kids!" Gail laughed heartily. We were just happy to be there, with new adventures ahead of us and loving parents to cushion the blows of starting all over again with nothing but each other, the clothes on our backs and, of course, Gail's books! We did come bearing gifts, though, because during our trip we had come across a train derailment that had scattered crates of fresh, firm Oregon pears along the tracks. The officials were telling passers-by to take as many boxes as they could carry since the fine fruit would otherwise go to waste. Gail found a way to tie seven boxes of pears on top of our already-heaped utility trailer.

The folks had a car port in which we parked the Cadillac, for we had realized after our trip that the engine had to be rebuilt if the car was to remain useable for our family transportation. Aside from a mechanic's class in school, Gail had no experience at this. He bought all the parts piece by piece, however, and followed an instruction booklet to rebuild the engine entirely on his own! It was a huge undertaking but he figured it out a step at a time and the car ran beautifully!

Doc and Hazel, Gail's folks, had a living arrangement with an elderly woman who needed in-home care. Her contract provided that the Bryans would inherit her home if they would take care of her until she died. "Auntie", as they called her, was a bit cantankerous and some of the kids were uneasy around her. She would get up in the middle of the night and wander into the living room where they were sleeping on couches or on the floor. She would stand still—like a ghost, except breathing—and stare. They could not see her eyes, but they could *feel* them and were unnerved by it. So as grateful as we were for their hospitality, we wanted to find a place of our own as soon as possible.

We met a lady who had a house for rent on the same street where the folks lived. She was willing to allow our family to move in right away and pay the rent as soon as we got the money. Gail was able to land a job at Gair's which was a fine clothing store for men downtown. In those days, a two-week paycheck could be as little as sixty-five dollars, which was the amount of rent we owed. Almost everybody knew how to budget during that era because if they didn't watch their spending they might run out of food before the next payday. "Shopping" meant buying only what was needed, and at the best possible price! We were settled right away in our little house and got the kids enrolled in school. The crates of pears had been green at first, but now that they were quickly ripening we had to decide what to do with them. A man who had come to help us unload saw them and asked what we were going to do with all those pears! I had given some to my mother-in-law, but I had no stove and no jars so I could not preserve any of them. This kind man bought us a second-hand stove and collected enough jars for me to can all of the pears. A dear sister in the church came over and taught me how to process them in the oven since I had sold my canning equipment long ago. These beautiful jars of pears were a pleasing sight in my little kitchen that we were still moving into!

We started services immediately for our fledgling body of believers in a small room of the local YWCA. This building was located on "church corner", as the townspeople called it. There was a church on every corner of this intersection: Presbyterian, Methodist, Congregational and Christian! Now Southside Assembly of God was added to the already crowded intersection where church-goers of all types gathered each Sunday. The YWCA building sat next door to the Christian Church and before long we outgrew the small room and moved into the gymnasium. We had Sunday School classes and Children's Church, with helpful and enthusiastic people serving in teaching and music ministry right away. From about a dozen at our first meeting, the congregation grew quickly into the thirties, forties and, finally, up to one hundred and fifty people in regular attendance. It was not until after we had agreed to pioneer this new church and had already made the move to Redlands that we discovered a small storm cloud hovering on the horizon! We knew that the local people had contacted the district about the need for another church in the community; and we knew that the district had approved it and, indeed, invited us to come. What we did not know was that the resident pastor of the area was not in favor of another church coming to town! So a cloud of tension was waiting for us when we got there and discovered that Northside Assembly was not in the mood to accommodate a Southside neighbor! Learning how to navigate these family schisms in a godly way is important, however, because they are a part of life in the Church as naturally as occasional rifts within our own families. Wherever people are present there will be perceptions, attitudes and strong opinions that are not necessarily pleasing to the Lord; we just want to be sure we are on His side of the issue! Gail always said, "If you ever find a perfect church be sure not to join; you will ruin it!" As time passed, these things were resolved naturally and without confrontation. Gail was a gifted communicator, always proficient at reaching out to other pastors to form a brotherhood of ministry leaders. He was a team player who appreciated the strengths of others; he believed that pastors could always help and encourage one another in the work of the Kingdom. Over time we developed good relationships and enjoyed all the normal area-wide activities together with our sister-churches, such as Fellowship Meetings and C.A. (youth) rallies.

During this time we had a prophet friend named John Gonerez who was another unique acquaintance of my father's, much like the aforementioned Brother Sivak, and who was also very close to our family. Brother Gonerez, commonly called Johnny the Greek, had power with God and many miracles followed his ministry. He was also an evangelist who preached on the streets of New York and Los Angeles, from coast to coast. His amazing stories were without end! Gail was so impressed with John's zeal for the Lord, and we had many conversations and times of fellowship with him that greatly enriched our family. Johnny the Greek led people to the Lord wherever he happened to be. Often, in restaurants, he would witness to someone who would then be overtaken by the power of the Holy Spirit and fall to their knees on site! Their public weeping would catch the attention of curious onlookers and Johnny would say, "Don't worry about them; they're just meeting God for the first time." One time Johnny the Greek and Gail were traveling to Mexico on an evangelism trip with another brother. As they rode along they came to a giant billboard along the highway. Johnny the Greek said, "Stop! We must get out and claim that board for our message of the gospel!" They parked along the road and went back to kneel in front of the sign and pray over that space to claim it for the Lord. One of them had a Bible in his hand and a State Trooper whizzing by in his patrol car thought it was a gun. Assuming there was a robbery in process he whipped around in the highway and raced back with lights flashing and sirens blaring. He and his partner leaped from their vehicle with guns drawn to stop this criminal act before anyone got hurt; only to discover that this "hold up" was nothing but a "hepped up" prayer time beside the road.

We invited Brother Johnny to come to our little start-up church in Redlands to preach a few meetings for us. Gail always revered and appreciated men of God and wanted them to share their gifts and wisdom with the people. David, our youngest, was about four years old at this time and still remembers the following exchange with the old prophet:

> I remember Daddy telling us that we were going to see a man who was a real prophet—like the prophets that stood before the kings of the Old Testament and whom God sent with messages to cities like Nineveh. I was really fascinated to see him and he was truly inimitable; a little bald guy with a colossal nose and woolly eyebrows. I remember just staring at him and being fascinated by his person. It seemed like somewhat of a potluck atmosphere where people were milling around getting food, when the prophet turned around and saw me. He motioned for me to come over to him and when I got close enough he bent down and said, 'If God allowed you to have lots of money, would you use it for Him?' When I answered, 'Yes,' he continued, 'Well, God knows this and he is going to let you have lots of money. You will always remember this. God wants you to remember that he gave it to you so you will use it for his kingdom.' Then he prayed over me and I have never forgotten what he said. I believe Johnny the Greek's prophecy was partly fulfilled when I came to Yuba City to pastor Glad Tidings church. There was three million in the Missions Fund, which we have invested in missionary activities all over the world. I also believe that this was only a partial fulfillment, and that there will be even more given in the years ahead for kingdom business.

Johnny the Greek also stood out in our back yard one day and prayed that we would find a building to hold our services in. He stretched out his hand and declared, "Lord, give them a church right down town!" Shortly after his visit, we found a building available in the very location that Johnny the Greek had pointed toward when he stretched out his arm in prayer. It was a cute little white church that would cost no more than the price we were paying to rent the YWCA. It was fully equipped with pews and pulpit, piano, microphones, and supplies. Even the classrooms were set up with chairs, tables and anything we needed to hold Sunday School and Children's Church. We could not have imagined such a complete package as the Lord had so generously provided for our growing body of believers. Aside from purchasing a few baby beds for our nursery, we had everything we needed. No more setting up chairs, pulpit and equipment for our singular Sunday afternoon services at the YWCA. Now we were free to schedule two services on Sunday, plus Bible study on Wednesday evenings. We changed our church name to Evangel Temple and painted it on a large white sign in front of the church. These were exciting times, experiencing the supernatural intervention of the Almighty as we watched the fulfillment of God's purpose right before our eyes. We were witnessing the truth that "Where God guides, He provides"; and I marveled at the faithfulness of the Lord in bringing us through such a wilderness to this place of blooming promise! My heart was grateful that I had followed the path set before us, despite my human misgivings; for who would want to miss such an exciting adventure as this had turned out to be!

Gail only had to work at the clothing store for about eight months. We didn't spend money on advertising, but the church grew by leaps and bounds through word-of-mouth alone. We had one Sunday School contest to bring in visitors. Gail constructed a six-foot candy bar as a prize for the person who brought the most guests. Several couples we had known previously joined us for the work in Redlands and we had a wonderful group of young families with children. Gail's folks, his little sister, Medora, and her family, and eventually his eldest sister, Bernice, all attended the church as well. Other family members came from time to time and with all of Gail's kin relatively close it was a meaningful period of building family relationships for us and for our children with their aunts, uncles and cousins. Paul and Caroline had some property about ten miles from Redlands with outbuildings and corrals. Mark loved to go anywhere with his dad, but he especially enjoyed the frequent trips to Yucaipa to see the livestock and hear family stories told and retold. We made many lasting friendships here and it was a happy and fruitful time of our lives; a strong family atmosphere and a good place for our children.

The churches had no custodians in those days, so the pastor's family cleaned the church every Saturday. All the kids had jobs to do and with everyone helping it was done in a few hours. Periodically, some of the church ladies offered their help for special projects. This was our livelihood and we wanted our children to take ownership of the place where God had planted us. As the Levites of the Old Testament accounts, we wanted them to understand the stewardship of the House of the Lord. Beginning at the young ages of five through ten, this season of their lives built the foundation for honoring pastoral leadership. During the next five years they would fill support roles that acquainted them with both the blessings and the challenges of growing up in the pastor's home, and what it meant to be a P.K.—Preacher's Kid.

When Heaven Came Down

After living in the little house on Grant Street for a year, we moved to a very nice home on Olive Avenue. I had not had a carpet on the floor in any house I had ever lived in; but this house had a nice carpet in the living room that was very cozy. We had a fireplace that we enjoyed all winter, and big pine trees out front that we could view through our large picture window. We also had a large front porch and a patio out back that was surrounded by a cinder block wall for privacy. The landlords were very friendly, and fond of our family. We were directly across the street from McKinley Elementary where all of the children attended grade school. Since we had only one car, it was a blessing to simply send them out the door and across the street each day for school. All the kids loved their classes which resulted in good reports from their teachers at every Parent-Teacher Conference. The girls' teachers bragged on what strong and able leaders they were among their fellow classmates; and the boys' teachers crowed as if each of them was the "cock of the walk"!

Before starting kindergarten, however, David had an amazing supernatural experience while we were living at Olive Avenue. He was a child who could be perfectly content playing quietly for hours with his toys. He had been busy for some time with his cowboy and Indian figures on the living room carpet as I worked in the kitchen. Suddenly, he came running from the other room and burst through the swinging café doors into the kitchen. Grabbing the corner of my dress he pulled me toward the door. "Mommy; Mommy, there's an angel in our house!" Pushing through the doors into the dining area he retreated slightly, backing against my skirts, and glanced pensively around the room. His wide eyes scanned about, looking into the corners and toward the place where his toys lay on the carpet.

"What do you mean, David? I questioned, puzzled by his behavior. With more confidence then, he ran over to his toys and began to explain what had happened. "I was doing this," he demonstrated, kneeling down and playing with his toys, "and I knew somebody was behind me. When I looked up I saw an angel there with his hand reaching over me. Then he just went up by the mailbox!" he finished with a gesture of his little hand toward the mail slot in our front door. "What did he look like?" I asked, hoping for more information.

"He just looked like an angel!" David answered plainly as if my question was totally unnecessary since everybody knew what an angel looked like! Not wanting him to be frightened, I took a joyful and enthusiastic tone as I exhorted him briefly about the possibility that his own Guardian Angel may have visited him. "So, don't be afraid," I finished.

"I'm not," he said cautiously, scanning the room again; and when I turned to go back into the kitchen, he followed me. He stood beside me for a while as I cooked; appearing to be just a little discomfited and wanting me close by. When Gail came home for lunch, David ran out to meet him, "Daddy; Daddy, there was an angel at our house today!"

Gail asked me what he was talking about and I told him that David had seen an angel. I asked him to tell his dad what happened and he told the story exactly as he had told it to me. Gail exhorted him about the wonder of it just as I had done. When David's siblings came home from school, he told them the same story with no variations. We were all awed by this and wondered what it meant. I know that many children have experienced supernatural visions and signs; but I suppose we will never fully comprehend them until we get to Glory. We will, as the old hymn goes, "understand it better, by and by."

The next year when David was in kindergarten, he took it upon himself to plan a fieldtrip for his class. He told his teacher that they were all invited to "his uncle's ranch" and that I would make cupcakes for refreshments. Approximately thirty-two kindergarteners were bussed up to Paul and Caroline's acreage in Yucaipa. They got to stand on the bottom rail of the corral fence and watch the horses, see the mother donkey, Bird, and her baby, Clementine, who was still young enough to be soft and fuzzy. Gail, his brother Paul, and their dad, Doc Bryan, dressed like cowboys in their Levis and chaps, vests and hats; complete with spurs and lariats. The three of them rode horses, demonstrated roping techniques with a lariat, and performed various cowboy stunts for the kids. Paul took them on horseback rides around the corral and Caroline even put on a dog show with her Keeshonds, which she had taught to do a number of wonderful tricks. She was very good with them and the children were delighted. It was a special event and an unforgettable day for all of us.

Life provides a variety of unforgettable experiences, and I had another one of a different nature while living at Olive Avenue. This one took place in my kitchen, and involved a very careless cockroach. These big bugs were common in southern California and, before pest control methods became popular, wives and mothers had to deal with these unwelcome guests on their own. I saw them skittering toward their hiding places from time to time when I would come into the dark kitchen and flip on the light; but for the most part they were not a problem. One Sunday I had poured my pre-made Tomato Bacon and Noodles into a large pan to warm up for our lunch. I stepped back into the kitchen a few minutes later to stir the pot and there on the top with legs a-kicking was a big, unfortunate cockroach floating on its back among the noodles! Seized with sudden mortification I instinctively spooned it up and dumped it in the trash, valiantly saving my supper. Scanning the bubbling surface I spied and retrieved one loose leg and realized that, like it or not, the only food available for the day had just been bug-spiced. Deftly flicking the last leg into the garbage I bravely decided to trust the Lord to bless my recipe, cleanse it, and make it nourish my hungry family, which I am very sure that he did.

Pressing through Dark Forecasts

I had struggled with kidney disease since our early years of ministry in Twin Falls; but after a severe attack the pain would finally subside and I would recover enough to carry on life as usual. While living at Olive Avenue, however, I was to learn some things that would shed a probing light on these incidents and verify their grave implications.

I have mentioned throughout this book the many times we were blessed by the fellowship and ministry of wonderful brothers and sisters in the faith. Gail valued opportunities to invite various pastoral and evangelistic colleagues to minister in his pulpit and enrich our congregation. It was one of these times when this nearly fatal attack began in my body. Our good friends, Ralph and Rose Mahoney, had come to speak to our congregation. Sitting on the church bench during the service, I suddenly had a flood of intense pain that went throughout my entire body. It was so extreme that I could not sit still and I finally lay down on the church bench. I could not stay in this condition so, with chills and a bad headache, I drove myself home and confirmed the tell-tale symptom, blood in my urine. After the service, the Mahoneys came to the house with Gail to pray for me. I remember Brother Mahoney saying, "Did you know that kidney disease is associated with the inner heart? It is usually brought on by deep grief or wounds of the soul."

Gail was visibly startled by the statement, and I knew by his face that he was sobered by this knowledge. I believe it was disconcerting to him that his lifestyle through much of our marriage was a likely cause of my ongoing physical trauma. The church was praying continually and for the first week the ladies took turns caring for me and the children. After that, they came and went and my mother-in-law helped whenever she could. Gail went to his office every morning and stayed gone all day. I could hear voices from where I lay bedfast in my room, but I was too weak to respond to anyone. I thought I was dying. I wanted to see my children and talk to them, but the ladies who were there would not let them come in. I think they believed that I was dying, too. I was too weak for words, and barely cognizant of noises and voices in the house. I knew that people were there helping with things but everyone stayed away from me. They brought my medicine and fed my children while I wasted away week after week until I was a frail one hundred and nine pounds. Finally, though I didn't think I could possibly do it, Gail forced me to get up so he could take me to a doctor. I was then referred to a specialist who described the disease as a low-grade infection always present in the body. He told us that it was incurable, and eventually fatal. His grave words to Gail were, "With this much blood in her urine, your wife could expire at any time." I hung on desperately and after about six weeks I began to improve. I was very weak and could not stand for very long at a time. I had to sit down between the smallest activities, such as getting dressed or doing a few dishes; it seemed like months before I could get my strength back.

Life went on with its constant challenges sprinkled with memorable highlights. Things were tight with twenty dollars per week for groceries and non-stop company. We were getting the evening offerings for our wages and I don't know how we did it. We even took the kids to Baskin-Robbins 31 Flavors for ice cream after services sometimes. Many of our favorite highlights were things we could do without spending money, though. Namely, our common family bicycle rides on Saturdays after cleaning the church. We also looked forward to special meetings as highpoints in our experience, such as World M.A.P. (Missionary Assistance Plan) camps and area camp meetings. The people and relationships that God brought our way were always considered highlights, not only our dear friends in the ministry but all the families that God brought to the church during those years. I have friendships that are still blessing my life to this day that were fostered fifty years ago at Evangel Temple in Redlands! One such friendship was a girl we took into our home for a while. Her grandmother had been a family friend of my parents during their church years at 87th and Avalon in Los Angeles. This lady came to our church in Redlands and brought her granddaughter to meet us. This beautiful, young teen was from a dysfunctional family and wanted a fresh start. We took her in to our home on Olive Avenue and she shared a room with the girls. Dorcas and Rebecca thought that Carla was the best! She was sweet and cooperative, cheerful, and helpful with household chores. She loved us and loved the Lord. We had some interesting experiences together and learned a lot from each other. Although she was with us for less than a year, she is still in touch with our family. During these years of our kids growing up we were purposefully involved with any activity we felt was worthy of family time and support. All the rallies, and regional organizations, Royal Rangers, Missionettes, Speed the Light, Christ Ambassadors, Women's Missionary Counsel, Boys and Girls Camps, and more. Church activities were number one whenever we were pastoring; but I was also involved with my children's school activities. I was a Room Mother for grade school classes, along with participating whenever possible in Brownies, Cub Scouts, Little League, and on PTA boards.

One needs only to plant themselves into a thriving church body to discover how much help is needed to keep good programs going! Yet, we often hear about the difficulties of being in charge of something these days; about the challenges of keeping volunteers inspired without bribing them with benefits or rewards, even in the church! Motivating people to help out isn't easy in our what's-in-it-for-me society. Yet, I hope that our lives can exemplify true servanthood to the world. God's people should always be inspired to give themselves wholeheartedly to whatever pleases the Lord. Our philosophy was always to give our very best to whatever we were involved with, which enlarged our boundaries with rich experience and rewards of the soul. Our guidance came from Colossians 3:23-24 (KJV), *"And whatsoever ye do, do it heartily, as to the Lord, and not unto men; knowing that of the Lord ye shall receive the reward of the inheritance: for ye serve the Lord Christ."* We must remember that only Heaven will reveal the true rewards, and that the crowns we have earned as overcomers in this world will gladly be cast at the feet of Jesus when we meet him face to face!

Torrents on the Zankie

After about two and a half years at Olive Avenue, Gail found a home for sale on Sylvan Boulevard that was surrounded by orange groves on three sides and had a shallow stream called the Zankie running in front of it parallel to the road. Gail was tired of renting from landlords and wanted to own a home. The church was doing well enough that we were able to buy this family home for $12,000. Our mortgage payment was only twenty dollars more per month than the rent we had been paying. We were excited, since we had not owned a home since our little house in Meridian, Idaho which we had eventually sold. This Sylvan house was an older home with dark wood everywhere. We immediately began to remodel, and my first project was to paint everything dazzling white. I also loved pink, which was popular for kitchens at that time; so I had everything from pink curtains and tablecloths to a pink dish drainer and wastebasket! It was cheery and beautiful and, most importantly, my very own!

We had a back porch and a huge tree in the back yard. Gail hung a long, thick rope from one of the branches for a swing. He fixed a large knot at the bottom that the kids could sit on to swing back and forth, which drew neighborhood boys and girls for blocks! Our sons loved playing in the orchards around the house and in the Zankie, which was about four feet wide. The bridge across it was low, and the kids could sit on it and dangle their feet in the water. It was just enough water to splash in, throw rocks across, catch water skippers and swing to the other side on a rope that hung from a tree along the bank. One time David jumped on the rope to swing across and fell. The fall knocked the

wind out of him so that he could not move, and Mark thought he was dead! He picked him up and hauled him all the way to the house shouting for help before David came to and we realized he was alright.

I enrolled all the children in swimming lessons when summer came. Throughout my own childhood, my mother had maintained a gripping fear of water, which lasted all her life. She often told us stories of people who drowned, and warned us continually of the "dangers of water". I think her fear must have latched onto me as well because throughout my lifetime I developed the same fear and was afraid of drowning. I had an excessive fear of deep lakes and rivers and, to make matters worse, the first funeral I ever attended was for a neighbor boy in Tujunga who drowned in Hansen Dam at age fifteen. Now that my own children were old enough to take swimming lessons, I decided this was the time to overcome my own water trauma. I enrolled all of them in swim classes not far from our house on Sylvan Boulevard and I learned to swim myself, which greatly reduced my anxiety. Before I could get my bearings about water safety, however, we experienced one of the flash floods that this area was famous for!

On a normal day in Redlands, I was doing some visitation while the children were gone to school. While I was sitting in the living room of this lady's home, a cloudburst surged into town spawning billions of heavy raindrops that danced in the streets. There had been some bad fires in the hills and I had heard about flash floods, but had never seen one. It only rained for about half an hour but the trickling rivulets in the gutters soon became rushing torrents that were leaping over the curbs and covering sidewalks! I knew that I should get back home as soon as the rain subsided but the flood arrived before I did. By the time I got there, the Zankie had become a wide, rushing torrent with logs rolling dangerously downstream. Our bridge was torn out by the log jam and the rabbit cages that we had on the edge of the lawn were caught in the gushing waters and tipped over. Neighbor men were rushing along the banks trying desperately to save the rabbits without getting caught by the current themselves! The kids had just come off the school bus and were standing agape at the scene before them. Since we couldn't get to the house, I took them all to Grandma Bryan's for the night.

Before it subsided, the flood cut a gorge that was twenty feet across and significantly deeper than before. The stream went back to its small size and Gail found a plank we could walk across on; but the sides were cut so deep that we had to climb up from the plank to get into the yard. We parked our vehicles on the street and, as soon as he could, Gail built a sturdy bridge that we could drive over. He hauled big logs and railroad ties to construct a wide, strong bridge across our own "great divide". We worked hard to clean up the debris and plant new grass in our ruined yard. We had planted bushes and flowers to create a nicely landscaped space in front of the house. Just as we were getting back to normal, another flash flood bore down upon us washing it all away. This time it was much worse because the gorge left by the first flood accommodated a deeper, wider torrent than the first. Another bad rainstorm brought rushing floodwaters down the bare foothills into our community. We were home when this happened, and safe inside the house; but the waters rose steadily until they were lapping at the top step of our front porch. It was about four stairs above the ground so the water was deep and quite swift. Our home looked like it was floating in the middle of a river and I even saw an old couch bobbing downstream. Gail was always calm and cool in emergencies, but when it seemed that the floodwaters would rise above the porch and overcome our living space we called for help. Men from the church came in their waders and found a shallow place through one of the orchards where they could carry the children to safety. Gail and I were able to wade out behind them and get to dry land. This time the flood did not wash our bridge away because Gail had built it so heavy and strong; but the bank was eroded enough to cause one side of the bridge to collapse. Our yard was littered with every imaginable kind of junk, wood and even old furniture that had been carried downstream from homes above us. Our home remained safe but by the time the waters receded there was lots of damage to deal with. All of our new plants and bushes were gone. The yard around the house was layered with sand and rocks. The skirting on the house had been torn away, causing our cellar to fill with water. It was half full of mud that we had to dig out before we could even see the shelves—let alone clean them. Becca was helping me sort through the rubble and we found a baby possum down there that had been separated from its mother. The possums lived in the orange groves and many times as our car rolled across the bridge at night we could see the mother's shiny eyes as she ran across the driveway with her babies hanging tightly to her belly fur underneath.

None of These Diseases

In 1967, while living at Sylvan Boulevard, I was miraculously healed by the Lord Jesus Christ of the kidney disease that had plagued me for about twelve years. We were having special meetings at the church and God was moving mightily. David received the baptism of the Holy Spirit during this time. The speaker we had invited was riding in the car with us one evening when he asked, "Do either of you have kidney trouble that causes pain right here?" and he touched my lower back exactly where my kidney pain had always begun.

"Yes," I answered. "I have had trouble with my kidneys for years."

"Well," he continued, "you will have another severe attack but when it happens remember to say, 'I was already healed.'" This was somewhat unsettling to me because if God wanted to heal me I wondered why he would allow more pain and suffering before he made me well. This man was acquainted with Major League Baseball center-fielder, Albie Pearson, who was a born-again believer and playing for the Los Angeles Angels at the time. He wanted to drive down to Albie's home so that we could meet him and hear what God was doing in his life. The Pearson's invited our family for dinner and the kids will never forget their gorgeous home with its unique décor; it was "baseball everything"! They had bar stools with round seats that looked like giant baseballs, and baseball bats for the legs. There was a large tile baseball mosaic on the floor of his swimming pool and, of course, his trophies were displayed everywhere. Albie gave Mark a personalized baseball bat as a souvenir. We had a wonderful time of fellowship with them, but we stayed very late and did not arrive back home until about 2:00 am. The next morning I was stricken by another acute attack of Pyelonephritis and once again came too close to death. I was sick for many weeks. One Sunday night while Gail and the children were at church, I lay on what I feared to be my death bed and began to pray. Suddenly, the Lord spoke to me very clearly, *"...who calleth those things that are not as though they were..."* It seemed like a very strange message to me. *Is this a passage out of the Bible?* I wondered. I had to find out, and I reached for the Bible on my bed stand. I still had fever and chills, a piercing headache, and was weak to the bone; but I had to know what these words meant! I used the Concordance at the back of my Bible to identify the verse and discovered that it came from the book of Romans. I turned to the passage in Romans 4:17 where the apostle Paul was speaking of Abraham's faith in believing; *"...God, who quickeneth the dead, and calleth those things which be not as though they were."*

Through those few words of scripture, the Holy Spirit gave me the confidence that God had healed me. Previously, I had been confused about this passage because I had heard "name-it claim-it" groups using it to declare that they were not sick when they were obviously very ill. I felt that they were false; pretending, and mistaking a foolish presumption for a statement of faith. When Jesus healed people, they did not have to pretend! Now, in bringing this fresh truth to me, God was opening my understanding to see that just as Abraham believed God's promise for a son when his one-hundred-year-old body told a different story, I could also believe God's promise for my healing though every fiber of my body screamed that I was on my deathbed. I believed that although I did not see the evidence in my body, God was quickening me, accelerating new life into every fiber of my being! With my head pounding, I sat up on the edge of the bed and thought, *"If this is God, I will be able to get up, get dressed and go to church."* Since I had my own car to drive, I decided to put this word to the test. The church people knew how sick I had been. I would barely recuperate from a bad attack, which required several months to regain my strength, and then I would have another spell. These were happening much more often and I had been close to death before. Consequently, when I walked into the building that night it was as though the people were seeing a ghost! Everyone was amazed and knew that I had undoubtedly experienced a miracle of healing in my body. I came in during the testimony service, and Gail was shocked as I stood there and gave my testimony before the congregation. As the days went by God's Word proved true, and I was able to resume all of my activities. Some days I had anxious thoughts, *"I hope this is real..."* because when we step out in faith doubts will always come to test us. But it *was* real and I got better and stronger until I became fully able to carry on my life as a busy pastor's wife and mother of four children. For many years following this healing I was able to work hard.

Later, when the children became teenagers, I worked hard on our ranch as well as taking double shifts at my cannery job—all with no side effects. Before my healing, extra exertion of any kind would always throw me into another painful spell. I marveled over and over again at the faithfulness of God in fulfilling His *rhema* word to me, the "quickened and living" word that brought life to my body, soul, and spirit that day.

Memories for Keeps

Our years in the ministry afforded us plenty of opportunity for hospitality. I believe it was one of my God-given gifts, and I'm glad because it certainly came in handy! By the time we were in Redlands, I was hosting full-scale holiday dinners with all the trimmings and inviting friends or family to our house. The kids were all in grade school by then, and always shared my enthusiasm. It was never a cause for stress to me, and I am always amazed to see how some women dread having company! I loved the cooking, the serving, and even the clean-up! It was all very rewarding. I have enjoyed cooking hundreds of meals through the years—to take to others, as well as for serving guests in our own home. I believe the Gift of Hospitality extends from the physical needs, to the emotional, through the soul, and straight to the spirit. Whether natural or spiritual nourishment is in order, I love to share anything that I have with whomever the Lord puts in my circle of relationship. There are many levels to relationships, and some of them are complicated; but there is a universal simplicity in serving, helping, and sharing that can touch anyone, anywhere, at any level. We took in another teenager when we lived at Sylvan Boulevard. She was rebellious and ditching school; her father came to us at his wits end and asked if we would consider taking her for a while to see if it would do any good. The only other option was reform school. We kept her for three months. She came to church with us because we required that of her, but she verbalized her disgust about how religious we were and before long she ran away. Years later this young woman gave her life to the Lord and sent me a thank you card. She wanted to make sure that we knew how much she appreciated everything we tried to do for her. Even in her disobedience and rebellion, she felt God's love from our family and knew we cared about her welfare. Hospitality is close to the heart of God because it requires a willingness to sacrifice our own schedules, comfort zones, and preferences in order to honor or defer to someone else. Philippians 2:4 tells us: *"Do not merely look out for your own personal interests, but also for the interests of others."* (NAS) Not only does Christian hospitality bless others, it is one of the greatest, and simplest, ways to bring enrichment to our own lives and a wealth of experience and knowledge to our families. A close family is a wonderful blessing; but if all we have is one another, we can also become severely ingrown, which limits our potential for well-rounded character development and responsible interaction with the rest of the world.

During our five years in Redlands we met many people through our ministry who had a lasting impact on our lives. Brother Jack Schisler held meetings for us many times and remained a close friend of our family, eventually becoming very instrumental in my son's life years later when David pastored in Yuba City, California. We shared times of rich ministry and fellowship with Ralph and Rose Mahoney, our wonderful friends and founders of World M.A.P. (Missionary Assistance Plan). We also became involved with the Full Gospel Business Men's Fellowship, where Gail spoke periodically. He was still in charge of the area wide monthly C.A. rallies and one speaker that he scheduled was Pastor Richard Wurmbrand, author of *Tortured for Christ*, the story of his fourteen-year imprisonment in communist Romania. He bared his back during the message to show the deep scars of his catastrophic torture, and it was something our children never forgot.

Brother Leland Davis also came many times and ministered with his prophetic gifts; one revival meeting lasted for five weeks. We had meetings every night which often ran until after 10:00 pm. By this time, the Charismatic Renewal had begun. We had attended the Dennis Bennett meetings in Los Angeles and were deeply affected and renewed by the moving of the Holy Spirit. People came from every church and denomination to our meetings with Brother Davis, and we counted more than five hundred visitors. He was exceptionally gifted in personal prophecy which was on target every time, amazing each recipient. These personal prophetic words were evidence of God's great power, but also of his keen and detailed interest in our earthly lives. Many were blessed and their Christian walk revitalized. These were often school nights for the kids but we felt that being in the presence of the Lord was more important than getting to bed on time. They would fall asleep on, or under, the pews and were never the worse for it! David once fell asleep on the pew and, in the bustle of joyful fellowship following the meeting, we forgot he was there. Halfway home when we realized he was not in the car, we raced back to the church to discover that he was still sleeping peacefully; probably in the presence of angels. It was an exciting time that our four children remember very fondly. Who could imagine that, a generation later, the church in general would become so calloused to the need for revival that these stories would become foreign to most? We could never have imagined that the entertainments and business of the world could generate such compromise and apathy that thousands would consider it adequate to attend church for two hours on Sundays mornings. My aim is not to criticize anyone who sets time aside to attend church on Sunday; this is good! Let us simply be encouraged to feed our spirits regularly, both at church and at home, just as we feed our bodies more than once each week!

The Kellys were another couple who enriched our lives while in Redlands. Glenn Kelly took our youth group to Tijuana, Mexico on a mission trip. They sang, told stories, and evangelized the poor neighborhoods with the love of Christ. Our acquaintance was with the Clark family afforded us another excellent missionary experience. Bob Clark, a pilot who partnered with another business man in ownership of a twin-engine Cessna, enjoyed flying supplies to an orphanage in La Pas, Mexico. The ladies of the church, in those days called the WMC (Women's Missionary Council) in the Assembly of God churches, made clothing, quilts, and many needed items for this orphanage. These things were included with food and other supplies that were purchased and packaged for transport. Gail and two other paid passengers were scheduled to go on this mission trip with the pilot; but at the last minute one of them backed out. Brother Clark called and said if I could get ready in fifteen minutes I could take this person's place and go along on the trip to La Pas! I stuffed one change of clothes into a small, paper bag and called my mother-in-law to see if she could stay with the kids while I was gone. Hazel rallied to the task, even though she was working in another town, and got to our house before school was out to meet the kids.

Traveling to La Paz was an amazing experience and, at nearly thirty years of age, my first time to fly in a plane! The view of the Baja Peninsula from the air was exhilarating, and we made many colored slides of our trip. We stayed for several days and saw the mission work at the orphanage, as well as visiting the pastors of a small Assembly of God church in town. We slept in a thatched hut on top of the orphanage roof! It was a place of extreme poverty and I gained a deep burden for missions from this experience. I remember giving out candy to the children, and seeing the joy on their faces while receiving our gifts of love. I was incredibly impressed with the obedience of these forty-two children as they sat with hands folded during a very long devotion before their meal. What a contrast to modern American life; and how we take our abundant blessings for granted!

Life in Redlands felt like five years of favor. Gail had his troubles but did well most of the time and stayed the course. We have wonderful memories from this place and so do our children. The people loved and respected their pastor and it was always very evident that God had gifted him for the work of the Lord. Gail's preaching was excellent and powerful. My husband was highly influential wherever we went; widely recognized as a chosen instrument through which God poured life-changing truth to his people. Much of the time he was that vessel meet for the Master's use, described in 2 Timothy 2:21 (KJV) *"If a man therefore purge himself from these, he shall be a vessel unto honour, sanctified, and meet for the master's use, and prepared unto every good work."* Nevertheless, I learned how to relish every period of peace and safety without taking anything for granted. I knew that imperfect vessels—which includes all of us—were prone to weakness; I had also learned to remain watchful for those small cracks that might surface in my husband's life and send him back to the Potter's Wheel for refurbishing.

Cast Down, but not Destroyed

In the middle of all the wonderful things that God was doing in the pioneer work at Redlands, Satan went on a rampage and came after the Shepherd of this flock. Gail slipped into a pattern of behavior that had been a former problem and weakness for him. The congregation didn't know about it, but after several months of struggle and personal failure he resigned the pastorate, confessing to the people that he had disqualified himself from leadership in the church and, once again, relinquished his papers to the Assembly of God district leadership. In those days, the response from the district was to encourage the prodigal to repent and seek the Lord; and when he felt ready to try again they would give him a two-year probationary period in which to prove himself capable of the ministry. Upon successful completion of this provisional period, they would fully reinstate his license to preach and to represent the denomination of the Assemblies of God. The process of restoration was left entirely to the individual at fault, with no particular accountability requirements or rehabilitative counsel provisions of any kind. Of our own accord, however, we had counselled with Jack Schisler and Ralph Mahoney who suggested that we move to Long Beach, California and sit under the ministry of Brother David Schoch, a prophetic man who was part of the Latter Rain movement of the 1950s and 1960s. He was pastoring a large church, Bethany Chapel, in Long Beach,[1] and it would be beneficial for us to soak in God's presence and receive the Word in a healing, refreshing atmosphere. A time to strengthen and restore the soul is healthy and necessary after a spiritual battle; refreshing would serve us well. As always, Gail was completely open to their counsel and willing to do whatever they thought was best.

Before moving to Long Beach, they suggested that we take our family on a vacation together. So we borrowed a camper from Gail's cousin and traveled to beautiful Bear Valley, Idaho. It was supposed to be freeing, but all I could think about was the hard work that would be wasted, the progress that would be lost, and the faithful people that we were leaving behind. With the children riding in the camper, I curled up on the front seat of the pickup in a fetal position and cried tears of despair. Gail was harsh with me, "Don't cry! Stop crying; I can't stand it!" He spoke irritably as if my natural emotional response was inconvenient to him. Why could he not acknowledge the legitimacy of my sorrow instead; especially when he was the cause of it every time? A person does learn to swallow the lump in their throat and to lock up their tears when they make no difference. I knew by now how to focus on my children and put my energy into things that would ease their questioning young minds. God's Word speaks often of putting the needs of others above our own, and when we do that we find in it a hidden treasure. By God's grace, we have been created to thrive on sacrificial giving and become better for it. I found that giving my all to my children's welfare and happiness was the best way to nourish my own soul. I was directly affected by their laughter and happiness; warmed by their sunshine; strengthened by their joy. We had a dog at Sylvan Boulevard that our children adored; Chief, an Australian shepherd with one blue eye and one brown eye. When we left for Bear Valley we told them that we would find a good place for him to stay while we were gone; but when we pulled up in front of the Animal Shelter, they knew it was permanent. David cried when Gail told him that there was no way to take the dog with us, and we would get another dog when we got settled again. "I don't want another dog," our little boy sobbed. "I just want to keep Chief!"

Life takes turns we don't expect, though, and part of success is navigating these changes bravely. I needed to help them re-focus and look forward to a wonderful trip. So they dried their tears and we were off to Idaho, all of us struggling in our own way to make the best of things. The girls were now thirteen and fourteen, and the boys were nine and eleven. Our first stop was Emmett, where our whole family picked cherries for two days in the fruit orchards around Emmett to make money for our trip. Once in Bear Valley, Gail created a wonderful "home in the woods" for our stay. He had borrowed a camper from one of his cousins, and a 9′x 12′canvas tent to sleep in. He also set up a cook tent for meals and created "log-chairs" from big stumps with a chainsaw. Other stumps with boards across them were used for benches around the fire pit. I kept our picnic table and utensils safe under a plastic mattress cover where they would stay clean and dry. We tied a rope from tree to tree that I used as a clothesline for drying things out. Mark and Gail kept the wood chopped and stacked nearby.

We did lots of salmon fishing in the Bear Valley Creek, and hiked in the beautiful mountain ranges of the Boise National Forest. We cured salmon eggs for fishing, and worked together to catch the big ones. The salmon swam upriver in large groups. There was a big tree along the bank of the river that leaned out over the water. The kids, usually Dorcas, would scamper up the back side of it to a lookout spot where they could see the salmon swimming upstream toward us. As soon as they saw them coming, they would sound the call to everyone else to get ready to fish!

David collected many chipmunk tails from hunting the area with his BB gun. The mountains were beautiful and the girls enjoyed picking wild flowers. We savored our warm campfires morning and evening, and talked about God at night as we gazed at starry skies above. Bathing in the cold river waters was a necessary activity, but not listed among the most pleasant memories of this trip! One special highlight was a long hike up Bluebunch Mountain with a picnic lunch. Gail always packed his pistol and on this hike he taught all of the kids to shoot. We got some great pictures of this outing and of the mountain meadows ablaze with wild flowers as far as the eye could see. When it was time to leave, Gail decided he wanted to fish a section of the river between our campground and another one farther down the road. Becca and David stayed with me to help pack up the rest of our camp, while Mark and Dorcas went hiking down Bear Valley Creek to the confluence of Marsh Creek near the pick-up point. They were to fish their way along this ten mile hike and meet me at a place called Cape Horn. I knew it would be gorgeous scenery but I did not know the extent of the adventure they would have in wading this rushing creek several times after the pathway ended. The water was up to Mark's middle in one place and he and Dorcas had to hang on to each other to keep from being whisked downstream. It took much longer than expected and when they finally made it back and I heard the tale, I was comforted to have us all together again safe and sound.

From Bear Valley we drove through central Idaho, coming down through the spectacular Stanley Basin beneath the Sawtooth Mountains, on our way back to California. Gail's younger sister, Medora, had allowed us to store our furniture in her garage; so we picked it up and settled temporarily in Garden Grove, California while waiting for a house to open up in Long Beach. We enrolled all the kids in school and Gail got a job with Foremost Dairies in Long Beach to which he would commute each day while living in Garden Grove. We had an old, heavy piano that Gail said we could not move again but I was not willing to leave it in the house. I got on Mark's stingray bicycle and rode down to the newspaper office to put an ad in the "For Sale" section. I was trying to pedal while standing because the banana seat was so hard; but I didn't realize that the handlebars were loose and, before I knew what was happening, I flipped over the front and onto the pavement. I was skinned up and I tore several holes in the knees of my new polyester slacks. Despite my wounds, I made my way to the newspaper office and placed my ad. The accident had flattened both tires so I had to walk a long way to a service station; but, thankfully, the tires were not ruined and I was able to fill them up again and ride the rest of the way home. With God's help and favor, I sold my piano for about sixty dollars—not much, but better than leaving it in the house.

Urban Paradigms

In a couple of months our missionary friends, the Schislers, left for the mission field and let their cozy home on Appleton Street in Long Beach to our family so that we could attend Brother Schoch's church. This was a difficult move, though, because the kids had barely begun to settle into their schools in Garden Grove. Mark was very happy there and his teacher loved and encouraged him, which he needed because of some dire school trauma in Redlands; now he had to leave. Also, Long Beach was a big city and the schools were not so good. The girls had to walk twenty blocks to their Junior High School and it was not the best side of town. We were facing our obstacles and getting through them together. Mark was very ambitious and had learned in Redlands that there was money to be had for boys who were willing to mow lawns! Now he wanted to work a paper route and since he was twelve years old Gail encouraged it. Mark was quite grown up for his age, but David was only ten and still small in size, though he wanted a paper route as well. The newspaper office would not give David his own route, but they would give two routes to Mark so that David could work with him and still earn the money. This was fine with the boys; but it was very hard for me because they had to do collections in the evenings when people were home from work and I was not comfortable with them being out alone after dark. We only lived two blocks from the beach and there was plenty of crime in that area—kidnappings, robberies, drugs—"front page stories" that we were unfortunately exposed to on a regular basis because of the boys' newspapers laying around the house! Mark got robbed twice by an older boy who knew he had a paper route. Once the boy stole a newspaper and the other time he took some money. When Mark had to go to that particular location again, Gail went with him and hid in the bushes to confront the thief; but he never came and never bothered Mark again. There was a large apartment complex at the end of the route where Mark had to stop every time in order to deliver several papers there. It was dark and dingy, and there was always a group of kids hanging around the grounds. One day when Mark stopped there, a bully that was bigger than all the other kids grabbed Mark's bike by the handle bars and stood in front of his bicycle, straddling the front wheel. "I'm going to beat you up!" he snarled. Mark spoke calmly, hoping to diffuse him, and told him that he didn't want to fight. The bully replied menacingly, "I'm going to beat you up anyway!" Then he stepped away from the bike and shouted to the crowd, "I'm giving this kid to the count of ten to run; and when I catch him I'm going to beat him up! One…Two…Three…" Mark fairly jumped on those pedals and put everything he had into that little bike. He was pedaling uphill, too; but he figured he was riding for his life. By the time the bully's voice said, "Five…" Mark was out of earshot and never heard the rest. He knew the burly tyrant could never catch him at this point and that he had safely escaped the threat. During this time, the girls—only thirteen and fourteen at the time—had a brush with a hippy that was high on drugs one day as they walked home from school with the neighbor girl. This naked driver with nothing on but a dirty bandana to keep his long, greasy hair off his forehead had pulled his car up to the curb. The three girls were waiting there to cross the street when he motioned them to the window and tried to entice them into his car! Another night the girls woke up to groans and cries outside their bedroom window where someone was having a bad trip on drugs in the neighbor's yard. This was a whole new world for the Bryan family, and a fairly dark one at that!

Meanwhile, we were thoroughly enjoying the church and the services were encouraging. The atmosphere was truly drenched in the presence of God. Health and healing were there in abundance, and the peace of God which passes all understanding soothed our weary souls. I remember how willingly the people stood in exuberant praise and worship longer than we had ever stood before. They were clearly consumed with the glory that filled this place and I could see why. The boys' perspective was a bit more practical. "Why do they have to stand up for the *whole* service?" David would exclaim; our youngest, and least-inclined toward vigorous postures. His legs would give out long before the people were ready to be seated! We agreed with him, but cooperated and made sure that he did the same, despite his pain.

The boys joined Royal Rangers at the church and Gail enjoyed working with them to build their cars for the Pinewood Derby and doing other father-son activities sponsored by the program. There were a lot of sailors in the congregation because the church was near a Navy base. They had a bus that picked up any service men who wanted to attend on Sunday. Our pastor had been impressed by the Holy Spirit that if he would take care of the service men in Long Beach, the Lord would protect any young men of his flock who were sent to Vietnam. They also had street meetings in the city, some of which I was able to attend. The girls were old enough to babysit and were utilized by the neighbors a few times, which I only allowed because they did it together and were right across the street from our house. We were all engaging in whatever we could do to make the most of our experience. At Christmas Gail had surprised me by having a new Spinet piano delivered to Appleton Street. We had enjoyed it all winter and this is when I taught Rebecca how to chord and play piano by ear. This is also where the girls and I began singing together as a trio, learning all the old gospel songs that Gail and I had sung together through the years as well as many new ones. We enjoyed working out the harmonies and we sang a lot, honing family music skills that we would use for years to come.

I got a part time job right away at a laundry service folding clothes. I worked a few hours per day to help with expenses. Our landlord also offered me a job cleaning a men's boarding house that he owned and operated. It was around the block from us so I could walk to work. I went every week to clean the rooms, vacuum, and scrub their sinks and toilets. The owner warned me often of the dangers lurking there, especially regarding one particular tenant. My boss gave me explicit instructions to never enter this man's room without a manager close by because it would not be safe; the gross pornography pinned to his walls was evidence enough to heed the warning. My own spirit confirmed it too, as I could feel evil hovering like fog all over that place. I saw this tenant in other parts of the building from time to time, and tried to be cordial. I even shared the gospel with him, and prayed for him, scattering all the seeds I could. He admitted that he had questions about "peace" but said he could never give up his life style. After we moved away, I called the manager about getting my last paycheck. He mailed it to my new address with a letter enclosed, telling me that the degenerate boarder had died of a lung hemorrhage. He left this world screaming frantically, "I'm going to Hell! I'm going to Hell!" His fateful last words were heard throughout the boarding house. The news was chilling, and I thought of the scripture in Hebrews 3:12-13 (KJV) *"Take heed, brethren, lest there be in any of you an evil heart of unbelief, in departing from the living God. But exhort one another daily, while it is called today; lest any of you be hardened through the deceitfulness of sin."*

I was intently seeking the Lord at Appleton, as the Charismatic Renewal was still in full swing and inspiring Christians worldwide to listen for the voice of the Lord and then share what He told them. *"Why doesn't the Lord speak to me?"* I wondered, because I had been open to hearing from Him as long as I could remember and couldn't understand why it should take a "renewal" to make it happen. As I pondered this concept and kept hearing testimonies of "the Lord told me" this and "God said" that, I realized that I regularly *felt led* or *was impressed* to do or say spiritually inspired things. So I decided to test it and see if "feeling led or impressed" by the Holy Spirit was, in fact, the very same as "God telling me" something. One day as I ran the vacuum cleaner at home, I felt a strong impression to go visit my neighbor. Wondering if this was the true "voice of the Lord", I responded instantly and turned off the vacuum cleaner, walking next door to see whether my impression was God-ordained or not.

"Hi!" I greeted cheerfully as an elderly woman answered the door. "I'm the new neighbor and my kids have already met Jeff and Melinda. I just wanted to come over and get acquainted with you!"

She immediately burst into tears, saying, "Oh! I'm so glad you came! I guess you heard that my daughter is dying of cancer."

I was stunned and answered, "Oh, no! I had not heard!"

"Yes;" she continued. "She is Jeff and Melinda's mother and the cancer is in the final stages. She's taken every available option, including traveling to Mexico for treatment. Nothing has worked for her and she only has days left to live."

"Well, I believe in healing because I was healed of acute nephritis of the kidneys only a year ago. I would love to pray for her," I offered. The grandmother was thrilled and asked if I would please go up to the hospital to visit and pray. I explained that my husband worked long hours and I didn't always have a car. She said that her ex-son-in-law would take me to the hospital if I was willing, so I bravely agreed. I was still young, in my very early thirties, and this man whom I had never even met drove up in a fancy sport's car to transport me. I left the kids at home with instructions, as Gail was still at work, and entrusted my journey to the Lord as we roared away from the house. I had no idea where the hospital was, and the trip seemed to be taking much longer than I had expected through twists and turns and freeways I was not remotely familiar with. Thankfully, his two children had come along also and sat quietly in the back. We finally arrived at a large hospital and rode the elevator to the tenth floor. The room was full of relatives and the privacy curtain was pulled half way around the bed so it was slightly awkward to burst in to what seemed like a very somber, personal scene. The Ex blended into the group and the children went to the foot of their mother's bed. "Oh!" she winced. "Don't touch the bed; I'm in so much pain!"

Feeling more awkward, I boldly decided that it was now or never; and since I had come to pray, I stepped up to the bedside. "Hello." I began softly. "I'm your new neighbor and my children have enjoyed meeting Jeff and Melinda. I met your mother today and she asked me to come up and pray for you."

"Oh, I'm in such terrible pain; I just want to die," she sighed. "I don't care about being healed; I just want out."

"Well, God is able to heal you. Would you mind if I prayed?"

"That's fine;" she yielded easily. "Go ahead." So I began to pray everything that I knew to say: that she would feel the comfort of the Holy Spirit, that she would come to know the Lord and that He would relieve all her pain and raise her up in health. After concluding my prayer, I acknowledged that visiting required energy and I was not there to tire her, but that if she wished I would ask my pastor to come and pray again, to which she readily agreed. When I turned around, the whole room was empty of visitors except the Ex, who leaned against the wall listening. Before I could leave, I heard a frail voice from the next bed. "Ma'am! Ma'am! Would you please say one of those prayers for me?" I went around the next curtain and, with the confidence that only comes from God, spoke boldly to this dear lady about Jesus, salvation, and healing; and prayed for her as well. Then I told both ladies 'goodbye' and rode home again with my chauffeur and his children. The next day I called Brother Schoch and he said he would go to the hospital and talk to her about her personal salvation, which he did. My pastor led this lady to the Lord on her death bed. She said the Sinner's Prayer and told her mother about it later; but she said something else that I never forgot, and which also confirmed that I had indeed heard "the voice of the Lord" about going next door.

"Yes," my dying neighbor told her mother the next day. "The pastor came to visit me. He explained salvation through Jesus Christ and I prayed the prayer... but I would give anything in the world to hear that little woman pray again." She died that night, and went into Jesus' arms for Eternity. I was so touched and awestruck that God could use me to influence the salvation of a soul—or maybe two—under such dire circumstances. I was nearly petrified the whole time, but *made* myself step out in faith anyway. How many of those relatives heard the gospel in that prayer? How might the Holy Spirit have tugged at the ex-husband's heart as he stood against the wall listening to every word? Later, he came over with boxes and boxes of her clothing. He had tears in his eyes, however worldly and calloused he had first appeared. "She had a lot of very nice things," he said; "and I know that she would want you to have them because of what you did for her."

The boxes held everything from scarves and belts to coats and furs; but all of it was riddled with the suffocating smell of cigarette smoke and I couldn't keep it in the house. I piled it all on the back porch and went through it a few pieces at a time. There were so many fine fabrics, and so much polyester in those days, that most of the items had cigarette burns in them and went to the Good Will. I found a few nice outfits that I could keep; but I left that big-city experience with a great confidence that I had heard God's voice, beyond a shadow of doubt; and with a deep fulfillment that my determination in that quest had resulted in lasting fruit for the Kingdom of God. I anticipate becoming well acquainted with my neighbor in Heaven someday, and talking to her about all the things that lady-friends enjoy—except this time they will be heavenly.

Getting out of Dodge

After about seven months of big-city living, Gail decided this was neither the best place to raise his kids nor to be refreshed in spirit—wonderful church or not! By June of 1968, Gail had "spring fever" and couldn't wait to get out of the city. He pulled the kids out of school a week or so early and packed up for Idaho. His Aunt Ruby and Uncle William still lived in Emmett and were delighted to hear that we were coming because they were taking a trip to Arkansas and needed someone to irrigate their farm and care for their livestock for a month.

The mare that Gail had purchased in Redlands, Squaw, had been boarded at his brother's place in Yucaipa and had since foaled, producing a darling colt which we named Twister. Paul and Gail had been welding a steel horse hauler to put on Gail's one-ton truck. Paul had also been talking up the money that could be made by selling goat's milk, so Gail spent one hundred dollars on a registered Nubian goat which we named Darlin'. He had also come home in late April, on Rebecca's fourteenth birthday, with a tiny beagle pup that someone on his milk route had for sale. We were not supposed to have pets at Appleton, but he knew we were moving soon and exhorted the kids to be very careful about the puppy's care until then. Once when the landlord showed up at the front door, I had Rebecca whisk her puppy out the back to hold still and keep quiet until the coast was clear! The move from Long Beach, therefore, was a doozy! Gail drove the truck with the horse hauler on it, housing Squaw and Twister. Mark and Dorcas rode with him and minded Darlin', on the floorboard of the front seat. Becca, David, and the puppy rode with me in the car pulling a trailer. This time the piano was not left behind and there was more than Gail's library packed into our trailer. It was a long trip and we had to stop overnight in the desert to sleep. Gail hobbled the mare. "She won't go anywhere with those hobbles on," he assured us. She was not happy about them, however, and began to scuffle and hop during the night. We were all sleeping on the ground and the kids were afraid that Squaw would jump on top of them. Becca finally became so frightened that we had to take up our bedding and sleep in the vehicles. When we woke up in the morning, the horse was nowhere to be found! Gail had left the colt free, knowing that it would not leave its mother's side; but they were both gone. He walked a long way and finally found a gully where she had hopped and pitched herself down to a fence at the bottom. He took the hobbles off, put a halter on her and led her back, loading her and Twister into the truck. We had to stop several times to let them get out and rest from the long trailer ride.

Close to our destination, we came over a rise and headed down what was then called Big Freezeout into Emmett valley. Gail had warned me that if the trailer got out of balance on this hill and began to swerve back and forth, the only way to pull out of it was to step on the gas until it straightened out on its own. It was very steep and the trailer was heavily loaded. I tapped the brake because it seemed that we were moving too fast; but that was the wrong move. The trailer began to swerve so violently back and forth that it was taking up the whole highway. I thought the car was going to flip because each time the trailer swerved to the other side of the road it lifted the wheels of the car on the opposite side. David had chosen to ride in the truck with the others so Becca was the only one with me and she began to scream, "Jesus! Jesus! Jesus!"

Meanwhile, I followed my husband's instructions and floor-boarded it, going seventy miles per hour down that hill! By God's grace, there were no other cars on the road as we careened across both lanes of the highway. Finally, we pulled out of it and made it safely to the bottom of the hill. Arriving at Uncle William's farm, we unloaded our trailer next to their barn and covered our things with tarps for temporary storage. We settled in for our month of transition. We got jobs in the cherry orchards right away and the whole family worked the harvest. Then Gail got a job at the local sawmill. He started on the green-chain but was soon transferred to the Bark Plant where he worked for seven years.

We looked for a house but they were few and far between. I finally found one in the newspaper and called to inquire about it. It was a small, two-bedroom house in town, situated close to a trailer park. The realtor said she would show it to me the next day so I was in her office bright and early. As I sat waiting my turn, I saw her give the keys to another customer and I knew it was the house I'd called about. She confirmed my fears when she called me in; I was devastated! It was hard to find rentals for a family with four children and I went away heavy-hearted. Gail was upset that night when I told him what happened, and retorted, "She can't do that!" but then conceded, "Well, honey; the Lord has something better for us." In my sudden nosedive from hopeful expectation to discouragement, I countered, "Well…it will probably be something worse;" but I later repented of those words many times over; for God was indeed working all things to our good, as his Word encourages us to remember!

CHAPTER TEN

Ranch Life

On June 29, 1968, our sixteenth wedding anniversary, we went for a drive. We had been staying at the Freeman's farm for three weeks, but Aunt Ruby and Uncle William were due to return in one more week and we still had no place to live. On the south side of town, past the Emmett sawmill, we turned down a country lane called Tyler Road and Gail spotted an old farm house that looked empty. He backed up and we got out of the car to look at it. We walked around the house and noticed that all the doors were open. It was definitely empty and very run down; but it had a shed, a tack room, and a big, old barn out back with what appeared to be some pasture land. "Hey!" Gail exclaimed. "This is just what I'd like to have! Let's ask about it."

We walked across the country lane to the neighbor's house to inquire, and got the name of the man who was in charge of keeping it rented for the out-of-state owner. Mr. Pratt, they told us, lived one road over so we drove straight to his house. The old man studied us inquisitively and asked a few questions. Deciding that we were a decent risk, he rented us the house on the spot for fifty dollars per month "as is", with part of the land—two fenced pastures—and all the out buildings. We were thrilled, and I had to eat my bitter words from before. *"Thank you, Jesus…you knew exactly what we needed and the price we could afford,"* my grateful heart whispered heavenward.

Country Castle

Moving into our new digs was exciting, but a gargantuan task. There was rusty junk piled everywhere; old tools, tires, and garbage. We took several big loads to the dump. Gail mowed down the weeds and irrigated the lawn. We trimmed the hedge and tidied the grounds. There was a deep well with a pump house that brought clear, fresh water into our home; and a hand pump in the yard for filling buckets. The pump house had lots of shelves that I soon filled with canned goods. We cleaned and painted the old two-story house inside from top to bottom and then we had to clean up our own furniture! The Freeman's farm was a country setting, surrounded by a lot of dirt, and the Idaho climate in June was also very hot and dry. Consequently, while we waited for other accommodations our furniture had become coated with layers of very dusty dirt! We had to scour everything we owned before moving it into our new home. We settled in with our kids and our animals and felt very blessed and cared for by our heavenly Father.

Little by little I fixed up the house and made curtains for all the windows. We didn't have a couch, but there was an old, worn sectional out on the screened front porch. So I made a cover for it out of a large, blue-flowered bedspread. I piped the edges and made a ruffle for the bottom. There wasn't enough fabric to cover the back, so I used old sheets since it would be against the wall anyway. It turned out nice and made our living room cozy with the wood stove on one wall and my piano on the other. We still had an old kitchen table and I told the kids that if they would help me take some orchard jobs we could save money for a Sears dining set. They were excited to help and we were able to purchase a very sturdy table with a Formica top and two leaves; the set included six swivel chairs. We were so proud of it! I kept that set for many years until I moved into a little apartment with a small kitchen that would not accommodate it. I found an old medicine cabinet at a garage sale and Mark helped me install it in the bathroom. He also helped me build a coat rack in the mud room with a place for hats and rubber boots. The mud got so thick and deep out at the barn and horse corrals that this little room just inside the back door became a life-saver! We made a walkway out of wooden pallets leading up to the back door where all the men could take off their muddy boots before entering. There was a huge cottonwood tree on the property that Gail trimmed about half way down, which was a huge job. That gave us almost a never-ending supply of firewood for the stoves. We had a wood cook stove in the kitchen and an Ashley wood burner in the living room. We used wood heat for five years before going to an oil stove to heat the house. Mark was in charge of the wood pile, chopping all the kindling, and bringing in fresh wood whenever it was needed. In his shop class at school, he made a wood box for inside the house that we kept in the family for years. It was about three feet long by two feet wide and deep. He had used a router to carve "Wood Box" into the lid, and had stained the finished product.

Gail didn't want to spend time or money on a rental; but it was my house, too, and I was inspired to fix it up. I would spend any extra money I was able to set aside from my wages on home repairs and updates. I bought linoleum for the kitchen floor and even cut and installed pieces for my kitchen counters, since they all had the old-fashioned bare wood surfaces. I cut an extra piece to fit the wood cook stove so it could serve as an extra worktop in the summer when we weren't using it for heat. I improvised with a quarter here and a dollar there, making my old house a cozy country castle for our family in any way I could. I eventually plastered all the ceilings upstairs, added some wall paper, and found carpet pieces for the wood floors. We had bunk beds in the boys' room and the girls shared a room with twin beds against each side wall. There was also a guest room upstairs and a large room-sized landing at the top of the stairs where I sewed. Sometimes we made beds in there, too, because we had lots of company at the ranch in Emmett. Most of my family had moved back to the area by this time; so we spent time with them and periodically hosted dinners at our house. We accommodated out-of-town guests visiting for reunions, or travelers coming through. Of course, Gail had numerous family members in the area and his folks had settled in Emmett by then, too. Grandpa Doc Bryan loved the horses and kept some of his own at our place. So he was there almost every day, which was wonderful for Gail and for the many special memories the kids were able to make with their grandfather. We also had many friends from the past, Redlands and other places, who stayed in touch with our family and visited periodically. Some of them would stay longer than a month, but all of them enriched our lives.

Gail's job at the mill was steady and I got a job at Stokely-Van Camp Cannery in early September, 1968. I had to work nights but I left for work after the kids were in bed and usually got home before they got up, until school started. The cannery was seasonal but the management wanted to keep all their good workers on board for the next season, so we were able to draw some unemployment benefits in between. We processed corn first, then peaches, applesauce and prunes, which ended the season; but there were breaks in between these runs where we had time off before the next crop was ready. My first job at the cannery was on the cutters and the trim belt; then I was moved to the huskers and eventually the canners. Soon I was promoted to Quality Control, which was the best job, and I stayed there until we moved. After the corn was tested it had to be discarded, and I hated to see it go to waste! I began bringing a small bucket to save it in so I wouldn't have to throw it out. Any time we had Grade A corn coming through, I brought home these test batches and put them in the freezer! We purchased the biggest freezer we could find at Sears and kept it full of produce and fresh venison.

I also worked for over five years at Ore-Ida Foods in Ontario, Oregon about an hour's drive from Emmett. Ore-Ida was a processing plant that produced and sold mostly frozen potato products such as french fries, hash browns, and Tater Tots. In fact, Ore-Ida's founders, the Griggs brothers, were the original inventors of the Tater Tot. These bite-sized plugs were made from the leftover slivers of potatoes from the French fry production line.[1] I started on a specking belt where peeled, chopped potatoes had to be sorted and purged of all the rotten pieces. Later I moved into Quality Control where I counted and measured french fries to ensure that the company's packaging standards were met. Since Ore-Ida was also seasonal, I could draw unemployment from this job as well;

every dollar counted.

Before I started working full time we planted a big garden with green beans, corn, tomatoes, zucchini, peppers and other vegetables. Each of the kids had rows they were responsible to weed during the growing season. The third summer a terrible wind storm came through and blew all of our corn stalks over. The hail flattened our other crops and beat down our beautiful tomato plants. By this time I was working enough that I could afford to buy the plenteous fresh produce from our local farmers in the area. Since the garden was so much extra work, and no longer our lifeline, we didn't continue it after that storm.

Bryan's Animal Escapades

We so enjoyed all of our animals during this stage of life. As previously described, we arrived in Idaho with our horses, Squaw and Twister, Darlin' the goat and Ranger, the beagle. By this time, the kids were all learning to save money. The boys had savings from their Long Beach paper routes and Dorcas had babysitting money. Mark used his money to purchase his first horse and his first gun. Gypsy was a little Welsh pony that was too feisty but perfect for learning to ride. The Savage lever-action was his second prize and a perfect first hunting rifle. David bought a calf and the boys began learning the art of keeping the stalls clean for our growing collection of stock animals.

We got some banty chickens right away to provide eggs, and Gail bought an old nanny goat for milking. We named her Granny, but she was mean and we didn't like her any better than she liked us. Gail staked her out beside the well house, and soon the eroded circle that she had worn in the grass around her post became off limits for the rest of us! Granny had a white beard and greenish-yellow eyes that always held the same expression: *"Try me..."* She had a natural telepathy that shouted, *"Git off my land!"* except, instead of brandishing a shotgun, she lowered her horns! Dorcas once got too close and, fortunately, caught the old goat by the horns before Granny could butt her to kingdom come. The old goat did succeed, however, in running Dorcas in circles for a while before the poor girl could find a way to let go without getting punished! Another time, when we had house guests from California, I was outside with my visiting friend standing near Granny. I bent over to pick up a bucket and Granny's bionic eyes zoomed in on her target—my behind! She lowered her horns and leaped for the bullseye, solidly hitting her mark and knocking me for a loop, which sent my city friend into gales of laughter.

Old Granny was too dangerous and unpredictable to ever let loose; but Darlin' was a pet and we allowed her to roam free sometimes. She was young when we first got to Emmett and would hop up into the truck with Gail whenever she could, just like a dog. Once she even bounded up the steps of the school bus following the kids! She loved hopping up on the tops of our vehicles, though, and when she began helping herself to my lilacs and other flowers, she had to be staked along with Granny. One day Darlin' got tangled in her rope and, while struggling to free herself, she fell forcefully against the steel stake.

Gail disinfected the puncture wound and gave her antibiotics every day until it healed. Another time we had been away from the house for a while and as I pulled into our driveway I heard a loud, warped bleat that sounded far from normal. I parked the car and ran over to Darlin' to discover the reason for her pitiful cry. She had pulled her chain so taut that it had strangled her. When I arrived on the scene she had passed out and her eyes were rolled back into her head. I picked her up and moved her closer to the stake to loosen the pressure of her choke-chain. Then I began to pray and, instinctively, cupped my hands over her little nose and started blowing air into her lungs. Suddenly her eyes popped open and she jumped to her feet looking startled and disoriented; but she was fine.

We didn't like goat's milk and since Granny was so incorrigible we only kept her until we bought a cow. The neighbors across the road had more cows than they wanted, so we bought Flossie from them. She was a nice Guernsey that gave lots of milk and we were happy to have her. Gail taught the boys how to milk the cow and the girls' job was to strain it into clean containers and clean up the buckets for the next morning. We not only had plenty of fresh milk to drink but enough to sell, at fifty cents per gallon, to neighbors and friends. I gave the money to the boys for doing the milking, although Becca commented later in her adulthood that dealing with manure-smeared straw stuck to the bottoms of those big buckets should have made the girls' cleaning job worth a few quarters at least! Flossie's milk was so rich that it had two-plus inches of cream in the top of each gallon jar by morning. We always had fresh cream for whatever we wanted, from enhancing our coffee to pouring over fresh peaches, to whipping up a garnish for a luscious dessert. We bred Flossie to a Holstein bull and she had a darling calf which we named Blossom. We raised Blossom to a full-grown milk cow and she produced very well. Her milk was not as creamy as Flossie's but the Guernsey genes made it rich and tasty just the same. By junior high, both boys had a cow to milk, morning and night.

I can't neglect to mention the kitten we found high up in the hedge. We named her Bush and she was a great mouser that lived in the barn, happily undomesticated. Dogs, of course, are always a part of the country landscape and soon the neighbor's dog, Charlie, buddied up with Becca's beagle. In this country setting there was a general attitude of accommodation regarding the neighborhood dogs and cats running free. One day, however, Ranger and Charlie turned up missing and never came home. We had heard rumors that Charlie was an egg-sucker and that they may have met the hot end of a rancher's rifle; but we never found out if they were stolen or sent to the pound, either of which would have been a better prospect than our first fear of their fate. We really wanted a good family dog but couldn't afford to buy one. One day I saw an ad in the newspaper describing a Norwegian Elkhound that was available free to a "worthy family." We drove to Caldwell to look at him and the people said that they feared someone traveling through had lost him because he was such a beautiful and well-behaved dog. We decided to take him home and when we opened the car door he hopped obediently into the front seat and leaped nimbly over into the back, taking a spot by the passenger window. His response was so smooth and automatic that it seemed he had been trained by someone else to do this routine. He sat alert and quiet all the way home as if he knew his place and was just happy to be there! We named him Smoky and everyone loved him. Years later when we moved away, we gave him to the neighbors but their house was not home to him. Whenever he disappeared they would find him lying contentedly on our old front porch where he belonged.

Another dog that joined our ranch life later was passed along by some relatives. This puppy was such a feisty little booger that he earned the name for keeps. Booger was part Australian Shepherd and Gail wanted to train him as a cattle dog. Booger was not the best watchdog because he loved people. Anybody who spoke to him and put out their hand was welcomed as a friend. Booger greeted strangers with a wagging tail and expected a pat on the back or a good scratch behind the ears, but all animals had to beware when he was in the vicinity. He cleared out all the neighborhood cats and, unfortunately, was a little too interested in the neighbor's chickens, which resulted in some angry complaints that we certainly understood. Whenever he growled and raised his hackles at our own chickens, however, good ol' Smoky laid an alpha paw across Booger's neck and pinned him to the ground as if to say, "Chasing *my* chickens comes with dire consequences; don't even think about it."

The boys remember how Booger loved to ride in the back of Gail's truck and utterly own the road. He was a fearsome stock dog that would chase anything on four legs. They said he probably would have taken on a bear because he wasn't afraid of anything. Gail would be clipping along at thirty miles per hour and if a dog rushed out to bark at the edge of the road Booger would jump on him. The truck would be going too fast for the stray dog to keep up with, but Booger timed his leap perfectly so that he would land right on top of the barking dog just as the truck got even with it. They would roll in the dust as he snarled and snapped until the startled stray could get out from under him and high-tail it for home with Booger on its heels. Gail would have to back the truck down the road and holler, "Boog! Get back in this truck!" Booger made it his business to let every barking dog in the county know the consequence of accosting the Bryan truck. He was a flying bundle of fur that inspired them to stay on their porches, or at least behind their fences, whenever they saw *his truck* coming down the road.

Booger also had a bad habit of chasing Gail's brood mares that were heavy with foal. One day Gail looked up to see Booger chasing one of the mares around the south pasture just for fun, so he yelled at him to stop. Just as Gail's voice met Booger's ears, that big mare kicked at Booger and caught him under the chin. It flipped him over in a complete somersault so that he landed on his feet going the other direction. If the mare hadn't kicked on the run, she would have hit him solid and knocked him silly. But since she was at a full gallop and didn't hit him full-force, Booger just learned a good lesson and ran off whimpering to get his bearings. Gail said the Lord was lending a helping hand that day because the timing was perfect for keeping Booger alive while making sure he never chased another mare. Yes, Booger has a book of stories all his own, but we had to give him to another family that turned him into a regular cattle dog. The last we heard, he was chasing bulls and finding ways to get them where he wanted them to go. They told us that he would get a mouthful of tail and hang on for the ride, bouncing from side to side behind the bull and hitting the ground about every five feet. The poor creature would bolt forward, kicking at air and bellowing to no avail. Booger was King with the bull at his mercy.

The second year at our little ranch we received access to the whole property, thirty acres, for eighty dollars per month! Gail was delighted because his desire was to keep brood mares and raise registered quarter horses. As a girl, I had experienced the common childhood longing of having a horse to ride. Living on the homestead at that time of my life, I look back wondering if the rolling hills and beautiful Idaho countryside spurred that desire. We never had horses then—except Coalie, my dad's work horse. Now, as my husband's enthusiasm for breaking wild broncs gained strength and took up residence in my back yard, I was not so anxious to be in the saddle! But the boys loved it and it cultivated some "wild west" skills, adventures and memories that they still cherish. By this time, Squaw had foaled again and her filly, Barbie Doll was added to our collection. Twister was raised like a pup and was as gentle as a lamb, but Gail broke all of our horses to ride and took on several jobs for other people doing the same. Lark, however, was a different story. He was one of those horses who could never learn, and his stories come later.

One day Gail and Grandpa Bryan came home from the auction with a pretty black horse for Mark. Midnight was half Arab and half quarter horse, strong and fine with plenty of endurance for upcoming hunting trips. Gypsy was passed on to David, and so it continued through the years. Later, when David was ready for a full-sized horse, he got Midnight and Mark rode Twister. Gail did such a wonderful job training the horses that the whole family was able to enjoy them, but this area of ranch life was more about the boys. They have many stories to pass along to their children and grandchildren, just as Grandpa

Gail would do if he was here.

More animals kept arriving, though some of them were temporary residents. Gail started buying a few calves to raise for beef, and we bought a couple of pigs to butcher as well. A large flock of pullets were purchased for the same purpose but, after attempting to butcher one chicken myself, I was more than willing to pay someone else to do it. The next time I saw them they were neatly wrapped and freezer-ready! Darlin', our Nubian goat, had a batch of four kids during this time and the children remember this event. Gail woke them up early that morning to run out to the barn and see the new babies. The three that lived were affectionately named Piper, Pepper, and Pippin. Darlin' birthed several sets of babies throughout the years, which we sold each time. So the little ranch at Emmett provided a full farm experience for our family. We learned valuable lessons together, gained priceless knowledge, and gathered cherished memories from every colorful characteristic!

Ranch life was not without its trials, however! One year we bought a bunch of Herefords and they all got pinkeye. We doctored them all through the summer, shooing away masses of vexatious flies and mosquitoes which were thick in the warm weather and spread the disease. The calves recovered and we were able to sell them at the auction, although our profits were cut significantly due to the money we paid out for medication.

Hunting Adventures

Our boys had many opportunities to experience extreme sports on high mountain hunting trips with their dad, Grandpa Bryan, and sometimes other friends. I was often on these trips with them but I stayed home when they went hunting with Lark. Lark was a horse that Gail had taken on to break for someone else. He believed there was no better training for a good horse than to get him "trail-broke" in a mountain setting. Mark describes this hunting trip as "the time Lark almost killed Dad and Grandpa." Grandpa Bryan was riding Barbie Doll and had Lark on a lead rope behind him. They were riding on a narrow trail beside a steep cliff when Lark decided to express his displeasure and began bucking toward the opposite side of the trail, wrapping the lead rope around grandpa's back. The rope became taut between his hand and Lark's harness on the opposite side and yanked him right out of the saddle. He and Lark both tumbled head over heels, literally, down the cliff. It was very steep and Lark's bucking fit sent him over the edge with zero control, landing him upside down in a bush far below. He fell so far that we could hardly see him from the trail. Grandpa didn't fall so far but was beat up pretty bad with scrapes and bruises. Mark relates Gail's response when he saw Lark's four legs sticking up out of the bushes below. "Well, either he broke his legs and will die down there or he's learned his lesson and might actually be a decent horse after this."

Mixing hazardous terrain with jumpy horses always terrified me; but these episodes were all part of the adventure for the men and boys. They figured that if they lived to tell about it they just added another great story to their collection. Jim came to pick up Becca for a date shortly after this incident and Doc Bryan answered the door. Jim saw his two black eyes and scraped-up face and exclaimed, "Oh, Doc! What in the world happened to you?"

"Why, Jim," Grandpa drawled; "you should've seen the other guy!"

The next time they took Lark along, Gail was riding Lark with a scabbard attached carrying Mark's rifle on one side. Lark went to bucking and veered off into a dry creek bed full of big rocks. He went down and Gail flew off. Lark rolled on the gun and broke the stock off. This time, as the story goes, Gail said, "He almost ended his own life this time because, if the stock hadn't broke off that rifle I'd have shot that fool horse in the head!" That was Lark's last hunting trip. Gail decided he was a "flat-lander" that could never learn the mountain skills and would keep having accidents and causing injuries to himself and his riders. He said Lark was dangerous and unpredictable and might kill somebody with his foolishness. Truth be told, I'm sure Lark was just as happy with that decision as Gail was.

Another extreme excursion happened one Fourth of July during the boys' high school years. Gail and a friend were taking the boys to Sage Hen Reservoir for a three-day horseback ride to Cascade, Idaho where I would pick them up. Gail and I were in his one-ton Chevy with two horses loaded in the stock rack on the back. Our friend, Curtis, was behind us pulling a two-horse trailer which carried another horse, plus our donkey, Byrd, for packing their gear. Mark was riding with Curtis in the other truck. Gail had borrowed the horse trailer and had cautioned Curtis to make sure it was securely attached to his trailer hitch before they left Emmett. We later discovered that the ball on his hitch was the wrong size for the borrowed trailer and didn't fit right; but Gail had trusted our friend to know better than to take such a chance.

Somewhere between Sweet and Ola is a spot where the creek is several hundred feet below the road. What saved them that day was a dirt berm about two feet high along the edge of the road. Mark says they were driving along and felt a bump. He looked in the side mirror and saw the trailer drifting to the edge of the road. It had come loose, but because it was a tandem axle the tongue didn't hit the ground. The stock animals inside must have been balanced just right because the trailer kept coasting down the road at about thirty miles per hour toward that drop-off. Suddenly, the tongue hit that berm and stuck fast, flipping the trailer. It did a complete somersault, flipping onto its top and then onto its wheels again, with a horse and donkey inside! Curtis stopped and they ran back to the wreck, thinking the animals would be dead or badly injured.

Meanwhile, up the road a ways, Gail had realized that Curtis' truck was not behind us anymore and we began to wonder if they had stopped somewhere. "I've been watching for them in the mirror and it's been quite a while," he inferred with concern. "If I don't see them soon I'm going to have to turn around and go back." Soon Gail found a place to turn the truck around and we went back to look for them. As we came around a corner, Gail saw the wreck and exclaimed, "Dear God! They've turned that trailer over!"

My heart sank into panic, thinking they were hurt or even fatally injured! Then I saw Mark standing beside the truck with his arms folded, looking at the wreckage and I refuted, "No, they didn't! The trailer is sitting upright!"

"Honey," Gail countered, "can't you see that the top of it is smashed in?" Then I realized that the trailer had come loose and was on the side of the road, badly smashed; but I still breathed a prayer of thanks at the site of my unscathed son!

"That trailer came loose;" Gail said, as cool as a cucumber. "I told Curtis to check that hitch." We parked the truck and got out to survey the damage. Gail walked around the wreckage, thinking it through and deciding on the best strategy. With a lot of effort he was able to get the back doors of the trailer open and reach Byrd's lead rope. The frightened donkey was hunched under the crushed roof but, with Gail's calming encouragement, she began to scoot backwards bit by bit until she got her hind feet onto the ground and pulled herself free. Her soft, brown eyes were worried and apprehensive as if to say, "Why did you let me get hurt?" Gail spoke comforting words as he patted her softly, and tied her nearby so he could focus on the horse. The trailer window near the horse's head had broken during the accident and now brandished shards of glass that protruded dangerously from its edges. Gail worked slowly and gently to encourage him to pull his forefeet back over the edge of the manger wall where both legs had been caught during the wreck. The horse also had one foot over its lead rope, which Gail could not get to. He removed the middle wall between the two stock bays to give the horse more room to maneuver, but realized he would have to startle him with loud commands in order to get him to move. The poor animal thrashed and jumped, pulled and bumped his head again and again on the compressed metal roof as he struggled to free himself. It was loud and traumatic for him and for me! I stood nearby watching anxiously and praying aloud in desperate tones, "Jesus! Jesus, help us! Jesus!"

Gail turned and looked at me. "Honey," he said calmly as he pointed across the road. "See that log over there? I want you to go across the road and sit on that log." My verbal anxiety, even in prayer form, was not helping my husband or the horse! So I took my intercession across the highway and watched the frantic commotion for some time. Unable to sit still any longer, I finally came back across the road, although there was really nothing I could do and Gail's directive had been the wiser choice! Finally the horse jerked himself free of the wreckage and backed out onto the gravel, muscles quivering and sides heaving. He had conquered his tangled trap, escaping with minor cuts and bruises. Both animals were banged up pretty bad, with cuts and scrapes, and obviously traumatized. We had to get them home but the trailer was no longer useable. "Getting them out of this wreck was the easy part," Gail observed. "Loading them up in another rig after what they've been through will be the challenge."

I was relieved to get back to the ranch in Emmett after such a close call. If the trailer had plummeted down that hill it would have killed both the horse and donkey. If it would have crossed the highway in the other direction and hit an oncoming vehicle we would have had human fatalities. Only by the mercy of God could we have rolled a horse trailer end over end—loaded with stock—with so little damage. We had cuts, scrapes and raw nerves, but no broken legs and no broken necks. Usually a broken leg on a stock animal is the end of its life because it never heals up strong enough for normal use again. We had the animals checked out by the veterinarian and they were both fine. I was so shaken after this near-catastrophe that I thought they would forego the trip. I said, "Well, maybe the Lord didn't want you to go."

"Absolutely, I'm going!" Gail retorted. "We're all here and ready for the trip and we're going." So they re-loaded, giving up their pack animal and finding a fresh horse to replace the injured one. We loaded up and drove straight back, arriving safely at the drop-off location where I left them to set out on their three-day ride. Gail had told me precisely when and where to pick them up at the end of the route. So, on the third day, I drove to Cascade with some old friends of ours who had showed up for a surprise visit at the ranch in Emmett. We had a wonderful drive along beautiful Highway 55 and I was glad for the company, wondering how long I might have to wait for my adventurers to arrive at the designated pick-up point. I could not humanly imagine that anyone could be so accurate about an arrival time when there were no guarantees against unexpected delays or mishaps along the trail. I was there on time, however, and as soon as I arrived and parked my vehicle, I looked up and saw my four riders coming down the trail on their horses with Smoky running happily beside them; precisely at the hour that Gail had expected them to return! I was utterly amazed, and so relieved that they were all safe and sound.

We all got out of the car to stretch our legs and greet them. The boys were all smiles and so excited about their trip. They had so much to tell, and when I noticed that our friend, Curtis, was black and blue on one side of his face, I knew that "the rest of the story" would be forthcoming!

Mark recalls, "Without Byrd as our pack animal we had all kinds of stuff tied to our saddles for the ride. Way up in the mountains, Curtis was riding Barbie Doll with a bunch of pans tied to his saddle. Smoky had been off exploring in the woods and had lagged behind, sniffing everything in sight as dogs do. We rode out into a meadow and when Smoky caught up with us he darted from the shadows out into the sunlight. Barbie Doll knew Smoky well, but when she saw his dark shadow slinking from the woods in her peripheral vision she thought he was a wolf. She jumped forward causing all those pans to bang together, which made her jump again. Curtis grabbed the reins and said, "Whoa!" leaning forward to correct his balance just as the horse threw her head up in response to the bit. She smacked him in the forehead and split him open from the top of one eyebrow right up to his hairline. Dad put a butterfly bandage on the wound but it was the least of Curtis's worries; all he could think about was how mad his wife would be about the scar it would leave on his forehead."

Life Abundantly

Life was full at Emmett, and the kids enjoyed things they would not have experienced in other places: our many animal adventures; floating the river; swimming and "boogie-boarding" in the big canals; outdoor adventures along the railroad tracks; playing basketball on our dusty half-court where Gail hung a hoop on the tack barn; their treehouse in the far pasture where an old tree had been split by lightning; rodeos and county fairs; livestock auctions; and the many friends and relatives who came to visit because we had room. The boys got a tractor tire tube somewhere and put it out on the front lawn. It must have been at least two feet thick and five feet across; they jumped on it like a trampoline. They had hours and hours of free, creative, outdoor play with each other and with friends. The memories are countless and each of the children could write about them in four different ways! After Rebecca was married, she wrote a nostalgic country song called "Home Again"[2] about her memories as a teenager on our little ranch.

> *"Daddy was workin' close by in the barn;*
> *An' Mama took the laundry off the line, whistlin';*
> *Sister was readin', and two brothers ridin';*
> *But I sat high on a fencepost…listenin'.*

> *"The meadowlarks flew and the mill whistle blew;*
> *A freight train rumbled way down the track;*
> *If somethin' should stop it, I might wanna hop it;*
> *But where was it goin'? Would it bring me back?*
> *Bring me home?*

> *"The grass was cool and the shadows grew;*
> *The water-skipper sat, not twitchin' a leg;*
> *And high in the hedge, right close to the edge,*
> *Sat a neat little nest with a tiny blue egg.*

> *"The hound dog frolicked in the pasture spring;*
> *The horses raised dust, racin' round and round;*
> *The little calf bawled, and the kitty-cat squalled,*
> *And I gathered memories from every sound…*
> *Memories…*

> *"On a hot summer night, when supper was done,*
> *The brilliant stars were so thick in the sky;*
> *But the day would dawn when they'd all be gone.*
> *To the home I loved, I would say, "Goodbye".*

> *"Then very soon, came the big, orange moon;*

I stood there wishin' it would never end;
But as it climbed higher, the Night dimmed its fire;
For the loveliest things have seasons, friend…
And seasons end…

Chorus: "Seasons come and season go,
And Time won't bring 'em back.
Things will change; but listen for
a "whistle" down the track.
Sometimes, that train comes rollin' in;
And, though it's not the same as then,
With memories, songs, and those I love,
I feel like I am Home again.
Home again; Home…again!"

Gail also learned horse-shoeing through correspondence and took shoeing jobs as well as keeping all of our own horses shod. He planted alfalfa one year and sold his crop. The kids had the tractor and hay-wagon experience—and the hay fever, too! We all learned and grew in ways we never thought we would; we had all kinds of opportunities and engaged in many activities that added a special dimension of wonderful to our lives. There were many times I cried and prayed, wondering if Gail's flight from the ministry had robbed our family of God's best. Yet here we were, and I knew my best course of action was to do what I had always done: take everything I had and do my very best with it. We worked hard and we played a little, too. We watched wonderful things happening in the lives of our children as well as good things in the many lives we touched along the way, not discounting all the precious memories of those who imparted rich treasures into each of *us*!

Mealtime around the table was important to us, whether it was spent with just the six of us or shared with family and friends. Our menus were always simple. We had lots of fish and wild game because Gail was a hunter and fisherman. For breakfast we had cereal and toast; lunch was usually a sandwich with milk, and sometimes soup; then a big meal for dinner of meat – venison or fish—vegetables, and various breads. Potatoes, gravy and biscuits were favorites at our house. We didn't have many salads because fresh vegetables and fruits were expensive; but I canned or froze fruits and vegetables as often as possible, as well as all kinds of pickles and relishes which we enjoyed year round. I was never into gourmet foods or looking for new recipes; just providing good nutrition for my family and taking care of everyone's needs. We also had a lot of cornbread and beans, usually pintos with hamburger and other chili ingredients. My mother's meatloaf recipe was a favorite, too. We had lots of enchiladas and spaghetti, tacos, soups and stews. We were all happy with the basics and—heaven-blessed by the hand of our Provider— every bite apparently provided all the nutrition we needed to thrive! Our family remained energetic and healthy. When we were first married Gail had favorite foods from his mom's kitchen, such as her famous Pineapple Refrigerator Dessert. Like most young men, however, after a few years of my cooking his favorites gravitated to the things that we enjoyed together. Our family was always fond of a good roast, usually elk or venison, with plenty of mashed potatoes and gravy! We added hot rolls with real butter, and Grape-up to drink—grape juice (sometimes home canned) mixed with 7-Up. Corn was a favorite vegetable; cherry Jell-O with sliced bananas was popular. These items created a favorite family menu that both of my daughters incorporated into their family meal planning as well. It even became the favorite "birthday dinner" of choice for several family members into the third generation—my grandchildren. Favorite desserts included Lemon Meringue Pie, Preacher's Cake (a moist, dense chocolate cake that needs no eggs), peach or apricot cobblers with cream poured over them, or ice cream on the side; apple-nut spice cake, carrot cake with cream cheese frosting, cheese cake, angel food cake with orange glaze, bananas and whipped cream. Our cookie favorites were always oatmeal or peanut butter. Many of these favorites from their childhood traveled with my daughters as they set up their own households later; particularly my mother's meatloaf, Preacher's Cake, peanut butter cookies, Lemon Meringue pie, and my vanilla-laced version of Pumpkin Pie, which is never without plenty of whipped cream and walnuts on top!

Homemaker, wife, and mother were my most cherished roles. I enjoyed every stage of raising my children but the happiest time was when they were all teenagers in Emmett. Even though I held some seasonal jobs at the local cannery and at Ore-Ida Foods during those years, I kept up on all the home duties, church life, and family life because these were my highest priorities. I considered my "outside jobs" not only as provision for making a few more ends meet, but God-ordained opportunities to witness to fellow employees. The most important experience gained during those times was seeing how God gave me favor with employers to receive promotions and advancements. Top performance was a personal goal that Gail and I both gained from the work ethic our parents modeled during our childhood. It was developed from Colossians 3:22-24, *"Servants, obey in all things your masters according to the flesh; not with eyeservice, as menpleasers; but in singleness of heart, fearing God: And whatsoever ye do, do it heartily, as to the Lord, and not unto men; Knowing that of the Lord ye shall receive the reward of the inheritance: for ye serve the Lord Christ."* We always knew that every job, whether paid or volunteer, was not only a service to God, but another chance to shine and to exemplify God's standards of integrity and responsibility to the world. We held these standards in our own jobs and passed them on to our four children. Consequently, they were always ambitious. Mark always had a job, beginning with his first paper route at age ten in Long Beach, California. When we first moved to Emmett, he got a job at his elementary school working for the janitor! He would get there early and dust all the floors with a commercial dust mop, shake out rugs and sweep around the doors. Later he got hired at Agg's Auto Parts and worked there until he was out of high school. All the kids worked seasonal jobs in the orchards and packing houses. David set sprinklers in the fruit orchards and did a variety of jobs for Sanders Packing. Dorcas worked at Roe Ann Drive-In for a while. In addition to part-time jobs, the boys played basketball and Becca joined the Color Guard in the high school band. When Becca was a sophomore in high school she won an old red Ford in a Sunday School contest. It was long, and had a black spot on the hood so, although she was disappointed by the look of it and rejected it as "her car", this jalopy provided an extra vehicle that could be shared for all their transportation needs. When they started getting their drivers' licenses they were able to drive to many of their teenage destinations on their own. Our kids usually enjoyed school and got very good grades, although some of them had to work harder than others. They were loved by their teachers and coaches and conscious of shining the light of Jesus to their peers. They were nominated for offices, particularly the boys, and participated in clubs and student government receiving honors and awards for their efforts. They all chose good friendships and had honorable reputations among their classmates, teachers and church leaders in our home town. We got high compliments from many people in various positions who worked or associated with our teenagers and praised their performance and character; we were proud to be their parents!

All of us enjoyed traveling, though Becca sometimes got carsick and had to get out and walk a bit in the fresh air. We couldn't afford expensive vacations but we loved the mountains and enjoyed camping. Gail loved to rough it, which was less expensive, so he never called ahead to reserve campsites. He loved to drive until he found a secluded, flat spot off the road where we could set up camp without paying the fees. He always put together a great campsite, but Becca hated anything dirty, dangerous, or scary. She always wanted to be safe and clean! So if anyone was not completely enthralled with the experience, it may have been her. Dorcas cooperated with everything and the boys were in the height of their glory! We had great times together.

One of the happiest trips we made was in our big Dodge truck when we went to Montana to visit my sister Dorcas' family. The kids thoroughly enjoyed their cousins as we picnicked and played in the water at Horseshoe Lake. It was a brilliant turquoise and very deep, but we could see to the very bottom because it was so clear and clean. Before going on to Glacier National Park, we crossed the border into Canada. Gail never traveled without his guns and we had a pistol and several rifles in our possession. I remember Gail being surprised that he had to leave his firearms at the border, which we had not expected. We ate dinner at a very unfriendly restaurant and kept our Canadian visit short, opting to spend our time at Glacier instead. The kids loved riding in the back of the truck and seeing all the gorgeous scenery and wildlife. We picked huckleberries and slept in a tent. I was slightly nervous about having bear visitors, as there were numbers of them in this national park and we had heard frightening reports of recent bear attacks. They must have been busy elsewhere because we had no unwelcome guests! We traveled down through Montana and came home through eastern Idaho. It was a memorable trip for all of us.

As much as we enjoyed our family getaways, "there's no place like home" and we were always glad to get back. I loved the routines of daily living and could never rest until everything was unpacked, washed, repaired and put away! The kids were always good helpers because we taught them that part of the trip was getting everything back in place when it was over. This was the most memorable excursion as a family during our years in Emmett.

Gail and I also made some life-long friendships in this chapter of our lives. We had cherished times with the Penix family from our church and Jim Penix was Gail's best friend and hunting buddy for many years. There was also a local ranch family who had several kids in the same grades as ours; Becca, Mark and David all had a Bryson in their class. The two younger ones, Alan and Joe, were best of friends with Mark and David up into their adult years. The Brysons also took Booger, our dog, when we moved from Emmett, and ended up with even more stories to tell about him than we had!

Faithful Pursuits

If I could choose a family custom to pass on to my own children and grandchildren it would be having family prayer and Bible reading every evening. I talked about it earlier as Family Altar, a practice that laid my own foundations. Everything in life was related to God, and our major focus was learning how to please Him. To know the will of God and to *do it* was what we were taught. My childhood experiences of worship, dedication to God's house, family camaraderie, industrious work habits, personal responsibility, and an orderly, well-supervised home were standards I continued. These patterns of my own upbringing were the same ones that I used in raising my own children. I followed all of these examples as my children grew up, to the best of my ability, through the various seasons of life. I was devoted to providing for them the building blocks of a strong foundation just as my parents gave to me. Sometimes I had to do it alone but, seeing my children now, I can say that it was worth every difficulty I had to endure in the hard times.

When we first arrived at Emmett, we had visited several churches and found that, although we had always attended the Assemblies of God, the Foursquare Church was more progressive at the time and a better fit for our teenagers. Gail was still in a state of discouragement from his personal failures of the past but he wanted a good church for the kids. He had no desire to get back into full-time ministry but was a strong witness to his co-workers at the mill. He eventually began to take periodic meetings at small churches in the area or speaking engagements for Full Gospel Business Men's Fellowship. The crowds were always blessed and encouraged and Gail's preaching was always anointed and powerful. He always loved the Word of God, and valued our Family Altar times with the kids every night that he was at home. We read the Bible, gave testimonies, talked about spiritual things that were relevant to the children's' current experience, and listened to Bob Mumford's messages on cassette tape. He was one of several popular and powerful preachers of the times who provided many wonderful teachings that enriched our lives.

We did a lot of family singing during this time, too. Back in Redlands, I had purchased ukuleles for all the kids with S&H Green Stamps. While we lived in Long Beach they all learned to play but Mark and Becca became quite proficient. They enjoyed recording all kinds of songs together on the old reel-to-reel tape recorder. Becca had also pursued piano on her own after learning chords at Appleton; she loved it and became quite capable at playing by ear. So by the time we got to Emmett, all the kids had an appetite for music and enjoyed singing together and playing their instruments. Gail and I had also taught Mark to play the guitar and he picked it up very quickly. He saved his money from cherry picking to buy an electric one. David had learned in grade school to play the big string bass and he later graduated to the electric bass guitar. He and Mark played their electric instruments together wherever our family went for singing engagements. We practiced all kinds of gospel songs to sing as a family group wherever Gail went to preach. The girls and I had several matching outfits and sang many trio numbers. Becca was writing lots of songs by the time she was in High School; but she was extremely shy about singing them as solos. She sang like a bird at home, but stage fright kept her safe inside the family ensemble in public. After the girls left home, the boys received invitations to sing at banquets, churches and even school functions. One time at a high school talent show, they wore matching outfits and played their instruments while Mark sang, "Pass it On" and "A Bright New World", two songs by Ralph Carmichael. The entire gymnasium gave them a standing ovation, whooping and whistling just as they would do at a basketball game.

All of our children were also growing steadily in their own relationships with the Lord. When the boys were thirteen and fifteen years old, Gail preached a two-week revival in a tiny mountain town called Sweet, Idaho. He fasted for three days, while working hard at the saw mill. Mark noticed that Gail wasn't taking a lunch to work and asked me about it. I told him that his dad was fasting for the revival meeting and on the last day of that fast Gail came home and said, "Well, I have the Word. I know what I'm going to preach." It made an impact on Mark that he still remembers because he learned that God will meet us when we seek him with all of our hearts; when we are persistent, God will answer prayer. The meetings were good and God was moving among the people. Both of our sons participated in ministry with the anointing of the Holy Spirit. David gave an exhortation and an altar call during which several people gave their hearts to the Lord. During one of the last meetings, Mark had a vision and he remembers it like this:

> The service went a long time and we were all standing, worshipping
> God. One of the reasons I remember that so well is because one of
> our cousins who had not been serving the Lord was there that night—
> standing with his hands in the air. To me it was a serious revival for him
> to be worshipping like that with everyone else. It was also new to me at

that time to stand so long with my hands in the air. We didn't do that a lot in our Pentecostal churches. We would stand and shout, or wave our arms and say, "Glory!" But to stand still with arms extended and just worship, as the Bible describes the scene around the throne of God, was rather unusual for all of us. So the worship had continued for some time and I remember looking around and thinking, "Wow! Something's going on!" As I turned back to worship again and lifted both hands, I looked up and suddenly I saw a vision of the Lord. There He was before my eyes! I could just look right through the heavens and see the throne of God. The Lord was looking down from the throne with a smile on his face; looking at me, and all of us.

"Just as I saw this, the worship began to die down and Dad said, 'It's been a wonderful day, and we thank the Lord for what he's done. At this time we need to bring the service to a close.' It was late because the service had gone almost an hour beyond the normal closing time. Nobody seemed to care about that because they were so amazed at the presence of God.

"I was still looking up at the heavens and, as the service came to a close, the throne began to turn. The Lord's face started to turn away, and a tear came in his eye. I had the overwhelming impression that the Lord was delighting in this communion, so pleased to shine down his love and grace upon us as we worshipped. He savored this time with us and when we became too weary to continue it just made him sad because He was treasuring it. He was wistful, and longing for us to stay. The scripture came to my mind, 'The spirit is willing but the flesh is weak.' It was so authentic, and these few seconds of spiritual reality made a lifelong impact on my heart. When the vision ended, nothing else seemed as real. The crowd was dispersing but it didn't seem as real; several times I looked back at the ceiling in awe, like there should still be something there because I saw it right in front of me.

"I was in the back seat on the driver's side, looking out the window over Black Canyon Reservoir on the way home to Emmett. I just stared up at the sky; I couldn't turn my face away because I kept expecting to see something. I had mentioned to mom on the way out of the church that I thought I'd seen a vision. So as we drove home she asked, 'Mark, do you want to tell us what you saw?' They were amazed and we all sat quietly. It was a holy recognition that the Lord had done something miraculous; he had been with us in a powerful way.

"As soon as we got home I went upstairs to my room and looked out the window again. My heart was still tuned to the supernatural and my spirit was saying, 'I know you're there; I saw you.' The next morning I woke early, threw on some clothes, and went outside. I walked down Tyler Road toward the railroad tracks watching the light of dawn appear in the sky, because I was facing East in the Sweet church when I saw the vision. The clouds were bright with the morning light as I walked all the way to the tracks watching the sunrise, and looking for something. The awe of what I had seen lasted for several days; it was a gift and a privilege that I will never forget.

Remembering Cherished Traditions

We had our family traditions as everyone does and birthdays were always special. We celebrated with a cake, the "Happy Birthday" song, cards and gifts from those who could give. As the children grew older, their gifts graduated from simple coloring books, puzzles, and games, to practical and useable things such as socks, shirts, or other clothing items. Gail always tried to get something manly for the boys, like pocket knives, flashlights, hats, ropes, hunting or hiking supplies. I often got personal items for the girls such as beauty supplies, perfumes and lotions. Our birthday celebrations were always simple and only with our immediate family. A few times I had birthday parties for each of the children where they could invite some friends, but not every year. On these occasions we had decorations, balloons, games and prizes, cake, ice cream, and punch. I was never over-indulgent because it was about honoring the birthday person, which could always be accomplished without putting on a big, expensive party.

One memorable birthday party for my girls, whose birthdays were only ten days apart in April, was a slumber party with their good friends from church. Dorcas was a senior, and Rebecca a junior, in high school. Together we planned the party and the girls each invited their two closest friends. They played games, laughed, told stories, sang songs, and just had a lot of fun together. I made dinner for them that night and then we had gifts, cards, punch, cake and ice cream. They stayed up very late, but Dorcas and her friends called it a night sooner than Becca and hers. The next morning we had a "grand slam" breakfast with pancakes, eggs and bacon, orange juice and fruit. All the girls had a great time and we took pictures to preserve the memories.

Looking back, I wish I would have started a new tradition: I would have taken a birthday photo of each family member and had them write a testimony to add to the scrapbook each year. This would have been a wonderful record to pass on to future generations showing a Christian perspective of their heritage. Other accounts to add would be dates of significant events, such as when and how they gave their hearts to Jesus; when and where they were water baptized and baptized in the Holy Spirit; times they were healed or experienced special blessings in their lives; or times of supernatural protection from God. The scripture tells us to talk of the wonderful works of the Lord, and to pass them on to our posterity. The busier life becomes the harder it is to remember all the miracles, answers to prayer, spiritual milestones and personal conquests in our family history. Yet these are the very foundation stones upon which future generations will stand in preparation for their own journeys.

Easter, always being on a Sunday, usually began with an early breakfast and often the tradition of Easter Sunrise Service where we would go to a hilltop and hold a short Resurrection Service just as the sun came up over the city. Sometimes a Sunrise Breakfast would be held at the church instead. In Idaho especially, the spring weather was often chilly that early in the morning, but it added to the excitement! We always wore our most special outfits to church, and once in a while got something new to wear. On this exhilarating spiritual holiday we often had friends or family join us for the Easter Dinner after church: baked ham, mashed potatoes with gravy, tossed salad or Jell-O, hot vegetables, rolls and butter, punch, cake or pies for dessert. This was a happy afternoon of visiting and celebrating Christ's resurrection, and sharing our Hope of Heaven with friends and family.

We didn't have a particular tradition for Independence Day with our children, other than putting up a flag and having a picnic in the park. When the kids were teenagers at Emmett, we tried to attend Camp Meeting at this time of year whenever possible. This had been such an important part of our own history together that we wanted the children to enjoy the same experience. However, working regular jobs was different from being in the ministry and we couldn't always get away to attend the meetings. We went whenever we could so that they could see this special event that was part of their legacy. When we moved back to Emmett the towns had expanded in the area and the camp grounds were not as rural as they had been in the early days. The location in Nampa was the same, however, and still full of nostalgic memories for Gail and me!

Our Thanksgiving meal was the traditional roasted turkey with cranberry sauce, mashed potatoes and gravy. Our stuffing was the main family recipe that was passed down. We made it with cornbread, onions and celery sautéed in butter, parsley, sage, salt, pepper, egg, and a few chopped giblets boiled before stuffing the turkey. Three of my children and several of my granddaughters still use this recipe for their holiday menus.

Over the years, I think we enjoyed the Christmas holiday most. It was the crowning celebration. We loved being together in the cherished, family atmosphere of our home. In our early years, we were distanced from our families geographically, so we became accustomed to celebrating with only our immediate family instead of other relatives. I always prepared a beautiful Christmas dinner with roasted turkey, cranberry sauce, cornbread dressing, mashed potatoes and gravy, corn, Jell-O salad, hot rolls with butter, and pumpkin pie for dessert with whipped cream.

The music of Christmas was always a big part of my life, growing up as well as in raising my own family. As a child I learned "When I was a Tiny, Wee Baby"—a cute children's song with the Christmas message of the Christ child. Another favorite was the song of how to spell "C-H-R-I-S-T-M-A-S", each letter representing a part of the story. These songs were passed on to my children and grandchildren. As I learned to play instruments, I usually ended up singing the carols that were the easiest to play. For that reason my all-time favorites are still "Joy to the World", "Silent Night", "Away in a Manger", and "O Come Let us Adore Him". I also love to sing "Tell Me the Story of Jesus", "Jesus Came from God Above", "Wonderful Story of Love", and "Come On, Ring Those Bells". I love to hear "O Holy Night", and many others that I don't play myself.

The famous carols that tell the true story of the incarnation are beautiful to me: "Hark, the Herald Angels Sing", "The First Noel", "It Came Upon a Midnight Clear", "O Little Town of Bethlehem"—I never tire of hearing or singing them year after year at Christmas time, and often in between.

I enjoyed decorating simply; we had a beautiful silver tinsel tree for several years with a rotating color wheel that changed the shiny tree to red, orange, green and blue as it turned. I always enjoyed nativities, candles, bells and stars. We never celebrated with Santa Claus, as Gail and I agreed when we were young to always make it a holy holiday instead, incorporating the family Christmas traditions from my childhood. Gail was diligent to teach our children the importance of focusing on Jesus and why He came as the Ultimate Gift for mankind, rather than commercializing the holiday with the aim of giving and getting personal gifts. We practiced the giving of simple items, wrapped with lots of love, and taught our children that the gifts were to commemorate God's gift to the world, his only Son for our salvation. Gail was a wonderful facilitator, initiating the reading of the Christmas story from God's Word, singing, sharing testimonies and sometimes having Communion together. We sang the Christmas carols and songs of the Savior, often recording them along with testimonies on cassette tapes—which was the modern media of the day when the kids were teenagers. Sometimes we even agreed to forego the exchange of gifts and to focus only on giving to others outside our family. We went Christmas caroling and took food baskets to families in need. This concept was the basis for the most meaningful Christmas we ever had, without a doubt, when we lived on the Emmett ranch. The kids were teenagers and we decided not to buy gifts for each other but, instead, to pool our money and make food baskets for poor families. Then we planned to deliver them and sing Christmas carols at each destination. It was a joy to all of us and all the families we visited were greatly blessed. Afterward we had a Christmas dinner at home and a peaceful time of singing, worship and communion together. It was a wonderful memory-maker that made a lasting impact on our teenagers during this impressionable season of their lives.

When our children were grown and could come home for Christmas we had such happy times. We made cassette tapes of the Christmases that we hosted after they were grown. Following our festive dinner we would gather in the living room, adults and children together. Gail would start by singing, "Oh, Come Let Us Adore Him", and other worshipful Christmas songs. After worship he read the Christmas story and other scriptures, followed by sharing and prayer. Each family with their little ones prepared songs, stories, or poems to share as a love gift to Jesus. We focused on Christmas representing His birthday and usually sang, "Happy Birthday" to Jesus as well.

The legacy that Gail and I wanted to pass on to our children and grandchildren was continued. I know that my children had spiritual Christmases in their own homes after they married, taking with them what we gave and adding some of their own traditions. One of them celebrated Jesus' birthday by having each person write a "thank you" to Jesus to hang on the tree on Christmas Eve. Then, in the morning, after the Christmas story was read, they would each take their letter from the tree and read it to Jesus as a gift to Him and a testimony to the rest of the family.

There are many creative and inspirational ways to celebrate the true meaning of Christmas and to honor the Lord while having a wonderful, memorable time with family and loved ones. When it comes to holidays, parents can give their children no greater blessing than to incorporate creative traditions that minimize commercialization and help them to practice things that celebrate our Christian foundations of faith—the birth of our Savior, and his glorious resurrection!

Our Young Adults

After Dorcas graduated from High School, she moved to Boise to help at the Stone House girls' home. This was a ministry for kids who had been saved out of drugs and the hippy culture. The Jesus People movement was going strong and this ministry gave some of these newly saved young people a place to live and be mentored in God's Word while getting their lives on track. They were required to sell peanut brittle during the day in Boise neighborhoods to earn their keep at the Stone House. The pastors who ran the place held meetings several nights each week that were open to the public; and our family participated periodically with songs, testimonies, and Gail's preaching. Dorcas lived there for about a year but this organization adhered to the Oneness, or Jesus Only, doctrine. They began to pressure Dorcas about getting re-baptized in the name of Jesus only and she realized it was time for her to come home. She was hired at the Gem County Courthouse in Emmett where she used shorthand to take notes in court proceedings; it was a very stressful job.

Meanwhile, Becca had taken a test in her senior bookkeeping class at school that placed her high on the list for clerical jobs with the State of Idaho. She was hired at the Capitol Building in Boise the summer after she graduated, and commuted in a car pool from Emmett until she got married a year later. Becca had met Jim at the Foursquare Youth Camp in Corbett, Oregon just before her junior year of high school. They started seeing each other in her senior year, and dated for a year and a half before they married and moved to Boise.

In May, 1973 our first fledgling left the nest to pursue her own dreams with the love of her life. I felt like I had an arm amputated. Our songbird was gone and I missed her music that had filled our ranch house these past five years. Our trio felt handicapped with her alto voice missing and nothing was the same again, although we improvised the best we could; Dorcas and the boys kept up the music. We knew the Howells, Jim and Josephine, from Full Gospel Business Men's Fellowship and other associations, and we really liked them. Jimmy was a wonderful, respectful young man and we liked him, too. Becca continued to work at the Idaho State Capitol until just before their first child arrived.

One of our last projects on the ranch was to take out a loan to buy some

Holstein heifers to resell for a profit. When they arrived from Minnesota, four of them were sick. Gail thought we could treat them so he decided to keep them, but two died in the night. Others were getting sick so Gail called the veterinarian and found out that they had viral pneumonia! We had to give them antibiotics, which were expensive, and the process was not pleasant. We took their temperatures with a rectal thermometer to see which ones were feverish and needed the medicine. Then we had to give a shot in the neck to all the sick ones. Additionally, they had infectious diarrhea which required that we rake out the barn and put down fresh straw every time they messed it up. Gail built small, temporary pens for these to keep them separated from the others because if a healthy calf should lie down on contaminated straw, the disease would spread. All this time, we were bottle feeding these calves because they were too young to thrive on hay and grain. We mixed the milk in an old agitator washing machine and used the drain hose to fill huge plastic "baby" bottles. In order to keep from getting trampled or pushed over, Gail created a makeshift chute for us to send them through one at a time so they would not crowd us. One person guided the hungry calves into this track while another person kept them from crowding ahead by sticking two fingers in their mouths as they waited in line, pacifying them until it was their turn for a bottle. Two people did the bottle feeding and one person filled the milk bottles. The 4-inch nipples were very stiff and hard to get on and off, especially with bucking, hungry calves lurching forward to get those bottles. It took the whole family to feed these calves and we did it twice each day for two weeks.

We were supposed to de-horn the calves at one month old, but they were still sick and the vet said it would kill them to go ahead with it. By the time they were healthy enough to undergo the procedure the horn buds had already attached to the skull and little horns were beginning to grow. If they grew too far past the bud stage, the gouger would not be effective in snipping off the horns, and alternative methods would have to be used. The de-horning scoop worked for most of them, though. It looked like a set of long-handled pruning shears, but had a sharp circle at the end that was hinged in half. The circle was placed over the little horn so when they pulled the shears open the sharp edges closed around the horn bud and scooped it off. Gail said that when they snipped off a horn blood would shoot five feet with every heartbeat. Consequently, the next step was of primary importance—applying blood-stop powder. Sometimes it had to be applied several times to pack the wound until the blood coagulated and the oozing stopped. It was a wild and gory undertaking, but our men kept after it and the calves came through with "flying colors", no pun intended! Out of the fourty-two Holsteins we had purchased, we only lost four. The rest of them were happy, healthy campers and the prettiest calves at auction when the time came to sell.

Dorcas had paid for one of them to raise and sell for a profit in order to make money for college. By the time we took our healthy herd to the sale, however, the national price had fallen. Ours were the best looking Holstein heifers in the whole place so we got a better price than some of the other sellers did, but not what we had projected at the outset of our venture. We realized it was the best we could expect under the circumstances; but when we went to pick up our check we discovered the outfit to be fraudulent and our check was only half as much as the price we had auctioned them for. When Gail went to contest it they made a lame excuse about being unable to find the proper markings on our cattle indicating that they had received their shots. Gail was very meticulous about these things and we knew this was not true but it was too late. They said the calves had been run through the auction a second time and had sold at a lower price. By the time we detected the error, the buyer was long gone. We didn't even have enough to pay off our loan. I literally sobbed about this disastrous outcome and later, when Dorcas saw me crying at home, she asked me what was wrong. "We lost more on these cattle than I made in a whole year of working at Ore-Ida…driving back and forth for nothing!" I practically wailed.

"Mother!" she chided; "I'm so surprised at you! We already prayed about the outcome; and you know that if Daddy had made money on this venture he would have wanted to do it again next year!"

I felt a little defensive. Dorcas had not been happy with her job at the court house, and had decided to attend a Bible school in Portland, Oregon. She had heard about it from a cousin and we had listened to some tapes of their worship services. She had invested in the calf project to make enough money for her tuition but had now lost nearly every penny of it. Reminding her that she was affected by this outcome also, I countered, "Dorcas, this is your Bible College money, too, you know!"

"Mom, I'm not worried about that;" she added reassuringly. "God is in charge of this and if he wants me to go to Bible College it will work out somehow." She was able to make a down payment on her first semester with what little money she had. Later she acquired a part-time job at the school to pay the rest of her tuition. She loved the Lord with all her heart and was excited to go and do something with her life that was more Kingdom-oriented! I was happy for her opportunity; she was pursuing what she loved in a safe place and I had peace about it. I was proud of her for trusting the Lord so completely, and having a mature perspective about losing her investment. I also smiled inside to think about her insight regarding how a profit may have dictated our future negatively. I certainly didn't want to experience another cattle venture and, after this big loss, it was likely that my husband would not try it again.

With Dorcas off to Bible College and Becca getting used to married life, it was just Gail and I with our boys. They were busy with school and activities and we were working our jobs and catching up after the debt we had incurred. We were happy together and all was well. During this time, our old Twin Falls church organized a reunion and invited Gail and I to come and bring our family to sing and minister. We practiced with the boys and prepared to sing, "The Family of God" by Bill Gaither. It was a good trip and our old friends enjoyed hearing us sing and play our instruments with our two fine sons.

In May, 1974 Mark graduated from Emmett High School. He sang at his graduation while he and David played their instruments and Becca accompanied them on the piano. Dorcas was also home from PBC for this joyous celebration. That summer, we made a trip to Montana for a family wedding. On the way home we stopped at Fenn Ranger Station in the Nez Perce National Forest. Gail had been researching some elk-hunting grounds on Glover Ridge and wanted to pick up a map of the area. As he waited for the secretary to get his map he asked, "You wouldn't happen to have a job around here for a young feller, would you? My son just graduated from High School and is looking for work." The boys and I were sitting out on the lawn and we noticed that there were several groups of men around the grounds that looked like they were being briefed by instructors. We looked up to see Gail coming toward us with a guide in tow. "Mark, these guys want to talk to you about a job!" he called, as they were joined by another man whom we discovered to be the District Engineer over the trail crews. What we didn't know—and only the Lord could have arranged—was that this was the Opening Day of the 1974 fire season and they were one man short. Due to the sudden transfer of one of their regular crew members, they had just started a late search to fill his position. They asked Mark some questions about his experience with livestock and whether he had ever handled a chain saw. His answers were strong, confident and complete and they handed him an application. After he filled it out they needed some time to review and discuss it, so we took a hike in the nearby hills and came back in an hour to see what the outcome was.

"You're hired," they told Mark. When he expressed great surprise, they added, "Yep; we need a guy on Trail Crew and you can do everything he needs to know." Mark told them that his high school counselor had said working for the Forest Service was impossible because the Civil Service Rosters were full months in advance of open positions. "Well, we do hire from the rosters," the boss explained; "but the next guy on the list is from Minnesota and if we contacted him right now he couldn't be here for a week or two. Our fire season starts today, so we need *you*!" They wanted him to start the next day, so we left him there and drove home. We packed up some clothes to send him by mail, along with a pair of Gail's White Packer boots for him to use until he had the money to buy his own. Mark's supervisor only had one good eye. He was the official Selway Ranger District Packer and Horse Wrangler and Mark loved working with old Al. He also worked with a new Christian who knew nothing about the Holy Spirit. Mark was able to share a lot; they had great talks and became fast friends. It was a great experience for him, working and hiking in the back country, building fires and sleeping under the stars—a young man's dream job. God works in mysterious ways!

Now that Mark was working in the Forest Service five hours away, only David was living at home. Dorcas, however, was on summer break from college until mid-August. I was always so happy to have her home again. Life was changing swiftly from our cozy and comfortable family of six to young adult schedules with school and jobs taking our kids away from home.

Fall arrived in style with the birth of our first grandchild. When Becca's baby, Angela Cheri was born on September 1, 1974, she sent birth announcements to Dorcas, who was back at school beginning her second year, and Mark at Fenn Ranger Station addressed to "Aunt Dorcas" and "Uncle Mark" respectively. Gail and I became grandparents at the young ages of thirty-nine and forty! As much as we loved having this vivacious little granddaughter to enjoy, the winds of change were beginning to blow and our cherished life in Emmett Valley was gradually coming to a close.

Gail was being drawn back to the ministry and we had been to Reno, Nevada with the Assembly of God pastors from Emmett for a Revival Fellowship Ministers Conference which stirred his heart. Mark came home from Fenn in early October and we heard that a man from Dorcas' church in Portland was the guest speaker at a meeting in Ontario, Oregon so the boys went with us to hear him. He was teaching on the restoration of the church and end-time revival. After the meeting, we talked to him and told him we were seeking the Lord for direction. He suggested that we contact a pastor who was heading up a ministry in Richland, Washington. We began to pray and seek the Lord about what we should do as life continued as usual.

David was busy with his high school activities and Mark got a job at Albertson's in town, cleaning the grocery store at night. Finally we decided to make a trip to the Tri-Cities with the boys to check out the ministry that we had been told about a few months before. Our good minister friend, Brother Leland Davis, had come to visit us at the ranch so we took him with us to Richland, Washington. Mark sang most of the way and it was an enjoyable trip. The meetings were good and the Holy Spirit moved among the people. When we got home, we decided to fast and pray about moving to Richland. We were also thinking about moving to Portland since Dorcas was over there. While we were considering these options, Mark had a prophetic dream. In the dream, our whole family was at an airport, standing out on the tarmac watching a jet plane arrive. We were waiting in line to board the plane as soon as it landed when suddenly it leveled off before our eyes, turned sharply, and went straight up for a few thousand feet. As we watched, two pilots bailed out and the plane disappeared. Then the scene changed and another plane approached. As the dream ended, Mark had the knowledge that this plane was the right one and it was going to a different destination than we had first anticipated.

The man from Richland called us and said that they had a house for our family if we were interested in joining them. We thought this must be the Lord's confirmation to us, so we gave notice to our landlord and made plans to have a big farm sale. We felt sure we would be moving so Gail quit his job at the mill and began making preparations, but we had not received much response to our ads for selling our animals. It was early spring and Mark was getting ready to return to Fenn Ranger Station for his summer job. He and Gail went to a

Full Gospel Business Men's fellowship meeting in Boise. Throughout this time, Gail had experienced several setbacks to his dream of running a quarter horse ranch together with his boys. Yet he was caught between wanting this dream to materialize and letting it go to return to the ministry. So, at this meeting, he felt the Lord telling him that it was time for a change. His heart response was, *"Lord, if you can sell all our horses, I'm willing to do whatever you say."* When they arrived home after the meeting, there was a man standing at our front door who was talking to me about buying some of our horses! Later, Gail told me that this buyer's visit was an absolute miracle in response to his prayer at the meeting, just hours before. Our transition had begun. We were able to sell all of our horses except one, and we gave other small animals away, including our wonderful dog, Smoky, who went to the neighbors.

Mark went back to Fenn for his second fire season and Dorcas came home for the summer from Bible College. We were getting ready to move but still trying to decide which direction we should go. Then this pastor from Richland called back and said their plans had taken a turn in a different direction and they didn't want us to come after all! When we got the call, we felt great relief in our spirits and believed that God had spared us from a mistake. Later we found out that Mark's dream had come to pass because two of the main leaders in Richland "bailed out" and left that ministry, and we ended up with a "different destination" than we had first planned for, just as the dream had predicted. At this point, the landlord had already rented our place to someone else so we were going to have to move out right away, but we had one horse remaining with a buyer who had not yet paid.

We had lived in Emmett from 1968 to 1975—seven beautiful years. We loved the old house that became our country home, and made many cherished life-long memories in that place. Our time at Route 1, Tyler Road in Emmett was an unforgettable country experience, even though we were only two miles from town. Seven years was the longest time to date that I had ever stayed in one house! Yet the time had flown by as we watched our children grow from children to young adults. Family life had never been sweeter, and we would be telling these stories for the next 50 years. *The steps of the righteous are ordered by the Lord,* and our gracious God had not left us wanting. We were full to the brim with blessings and rewarding experiences to take with us to our next segment of Life's Pathway.

Gail had talked to Jim Howell, Sr. at a Full Gospel Business Men's fellowship meeting in Boise. The Howells were realtors and owned several properties. One of their houses on Cole Road in Boise was vacant at the time and they said we could rent it month to month until we decided what to do. This was an answer to prayer because it had a small pasture for the one horse we still owned. We were only in the Cole Road house for one month, as a place had become available for us in Portland. Since we didn't want to pay another month's rent in Boise, we contacted the man who wanted to buy the horse to finalize arrangements.

He said he would come and get it, since we needed to move, if he could send us a check for payment in two weeks. We decided to trust him and, by the time he came to get the horse, we were packed up and ready to leave. Things were moving rapidly to boost us out of our beloved Idaho home. With David in his own vehicle, Gail driving the U-Haul, and Dorcas and me following in the car, we caravanned together over the Blues in search of new territory that only God could secure. Most of us were looking forward to it, although Becca was sad to see us go. We would not be nearby to watch our first grandchild grow up; but she and Jim had their own life now and they were very happy. David was the one who had to be most courageous. He was giving up his senior year of high school as a basketball star, surrounded by many friends that he had been with since fifth grade. He was Student Body President-elect for the coming year. He had approached us with the idea of living with Grandma and Grandpa Bryan to finish his senior year in Emmett and graduate with his class; but we felt that he should be with us, even though we knew the move would be hard for him. His basketball coach even offered him accommodations in order to keep him on the team; David was a valuable player for the Huskies. He was learning that the Road of Life can take some very sharp turns, and dump you into a bog where you may flounder until you get your footing again. He cooperated, but we knew it was painful for him to be uprooted in the prime of his teen years. We headed west again, but this time it was not the southern route to California; it was northwest on I-84, over the Blue Mountains and along the windy Columbia River Gorge.

We were moving again, but this time we were not running from anything. The circumstances of this move had been a mixture of natural change, as our young adults began venturing out on their own, and supernatural intervention with the curious happenings of recent months. We were intentionally relocating to a large metropolis, which was miracle number one. I didn't know what awaited us in Portland, Oregon but my anticipation was not muddied by anxiety this time. Instead of the apprehension and dread that had surrounded past moves, this transition possessed a sort of happy exhilaration, more like the moves I remembered as a girl. We were being drawn by the Holy Spirit instead of pushed by pain and failure; advancing instead of retreating. We had gathered what seemed like a lifetime of memories during our seven years at the little ranch in Emmett; but this wonderful season had come to an appropriate close, in God's time. It seemed that we were progressing toward the next step in His plan, and progress was a good feeling—for a change!

CHAPTER ELEVEN

Over the Blues and Beyond

Roots of Renewal

When we arrived in Portland we had a furnished house waiting for us. The man we had met in Ontario lived with his family in one of the properties owned by the church and said we could stay there while they were away in ministry. We were grateful for a place to land, but since it was furnished we had to find storage here and there for all of our belongings. Gail looked diligently for work every day, but he had no college education and only minimal work experience because of being in the ministry most of his life. Dorcas lived with us in what we called "the gray house", and started her second year at Bible College. We were glad to have her back with us again after her first year challenges in the dorms. Mark had worked for two summers at Fenn Ranger Station, and had decided to attend Bible College as well. He enrolled, and arrived in Portland a week after we got there. He moved into a ten-plex dormitory on campus, which was a requirement of first-year students.

David enrolled at Madison High School and finished his high school credits in one semester. He had requested to go back and walk through the graduation ceremony in Emmett with his graduating class; but they said it was against their policies. He was very sad, but tender-hearted toward the Lord and he prayed earnestly about everything. Even in Emmett, as a busy high school student, I remember hearing his voice in fervent prayer coming from his room at the ranch house. He was hired at Fred Meyer after finishing his diploma requirements at Madison, and was happy to be working while he decided what to do next. We also had a niece living with us that first year in Portland. The gray house was a busy place as everyone plunged into their various new activities, and the Bryan family settled into life in the big city.

We had some money from our farm sale in Emmett and Mark loaned us some from his savings to help out while Gail was looking for work. The church accepted our over-sized freezer in exchange for our home electricity costs. Eight months went by before Gail found a job; he was finally hired by United Parcel Service to wash their trucks at night. Meanwhile, the people whose house we were in returned to Portland and moved all of their furniture so that we could move ours in. To our dismay, we discovered that quite a few things had been stolen from the various places we had been using for storage. As we brought our belongings one load at a time and moved them into the house, we kept noticing that things were missing. This dilemma remained a mystery and, with no clues as to who had been snooping through our stuff, we carried on.

Another mystery, or more likely a gross misfortune, was that the man who supposedly bought our horse just before we left Idaho had never sent a dime. We had not heard from him since the day he loaded up the mare, yet a year had gone by. We realized long before this that we had been lied to and as soon as Gail had a weekend off he decided to go get his horse. He was not about to let this man steal it from him. He could not track him down but was able to locate the man's son. By telephone, he revealed that this behavior was common for his dad, and told Gail where he might find him. After driving to Emmett to pick up his father, they traveled on to Battle Mountain, Nevada—a small mountain community somewhere between Reno and Elko—to undertake a "private investigation" mission of their own. Their first stop was the US Post Office, where they swaggered in dressed like area cowboys and asked for the man by name. Assuming they must be close companions, the clerk told Doc and Gail exactly where the man lived! On their way to his ranch, they passed him going the other direction. Just as Gail said to Doc, "There he is," the man also recognized Gail and pulled over to the side of the road.

"They say horse thieves are hard to find!" Gail jested as they walked toward each other. The fellow was hardly discomfited at all and began to make the same types of excuses he had given before as if he was honest and dependable as could be. He back-tracked and apologized, then said he would make arrangements to pay; but he still wanted to keep the horse. Gail told him in no uncertain terms that his gig was up and that he was not leaving without his horse. They followed him to his ranch and loaded up the mare. Gail's father was willing to buy her since he lived in Emmett where he could board her easily. Gail came home with the money, thankful that the Lord had helped him to track down the thief and kept him from another financial loss that we could not afford.

We had lived in Portland less than a year when we heard about a young man in the Bible College who wanted to start a church in his home community of Aberdeen, Washington. The church leadership appreciated his zeal but didn't want to send him out alone. They talked to Gail and said that if we would lead a team to assist this young couple the church would approve it as an outreach location. We agreed, and began immediately to make trips every weekend to Aberdeen where we met for Home Group meetings in this young couple's home. Gail was working nights for United Parcel Service but had weekends off and was able to make these trips. He was also doing odd jobs for the church, working on their properties as a volunteer groundskeeper.

There was a wonderful move of God during these years that provided times of refreshing in the presence of the Lord. We were soaking up the inspirational worship services and enjoying the good teaching. I was enjoying night classes at the Bible College, enrolling in every free course that became available. I loved the studies and took notes on everything. This move of God had come with refreshing revelation about the restoration of the church and its current purpose in the timeline of God. They taught classes on present day truths and the gifts of the Holy Spirit in the last days. We were happy to be here and to see our young adult children thriving in a place where solid foundational principles were taught and godly practices were encouraged.

In June, 1976 Dorcas married her college sweetheart, Ed Mason. All of her siblings were in the wedding. Jim and Becca traveled from Boise to attend with their small children. We were now grandparents of two. Benjamin James Howell was born in Boise on April 1, 1976 and was on his first trip where his big sister Angela, who was not yet two, was to be the flower girl in her Aunt Dorcas' wedding. The ceremony was beautiful and we rejoiced to celebrate the marriage of our daughter to a fine, Christian man who was already involved in Kingdom business. Ed had graduated from Bible College and Dorcas had earned her two-year certificate. They would start their married life on a good foundation and our hearts were joyful for them, and in having all of our children together again.

Shortly after the wedding, our church needed the gray house for another family. Gail and I moved into a large apartment complex on Glisan Street whose owner had advertised for a resident manager's position and hired us. She was a very liberal older woman who had an interesting but precarious past. "You can't run apartments by the Golden Rule!" she had drilled me, because I was kind and caring to all of our tenants. Betty was not easy to work for, but she respected our family and was very impressed by the good character of our young adult children. She despised her children because she thought they were all after her money. I planted many seeds of truth into Betty's life and, although I was not able to lead her to the Lord at that time, I am confident that the Holy Spirit carried on the work because God has told us in Isaiah 55:9-11 (KJV) *"For as the heavens are higher than the earth, so are my ways higher than your ways, and my thoughts than your thoughts. For as the rain cometh down, and the snow from heaven, and returneth not thither, but watereth the earth, and maketh it bring forth and bud, that it may give seed to the sower, and bread to the eater: So shall my word be that goeth forth out of my mouth: it shall not return unto me void, but it shall accomplish that which I please, and it shall prosper in the thing whereto I sent it."* When we are faithful to shine the Light of Christ into our needy world, our confidence is sure because we know the truth of the scriptures. I Corinthians 3:7-9 assures us, *"So then neither is he that planteth any thing, neither he that watereth; but God that giveth the increase. Now he that planteth and he that watereth are one: and every man shall receive his own reward according to his own labour. For we are labourers together with God: ye are God's husbandry..."* (KJV). We labor with the Lord of the Harvest, but he is the one who gathers the souls into his Kingdom of Light.

This was a hard time for me because all of our children were out of the nest for the first time. David had enrolled in his first year at the Bible College and he and Mark were both living in the dorms. Mark had made me a beautiful chiming clock in his high school shop class which was my only comfort in the absence of my children. My mind often turned back to the happy years of mothering my little ones through the ups and downs of life and I thought, "What is Life without my children?" God knew the answer to that question, and I would do all that was set before me with a servant's heart and see where his plan would lead. We were building relationships with the small flock in the Aberdeen Home

Group and since Ed Mason grew up in this area he and Dorcas would often travel with us to these meetings.

We were also able to take a wonderful trip with our son, Mark, during his Christmas break from college. David had a part-time job and was unable to go with us. Betty had given Gail and I a week off from our manager duties at the apartments to go to Fresno, California for a speaking engagement. After the meeting, we had opportunity to visit many old friends over the next few days. We saw Ralph and Rose Mahoney, and friends from our church in Redlands, the Rogers, the Kellys, and our dear assistants in that work, Haskell and Shirley Pride. We also got to visit relatives, Paul and Caroline Bryan, who lived in the vicinity. We were able to stay with, and often dine with, the people we visited, so the trip was very affordable and full of great fellowship. Our "big gold boat", which is what our kids called our recently purchased Mercury Marquis, was cushy and comfortable for a road trip, and featured a nice cassette tape deck that we enjoyed all the way!

Almost a year after Dorcas and Ed's marriage, spring of 1977, a ceremony was held at the church in Portland ordaining us as ministers with their organization. The leadership team commissioned Gail and I to move to Aberdeen and pioneer the new church with the young team that was already assembled there. The next weekend Gail and I went up early to scout for housing. We found an old, run-down house that we thought may be available to rent. It did not look very inviting, but we were veterans regarding old houses and willing to take whatever we could find. At the Home Group that evening, we heard that someone had come upon a vacant church building in the neighboring town of Hoquiam. So we decided to go take a look. It was an old church on the corner of Garfield and Karr; quite shabby and in a state of great neglect, but definitely unoccupied. Our little group held hands on the lawn and asked God to give us the building if it was the property of his choice for our fledgling church body. The next weekend, Gail was invited to preach at Taholah, just under fifty miles north of Hoquiam, on the Quinault Indian Reservation. Our son-in-law, Ed Mason, went with him to this meeting and witnessed the miracle that God had ordained. After the meeting, a man came up to Gail and said, "As soon as you walked into the room, the Lord said, 'This is the man I want you to give the church to.'" Brother Ralston gave Gail the key and told him to check out this building on his way back to Portland. When Gail and Ed drove up to the address they were given, it was the same little church in Hoquiam where our group had stood on the lawn the week before and prayed! Gail got home very late from that trip, but he was incredibly excited and told me the whole story. God was already working miracles for this new undertaking. He had a plan for Hoquiam-Aberdeen and his hand of blessing and provision had gone before us to prepare the way.

The Church at Hoquiam

Dorcas and Ed moved to Aberdeen ahead of us to live in a darling little green house that they had been able to rent from long-time friends of Ed's family. As soon as we secured the building and all the documents had been signed, Gail and I packed up and moved out of the big city to the little bay town of Hoquiam. The church had a large, four-bedroom, two-story parsonage that was part and parcel of the deal, but it was not currently available. The owner had allowed some of his kin to live there and they were not inclined to move out of these free and roomy lodgings! Consequently, we moved into the church basement! We set up our beds in a Sunday School room, cooked in the church kitchen, and washed up in the big commercial sinks or went to Mason's house for showers. We covered the windows with extra bedding and camped out in our miracle church building, praying and waiting for God's timing. Gail was so excited, and worked diligently to set up his office right away. Despite our temporary accommodations, everything else came together quickly and our home group met in our church building from that point forward. Rhema Fellowship was born! We had twenty-five people at our first meeting and, just by word of mouth, attendance grew to forty by the time we met a second time in our church building! At the same time, we were having a stream of company that came to visit from various places to see what was going on in Hoquiam! We had plenty of room for them to throw down their sleeping bags in the church basement where we lived. It was a time of great enthusiasm and excitement for all of us! Our group was dedicated to preparing our building for the people whom we knew the Lord would send. The ladies of the church sewed long drapes for the sanctuary windows where the scorching afternoon sun came through. Everyone pitched in and found ways to help get the place cleaned up and organized. Ed acted as foreman to supervise volunteers whenever they were available. All of our young men held regular jobs and had to find time to volunteer whenever they could. Our young body of believers was growing rapidly! People were getting saved and there was a great hunger for the truth of God's Word. I started a Women's Bible Study right away to teach our young women about godly character and modesty, Christian disciplines, how to raise their children biblically, and learning God's way of family living.

Right in the middle of all the excitement, another granddaughter came along. Christina Joy Mason was born on June 9, 1977. Dorcas and Ed were starting family life with their first baby and I was overjoyed to be close enough to adore her, especially since my other grandchildren were so far away.

During the three months that we lived at the church, the previous owner had told his relatives and their friends—multiple times—that they had to move out of the house since he no longer owned the property. They flat refused, however, and became very rude and threatening to us. The house and the church were separated only by a paved driveway with a short, covered walkway between the garage and the side door of the building. We were, therefore, in very close proximity to the occupants. One day I looked out the kitchen window and saw a large Native American man looking angrily back at me from an upstairs window of the house, and shaking his fist. Another time, he progressed from shaking a fist to brandishing a pistol! We were as friendly and polite as possible whenever we saw any of them, but they remained hostile and we thanked God for his angels that we knew were encamped round about our dwelling. We often witnessed late night exchanges with questionable characters that showed up next door, and regularly saw our neighbors exclaiming over their wares as they unpacked items from their vehicles at all hours of the night. We assumed they were stolen, and would be sold or traded for drugs. Eventually, some of the men were arrested and jailed for their thievery, and the other occupants moved out.

Ed began to clean and fix up the parsonage immediately whenever he had time off from his regular job. He was a whirlwind of talent and energy that we could not have done without! Ed could do anything that needed to be done in the church or parsonage, and was willing to give his time to the work. We found the house to be full of garbage. We had to rent a forty-foot dumpster which we filled over and over again. There was a gallon of paint spilled on the floor with footprints going through the puddle and up the stairs. There were dirty handprints everywhere and grimy smudges on all the window sills and stair railings. We threw out all the carpet and vacuumed piles of dead flies from the corners of the windows. There were arrows sticking into a target on one of the bedroom doors. We found live rats in the garage and a dead one in the pantry. There was a mouse in the garbage disposal, broken dishes strewn about and shattered glass everywhere. Every lightbulb was burned out and all the curtains were filthy; we threw everything away. It took us a whole week to get rid of all the trash before we could start remodeling. New carpet was donated by someone and Ed installed all of it. After a month of hard work, the house was livable and we were able to move in. Our parsonage was a wonderful house! Sometime later the girlfriend of one of the previous occupants came to one of our services and cried at the altar. Afterwards I talked with her and asked her if she would like to see the house. She was in complete awe and said, "God wants to do in my life what you have done to this house."

Shortly after we got settled, we invited a young man who was part of our team from Portland to board at the parsonage. I had a constant stream of company come for refreshments and fellowship, or for family dinners. We often hosted overnight guests in our home, many of which were special speakers that we had invited to minister to our growing congregation. We had friends and co-laborers from other places come often to visit and share with our people, as well as inspirational choirs and other group ministries. The first year living at the parsonage we served one hundred and eighty-five meals to visitors and overnight guests.

Gail and I were only in our forties when we started the work in Hoquiam, but we felt old! The bulk of our growing congregation was under thirty years of age! Most of them were new Christians, and many of them had come from un-churched backgrounds or out of the hippie culture. They needed all the basic concepts of the Bible, so it was easy for our team to find subjects on which to teach. One young convert came to me and said, "Sister Bryan, I don't want to take years and years to learn. Just tell me what I'm doing wrong right now so I can start doing right! I've never seen a godly woman and I want to know how to be one!"

Jesus said, *"...they that are whole need not a physician; but they that are sick. I came not to call the righteous, but sinners to repentance."* Luke 5:31-32 (KJV). We spent hours counseling people in the parsonage and Gail's first messages were on subjects necessary for discipleship training. Our entire team worked together to teach these new believers the valuable principles of Christian living and the necessity of being filled with the Spirit in order to walk in God's ways and experience freedom from the bondage of sin. Lives were being changed and revival was happening in the hearts of the hungry that came to Rhema Fellowship to take part in the outpouring of the Holy Spirit. That first Fall in Hoquiam we realized that the spiritual ground that had been softened by the Holy Spirit in people's hearts was now prepared for a deeper planting of the Word of God. We started Rhema Bible College as soon as we were settled into our parsonage. A wonderful Christian brother from Portland came to help us set up the program and the curriculum. He was a brilliant man and a great help to us in launching this significant stage of our outreach in Hoquiam. Our own small Bible College was the most important period of my personal education and ministry training. I took Bible College classes right along with our first seventy students. We only had night classes available the first year because so many of our students worked regular jobs during the day. They were all young, energetic, and hungry for the things of God. We offered classes such as Basic Doctrine, Spirit-filled Life, Bible Survey, and more. I loved every class I took and received the maximum benefit from all my studies and research. I was always inspired to do even more research than the courses required; I was so intrigued by the material that I could hardly stop. I felt like a porous vessel that needed constant re-filling as God blessed the Word to my heart and spirit. These years were the most fulfilling and enriching time of my educational experience and pastoral career. I gained a broader understanding of foundational truths and a greater ability to impart them to others. God greatly enlarged my heart with the knowledge of his Word and I earned my two-year diploma in 1981. After finishing my two-year program, I taught in the Bible College, offering classes such as Women's Role and Practical Womanhood. Our young women were enthusiastic and anxious to learn. I had forty to fifty students in each class. With papers to read and grade, along with my preparation for our Tuesday morning Ladies' Bible Study and my other pastoral duties, my life became very full!

In the summer of 1978, Dorcas and Ed moved out of their little house and came to live with us in the parsonage while saving money to build a house of their own. Ed was on staff at the church by then. His dedication and skill had been such a blessing on a volunteer basis; now we were only too happy to be able to pay him for it! They had another baby on the way by this time. Christy's little sister, Faith Esther, was born to Ed and Dorcas on August 18, 1978, our fourth grand! Our family was growing every year and we were about to stretch our boundaries even farther. For, back in Idaho, Jim and Becca had moved from Boise to Burley so that Jim could take a State Police position at Cotterell Weigh Station about 47 miles from the Utah border. They had lived there for almost a year when they decided to move to Washington and join us in the work at Hoquiam. They arrived in September of 1978 while Dorcas and Ed with their two little girls were still living with us. Jim and Becca had sold their house in Burley, but the sale fell through the day they left. They would have to wait for it to sell before they could buy another home of their own. So we became one big, happy family for the next couple of months! I loved every minute of living with my daughters and my four grandchildren in such close proximity. We all got along great and the big parsonage provided plenty of room for our temporary arrangements. The next month, however, Ed and Dorcas decided to purchase a nice mobile home for their family. Jim and Becca were not able to move out until the following May when their home in Idaho finally sold and they purchased a house in Hoquiam. Ed was eventually able to build a beautiful home for his family in the nearby community of Cosmopolis when their girls were preschoolers. Dorcas and Becca were happy to be living nearby to each other so that their children could be close cousins. They were both very involved with the church, too. They were instrumental in getting a wonderful Children's Church going and took sole responsibility for creating curriculum and song sheets. They made a recording of all the children's songs and provided these to all of the volunteers who wanted to help with the children's ministries. Most of our church families were young couples with babies and small children, so we had full Sunday School classes and the Children's Church was thriving. Our nursery was also bursting at the seams so we had to purchase stacking cribs in order to accommodate the growing numbers of infants.

Growth and Expansion

Over time, we had been able to accumulate all the equipment necessary to hold services. We had a good group of volunteer musicians who played piano, violin, and various horns and drums. The young man we had joined with to start the Aberdeen-Hoquiam outreach was our worship leader, and did a masterful job. He was anointed and capable of leading the congregation joyfully into the presence of the Lord. Sunday morning, evening and mid-week services were packed out, and we expanded the sanctuary on one side to accommodate more seating. The rapid growth of the Hoquiam church was miraculous; it was a sovereign move of God! The Holy Spirit was drawing people from all over the area and it was both shocking and encouraging to see so many rescued and saved from sin. Lives were changing before our eyes and, as I looked around at all that God was doing in this place, I realized it was worth it. This beautiful scenario was worth every tear and midnight prayer during the many years of struggle that we had endured. Gail was dedicated and strong, walking in victory and preaching with great anointing and insight. We were both very fulfilled in the ministry God had led us to. I was glad that my husband could finally reach the desire of his heart, to be profitable for the Kingdom of God after all of his challenges.

We joined a minister's fellowship that included Whidbey Island, Olympia, Tacoma, and Seattle. We met many wonderful co-laborers in the field and frequented each other's congregations during those years to share the wonderful things the Lord was doing throughout the area. We also sponsored the A.C.E. school program in the fall of 1978 for the school-aged children of Rhema Fellowship from grades one to eight. Our staff had gone to Portland for training in the summer and we had a certified teacher and several classroom monitors ready to begin the first semester. We set up a Learning Center in the church basement with small cubicles around the room for our first forty students. Gail had attended some additional training to take on the job as Principal for the first year of our new school. Meanwhile, our sons were beginning their third and fourth years at Bible College and doing well. They came up to visit whenever possible and joined us for their holiday breaks. We also had both of them come as guest speakers from time to time. We continued to have a variety of special speakers to share their biblical knowledge and experience with our young flock.

One guest who made a great impact was Evangelist Francis Anfuso, founder of Christian Equippers International, who came and taught a seminar. At that time, however, he was with Glad Tidings School of Evangelism in California. After the teaching on evangelism, everyone who took the course went out two by two into the local community to witness door to door. It was a great experience for our church, and a prime time for these growing Christian disciples to learn the importance of sharing their faith with the world.

The summer of 1979, after we had been in Hoquiam about a year and a half, the church took a love-offering to send us on a vacation. They mentioned Hawaii, but Gail wanted to go to Alaska. I said, "Oh, not Alaska! There are so many beautiful places in Washington and Oregon; and besides, the airfare is too expensive for Alaska." Gail had always wanted to go to Alaska, however, so my pleadings were to no avail! After this "vacation" he never talked about it again, for it was indeed a trip we will *never* forget! Mark was free to go with us and we thought it would be a great way to celebrate his graduation from Bible College. We were all looking forward to a special time together. The first mishap was that the travel agent made a simple mistake denoting "AM" instead of "PM" on our tickets and we arrived at the airport twelve hours early. It was our anniversary, so we found transportation to the Space Needle in Seattle thinking we could enjoy a nice dinner with a view from the top. The food was too expensive so we went to a deli instead, but still saw the scenery from its windows. We were already very tired from our trip and our long delay, so it was excruciating to discover upon our return to the airport that our flight was delayed five hours longer! Before it finally arrived everyone was sleeping on the floor. Gail had depended on his nephew to arrange our details and when we landed in Anchorage we found that there was a glitch in the plan that required the purchase of another flight across the Kenai Peninsula. Then we would be dropped off for four days at Twin Islands Lake. We were told we would get a mosquito-proof cabin, furnished with a stove and all the necessary utensils, plus a fishing boat with plenty of gas. When we got there, we were greeted by a tent on an old wooden frame. The door was wide open and sported a sign which said, "The Hilton". The place was so thick with mosquitoes that Gail quipped, "Its mosquito proof alright...they can't get out!"

There was a tiny gas burner for cooking that was coated with grease and all the utensils were filthy. There was no clean water anywhere and the lake was floating with moss and crud. We didn't bring water with us because we thought there would be plenty at our vacation spot. Now we were in survival mode; we got in the boat and motored off to find a fresh water source. We finally found an inlet but we only had a small tin coffee pot to fill. It would be a challenge to clean dirty skillets and still have enough water for drinking. The weather was nice at first but since we didn't bring insect repellant we had to cover ourselves from head to toe in self-defense! Jillions of mosquitos buzzed at our ears all night long, for we were the only skin on the island that they didn't have to work through a layer of fur to get a bite of! We had cots, but no mosquito netting, and we had to sleep down inside our sleeping bags to protect ourselves. Gail had found an old newspaper and rolled it up to use as a torch; but when he lit it the mosquitoes were not affected. We were the only ones who got smoked out! Some of these invaders were as big as water skippers! Later we saw giant mosquito souvenirs in the gift shops, and realized what this place was *really* famous for. We finally discovered that the only way to get away from them was to get in the boat and zoom across the lake faster than they could fly! Gail had declared that he wouldn't vacation anywhere in Washington because he didn't want rain. This became the second plague of our vacation spot, for it rained the whole time we were there. Gail fished anyway; but Mark and I didn't have licenses so we had to find other things to do. We spent lots of time in the boat fleeing from mosquitoes. We saw lots of moose and one charged us from the bank of the lake. He swam after us but the boat was faster and we got away. With no electricity, there was nothing to do, and we were mostly miserable. The fishing was no better than many beautiful places we had found in Idaho and Washington. Consequently, there was nothing about Alaska that we found to be worth the trouble we endured. We were packed, ready, and waiting eagerly when the float-plane finally landed on the lake to take us back to civilization. I felt like I was being rescued from a war zone!

In Anchorage, our nephew, Dan Bryan, picked us up and we stayed a couple nights with him. A friend of ours had suggested that we take a drive down the Kenai Peninsula where we were to meet some pastors that he knew. So we rented a car from the Ugly Duckling Car Rental and drove far out in the boondocks looking for this church. The Ugly Duckling car had a leak and I was sitting right under the drip; I felt very much like a drowned rat by the time we got there and went into their church service! Afterwards the pastor had a place for us to stay. A lady in the church had offered her trailer out in the country while she was away. This proposal brought back nightmares from my past but the pastor sounded perky and pleased so we followed him and hoped for the best. When he turned the key in the lock and opened the door, three frightful greetings awaited us: a huge, Siamese cat; a bowl of cat food big enough to feed a feline army; and the smell of cat poop strong enough to blow our hair back. The lady had been gone for six weeks with her cat locked inside the trailer. The horrified pastor promptly locked the door with a stifled gag and took us to someone else's house. The next hosts were nice but in a temporary bind. They had taken in a homeless man who was sleeping in their living room. We were out of options at this point, so they gave Gail and I the extra room and Mark shared the living room with the hobo. The next day we drove back to Anchorage in our dripping, Ugly Duckling rental car, and were ever so happy to board the plane for home. Most of that trip I would be happy to forget, but we both thoroughly enjoyed spending the time with our wonderful son, and laughing together about making the best of it.

The next spring, April 15, 1980, a tragedy enveloped our growing family. Dorcas and Ed's third child, Sarah Elizabeth Mason, was stillborn. She was whisked away to the arms of Jesus before her family had a chance to welcome her to their world. I grieved for my sweet daughter and dear son-in-law in their unimaginable pain and loss. A large group from our church was planning to fly to Washington D.C. for the Washington for Jesus Rally and because the new baby was due Dorcas and Ed had not planned to attend. We encouraged them to come along and they agreed, sharing a motel room with Jim and Becca. It was inspiring to be a part of it, and amazing to see all those Christians in one place for one cause! Speakers focused on prayer and fasting, repentance, and seeking God for a great outpouring of the Spirit on our nation. There were parades, special speakers, singing groups and much celebration. Nearly a million Christians gathered at the Capitol Mall in Washington D.C. to pray for our nation. It was supposed to rain the day of the main rally, but although dark clouds surrounded the area, there was a patch of blue above the million voices gathered to pray. History was made that day, and it was a great experience for all who were privileged to be a part of it! As happy as we were to be able to surround Dorcas and Ed with love and support in this great atmosphere of prayer and praise, losing a child is not something that can be eased by focusing on other things. The Waters of Sorrow must be navigated during the course of every life, and I had waded through some of my own; but this was a weight of grief that I had never borne. I could identify only from a mother's instinctive understanding that there would always be a special place for Sarah in Dorcas' heart, that the raw vacuum could only be softened by the protective cocoon of Time, and that our hope of Heaven would be her comfort. The perpetual message of I Thessalonians 4:13 reminded us, then and now, that we need not sorrow as those who have no hope. We knew that Sarah would be eagerly waiting to greet us on the other side; that she had passed over the difficulties of earthly life and entered the gates that the rest of us can only look forward to at our journey's end. I Corinthians 15:51-52 (NLT) *"But let me reveal to you a wonderful secret. We will not all die, but we will all be transformed! It will happen in a moment, in the blink of an eye, when the last trumpet is blown. For when the trumpet sounds, those who have died will be raised to live forever. And we who are living will also be transformed."*

In May, our son, David, graduated from college and married Cheryl Allen, granddaughter of famous healing evangelist, A.A. Allen. At the end of the summer, they moved to Grays Harbor to join us in the work. We now had a full plate of pastoral responsibilities along with our Bible College, Christian school and many counseling appointments. In addition, Gail and I were both receiving numbers of speaking engagements around the area due to our continued fellowship with the aforementioned co-laborers in neighboring cities. We had branched out in our own congregation to provide leadership training for all who would give themselves to the ministry of the church. We had seventeen thriving Home Groups around our small area of the harbor. By 1981, our church, school, and Bible College were all thriving. We had hired another teacher for the A.C.E. school and Gail and I bought a personal residence in Aberdeen so the parsonage would be available to use for our first grade classroom. Some of the young men on our ministry team were teaching in our Bible College. God had blessed us with a dedicated church and school staff for which we were duly grateful. In addition, our son, David, began teaching in the Upper Learning Center, the higher grades of our A.C.E. school, and also filled the position of Principal. Becca had come on as Secretary for the church and school combined, and Ed Mason was doing a great job as Church Administrator.

The congregation soon outgrew our little church building and we began renting an old gymnasium across the street for our meetings. This required crews to set up and tear down all of the equipment and seating necessary to conduct Sunday Services every week. The last year we were in Hoquiam, our attendance record hit five hundred and twenty-five. Our wonderful volunteers were dedicated to their contributions in the work, using their God-given talents to bless and enrich the Body of Christ by music, teaching, preaching, and administration; as well as laboring with loving hands on our buildings and grounds. We were all rejoicing together in the great harvest and sharing the benefits of the work of the Kingdom, reaping the rewards of lives dedicated to God and His eternal purposes, just as the scripture describes in portions such as Proverbs 3:1-2 (NLT) *"My child, never forget the things I have taught you. Store my commands in your heart. If you do this, you will live many years, and your life will be satisfying"*; and Isaiah 26:7-8 (NLT) *"But for those who are righteous, the way is not steep and rough. You are a God who does what is right, and you smooth out the path ahead of them. LORD, we show our trust in you by obeying your laws; our heart's desire is to glorify your name."*

Guests were streaming in and out of our second home, on Scammel St. in Aberdeen, even more than we had hosted in the parsonage. One year I decided to keep track and found that I had served three hundred and seventy-eight meals in our home in twelve months' time!

That holiday season we had tragedy strike again, sandwiched between two joyful occasions. Our first great joy was the marriage of our son, Mark, to Diane Iverson in early November. We rejoiced that all of our children had found life partners from strong Christian backgrounds. The tragedy happened ten days later when our five-year-old grandson, Ben, had a home accident that injured his left eye and caused permanent loss of sight. That Thanksgiving, we counted our blessings and thanked God for his mercy and comfort. "Protection" was not in the mix at first because Becca struggled with why God would allow such a tragedy to begin with; but in the hospital God spoke to her heart through the eyes of a child. As he awoke from surgery Becca asked little Ben if he knew where he was and if he remembered what had happened. "In the hospital?" he carefully supposed. "But, Mommy, I know that my Guardian Angel was with me."

Struggling with tears and words that wanted to seep out, but would not be helpful, his grieving mother answered, "You do?"

"Yeah, cuz," he continued with assurance, "I had two curtain rods and I only poked one eye."

A week later, our second joy arrived to sandwich our sorrow. David and Cheryl were blessed with their first son, James David Bryan, who was born on December 5, 1981 in Aberdeen. Now we had three granddaughters and two grandsons! Time was marching on.

Undercurrents

By the spring of 1982, we had enjoyed five exciting years of pastoring the church in Hoquiam, when the spiritual temperature turned cold. A young man in our congregation, Bill, had a vision that he shared with the congregation. Ephesians 2:1-6 (KJV) depicts the precedent for his revelation:

"And you hath he quickened, who were dead in trespasses and sins; Wherein in time past ye walked according to the course of this world, according to the prince of the power of the air, the spirit that now worketh in the children of disobedience: Among whom also we all had our conversation in times past in the lusts of our flesh, fulfilling the desires of the flesh and of the mind; and were by nature the children of wrath, even as others. But God, who is rich in mercy, for his great love wherewith he loved us, Even when we were dead in sins, hath quickened us together with Christ, (by grace ye are saved) And hath raised us up together, and made us sit together in heavenly places in Christ Jesus."

He saw a large Ruling Prince looking down upon his assigned territory with muscular arms crossed over his chest in the defensive position. His image suggested a guard-like stance, suggestive of arrogance and superiority. He turned and looked over his shoulder, casting his angry eyes down upon our town and then fastening them on Rhema Fellowship. His gaze exhibited intense dislike, with a cold and calculated stare that remained fixed upon our little church. The excitable goings-on had gotten his attention, enough to decide that he had to do something about the regenerative changes taking place.

Our people took it all to heart; but none of us knew the full implications of this malicious concentration directed toward our happy little spot on the planet. Satan makes it his business to look for loopholes in our defense, for he knows that a crack in the armor is all he needs to smite the shepherd and scatter the sheep. He found an old weakness, and conjured up a hurricane from Hell. The last eighteen months of our ministry at Rhema Fellowship in Hoquiam were stormy and turbulent.

I felt the undercurrents of trouble swirling beneath the surface of what looked like a placid sea of grace and blessing to the outside world. I started feeling the dark struggle in my husband's soul and I saw it on his countenance; expressions that I dreaded to recognize but could not deny. The behavioral symptoms were beginning to surface again: disappearances, long absences, refusal to answer questions, scorning my attempts to encourage, and casting off any confrontation with angry resentment, even cruelty, toward me. Once again I was bombarded with deep suspicions and a grave sense of danger for Gail and our marriage, not to mention how another outbreak of this plague would jeopardize the church and the ministry that God and others had entrusted to us. Additionally, our children were now adults with families of their own. This was the very thing that I had feared when they were young—their father's addiction returning with a vengeance to puncture their souls and shatter their tender hearts. This would be worse for me than the punishment my own soul had endured so many years before. I could not assuage the hard truth that was about to hit them head on. No longer could I take their little trusting hands and lead them to a safe place where I could protect them from seeing the hard realities of life. It was time to trust God to cover them, and trust them to follow His path in this dark and gloomy rain forest of suffering another's consequences. I was deeply troubled but, again, had questions with no answers and theories with no proven facts; worries without evidence and problems without solutions.

God says that everyone will reap the consequences of their own sins. He assures us that a son will not be punished for his father's sins, and a father will not be responsible for the sins of his children. What is inescapable in this scenario is the probability of being burned simply because of one's close proximity to the fire that they did not start, and refused to fuel. By virtue of God's order of things, members of families and of the Body of Christ bear each other's burdens in obedience to his commands. Like it or not, we feel the pain of those we are connected to; we crumple beneath the weight of their burdens, and we are delayed by one another's failure to thrive. All of God's people whose names are written in the Lamb's Book of Life will stand as individuals before the Bema Seat Judgement of Christ one day and be rewarded according to the fruit of their lives, but on earth we experience the daily "touch and go", "fast and slow", ups and downs on our Pilgrim Pathway. This is where the things we do and say, the way we choose to live, affects many who travel with us. Here is the place where, by God's grace, we learn to take full responsibility for our own actions while extending forgiveness and mercy to others who don't. I had been burned by Gail's wildfire many times, picked up the pieces and rebuilt family life from the charred remains. The same God whose grace and power enabled me to carry on would now do the same for my children, their spouses, our grandchildren, and members of this new body of believers who were, by no fault of their own, in the line of fire.

Suspicious incidents began to press in upon me, sometimes resulting in confrontation and sometimes ending in buckets of tears concealed by closet doors. But morning would always come with duties to perform, speaking engagements to fulfill, and young lives to teach and guide, regardless of my own dark nights or anguish of soul. One night I drove all over town looking for Gail, knowing that something was terribly wrong and that Satan was gaining the upper hand. It was very late, and as I roamed the dark streets I was stopped by a policeman who questioned my reasons for being on the road at this hour. I was probably driving not-so-attentively since I was distraught and looking for my husband, for a clue, for anything to give me footing to take the next step. I needed validation for this penetrating dread, or substantiation to let it go.

All through these years, as was his pattern, Gail had strong seasons of fasting and prayer, hours of study in the Word, powerful preaching and strong leadership. The reality of the intense spiritual battle being fought for his soul was more evident to me now than ever before. I was reminded of near death experiences that his mother had told about. He was a "blue baby", born with the umbilical cord wrapped around his neck, but his life was saved before the spirit of Death could snatch his last breath. As a young child, he became very ill with pneumonia and lay in the hospital, close to Death's door. The nurse had been coming in periodically and as Hazel Bryan sat nearby, with her head bowed in prayer for her son, she heard footsteps enter the room and stop at the foot of the bed. No words were spoken, yet she felt such a strong presence in the room that she looked up to see who was there. She saw nothing but had a great sense of peace and assurance that little Gail would be healed. Almost immediately, he sat up and told his mother that he was hungry and wanted something to eat. He improved daily until his health was restored and his mother always knew that God had brought a miracle to save Gail's life. He was once kicked in the back of the head by a horse when he was a young boy. Although he was bowled end over end and left stunned and raddled, he was not killed. Another story sets the near-death scene in San Mateo Canyon where his family lived. There was a deep and wide, rocky wash on one side of their acreage that had been gouged out by California's famous flash floods. Another raging surge came through the canyon and Gail with his older brother, Paul, had run to the edge of the gorge to watch the torrent of water racing past. Fascinated by all the debris bobbing on the roaring river—including furniture, and a house—Gail leaned too close to the edge, peeking over the precipice. They had no inkling that the rushing water had undercut the bank on which they stood. Paul instinctively hollered, "Gail! Get away from the edge!" and grabbed his little brother by the collar, pulling him to safety just as the bank gave way and tumbled into the violent floodwaters below. Such happenstance is often credited to common life experience but, as the battle raged, I realized more and more that Satan's strong desire was to snuff out his life so it could not be used for the Kingdom of God; because he knew it would make a difference.

One night, shortly after we moved to the Scammel house, I had a terrible nightmare that was very revealing. This dream woke me out of a sound sleep and left me crying for help and shaking like a leaf. I saw the church in this dream, and the gymnasium across Karr Street that we had been renting for our school sports programs. This was before we began having our Sunday services in the gym. All the people of the church were standing outside on the lawn. Some kind of formidable evil was fast approaching and I could feel the dread and danger all around me. Our congregation was exposed and vulnerable to this peril and two of our faithful young leaders were scrambling to get everyone into the safety of the church building. For some reason, they could not enter through the doors and were instead being ushered toward a tall ladder where they must climb to safety through an upstairs window. The people were milling around and the children were playing about the grounds, unaware of the imminent hazard that swiftly approached them. I was helping to direct them toward the ladder and was the last one in line when, suddenly, they pulled the ladder up through the window and left me standing alone outside. My heart sunk as I realized that they had intended to save everyone except me. I turned around and there before me stood the Devil. He was dreadfully black and incredibly muscular. He brandished big horns from his ugly head and had a huge tail that flicked from side to side like a downed electrical wire that pulsed with destructive power. He had long, sharp fingernails and he pointed at me with a curved pointer finger and sneered, "You! I hate you! I hate you and I'm going to kill you!" His face was masked with great fury and his eyes burned with hate as he raised a spear that he held in his other hand. He pulled back with menacing intent and held his intimidating aim with malicious glee. His malevolent glare sported an arrogant assurance that I was as good as dead, and that he would relish in my demise.

I cried out to the Lord to come to my aid, and confronted my enemy with the Sword of the Spirit, "I resist you in the Name of Jesus!"

He laughed, and reiterated his threat with mocking scorn, "I hate you. I hate you and I'm going to kill you!"

The only thing within my reach was a shiny thread that hung like a silky spider web stretching through the air. I grabbed at it in desperation and it became a strong nylon-type bungee cord. I bounced a couple of times and the cord sprung me up from the ground to the rooftop of the gymnasium across the street. Satan stood below me on the ground and continued with his threats, which I persisted to answer with the truth of God's Word. "In the Name of Jesus, I rebuke you!" As I continued to cry out, several men came out of the church in response to this confrontation. One of them had a bow and arrow which he pointed at the Devil, taking aim to shoot. Suddenly, Satan's expression began to melt away and bizarrely morphed into Gail's face as I watched. He looked up at me with pleading eyes, as if he was held captive and could not escape. He was extremely distraught and sweating profusely. In a panic, I called out to the young man with the bow, "Stop! Don't shoot!" Then I turned to Gail and shouted, "Honey, run! Run to the altar!" This is what I was saying when I sat up in bed, wide awake with my heart pounding. Gail was awakened also. "Eunice! What's wrong with you?" I was traumatized but I told him the dream. His response was indifferent and he seemed unaffected. "Well, I'm not the Devil! It's just a nightmare; go back to sleep."

I lay quietly beside him as he began to snore, and I silently cried to the Lord. I knew God had given me the dream, although it had fallen on deaf ears and Gail had disregarded it as a fantastical account that was nowhere close to reality; I knew different. For the first time it became clear to me that the bane of his life was indeed a solid stronghold; the deadly result of opening the door to the enemy too many times. Weak moments combined with strategic circumstances arranged by Satan had piled on top of multiple bad decisions to create a nearly impenetrable Fort of Failure that could only be escaped by supernatural intervention. This was the first time I saw Gail as a victim of Satan's power instead of just a man choosing wrong over right. It was also very apparent that the danger was affecting the whole church, and that the leaders would want to shoot Gail and blame me. I prayed differently from then on, knowing that Satan's course was to destroy much more than one man's life. Soon after this dream occurred, Gail's cousin called one afternoon. "I am so burdened for Gail;" he spoke with great concern. "I need to talk to him." When Gail took the call and heard that his cousin had been very worried about him and was asking if there was anything he could pray with him about, Gail eclipsed his concern with false optimism, pretending that all was well, and missing another opportunity for accountability and helpful support. We can love, encourage, exhort, and offer to share a brother's burden; but his will is his own. No one can choose for someone else. All must choose for themselves; and Gail chose wrong. Finally, I shared my concerns with others on our leadership team and, in the course of time, enough evidence came to the forefront for the elders to contact the church that had sent us out to pioneer the work in Hoquiam. The leaders there were surprised for, although they knew some of Gail's troubled history, they believed that his strong family, his spiritual stature, and the fruit of his ministry proved that he was in good standing and biblically qualified. They trusted him; we all did. Now they were advising us to come back under their covering for accountability and discipline.

Retreating to Portland

On Sunday, December 11, 1983 after seven years of ministry in Hoquiam, Washington (including the preliminary start-up meetings before we moved there), Gail stepped to the podium and resigned his post as Senior Pastor of Rhema Fellowship. It was a shock to our congregation and most of the people were sad. Many considered us their spiritual parents who had brought them to salvation through Jesus Christ and had mentored them just as parents teach young children. They told us that they loved us and wanted us to stay. Many had come out of such troubled life-styles that they were ready and willing to forgive and keep moving forward together. Others were hateful and vindictive, anxious for us to leave. After we were gone, some were even so cruel as to charge our children and loyal friends with "having the Bryan spirit" and concluding that our grandson's eye accident was a result of his grandfather's sins. There is never an end to what Satan will do to kick us while we're down. He will gleefully take advantage of our failings in every possible way to batter anyone in proximity—from the center of a hurricane to the outer bands. His object is to steal, to kill, and to destroy. Another young man in the church had a vision of a beautiful cliff that looked wonderful for climbing, but down below were sharp rocks, which then became a huge, ugly mouth. A tongue came out of the awful mouth and the tongue became a river, a raging torrent rushing down into the dark cave mouth. The Holy Spirit gave him the interpretation that a deceptive spirit was working to wash many into darkness by that tongue. This vision was given after we were gone; but the substance of it was beginning now, on the eve of our departure.

Our move back to Portland was hard, cold, and heart-wrenching. We were leaving behind our children, grandchildren, and the people we had grown to love so dearly, in sorrow and confusion. David and Cheryl had been blessed with a second beautiful son barely a month before. Joshua David Bryan was born on November 16, 1983 in Aberdeen. I was being pulled away before I could even get to know our newest Bryan baby, and the winter weather depicted the severe unfairness of it all. Western Washington tended to produce weather combinations that would often chill to the bone. Seldom turning to snow, which would have at least lessened the gloom, the extreme levels of moisture in the coastal air became an icy wetness that felt *colder* than cold! That's what the weather was like that sad day; the day our kids and many church friends came to our Aberdeen home to help us load up our moving truck for the trip to Portland. The name of that place—Grays Harbor—was never so fitting as then. Brutal cold, biting wind, and dreary gray described not only the weather, but the gloom in so many hearts as we worked with frozen fingers, stinging faces and despairing thoughts that tumbled over each other. Satan's attacks had been fierce and relentless, and terrible mistakes had been made, leaving many hearts wounded and bleeding, including my own. The future looked grim and hopes languished in a sea of tears and mournful sorrows. December 23rd, my fiftieth birthday, we left Aberdeen, Washington in an ice storm. Gail drove a pick-up, Dan Davenport—whose kindness and generosity I will never forget—insisted on driving the U-Haul so he could bring it back and save us one hundred dollars, and I drove alone in our car. The roads were bad and the two and a half hour trip to Portland, very precarious. I was still in shock, drenched by grief, and now a skinny one hundred and twelve pounds from being unable to eat in weeks past. The agony of my soul was unbearable; I was devastated and deeply hurt, with vicious tongues wagging behind me to add insult to undeserved injury. They could not know how they had re-opened my wounds, or how their shallow conclusions had bludgeoned my heart, the heart that had loved and served them for seven years. *"Lord Jesus, forgive them. They don't know the half…"* my spirit whispered, for my lips would not move. The icy wind and bitter cold of that day were uncanny, yet a perfect picture of the numbness shrouding my heart and soul. The sunless horizon shouted that Hope was imprisoned, and my frosty breath seemed fitting for the end of something: weak, soundless, and cold.

CHAPTER TWELVE

Unsettled Weather

When we pulled our gloomy caravan up to the curb in front of the cute yellow house we were to live in, we found two inches of ice on the front door that had to be broken off before we could even get inside. Was this a sign of the difficulty we could face in getting through the next door that God would open for us—somewhere down the road? Pressing past the first of obstacles, we got in and began to unload. Inside the U-Haul truck we discovered that all of my houseplants had frozen completely during our road trip. Seeing them drooped over the edges of their pots and lying wilted on the floor was a depiction too close for comfort. I felt like my own life had just undergone the same exposure to the elements; I could identify with their soft, rubbery stems and drooping heads. In I Corinthians 10:12-13 (KJV) Paul speaks of the Israelites who were overthrown in the wilderness, and exhorts us to beware that we do not experience the same fate. *"Wherefore let him that thinketh he standeth take heed lest he fall. There hath no temptation taken you but such as is common to man: but God is faithful, who will not suffer you to be tempted above that ye are able; but will with the temptation also make a way to escape, that ye may be able to bear it."* I knew where my help would come from, and that in my weakness God would show himself strong. We unloaded, and set things up enough to spend the night, but at some point the power went off and we had no electricity. The ice storm was severe all over the city, downing power lines and leaving our part of town in darkness and without warmth. We stayed with our son and daughter-in-law, Mark and Diane, for a few days until power could be restored and we could finish moving in.

On Probation

Since we had been called back to our church in Portland for a time of discipline, accountability, and restoration, this was announced to the congregation on Sunday morning as we sat there in the church service. A few people came up afterwards with compassionate hugs but most didn't even look in our direction and nobody knew what to say, so it was quite awkward and embarrassing. The discipline and accountability were delivered as promised, for it felt like we had been brought forward to stand in the corner in front of the class. Restoration? Not that day, anyway. We felt very little warmth or welcome, so I was not sure how that part would play out. Gail had been told to get a job and forget about ministry. He was almost suicidal; he said he had ruined his life and wished he could die. It didn't help that attitudes of disgust from some of the leaders so closely resembled the accusations of the enemy of his soul. He was often treated with condescension, as if his failures in one area made him untrustworthy with all things. I struggled under the same burden, feeling as if I was automatically thrown into a "less than" category by association. I received awkward looks and superficial greetings from people I had known as friends and colleagues for years. Gail's own attitude was very humble and compliant and he usually said, "I deserve all of it." He gladly submitted to everything he was asked to do but, other than that, both of us were left completely alone. The atmosphere of relational circumstances closely resembled one of those *unsettled* weather systems: no major movement to bring in big change, but many small disturbances causing periods of clouds and spotty storms. Just like a weak weather system that can't decide which direction to go we could receive a burst of sunshine one day and a biting wind the next. I didn't know what to expect, and could only hope that a better pattern would develop soon. I understood clearly, however, that our surroundings and circumstances should never be the source of our comfort, and that another's opinion of what we needed to thrive may or may not be sufficient for progress. Human understanding is limited; and life teaches us that being in close proximity to someone in crises is not the same as walking in their shoes. Our victory is found in Jesus alone; for only he can see every obscure detail of our situation, or clearly hear the lamentations of the soul. This was the setting in which the Lord gave me a song, "Jesus has Triumphed in Me."[1] I awoke on January 28, 1984, singing these lines in my spirit.

Jesus has triumphed again,
Over my heartache and pain.
If I let Him reign, he'll put an end
To all of the striving within.

Chorus: Peace! Be still!" His voice speaks to my spirit;
If I but listen, I can softly hear it.
Then comes the calm; His healing balm;
And I know He has triumphed again!

Jesus is reigning in me!
He sets my troubled heart free
From the fear and distress that have robbed me of rest.
Now I will worship my King.

Jesus is Master of me!
He wants me to have victory
Over each situation that brings me frustration;
So others, His glory will see![1]

The scripture came to me from Matthew 10:39 (KJV) "*...he that loseth his life for my sake shall find it.*" I felt like I had so much to give but had lost every outlet through which to give it. David of the Bible ran for his life, and hid in caves, for years after he had already been anointed King by the prophet, Samuel. No one wants to experience the difficult scenarios our Bible heroes endured, yet they are recorded for our education in the realities of life. We can be full of spiritual riches and still be thrust into wilderness experiences; and God is faithful to use all things for our good and for his glory. Shortly after receiving this song into my spirit, I had an invitation to attend a women's retreat with a dear friend who had been invited to speak. The location was in Washington State, and the event was sponsored by churches that we had been in close fellowship with while pastoring in Hoquiam. I had also been contacted by faithful friends from our previous church who hoped to see me there. I decided to accept, and I was looking forward to seeing friends and church family again. Little did I know that there was more waiting to greet me than sweet Christian friendship; darkness had also found bitter hosts in which to hide. I was approached by a group of women from Hoquiam-Aberdeen who demanded to know why I had come there and told me in no uncertain terms that I was not welcome! If their words had not delivered such a nasty sting they would have been laughable—representing a mock court that had banished me to an island of eternal punishment from which I had somehow escaped! I was shocked and hurt by these false accusations and I identified with David's grief as expressed in Psalm 55:12-14 (NIV) *"If an enemy were insulting me, I could endure it; if a foe were rising against me, I could hide. But it is you, a man like myself, my companion, my close friend, with whom I once enjoyed sweet fellowship at the house of God, as we walked about among the worshipers."* On the other hand, the sadness I felt for them was deeper than the rejection they hurled out; because I knew that the bitterness cast against me would only ricochet back to my accusers and poison their character more deeply than I would ever be affected by their angry words. Others, who were filled with the love of Christ, were glad to see me and came to embrace me with kindness. The song God had given me was a timely buffer; it was already settled into my spirit as a shield against the spiteful onslaught of the enemy. His darts did not penetrate with the force he had presumed, nor left the wounds he had purposed for my pain.

Hacking through the Jungle

Gail had a pickup that he had bought from, and was making payments to, a man in the Hoquiam church. With this truck and his chainsaw, he thought we could go into the forest to find wood that we could cut up and sell in town. It was January, and the weather was very cold; but at least this was work that we could start immediately. We drove around on dirt roads looking for slash piles that were free to the public. He wanted me to go with him and help load the wood in the truck as he cut it into small logs and pieces. We had gloves and coats, so we prepared the best we could for an outdoor job in winter time. One of the big logs hit me on the leg and was very painful. I was freezing, and miserable; and the work was really too hard for me to do because I was very thin from trauma-induced weight loss. We worked hard all day long, however, from morning until dusk. When we finally got home, we had to unload all the wood into our driveway and stack it in cords. We made a sign that said "Firewood for

Sale", but didn't sell much of it and made very little money. We had rented a trailer for this venture so we had to take that and our gas costs out of our profits. We really needed the money because we had only gotten a small severance pay from the church in Hoquiam and we had to pay rent and utilities. We realized right away that we would not be able to make enough to keep the truck, so that venture ended with arrangements to take it back to the man we had bought it from.

The next opportunity was presented by a young man in the church who was with an insurance and mutual fund holding company and needed to build his pyramid. Consequently, right on the heels of the wood-cutting project he got Gail to go to a meeting with him. At fifty-two Gail figured this was at least something he could do that was not so physically demanding. He attended all the meetings only to discover that everything was voluntary while he was learning the ropes. It cost us about one hundred and fifty dollars to get the training he needed before he finally passed the test and got his securities license. Immediately he wanted me to get the training and get into the business beneath him, which would help his young up-line as well. This was the last type of business I wanted to be involved in, but I went through all the training and got my license. I was grieved about it because we didn't remotely agree with these concepts of depending on insurance plans. We had always trusted God for everything and I saw the entire scheme as a waste of time and money. I only sold one policy. We tired very quickly of the philosophy behind it because every meeting was filled with the same old hype, "Take charge of your destiny! You can have what you want! Put your dreams on your refrigerator and say 'I *will* have a new home!' The verbiage and coaching continually promoted greed, covetousness and things we didn't want to identify with so after a few months Gail decided to look for another job. Besides, we weren't making any money.

Now it was summer time and Gail found out about a man in the church who had his own construction business and needed some help. This man was very kind and had a nice family. He hired Gail to work with him part time for a minimal wage. Meanwhile, Gail had also been asked to do volunteer work for the church as a means of "proving himself." There was a lot of tree and shrub trimming to maintain on the new church property on the hill. His experience from the tree business with his brother in California enabled Gail to do an excellent job, and his good work led to a few side jobs for other people needing these professional services. I was not working a job during this time but often helped my husband with some of his odd jobs while staying busy with volunteer services. I worked in the church nursery on Sundays and Wednesday nights. We were expected to be at every service which, at least, provided part of the "restoration" component through worship and preaching of the Word; but there was no effort by anyone else to facilitate the help we had been summoned back for. We were just *there*—staying busy and being faithful. I remember Gail mentioning that we probably could have done better by going somewhere else where there was a small church that could benefit by our experience. Even though he was submissive to the whole thing, it was plain that no restorative counsel or directive input was forthcoming, and that we would be praying through this transition on our own. He fasted quite a bit, and would often be down on his knees engaged in sincere prayer. He would say to me, "Nobody here has time to mess with me; they're all too busy." They had a strong focus on training up the next generation for leadership and kingdom business, which we could appreciate from our own experience as pastors. Consequently, however, anyone with enough experience to work with people like us was engaged in meetings, dinners and fellowship with their younger associates and mentees. One time the pastor's wife stopped in for a few minutes on her way to another meeting to say, "Hello". Another time the senior pastor saw me coming and asked in passing, "How are you doing?" I took the opportunity to tell him that I was disappointed because the "help" that we had been assured of in coming here had never been brought up again. His response was, "Well, I don't really know how to help Gail. In most areas he is as experienced as I am. He is a mature Christian who understands the Word of God, and he knows what to do. He probably just needs some accountability, and I don't have time to do that. Do you think he would be accountable to someone else?"

"Yes!" I answered confidently. "Gail has always been open to counsel." Then a couple who were elders at the time invited Gail and me to come to their home for dinner. They were both kind, and showed Christian love to us; but they talked in general terms all evening and avoided any personal conversation. No appointments were ever made with us by anyone else in a leadership role. They were busy with more important things, and their schedules were full of ministry opportunities that were undoubtedly more appealing—and much less complicated than our dilemma.

One sad day I was sitting on the front steps of the yellow house grieving my heart out. I was feeling that life was over and hope was very dim. Suddenly a tiny, cute girl came down the sidewalk and walked over beside me. I smiled and said, "Hi. How are you today?" She answered, "Fine" in her sweet, tiny voice. She just talked to me and let me hold her little hand. There was no adult around and no one else with her, which seemed odd in a big city like Portland. I don't know if she was an angel but it was the most healing experience I've ever had; and I thought, "There will always be happiness where children are; and there will always be a future if there are children." I was comforted, simply by the presence of a sweet, innocent child.

The church owned several houses up and down the street on which we lived right across from the church building. Several couples that were part of the church leadership lived in these houses and would walk back and forth to the meetings. I specifically remember one Minister's Fellowship where I could look out the window and see all of our former ministerial associates and friends walking by in groups on their way to the meeting. A deep sadness enveloped me as I watched from the inside out. Nobody noticed; no one stopped by to see us or seemed to care how we were doing. They needed additional volunteers at that fellowship meeting so I was asked to serve, and I remembered a verse by Edwin Markham that I had learned as a child.

> *He drew a circle that shut me out —*
> *Heretic, rebel, a thing to flout.*
> *But Love and I had the wit to win;*
> *We drew a circle that took him in!*[2]

As I poured coffee from table to table where many of our former friends were seated, my heart grieved the loss of the camaraderie I had enjoyed only months before. People avoided eye contact because they didn't know what to say. I walked among my friends without speaking to a single soul. It seemed that the stripping of my husband's title had placed me on probation by association. I had somehow been assigned jail clothes and kitchen duty! The servant's heart I'd always had was just as willing to attend here as anywhere, but the superficial treatment from others who could not see me as the same Eunice that I had always been magnified the hurt of a very lonely season. I was Gail Bryan's wife; but that's not all I was. Yet, this place of restoration and healing felt more like a jungle of isolation; and it seemed that my God-given identity was trapped behind the door of someone else's Scarlet Letter.

Gail and I had a lot of conversations at home about these things. He openly talked about what a big failure he was and what a disappointment he had been to everyone. He could see that the pastor was a very strong man who appreciated strength in others who could benefit the work, but had no forbearance toward weakness, or patience for the process of restoring the fallen. There was a disdainful attitude toward us from many of the leaders there. One time we were invited to a meeting—and this was after we'd been back nearly four years serving faithfully in every way we knew how. One of the most prominent leaders looked at Gail and said, "You know, with your record, I wouldn't even trust you around my kids." My husband was always able to handle inappropriate comments with grace and dignity, and this time was no different. Later, though, Gail just shook his head in disbelief and said, "My goodness, that young man has barely begun to parent his children and ours are not only well-raised, but all serving God faithfully as adults." Despite his periodic downfalls as an individual, Gail always had very strong family values and child-rearing concepts. We always agreed on how to raise and discipline our children as they grew up in our home, and whenever he dealt with the kids on anything his parental advice was wise and biblical. He loved his kids, and they loved him.

Healing Balms

Our son, Mark, had written a beautiful song for us during those first excruciating months. It came at Gail's most discouraging time when he simply wished he could die. It was a God-send, anointed by the Lord, and we listened to it again and again. "He's Ever Interceding"[3] was like the Balm of Gilead to our souls. It was inspired by Hebrews 11:25 (KJV), *"He is able to save to the uttermost those who draw near to God through him, since he always lives to make intercession for them."*

Walking through the shadows at the closing of the day,
I wonder if I've strength to carry on.
I wonder if these armaments have strength enough to stay;
A shelter when the battle rages on.

Looking up through tear-stained eyes in search of God above;
Crying from a war-torn heart for His power and His love;
As the cry ascends the blackened night and darkness falls,
His voice bursts through the darkest night, "My child, I'm Lord of All!"

Chorus: Don't you know I'm ever interceding?
Don't you know, I know your every need?
And, though the battle seems unending,
Don't you know that I care for thee?

Rising up with morning light, I see the road ahead.
It's crooked, and it's clouded, and it's long;
But now I have the will to live and the strength to lift my head.
And, rising from my heart, there is a song!

Chorus: 'Cause I know that He's ever interceding!
And I know that He knows my every need.
And, though the battle seems unending,
Yes; I know that He cares for me.

So, pilgrim, if you're weary and your battle rages on;
You've tried and failed; and now all hope seems gone.
Lift up your eyes and see the Lord! He's seated on the Throne!
He's tried, and He's true, and He's faithful; and your battle He has won![iv]

Thus, the first year back in Portland was largely a time of recurring shock, embarrassing circumstances, and unexpected reproach; yet we willingly humbled ourselves to do all we were asked and we were sincere in our commitments. It bodes well for everyone's future to remember that in every circumstance two roads lie ahead of us; and the road we choose will determine not only our consequence, but our character. We chose to be there for all the services, pre-prayer before the services, and everything in between, even though it was difficult to be *present* and *invisible* at the same time. Nobody talked to us, or even looked our direction. So I decided to take the initiative myself and I started inviting people to our home. We met more friends this way, and began to build lasting relationships based on our whole identity rather than fragments of our recent past. People from Aberdeen and Hoquiam were also coming down to visit and spend time with us. Many families from our church in Washington loved us and missed us, and drove down often for fellowship and to attend services with us. We had been told not to contact anyone from the church up there and it was very hard, like leaving your baby with someone and not being allowed to communicate with them. We complied with this, but we couldn't control the flow of guests who contacted us and came on their own, so we had some good times of refreshment and healing through these visits. They didn't talk much about the church, anyway; they just missed us and wanted to be together again.

In September, Mark and Diane had their first child. Kari Marie Bryan was born on September 13, 1984 in Portland, Oregon. Gail had a job selling aerial photos of ranch properties, which required a lot of driving around in the country to show the photos to the property owners in hopes of a sale. I went with him on one of these drives, but was reluctant because Diane was due any time and I was afraid the baby would come before we got back. Sure enough, when we returned to the city we found out that they were all at the hospital celebrating the arrival of our fourth granddaughter. Diane's folks were there with them, and when we got to the hospital we saw the baby and heard about the birth. I really got close to Kari during these first years in Portland because we had to leave our other six grandchildren in Washington when we resigned.

I was able to babysit for Mark and Diane when they had meetings to attend, and it was so fun to see little Kari at every service and watch her grow. The sweet innocence and joy of a small child brings warmth, like sunshine, to the soul; pure wonder, genuine smiles, and miniature perfection.

I will never forget the Christmas of 1984, exactly one year after we had left Rhema Fellowship. Dorcas and Ed invited us back to the harbor to spend Christmas with them at their beautiful newly built home in Cosmopolis. Everyone was still trying to heal and regroup from the cyclonic events of the past year. Even with the many questions remaining, however, and all the raw feelings and loose ends, it was healing to spend quality time with our children and grandchildren. The singing, hearing poems, exchanging gifts, and sharing meals was soothing to our souls. The welcoming arms, I-love-yous, warm smiles and even some glistening tears all pooled together to soften the glaring reality of what had been lost. There was a piñata for the kids, and the atmosphere was filled with laughter, forgiveness and hope. Each testimony, every prayer, and the timeless story of our Savior's birth from the book of Luke went a long way toward soothing our spirits and rebuilding bridges that the enemy of our souls had so furiously sought to destroy. We experienced firsthand how "the family that prays together stays together."

Very often, when we would see the kids or old friends, Gail would later talk to me about his regrets for what he put the rest of us through. He was remorseful, and apologized that I had to endure all these consequences for things that were not my fault. He wept a lot in church; but he also found many encouraging scriptures about rising up and going on in God instead of allowing the enemy to gloat. One of his favorites was Micah 7:8 (KJV) *"Rejoice not against me, O mine enemy: when I fall, I shall arise; when I sit in darkness, the LORD hall be a light unto me."* This verse was also made into a chorus with a catchy tune that we sang often at Rhema. New paths are always possible on this pilgrim journey and, step by step, we were forging our way.

Closer to Daylight

We had been back in the big city for over a year now, most of which had been a struggle that felt like eking our way up the muddy walls of a deep pit toward the edge of daylight. We had been exhorted that "this is really the safest place that you could be". I fully understood that just because something is hard doesn't mean it is not God's will, yet the picture didn't seem complete. Our experience thus far seemed very much a fulfillment of the discipline and accountability piece, but not all that 'safe' and, in fact, somewhat removed from anything that I would call being restored to fellowship. Nevertheless, with no apparent options at hand, we pressed on with whatever was set before us to do, and things began to get better.

On June 18, 1985 Joseph David Bryan was born in Aberdeen, Washington. He was the first grandchild born in Aberdeen after we left, and the only thing I remember about his birth is that I missed it all. It wasn't that I had never missed the birth of a grandchild before; it was just hard because we were instructed to stay away from there and to not interact with any of the people in any way. We'd been in Portland for a year and five months and we were both trying to hold down jobs; so the timing may have been a contributing factor as well. Mainly, however, we had been taught to come under authority and obey those that were over us. Basic Youth Concepts was popular then and taught that if you were treated wrongly by leaders God would make it right in His time. So we were submissive and didn't question anything. Looking back, I see that perspective as quite controlling, but we were shattered and struggling to survive however we could. We probably didn't think twice about the restrictions. We were just happy for David and Cheryl. Our youngest son had three little boys of his own, James, Joshua and now, Joseph. They gave all of them his name, David, as their middle names. We all laughed when Cheryl said, "Well, I didn't want any of them to have an identity crisis so I named all of them after their dad!"

Later that summer, Dorcas and Ed moved back to Portland from Aberdeen, Washington. We were not apprised of the circumstances under which they came, but I knew they had carried too heavy a load at Rhema Fellowhip following our departure. The young men on our leadership team had been left to clean up a mess that they had not made, and our son-in-law was faithful to his duties as an elder. During this past year and one half, Ed and Dorcas had done everything they could to help with the transition, staying on board until new pastors had been installed. Now they were invited to return to the place where they first met and began their ministry journey together. There was much work to be done on the new church buildings and grounds. Ed was placed in a supervisory position for the ongoing construction projects, and it seemed that he was busy from daylight until dark. They lived in a duplex across the street from our house. It was not only enjoyable to have my daughter and two granddaughters so close, but a relief later on to have Ed nearby when Gail worked nights. One time my phone rang in the middle of the night and I ran to answer it thinking that it was an emergency with Gail or one of the kids. Instead, a spine-chilling male voice told me in guttural, menacing tones that he was going to kill me. I tried to call for help, but he called back so quickly every time I hung up the phone that I couldn't dial a number. Finally, I let it ring and ring until it stopped and then I tried to call Gail. He was at work, but there were no cell phones in those days so I couldn't reach him. I called Ed, my son-in-law, and he walked across the street from their duplex and brought me over to their house to spend the night. He called the police immediately to report it and they asked me a lot of irrelevant questions, thinking I may have brought the threat upon myself somehow. When they were satisfied that this was not the case, they informed us that these calls had been more common recently and that it was most likely a perverse and cruel prank. I was grateful to be safe on my kids' couch that night but I shook like a leaf for some time from the trauma of it. I remember being fearful of staying alone at night in the big city for a long time after that because the house we lived in was not secure and the locks were unreliable. I would play my Bible cassette tapes until I fell asleep, and I was always relieved to see the sun rise on another day. Finally, as I pondered Psalm 3 about "David's many and vicious enemies, God took away my fear. Verses 4-6 say, *"I cried unto the LORD with my voice, and he heard me out of his holy hill. I laid me down and slept; I awaked; for the LORD sustained me. I will not be afraid of ten thousands of people that have set themselves against me round about."*

Dorcas and the girls came over a lot, and sometimes I kept my granddaughters, Christy and Faith, while their parents were engaged elsewhere. One of my favorite activities was to make cassette recordings of the girls' tiny voices in conversation and story-telling. Listening to these tapes brought me joy again and again through the years, and I have kept them to share with my great-granddaughters someday. I also began teaching Christy to play a small accordion, which she picked up very quickly—quite a feat for a small child with such a difficult instrument. She practiced a song for an assembly at school and knew it perfectly; but she got stage fright at the last minute and didn't perform well. After that negative experience she had no interest and, as far as I know, she never played again; although she definitely had the knack for it and, I believe, could have become proficient.

One day I was sitting in church and noticed a business man in the balcony who kept glancing over at us. He came over after the service and described his business, asking if I would be interested in working part time for him. He sold security doors and windows and displayed his products at Home and Trade shows in the area. He needed someone to be on call to work his information booths on weekends whenever he had a show. So they trained me to work in the office and to work the trade shows on weekends. The work was easy and the pay was just as good as any I had been accustomed to. I talked to many interested people who stopped at our booths, gave them pamphlets, and took their contact information if they wanted more material sent to them. When the shows concluded, I followed up with all interested customers and made appointments for the salesperson. We had kiosks in malls or shows at fairgrounds, such as the Oregon State Fair or local county fairs, and other public event locations. I did not work every weekend; and when I was scheduled on a Sunday I never had to miss church because the events were in the afternoon. I loved this job and it was a wonderful outlet for me during this time. I was glad to go back to work and help with the expenses. I had always enjoyed working at every job I had but I always knew they were temporary because my life's work was in the church. So anywhere I was employed I did my best to lead an exemplary Christian life and to leave a good testimony to others, spreading God's love to my fellow employees. Happily, I can say that I have some "sheaves" from these endeavors to place at the feet of Jesus someday—people I worked with who came to the Lord. Others I won't know about until I see Jesus because we never see all that God is doing through the testimony we are daily living out. We trust God for "fruit that will remain" in lives that were impacted for the Kingdom by our own. This job was another opportunity and, once again, the Lord gave me an anointing to witness to everybody that I worked with as well as many of the people that I talked to at our home shows. I remember people making comments like, "What is it about you?" or "I wonder what it is about you that is so intriguing to me?" One man said, "I'm an atheist, but everything you say makes so much sense that I want to believe." I answered him, "That's because I'm telling you the truth! The Holy Spirit is working in you." Every time I went to work I prayed about who I would witness to next. I eventually talked with all my lady co-workers and finally one of them asked if she could go to church with me. She'd been reading her Bible and had brought it with her. She knew we had services on Sunday nights and was prepared to attend with me. She became a Christian immediately, and I mentored her for several years until we went our separate ways. She married a minister and they continued to serve the Lord together.

When I started this job Gail was still working in construction part time and on the church property. He was looking for work all the time, but never found anything permanent and he needed to stay busy. Our son, Mark, was taking flying lessons and had talked to Gail about it, but we didn't have the money for it so I never gave it a second thought. Gail had purchased a beautiful $2400 guitar while we lived in Aberdeen and had promised me that he wouldn't sell it like he did the last one. One day I noticed that it was gone and I said, "Where is your guitar?"

"I sold it to pay for my flying lessons," he said matter-of-factly. "I have to do something or I will go insane. You don't know what I'm going through. I've got to keep busy." I knew this was true, but I wished he could have done something that was not so costly. He finally had a chance to talk to the senior pastor who told him again to look for work as if he had never been in the ministry. He had been looking for a job ever since we had arrived back in Portland but had not found anything full-time. At home, Gail told me, "Well, I've always wanted to work with guns so I guess I should pursue that as a business."

He began to study all kinds of books about gun-smithing and started buying components for a Gun Shop. Our only income was mine so everything he put into the Gun Shop was purchased on credit. He built cabinets downstairs where we lived and got the tools he needed one by one until, before he realized it, we were $25,000 in debt! When I found out about it, I was furious with him; especially since he had recently sold his guitar in order to take flying lessons. The interest was so high on the credit cards that I wondered if we would ever pay them off. Gail was such a perfectionist that he did everything in detail and of the highest quality so it took more time and more money; but both activities were a god-send for him. He loved flying, and thoroughly enjoyed working on his Gun Shop at the same time. I had trusted the Lord to manage our finances all my life; I could trust Him with this, too.

Working at the School

That fall, there was an announcement in the bulletin about a job at the Christian high school. They needed a secretary for their office. I thought I might like to do that, but didn't feel that I was really secretary material. I talked to them about it anyway and they asked if I could type, which I could but not very fast. So they decided to hire me as a Monitor because they needed another one for their Learning Center in the high school. These were helpers who walked around the classroom, answering questions and helping the students all day—kind of like teacher's assistants. The man who interviewed me for the position said that I had everything they were looking for. The one I worked for was the supervisor over the high school, who I still believe was one of the finest men I've ever known. The job was easy for me and I loved the people I worked with, but I was only a Monitor for a short time. They wanted to move the school secretary over to work in their Bible College instead, leaving her position open. I took the Secretary job, but wasn't as experienced or efficient as she was so I helped with a variety of miscellaneous duties in the beginning. It seemed like I answered the phone a million times a day! I also had to deal with all the students who were delinquent or tardy. I had to write out their detention slips when they came in late. I said to one boy, "D, why are you late for the third time in a row?" He said, "What am I gonna do? I'm depending on my mother to bring me and she's always late; so I get another detention." I enjoyed all of the students, but some of them were quite ornery. Even the ornery ones liked me eventually, and I kept this job until we moved from Portland. When I left the school much later, after working there for five years, the staff and students gave me a lovely going-away party with nice gifts and the kindest of words, which was very rewarding and considerably healing after the wounds of my recent past. Many cards from the students included words of honor and respect such as, "To the godliest lady I have ever known." They also presented me with a beautiful plaque that I still have. It pictures a woman in a country setting with a scriptural caption that reads, "Her ways are ways of Pleasantness, and all her Paths are Peace."

To Counsel…or Not

We had been back in Portland for two years, gladly doing whatever our hands found to do. Gail had attended every service, doing all he was asked. We were not only part of a Home Group, but were hosting it as well. We had finally made a few friends, but not especially close. We were never again invited to take part in any leadership activities, although before we went to Aberdeen, I had been invited to speak at retreats and participated in all things pastoral. Guilty by association, I donned a stigma that, in some circles, would stick for the rest of my life even after my husband was gone. I would later discover that the work God has for us to do in His kingdom is not restricted by man-made titles; and that our callings from God need not remain locked behind man-made doors. All the time we were in Portland, regardless of popular opinion, people came to me regularly for prayer and advice. God sustained his ordained ministry of counselling and discipleship through me by his own means. I enjoyed many thrilling sessions taking new converts through a basic Christian principles course, and I spent countless hours in exhortation and encouragement to those with needs. I initiated these relationships on my own and we continued to enlarge our capacity for hospitality as well. I was already in the habit of preparing dinner for guests on Sundays so this practice was sustained. We had people over regularly, and it was a great joy to us, as well as a blessing to our guests.

Eventually, a young man on the church's counseling staff was asked to work with us. He talked to Gail a few times and told him to humble himself and to be a man of God, but to forget about the ministry. We had heard this before, and the "counseling" was short-lived. Every question the young man asked, Gail had the right answer for. He'd had good up-bringing and supportive parents, a wonderful wife, a good marriage, and all the rest. There was nothing in his background to blame his failures on and everything Gail talked about was from the perspective of a mature Christian man. Finally, the young man told Gail, "You know more than I do; you should be counseling me!" He decided it might be better to focus on me and I was invited to one session where he questioned me about my parents. I just cried, remembering their godly lifestyles and reciprocal loyalty to one another. Everything in my childhood home seemed so good and right. So the counselor suggested that Gail should do something nice for *them* because it would mean so much to me. He told my husband that he needed to heal the wounds that he had caused. Gail was instructed to make some new covenants with *himself* in order to mend our relationship and to live more for me. He told him to do things like buy a music box, put hand-written promises inside, and fulfill one each week. This young-married man was probably going by the book, but we felt like he'd been thrown a curve ball and would appreciate being off the hook. He finally told Gail that he didn't think these sessions were needed, and that we would probably benefit more by engaging in the church body and staying active in service and fellowship—which we had been doing since we arrived. Therefore, the counseling stopped; but nothing else changed. We gladly continued to attend all the services, host the Home Group, and volunteer wherever we could.

While Gail worked on his custom rifle business he still took a few odd jobs to bring in some money until he could finish and sell some guns. One of these jobs was selling aerial photographs of rural properties. The second winter, 1985, he had gone out driving in the country to sell some of his photos and had slid off the icy roads and wrecked his car. He had become acquainted with a chiropractor who was interested in purchasing several of his guns and had frequented the shop enough to be on very friendly terms with us. When he found out about Gail's wreck, he said, "Well, why don't you borrow my Corvette? Your wife can drive it to school." When I roared up and parked that sports car at the school, those high school boys stood gawking in complete disbelief! "Mrs. Bryan! What are you doing in that Corvette?" They thought it was fabulous, and I enjoyed keeping them in suspense for a few minutes until I told them it was borrowed. My job at the school was good, but the time commitment was a heavy responsibility because every employee was needed onsite for extra-curricular activities as well as during school hours. There was too much to do and no one else to do it; we were it! Every quarter we would stay after school until at least 7:00 pm recording grades and preparing all the report cards for students. There was no overtime pay, but I was more than glad to get my eight hundred dollars per month! We needed every penny!

Thus, time was passing by and we were filling it up with whatever our hands found to do; but sometimes I felt that we were keeping time to a drumbeat that was not our own. Yes, there were obligations to fulfill, bills to pay, and duties to perform; but there were intervals when I longed to see what God's calendar looked like. What was ahead for us? I knew there was more. Gail and I used to sing a cheerful duet called "God's Calendar of Days". Some of the lyrics went like this:

> *In looking o'er God's Calendar of Days,*
> *I was surprised to see how blind I'd been.*
> *For in it I saw times for prayer and praise,*
> *But not a single moment left for sin.*

> *Chorus: In God's Calendar of Days there are times for prayer and praise,*
> *And the joys we find in service are like golden holidays!*
> *Not a Blue Day on the list; every cloud by sunshine kissed!*
> *Dwelling 'neath Hope's gleaming rays; in God's Calendar of Days.*

> *In all God's Calendar I failed to see*
> *one single day when we should idle be.*
> *And then a song of joy burst from my heart*
> *to think that he might use even me.* [4]

It was about God's calendar having plenty of times for prayer and praise; and the days of service to him were like golden holidays. It was full of hope and joy, with no sadness—or blue days—in sight. I had lived a lifetime of serving joyfully in whatever capacity was required of me. Yet, during these years I had to focus on prayer and praise, for although I was never idle, the "golden holidays" did not seem so evident. I actually had my "blue days" during this season, but every one of them was followed by a *Song in the Night* that left an indelible refrain upon my soul declaring God's faithfulness to be the same now as it had ever been to me. I knew His thoughts would always be higher than mine, and His ways mysterious; but there was never a doubt that my times were in His hands, or that he was working all things for my good.

Meanwhile, there were other joys along the way! Early in 1986, Dorcas and Ed had moved out of the duplexes onto the church property where Ed worked. They had an opportunity to build a house and built it right into the hillside— amazing to me! Dorcas and Ed had always been a team, and she was used to working hard; but this project took the cake! I remember her carrying buckets of broken cement and plaster board up and down a very steep staircase to the dumpster. When their home was completed it was time to rejoice, and they had more room for their family. They had decided to adopt a son after losing Sarah Elisabeth eight years before. Philip Edward Mason was born in Aberdeen on February 17, 1986. They were excited to bring him home to Portland, and his big sisters, Christy and Faith, couldn't wait to help with their new little brother. He had a little king's welcome that came with, not a personal "valet", but with two mini-maids-in-waiting!

Burnside Burglars

After several years in the yellow house, we were given notice that this residence was needed for another family and we were asked to find another place by a certain date. Gail was still working for the church, but by this time he was getting compensation. A lot of supplies were being stolen from the property outside of business hours when no one was around so they hired him as a night time security guard. We found an older house that was so run-down and neglected that the landlord said if we would clean it up and trim the yard we could have the first month rent-free. So we moved to this house on Burnside Street and took in two boarders from the Bible College to help pay expenses. The house was in a bad area of town and was very dirty. It was a place where drugs and prostitution blatantly walked the main thoroughfare close by, and sirens were as frequent as clock chimes. We got robbed the first day we moved in. Gail's mother had come to visit and the three of us were out in the back yard where Gail and I were trimming and cleaning things up. Thieves apparently lurked nearby, calculating how much money they could make selling all of our nice tools! Before we went inside for lunch, Gail put all his yard tools in the garage and locked it with a large, heavy-duty padlock on the outside. By the time we came out again, the lock had been cut off and tossed to the sidewalk. The garage door was open and everything was gone. Our lawn mower, two chainsaws, and all kinds of expensive tools were practically stolen before our eyes, in broad daylight! Later we discovered that the place next to us was a drug house. The tenants played toxic rock music from the basement, with loud drums, late into the night and I was anxious the entire time we lived there. Portland was a big city and, consequently, had much more crime than we had ever been close to. Even at the first house, which was a much better area, we had been robbed. Gail had contracted some tree jobs and bought a small chainsaw that he could climb trees with to do his trimming. It was brand new and had a nice case. The next day it was stolen from the trunk of our car, parked right in front of our house on the street. There were some questionable characters two houses down and we always thought they must have seen us put the chain saw in the trunk because of how quickly it was stolen. The house on Burnside was right next door to The Matterhorn restaurant and their back parking lot was against our fence. We could look out the dining room window and see cars parked where people would stand around and smoke crack cocaine. I didn't realize what they were doing until our college boarders moved in. When the boys saw what was going on, they told us what it was. There was plenty of evidence that this location was a bad place for a Gun Shop; but we had no choice. Despite the smaller space, Gail got it set up nicely and added jailhouse bars to all the windows. We would trust the angels of God that encamped round about our dwelling to keep those druggies from discovering what we had in the basement. The old Burnside house was built well, at least, and between the bars and the angelic barricade, we had no more break-ins while we lived there.

Gail had built several rifles by this time and had gained some return customers. His work included purchasing all the components for creating custom-weapons, including glass-bedding the barrels to enhance shooting accuracy. He tested every gun several times before selling, and could put five holes in a quarter-sized bullseye at 1,000 yards. He also owned all the necessary equipment, brass, and powders for creating the custom-loaded cartridges. He was conscientious and detailed in his work, well-worth his hire. Yet customers would often wheedle a bargain for themselves, trading services for firearms. One chiropractor who wanted several guns discovered that the only way to get a lower price was to throw in a package of one hundred dollar treatments with his cash. Gail usually accepted them because he had a lot of headaches, neck, and back pain that was relieved by the chiropractic treatments, which we could never afford to pay for on our own.

One day, while working at the school, I received a surprise phone call from my husband. He had been partly-employed selling permanent siding with a friend and they were having lunch together that day. When I answered the phone, he asked, "Eunice, did you come and pick up the car this afternoon?" Thinking that was an odd question, I answered, "No; where was it?"

"Well," he rejoined. "It was parked in front of The Matterhorn, but when we came out after lunch it was gone." Once again, we had been robbed in broad daylight. Our car was stolen as it sat parked in front of our house! Have you heard it said, "When life gives you lemons, make lemonade"? These years were uncommonly well-stocked with it!

Gail's business was slow-going, but he was making some money at it. In addition, he had really tried to do every kind of job possible. He was praying a lot at this time, too—at home and in the prayer room—always tender-hearted, believing God and always loving Jesus. As long as I had known him, Gail had been fervent in worship and a student of the Word. He loved godly people, too, and could never abide crooks or questionable characters. I wanted so desperately for him to get the right kind of help to conquer the vices of his past that had toppled his ministry and life's work; but it was not happening here. Gail always had an understanding about that. Whenever I would express frustration about not being "surrounded with help and encouragement" as pledged when we were brought back to this place, he never shared my disappointment. His gracious and mature response would always be, "Honey, they don't know what to do. And, can you blame them? What could they possibly tell me that I don't already know?" His honor and respect for all the other players in the arena never wavered. He never expected anything from them. I was the one who felt cast off and left floundering.

Honor and Progress

Summer of 1987 delivered an unforgettable surprise for us. Dorcas and Ed had made an appointment for a family portrait and asked me if I could get off work for it, which my boss agreed to. So I went from work to their beautiful home up on the hill and met Gail there. We were walking up to the house together and saw one of our young men from the Hoquiam church walking across the property. We wondered what in the world he was doing in Portland! Then we saw another couple from there and soon we began to see numbers of cars parked along the road. As our curiosity increased, I suddenly remembered, "Our anniversary!" Gail exclaimed, "You don't mean it!" Then we saw flowers, and a big banner that said, "Happy 35th Anniversary!" We opened the door to find that Mason's home was packed out with many friends from Hoquiam-Aberdeen, quite a few relatives, and new friends from Portland. Our children had been working toward this celebration in our honor and the walls were decorated with poster-sized photos from our past. We were never so surprised about anything; and we felt loved and celebrated. All of our kids and grandkids were there and spent the weekend so we had several meals and family times together as well. The whole clan dressed in western wear one day for a family portrait that we have cherished over the years. Our children were such a blessing to us during these years. The events that had separated us could have caused a permanent breach in our family, but we had spent too many years loving each other to stop now. The kids were hurt and disappointed, but mature and forgiving, wanting God's will to be done through this storm and beyond. They were kind and encouraging. Every time Becca wrote a song that she thought God gave for her own journey and encouragement—although she did not realize—it was for me. "I See Your Tears", "Patch of Blue", and many others that she recorded and sent to us during those years were special deliveries from Heaven! I played them a thousand times and cried. God sustained us in ways we never could have devised or imagined. As the pain began to subside, and life went on, we counted our big city blessings along the way. Our children were busy with their own families, their jobs and ministries; all of them were doing well. We enjoyed Dorcas' and Mark's families locally, and looked forward to visits from Becca's whenever they could come to Oregon. David and Cheryl had been offered an opportunity in California and had moved from Aberdeen in August of 1987. They would be farther away now, but God was guiding their lives and we were happy for their progress. We were also beginning to experience some progress of our own.

We had been serving and cooperating with everything expected of us, attending faithfully and not dependent on the church for anything. I had worked at whatever jobs I could find and Gail had also, and was now busy working in his Gun Shop; we were on our own. There was a pastor in Mt. Hood, Oregon that Gail had met and talked to during one of the meetings in Portland. He wanted Gail to come and preach for him, which we had done twice. One time that we went, Gail was planning to teach on child training and he told me that he had a strange dream. This was the morning before we left to go there, and he said, "A young couple was at the church and they had a two to three-year-old child that was misbehaving so badly that the parents were ready to leave. When I gave the altar call, I prayed for the man and was able to help him with his little boy." He said that the dream was very powerful, and he wondered what it meant. When we got there, and were sitting in the first service, Gail saw the same man and wife with their little boy, just as his dream had depicted! He preached on child training and the man came to the altar where Gail was able to pray with him and exhort him as a young father. We were amazed, and thanked God for this confirmation regarding our ministry.

Whether this prompted some action from our own leadership, or whether it was coincidence does not matter now; but at this time Gail was informed that he was no longer under discipline. He was told that his probation was over and that he was free to accept invitations to preach. Good thing; since we were already receiving requests and had taken meetings here and there. My work, however, was full time and we could never be gone more than a few days. As glad as I was about these opportunities I had noticed that Gail's preaching was not the same, and I believed he had lost much of his confidence and spoke with a lesser anointing. He was still ashamed of his personal failures and struggling with guilt. Like a wounded soldier that had fought with amazing skill and taken much ground, he had made foolish mistakes that had stripped him of his position and respect. His lost battles had cost him his confidence and drained his enthusiasm. He was paying the price of careless stewardship, and I was paying for it right along with him. Nevertheless, this same pastor from Mt. Hood had an outreach in Cutbank, Montana and wanted Gail to travel there with him as well. He did not enjoy the drive so they had decided to go by train, which afforded them the convenience of great conversation all the way there and back. As we became better acquainted with these people, they invited us back later to hold a longer revival. This time we went out on the Indian reservation to give out gospel tracts and witness about Christ in between services. We knew these opportunities were from the Lord, and we were excited to see God moving in other places. Sometimes we were invited to preach at smaller churches around the Portland area and other times the Lord took us to different places. God's eternal work is always in motion, and good things were happening behind the scenes, despite the odds.

On September 11, 1988 our sixth grandson was born in Portland. We were so excited that God had blessed Mark and Diane with a baby boy. Kari was now four years old and I had become very close to her from working in the church nursery and volunteering with the Children's Ministry, over which our son, Mark, and daughter-in-law, Diane, were now pastors. I so appreciated the opportunity of working with the children. This was always a joy to me, and filled the void left by some of my sorrows; just as filling my time with my own small children had helped me through some of the hardest times of my earlier years. The acceptance and wonder of a small child is a healing antidote for soul pain. Their playful laughter and sweet innocence can alleviate the nagging residue of past or present wounds, and provide a powerful dose of affirmation and hope; like walking into a sunny field of flowers from a dark, damp forest. By God's grace, we had weathered the storms of these last five years with grace and dignity. We had moved with the flow of this place, enduring the many adjustments while seizing the value of every blessing we found along the way. We had remained faithful, waiting on the Lord in the face of varied and unexpected difficulties that were mingled with fairly consistent disappointments. God had sustained us and walked this path with us; now he was preparing to open another door. We were being released into new territory, for He is the God of perpetual forgiveness, boundless love, and infinite opportunity. We had always understood the benefits, and accepted the challenge, of Colossians 3:23-24 (KJV) *"And whatsoever ye do, do it heartily, as to the Lord, and not unto men; Knowing that of the Lord ye shall receive the reward of the inheritance: for ye serve the Lord Christ."* What would our next assignment be?

CHAPTER THIRTEEN

Last Chance to Thrive

A Gorgeous Advance

Along Highway 101 on the Olympic Peninsula there is a small community called Sequim, Washington. Located on the Dungeness River and seated at the base of the Olympic Mountains, Sequim is the gateway to the Olympic National Park which accommodates four magical rain forests—some of the wettest in the United States. Yet, this charming town has the nickname of Sunny Sequim because its annual rainfall is about the same as Los Angeles, California. Cool fogs coming off the breezy Juan de Fuca Strait generate a humidity uncharacteristic for this low-precipitation climate; a climate that crowns this pacific northwestern area the Lavender Capital of North America, rivaled only in France.[1] Discovering this beautiful retreat to be our next place of residence was a complete surprise, and the events that made it possible were unexpected.

A sweet, dedicated couple that pastored a small church in Sequim was interested in becoming a part of a minister's fellowship group which was based out of the church we attended in Portland. They were declined, but in the process were put in touch with some good friends of ours who were recommended as candidates for that pastorate, since the original pastors wanted to move out of state to be closer to their family. These friends that had been recommended to Sequim had been close to us from the very beginning when we first moved to Portland. We used to have them come for dinner and I remember this brother saying, "Well, I know that Gail must be a wonderful man because he has to be in order to have such a happy wife!" He didn't know the half, but apparently my countenance showed the right kind of light, for which I was grateful. Gail loved this brother and always had a wonderful time laughing and talking with him. So when the church at Sequim was turned over to them they invited us to come up and visit. We discovered that it had been a struggle for them because the church was far from thriving when they had arrived. It included a Christian school that was breaking their small budget and keeping them in debt. Our friend had military experience and knew how to keep things in order. Additionally, he and his family were well-acquainted with the disciplinary practices of the private schools where their own children had attended. His own kids were very well trained and his wonderful wife was a woman of excellence. They soon tired of this struggle and moved back to Portland so that their children could finish school there. Meanwhile, through our association with these dear friends, the previous pastor heard about us and contacted us about coming to Sequim to preach at his church. Before inviting us he had contacted our Portland pastor for his input and he had approved, so we went. Then they invited us back to participate in a camp meeting where Gail would be the main speaker and others, mostly singers, would be sharing in ministry. I was off for the summer from my school job, so we decided to go.

When the camp meeting ended, the pastor asked us to stay and help with the church. He said he would give us an apartment to live in plus five hundred dollars per month for expenses. He had built fifty churches and knew how to construct roomy facilities for less money. To accommodate the Christian school he had built a gymnasium with locker rooms and showers, as well as numerous classrooms on the upper level. The finances had not come in for operating the school, so the entire facility was available for other uses. He showed us around the property and offered Gail a big room for his Gun Shop. The apartment he presented to us was a one-bedroom unit in the upper corner of the gym. It had been built to house guests, teachers or visiting speakers so, although small, it was a complete living unit with a deck on the outside. Additional upstairs rooms were available for any storage we needed while living in the apartment. This pastor was very accommodating because he was anxious to leave for another out-of-state trip. He and his wife still had a house in Sequim, so they had traveled back and forth to keep the church going after our friends had given up the pastorate. Their plan was still to retire and move closer to all of their children. Now he wanted us to come to Sequim to assist them while they made plans for this eventual transition.

It was the spring of 1989, and Gail was diligently praying for direction at this time. He was busy with his Gun Shop but after all these years of being at Portland, he was sincerely asking God what we should do next. Most of my paycheck from working at the Christian school was going toward feeding our two boarders, and the power bill had more than doubled with these boys living there. One of them took half-hour showers twice a day and the other one had an odd habit of plugging in an electric heater while lying on the couch with his shirt off! So when we got this offer from Sequim we were ready to go; and we knew it was the direction we had been praying for. We told our pastor in Portland and he gave us a letter of recommendation saying that we would be excellent assistants, and that he approved of the opportunity. We had another giant yard sale and got rid of everything that wouldn't fit in the small apartment we would be living in. Our two children who lived in Portland helped us, and within a matter of weeks we were packed up and on our way to Sequim, Washington for our next assignment. Some had mixed feelings about our going and had expressed strong feelings to Gail, disagreeing with any option allowing him to pastor again, even as an assistant. We understood their concerns, yet knew beyond a shadow of doubt that our hands would be forever tied in this place as far as fulfilling any calling of our own for the rest of our lives. We were restricted to support roles, with no freedom to pursue anything else that God had ordained for us individually. Dorcas and Ed made the drive with us and stayed overnight in Sequim to attend our first church service that Sunday.

Working with the pastors at Sequim was a wonderful experience after all we had been through. They were generous and kind to us, accommodating and appreciating us in every way. Sequim was a new beginning for us and, true to its nickname, the sun was always shining! It was a beautiful, restful place where the birds were always singing, along with my heart, and we were glad for some different scenery—in more ways than one. Many of the people in the church were our age so we made many new friends right away and developed some lasting relationships. The people were loving and kind, and glad we came. We made one of the extra rooms close to our apartment into a guest room with two double beds in it. We had a lot of overnight guests come to visit. Our friends and family were excited to see what was going on in Sequim, and happy about our new opportunity. The pastor was a wonderful, fatherly man who went above and beyond by willingly sponsoring needs of the church with money from his own successful, full-time construction business when funds were low. His health was not good and, although they were living there and occupying the pastorate, they were not able to do very much and expressed their gratefulness that we were there to fulfill most of the ministry needs. Consequently, we became very busy in a short time. We had goals for evangelizing the area and building up the church congregation. I started a Ladies' Bible Study right away that was well-attended. We began to see progress immediately, both in the church and in our ministry. After selling his beautiful guitar for flying lessons in Portland, Gail had later traded a pistol that our son-in-law wanted for a guitar that Ed was not using very much. So we were able to play our instruments together again, and we sang often. I also played the piano for worship, and started a children's church for the young ones that began with about eight children. Kingdom business was increasing; our assistantship was off to a great start, and time flew by. Before we knew it, summer began to wane and fall was in the air.

Another Crazy Adventure

So often, when Gail wanted to do something that he knew I would not agree to, he would simply neglect to tell me about it. One of these events was when he made arrangements with Jim, his best buddy in Emmett, Idaho to buy a horse from him. This was a young horse that had not been broken. He had decided to take this horse on a hunting trip and made a plan to go to Emmett a week early to break this bronc beforehand! Of course, he had to tell me about it in order to make the trip to Emmett. I was exasperated. "Why did you buy a horse without telling me?"

"Because," he answered without a hitch, "I knew that you wouldn't want me to buy it. So, I made a deal with Jim to keep it for me and I've been making payments to him."

"You can't break a horse in a week and expect it to be trustworthy!" I exclaimed.

"Well," he said with resolve, "I'm going to try." He had a rifle that he wanted to take on this hunt that he had worked very hard on. He had spent hour after hour in his Gun Shop checkering the stock and getting everything perfect. Also, there was a twelve-year-old boy, the grandson of our pastors, who had heard Gail's stories and had begged to go on a hunt with him so he decided to take him with us.

When we got to Emmett, I stayed with Hazel, Gail's mother, while he went out to a corral every day to work with this new horse and get it ready for the hunt. The animal was completely green, with no training whatsoever. He had also bought a horse trailer from Jim so, when the week of training was over, we loaded everything up to head out for our trip. When we got there, it was just a wide open, barren wilderness, high desert. It didn't look like a place that any smart deer would ever frequent! We drove for miles and miles before we got to our destination. I was nervous about being out in the middle of nowhere with a wild horse and a young boy! There was another friend, however, who was familiar with this eastern Oregon location and had planned to meet us at the chosen hunting site in a couple of days. I would feel better when he arrived but now it was time to set up our camp and get some rest. In the morning, we got up early and Gail saddled the horse and put his new rifle in the scabbard. I made a lunch for him and the boy, packing it in a plastic sack. I didn't even think about the noise it would make, but when Gail went to put the lunch sack down into the saddle bag, it crackled loudly and spooked the horse. He panicked and went wild, bucking and rearing up on his hind legs. Naturally, the more he jumped and twisted the more noise that sack made. Gail had hold of the lead rope and was hanging on desperately to keep the horse from running away, but to no avail. The horse jerked him around until it pulled his shoulder out of joint. The frantic steed kicked until he got away and went running out across the landscape, bucking all the way. He cavorted and carried on until he was so far away that he looked as small as a Lego piece where he finally stopped. Gail didn't say a word. He just watched him disappear as if to say, "Go ahead and buck your life away. I'm not chasing after you!" He was never a reactionary person about things he couldn't help. Then he said to me, "Well, honey. I want you to get in the van and drive me down this road until we get across from the horse. I'll take a little bit of grain with me and catch him; I'll bring these hobbles with me to keep him from running again." We got in the van and drove down to a point in the road that was across from where the horse had stopped. He was just standing there, all worn out, about a quarter mile away from us. After I dropped Gail off, he started walking slowly toward the horse and I drove back to the camp. He told me later that when he got to the horse it was shaking all over, scared to death and dripping with sweat. He kept moving slowly toward him, speaking in low tones to calm his nerves; "It's OK; whoa, boy," until he got close enough to reach the lead rope. He began to stroke the horse's neck and gently pat him to calm him down. The animal was so scared and worn out, he never moved. He even stood still while Gail put the hobbles on him. Then Gail stood there talking to him for a while and fed him a little bit of grain. Finally, he called to me, and I could hear him from the camp. "Eunice, follow his tracks and see if you can find my rifle."

I followed the tracks and hollered back, "I found your gun!"

"Good!" he called back, to which I replied, "It's broken in half!"

He bellowed from far away, "It better not be!" I started laughing.

"He stepped on the stock!" I called back. There was no answer this time, but Gail walked back with the horse and tied him up at the camp. I said, "Honey, are you hurt?" He told me, yes, that his shoulder was in bad shape; but when I said that maybe he should not continue, he insisted, "Oh yeah; we're going." He got another rifle and took off on that horse with the boy walking beside him. I was so worried. I was out there all alone in the wilderness, with no way to know how they were doing. The horse could spook again and Gail was already in terrible pain. If anything happened I knew the boy couldn't help him and I would have no way of knowing how to find them. I watched them until they became tiny figures cresting the hill; then I prayed diligently and fervently for Gail, the boy, the horse and everything in between. I sat out on that high desert landscape for hours, watching and praying, until another hunting party showed up. They parked about fifty yards away and I could hear them laughing and swearing; I could see that they were drinking, too, which was a bit unsettling since I was alone. I had looked at the gas gauge in the van earlier and discovered that it was almost empty. I found a gas can, but there was no gas in it and I realized that we were stuck out there with no extra fuel. I had to figure something out before they got back, so finally I got brave enough to walk over and ask those men if they could sell me a little gas. They didn't want to, but they sold me a can of gas and I poured it in the tank. I didn't tell them that I was out there alone; I used pronouns like "we" and "us" so they would know my hunting party was close by. Praying and crying as I waited for any sign of Gail's return to camp, I wondered why people have to go through things like this. I got my mind on other things by singing songs and puttering around the camp. I cooked some food, trying to pass the time, and hoped that Gail and the boy would make it back. When they finally did, they had not seen a deer all day, and Gail's pain was so intense that he looked quite sick. The boy had walked all day, but never complained. We ate supper and tried to sleep but, in the middle of the night, Gail developed a terribly high fever and was in bad shape. The next day our friend arrived to join the hunt but Gail was too sick to continue. Instead, Bill took us to Vale, Oregon where his brother lived and they gave Gail some medication to relieve his pain and fever.

We headed home then and when we got close to La Grande Gail saw a deer going up the side of a hill. "There's my buck!" he exclaimed, and jumped out of the van, took aim, and shot it. "Gail, what are you going to do now?" I questioned with added consternation. The hills sloping up from the highway were so steep that I didn't know how he would manage to get to his game. Naturally, however, there was no question in his mind; he and the boy hiked up there, butchered the deer, packed all the meat in a backpack, and brought it back down. I just sat there and waited, for it took them several hours to accomplish their feat. Gail was happy as a lark that he got his meat, even though it was a small one, and acted as though it was more than worth all the trouble. It was a painful trip home and he went to the doctor as soon as he could. His shoulder was damaged, and pained him for over a year. He couldn't lift his arm for a long time, and I never trusted that horse again.

When we got back to Sequim Gail set up a temporary place to keep the horse near a barbed wire fence on one side of the building under some trees. He had to tie it out there because there was not a space anywhere that was fully enclosed where the horse could run loose. One day, while I was practicing songs in the church with some other ladies, he decided to go for a ride. He saddled his bronc and rode out across the fields around the church but, alas, something spooked the horse again. A busy highway ran along one side of the church property and the horse was barreling straight toward it. He had new shoes on and Gail realized that when he hit the highway he would slip and go down. Consequently, and to his own peril, he decided to jump off, since comparing a run-in with a speeding truck to a self-propelled drop-and-roll seemed an easy choice at the moment. When he made his leap, he landed on his hip. One of the ladies looked out the window and cheeped excitedly, "There's a runaway horse heading for the highway with its reins dragging behind it!"

I thought for sure Gail got hurt and we jumped up to see what happened. Here he came, walking alone across a plowed field—without the horse. Suddenly, as we watched, he began to hobble so that by the time he reached the house he was limping badly. We called the sheriff to report the horse because there was a high possibility that it could cause an accident on the highway. After several hours, the pastor offered to take Gail to the hospital and helped him get into the van. He had twisted his spine and was prescribed some potent pain medicine that affected his mind and emotions, making him extremely hateful toward me. I had never seen the evil side-effects of drugs like that on someone's personality. He was so mean; he spoke very harshly and became terribly difficult and irritable. At first I didn't realize it was the drugs, so I was mystified by the sudden change in him. Anyway, a lady called the next day and said they'd caught a horse that had run to the edge of their property next to the Juan de Fuca Straight Gorge. They had corralled him so Gail went to pick him up in the horse trailer. My husband, despite his frequent thoughtless decisions, was usually willing to recognize when his sneaky strategies of getting what he wanted produced rotten fruit. He didn't really admit it this time, but the outcomes spoke for themselves; although this was not the bronc's final escapade!

Mark and Diane, our son and daughter-in-law, brought Kari and Jonathan up to Sequim to spend some time with us while they went on a short trip. The kids were little; probably around ages six and two, respectively, and they wanted to see the horse. Gail brought the unpredictable critter up behind the church where there were big logs lined up as parking area boundaries. There was a basketball hoop out there with a huge backboard on a telephone pole. Gail tied the horse on that pole and started to saddle him up. He said to go ahead and bring the kids outside so they could watch. Jonathan was an active little boy and I didn't think it was safe for him to be out there. I felt a strong caution that we needed to be farther away, so I took them up on the balcony to watch from a safer distance. Suddenly, I heard a terrible noise and saw that the horse had gone wild and was kicking and jumping for some reason. Gail was standing there looking at him with his classic calm when the horse suddenly jerked back so hard that he pulled the telephone pole out of its ground hole and toppled it onto his own head. Now he felt attacked, and thought he was fighting for his life, so he kept bucking and jumping until he got himself tangled up in it. He was dragging the whole pole behind him with the backboard, hoop and all. It looked like the worst rodeo mishap in history; yet, with his inborn unruffled composure, Gail just said, "You crazy fool; just buck yourself silly." I was shaking with fright because I thought the horse was going to kill himself or hurt someone else. Instead, he finally got so tangled up with the contraption that it knocked him down, pinning him under the telephone pole. Gail never got excited or worried; all he said was, "Well, good; he wore himself out." When the wild bronc never moved a muscle, I thought he might be dead; but Gail said, "He's not a bit dead; he's just resting." He waited until the poor beast was finally calmed down enough to accept some help; then he gently and patiently got the horse untangled and guided him back to tie him up.

I just knew that wild horse was going to kill somebody, probably Gail. God intervened, however, and out of the blue our friend, Jim, called Gail to say that it had been a mistake for him to sell the horse. He wanted to know if he could buy it back, with the trailer, and Gail readily agreed. If not for this turn of events I believe that crazy horse could easily have been the death of Gail. We planned a trip to Emmett to return the horse and trailer, and I was never so glad to set out on a spur of the moment road trip!

An Unexpected Treat

In late January, 1990, we were invited to go with a group of other ministers on a trip to Israel. It was called a "familiarization tour", and was organized with the purpose of inspiring ministers to bring their own tour groups back to Israel. We did not plan to do that, but we enjoyed a trip of a lifetime, and a great educational experience. Our son, Mark, was also along on this trip and was such a delight to travel with. We visited sites where biblical history had been made centuries before, and the Bible stories I had heard all of my life came alive! The meals we ate, and the nice hotels we stayed in—including The Kibbutz— were so enjoyable! The company of other ministers was wonderful and the tour guides explained everything thoroughly and with great enthusiasm. We saw Masada, the Dead Sea, Jericho, Nazareth, Bethlehem, Mount Carmel, Solomon's Stables, the Valley of Megiddo (or Plain of Jezreel), the Garden of Gethsemane, the Mount of Olives, Golgotha, Calvary Hill where Jesus walked to the place of his crucifixion, Jesus' sepulcher, and the Dead Sea Scrolls in Israel Museum's Shrine of the Book. We went in a boat on the Sea of Galilee, shopped in Jerusalem, and visited The Upper Room. We bought lots of souvenirs and enjoyed a wonderful vacation in the place where Jesus walked the earth. There was a big storm while we were there, with snow and wind, so it was too cold for comfort; but I loved seeing the snow-covered Swiss Alps from the plane! It was somewhat comforting to join in the company of other ministers again, although still a little awkward with those who had attended church with us in Portland, since we were still outsiders in their circles. Our main fellowship focus was spending time with our son, hearing about his own ministry involvements at the time and supporting him in his endeavors. He was very sweet, and we had a very close relationship with him at that time. Good memories were made and we enjoyed the entire trip.

Questions Considered; Answers Unforeseen

After almost a year of working and staying very busy with the duties of pastoring, we needed to make some decisions. We had not yet committed to stay on and take the church permanently because we were noticing that our standards and policies regarding some church practices and congregational values were markedly different than what the resident pastors and their congregation were accustomed to. They were overly accommodating to people wanting to live on the premises for long periods of time free of charge, some with no intention of committing to a Christian life-style or contributing to their own personal progress. We were questioning whether we could work with those conditions much longer and we decided to get away and take some time to think everything through. We knew the pastors were waiting to transition out-of-state and after all their kindness to us we wanted to make a thoughtful decision and have a solid answer for them by the time we got back. There were other options and, now that we had been released from Portland, we had thoughts of other places we might like to go and serve. At the same time, Gail was concerned about his aging mother because she had moved back to Emmett after living in California and he wondered if we should live closer to her.

This time-away trip we planned was the result of several requests that we had received from other places to come and minister at various churches. The pastor of Gail's Aunt Fern had called and asked him to come back to Arkansas for another revival meeting. His mother's pastor had also asked us to come and preach a revival meeting in Emmett, Idaho where she lived. David, our son, was pastoring a church in Yuba City, California by this time and had expressed gladness that his dad was back in the ministry. He had mentioned that he would like Gail to come and preach at their church as well.

As a result of all these opportunities, and our need to get away and think, Gail decided this was a good time to plan an evangelistic trip. First we would travel back to Emmett to visit his mom and preach at her home church for a week. Then we would go on to Dover, Arkansas and hold a revival meeting there. Finally, we would come back across the country to Yuba City, California to visit David and Cheryl's church. After preaching there, we would return to Sequim and give the pastors our decision about whether or not to take the pastorate there. They were on board with this plan and ready to carry on with all church responsibilities while we were gone. They donated a big van for us to use for our trip with plenty of space to pack whatever we needed, including our instruments so we could minister in song as requested. We packed for a long road trip and headed for our first meeting destination in Idaho.

When we arrived in Emmett, we stayed with Gail's mother, Hazel, and his sister, Bernice. The meetings went wonderfully and the week had come to an end. It was Sunday and the morning service would be the last one before we would set out for our second destination in Arkansas on Monday morning. We were awake, but had not yet dressed for the day, when Gail began to groan in pain. We prayed for him, and called the pastor of the church where the revival meetings were being held. He came over to pray for Gail and said he would take care of the service and asked us to keep him posted on Gail's condition. Our best friends in Emmett, Jim and Goldie Penix, had dealt with all of this previously when Goldie had a heart attack; so I called her and described Gail's symptoms. She exhorted me to get him to the hospital immediately, but he was not about to go anywhere without a shower! As soon as he was showered and dressed we took him to the ER and the medical staff put him on an emergency Life-Flight to St. Alphonsus Hospital in Boise. Jim and Goldie said they would go with us, so I did not ride in the helicopter with Gail because they drove me to Boise. The paramedics kept him alive during the flight and when they examined him at St. Al's the blood tests revealed enzymes that verified he had undergone a massive heart attack. Gail remained in the Intensive Care Unit for ten days. Many people were praying and he had lots of visitors. We had no insurance and we had no idea what these hospital bills would add up to. I wasn't afraid, and I didn't expect him to die; but I wondered what the future held and I knew that the Lord would help us with whatever challenges were ahead. Naturally, our ministry trip was cancelled and we felt like we needed to get home to Sequim. Hazel, his mom, didn't want me to take him home. She wanted me to drive back by myself and take care of the church while she kept her son in Emmett to take care of him during his recovery. Her mother's heart had gotten the best of her mind! Gail was not about to stay anywhere without me. "Why, Mama." he said. "Eunice has been taking care of me all my life! She's the best nurse I ever had!" So I drove him back to Sequim in the van with the passenger seat laid back as far as it would go so he could rest. It was a ten hour drive, and very taxing. We were glad to get home.

Gail's recuperation was lengthy. The pastor at Sequim preached the first two weeks and the third week Gail was feeling good enough to share his testimony with the congregation. He told how the heart attack had sobered him. He said that God had spoken to him while we were living in Portland. One day, as he was trimming trees on the church property he had heard the voice of the Lord warn him clearly, *"Set your house in order, for your days are numbered."* This worried him because he had accumulated quite a bit of debt while setting up his Gun Shop there. He never meant to do this, but—as is the nature of debt—it happened gradually as he added one component or piece of equipment at a time. I had prayed earnestly that God would help us find a way to pay this off. Now we not only had over $20,000 worth of credit card debt at high interest, but we were also accumulating hospital bills! It was $1,500 for the helicopter flight alone! He had sold a few more of his custom rifles since moving to Sequim, but had not fully applied himself. Now he believed that God had allowed the heart attack to remind him that he had dropped the ball, and needed to get back on track. From this point forward, he focused on paying down his debt as quickly as possible. He repeated often that he knew he was going to die and that he didn't want to leave me with all his debt. Meanwhile, his condition was being monitored by medical staff at a Port Angeles hospital.

Previously, while he was in the Boise hospital, our pastor's wife had retrieved an old address book from our apartment in Sequim and, unbeknown to us, sent cards to every name in the book! She informed them of Gail's serious condition and requested financial help from anyone who was so inclined, giving our Sequim address as the place to send donations. By the time we got home from Idaho and began paying on our hospital debt, money started coming in the mail every day from people we had not heard from for years!

Then I remembered a dream that I had before our trip to Idaho. In the dream I was standing in the church parking lot, looking up into the sky. As I gazed upward, I saw a tiny object high up in the sky, shaped like a bird that was approaching from very far away. Suddenly this creature swooped down and landed in front of me. It was a huge angel with massive biceps. He wore a cream-colored robe with a tan sash. Startled, I asked, "Are you an angel from God?"

"Yes," he answered, and as we talked briefly I looked directly into his face. Almost immediately he turned and began to ascend into the heavens once more. He had no wings, but just rose swiftly into the air, leaving me in awe. Then he turned toward me in flight and spoke these words to me as he soared ever higher, "Supernatural intervention!" Then he was gone and I woke up speaking in tongues.

Now—as these kind condolences, letters of encouragement, and generous funds poured in—I believed this must have been the meaning of the angel's message. Who knew that our trip would be cut short by a heart attack? Who knew that our dear pastor's wife would be able to get into our apartment in our absence and randomly run across an address book that I had not used for years? Who knew that this many people loved us this much, and would respond with such care and concern for our welfare? It was, indeed, supernatural intervention for a desperate time. Another twist that was even more curious was the result of a telephone call from the welfare nurse. We had applied for SSI, Supplementary Security Income, to pay his hospital bills and she was advising us not to pay any more while we were waiting because the SSI would be retroactive. So we used the money we received in the mail to pay off some of the Gun Shop debt instead. Months passed before our SSI finally kicked in so we followed her advice and let the bills pile up during that time. When the assistance became available, all those bills—representing thousands of dollars in medical treatment—were paid at once! We were overwhelmed by God's timely care and provision; He had truly intervened in mysterious ways to meet our needs.

Months passed, and we were thoroughly involved in our church work and pastoral duties again. Gail had lost some weight, but was feeling quite well and seemed to have energy for his responsibilities, although he was definitely in recuperation mode and had times of weakness, too. We went to Port Angeles for more X-rays, which revealed evidence that he had experienced another slight heart attack since the first one in Emmett. This explained his physical weakness and his gray complexion. They kept him for a few days in the hospital at Port Angeles before referring him to a cardiologist in Seattle. The specialist informed us that Gail had lost one third of his heart function at the time of his first heart attack in Emmett and that it was imperative for him to schedule a double bypass surgery immediately. The hospital had family rooms available and our daughters, Dorcas and Rebecca, both came to stay with me there. We were there for ten days and Gail came through the bypass surgery very well. Mark was there for part of the time also. I was glad to have the support, and to be with some of the kids during those days. Back in Sequim, Gail was prescribed a rehabilitation program and strict diet, which he was very diligent with. He finished his rehabilitation program in good time and with great progress toward a full recovery. He wanted to go hunting again, and was determined to work up enough strength to do it. He began walking with a backpack and taking short hikes in preparation for hunting season. At the same time, the pastors felt that things were stable enough for them to make their move and retire, so they turned the church over to us and said their goodbyes. By the fall of 1991, we were on our own to pastor the church at Sequim. We moved from our tiny upstairs apartment to the roomy double-wide that was considered as the onsite pastor's quarters.

Failed Boundaries

It is well-known that "the grapevine" is the fastest way for news to travel, and when the church in Portland discovered that the senior pastors at Sequim had moved out-of-state and turned the church over to us, they sent a letter of discipline that said, in so many words, *"We did not release you to be senior pastors, and we do not approve of this decision. You are on your own."* We had, however, been "recommended as excellent assistants" which we had diligently fulfilled for over two years in this place. In most leadership climates it is not only common, but expected, that excellent assistants may unquestionably step into higher positions when senior leaders step down. Encouraged to move to Sequim with everything we owned, we had served faithfully; and now that our pastors were gone, here we were! As for being on our own, we had been in that position—realistically speaking—from the time we had left our pastorate in Aberdeen. In addition, our time in Sequim had not been monitored in any sense of the word! Our pastoral activities were not dictated nor controlled by anyone else. We were given the reins to seek the Lord for direction here and to pursue it without restraint, which we had done wholeheartedly—and successfully. All of our children and their families had visited several times, and our sons had gladly preached in our pulpit, rejoicing in what God was doing in our midst. We, indeed, felt alienated from the Portland group following this vindictive letter, but at least it appeared that any strings still attached had been severed; and that any virtual boundaries that had been on file were finally erased. Still, we were impugned for taking these logical steps of progress and responsibility and had to simply move on.

After all that I had been through with Gail from the time I married him, plus the trials of Hoquiam and then the humiliation of Portland, I was hoping against hope—more than everyone else put together—that things would go well this time. I wanted him to really be victorious over his vices and free of the strongholds so we could finally be free to minister and do what we knew that God had called both of us to do. The perfection of God's plan for the human race is not in sticking a weak, vulnerable human being in a place where he can easily fail, but in giving him that same opportunity with the promise of victory through Christ. It is never by our own power that we succeed in life anyway. The only way we can "do all things" is through the power of Christ working in us. The scripture is plain: John 15:4-5 (KJV) *"Abide in me, and I in you. As the branch cannot bear fruit of itself, except it abide in the vine; no more can ye, except ye abide in me. I am the vine, ye are the branches: He that abideth in me, and I in him, the same bringeth forth much fruit: for without me ye can do nothing."* I believe that as long as we tread our pilgrim pathway on this earth, God wants us to keep pursuing Him with everything we have. He will never put obstacles in our way to deter us from what should be a life-long pursuit; a race toward the finish line. He does not want to take us out of the race but, instead, desires to encourage us to continue through thick and thin until it is finished, never giving up.

Because I had been through every failure with my husband, and knew all the signs of trouble and danger, I was blamed many times for "allowing" it to happen. Really? If we support someone in a race and we see that they are forgetting to hydrate—again—do we angrily jerk them to the sidelines and say, "You're done. I'm not going to let you embarrass me by falling down on the course again"? No; we call encouragement from our place on the route, "Drink water! You are suffering from dehydration! Come on! You can do this!" Any time we commit to helping someone succeed whether in a marriage, a training program for our employees, teaching our children what they need for life, or even mentoring new believers we make ourselves vulnerable to their mistakes and failures. Because we have taken ownership of their journey to success, we are affected by their failures along the way. The minute we attach their progress or success to our own image, we fail; proving that our "support" was not genuine. We cannot own the success without experiencing what it takes to get to the finish line. Our job is to coach with dedication and give the outcome to God, who judges all men perfectly.

There was a woman in Sequim whose behavior was questionable and I saw some things that needed to be addressed, so I had gone straight to Gail and asked him about it. He had admitted that she was very lascivious and seeking ways to create an attachment, but then he would minimize it by reminding me that she was a brand new Christian and from a bad background. He had taken the perspective of giving her a chance to learn and grow. She played piano by note but wanted to learn how to play by ear in order to assist during worship. I didn't want to allow it because this would open the door for her to come to the church and practice her music. I told Gail it was not a good scenario and he agreed. He always agreed with me because he knew what was right, but he still let it happen. Before long, she was coming all the time to work on her music and, consequently, I felt like I could never leave. I was in turmoil because I never knew when she might show up to practice. I tried to be wherever Gail was, or at least close by, because I knew this was another strategy of the enemy. She was seductive, and had designs on him. I always cautioned him about anything I felt could be a problem, as much as I could without being overbearing, but I couldn't be there every minute of the day. Success on Life's pathway is very personal, which is how God designed it to be. For we will each stand as individuals before the judgement seat of Christ. Whether our personal race ends in defeat or a trophy, it is ours and ours alone. The coaches and cheerleaders are still on the sidelines.

Within a few months' time, therefore, this promiscuous activity had progressed to a point of trepidation for Gail, and he decided to back off from her. When she realized that it was just a foolish attraction that meant nothing to him she became angry and decided to expose him. By this time, we had a young man from our church in Hoquiam who had moved with his family to Sequim to help us in the ministry; so she went to him. He came to me very sadly, and with merciful kindness he revealed to me what had been going on with Gail, as well as this woman's intent to expose him. It was pure torture for me. I couldn't eat for a week, and I was skin and bones.

The Beginning of the End

This faithful young man took the initiative to call our former pastors, who then came back to Sequim to steady the church during the transition that was warranted. I don't know if they were sent or if their coming was voluntary, but somehow, two of our children and their spouses arrived from Portland and divulged to us that a meeting had been arranged with our pastor to decide how to inform the congregation of these developments. We were instructed to make ourselves scarce, and then informed that we would not be allowed to return. We drove quite a ways, to a place where we could sit by a creek in the peace and quiet of God's handiwork. We were both sad; but I felt like I had been branded for the umpteenth time, and banished once again by association. At this point in the race, the support staff is often nonverbal. I had spent forty years saying everything I could say and doing everything I could do to encourage him on the right path. I was grieved to the point of silence; all my words had been said long ago. We also felt the smothering "we-told-you-sos" and "what-did-you-expects" hanging in the atmosphere from those who had expressed various forms of disapproval in the first place and now felt justified by this outcome. We were told that we should go back to Portland but we had already decided we would not do that again. We didn't know what to do, but we talked about going back to Idaho. Our son, David, had also invited us to Yuba City, California. As disappointed as he was about his father's recurring collapse of character, he had chosen kindness and love over condemnation, even now.

Gail always took people's responses on the chin because his guilt was semi-absolved by verbal punishment and condescension. Yet I stood beside him, feeling bruised and falsely accused all over again. Traveling with a reckless driver will always put you in the line of fire. I felt the full impact of the wreck each time, and my wounds took just as long to heal as his. Through the devastation, I clung to God's grace and strength each time and, once again, I was not only alive, but still in the passenger seat. No one else needed to understand all the reasons I had "fought the fight and finished the course" over the years. I was doing what I knew God wanted me to do, and this was one of those painful times of staying the course.

At this time, probably the summer of 1992, our daughter from Idaho called to inform us that her in-laws had a large house available that had been unoccupied too long. They were willing to rent it to us at a reduced rate just to have someone live there and maintain the place. We felt it was an option born of God's generous spirit of love and mercy. Gail said, "Let's just pack up and go back to Idaho. I'm going to die anyway; the Lord has told me my days are numbered. I don't want to die out on this peninsula. I want to go home."

CHAPTER FOURTEEN

The Last Lap

Five Sides of Time

The clock was ticking. At the time of Gail's initial, life-changing heart attack in Emmett, our son Mark saw a bulletin board in a Boise hospital with this inscription on it:

> *"Time is too slow for those who wait,*
>
> *Too swift for those who fear,*
>
> *Too long for those who grieve,*
>
> *Too short for those who rejoice;*
>
> *But for those who love,*
>
> *Time is Eternity."*[1]

I had experienced all these facets of Time during my life, sometimes all at once. I had waited in agony for things to get better, but simultaneously feared that Time would only make them worse. I had suffered through painfully slow hours and days of grief over my husband's frequent moral failures, while clinging to sweet times of rejoicing when things went right; wanting the good times to last. The scripture is plain, however, in Isaiah 40:6, 8 (KJV) *"The voice said,…All flesh is grass, and all the goodliness thereof is as the flower of the field…The grass withereth, the flower fadeth: but the word of our God shall stand for ever."* Human life, whether lived for selfish gain or in service to others, is fleeting and corruptible. Only when our souls are infused by the incorruptible seed of Truth through receiving the gospel of Jesus Christ will our lives on earth have merit and reward for Eternity. Everything else we encounter along the way is very transitory. Only when the love of God is at work within us can we understand his purpose for life and become everything we were born to be, both now and forever.

Even now, as we prepared for what would be our last move together on this earth, I waited for what lie ahead and feared it at the same time. I grieved over what we had lost and what life could have been, while rejoicing over what we still had and the opportunity ahead. Gail was always such a mixture. So many times throughout his life and ministry he carried a deep passion for the church, caring for God's people and reaching the lost. In every place we had ministered there were many who highly honored him, who loved and appreciated his pastoral input to their lives, and grew into vibrant Christians. Yet, without question, debris was often scattered on the trail he left behind, where wounds and disappointments that he caused would require damage control by leaders coming after him. How well we could all be served by learning more from the mistakes of others rather than making the same ones ourselves. How much we could benefit by seeing another's failure with less criticism and more determination to finish our own journey well. Positions of leadership draw the spotlight in society, yet we could all retrace our own footsteps and see times when we missed the mark. People in every walk of life make choices every day whether to walk away or stand beside; crush a soul or encourage them; ignore instead of attending to, or lift up instead of put down; speak words of life or death; live exemplary or carelessly exist; respond in love or react in anger. Every day of our lives brings a plethora of opportunities to do the right thing, or choose wrong; and either choice inevitably affects others.

God helped us to pay off our debts before we left Sequim; but Gail still had his Gun Shop so it took nearly an entire U-Haul truck to move it to Boise. He packed his shop equipment and all of our furniture in the biggest U-Haul truck available. He would drive this vehicle, towing our car behind. I would drive the pickup with the camper on it, which was also packed to the gills with bicycles and other items filling up any extra space inside. I used all the upper cabinets to pack Gail's books. When he saw what I was doing he cocked his head sideways and said, "Oh, honey; I don't think it's a good idea to fill up those cupboards. It could make our load too top heavy." Now that it was already done and I had nowhere else to put them, I left it that way. We were loaded up and the double-wide we had been living in was cleaned and shined for the next occupants. We had our best clothes on and were ready to begin our journey. Gail instructed me to follow behind him and said he would be watching me in his rear-view mirror to make sure I was keeping up. It was a beautiful day driving along the edge of the gorgeous Olympic National Forest through Washington on Interstate 5. Leaving more sorrow behind, the beauty of God's creation brought songs to the surface of my heart—his life-long gift, to Eunice with love. Because God held my destiny securely in his hand, he had carefully planned that my mind would be able to soak up lyrics and melodies of praise that would forever remain in reserve. My heart full of music was a live demonstration of Isaiah 58:11 (KJV) *"And the LORD shall guide thee continually, and satisfy thy soul in drought, and make fat thy bones: and thou shalt be like a watered garden, and like a spring of water, whose waters fail not."*

Roadside Misadventures

Meanwhile, back to the mundane, I had a can of white Verathane that was full. This durable paint was a tough polyester urethane that would cover any surface and retain its high gloss. I thought I might need to touch some things up when we got to our destination, so I didn't want to waste it. Gail had told me not to bring it; but it had cost seventeen dollars and ninety-eight cents and I couldn't stand to leave it there. Consequently, I sat it on the floorboard of the pickup beside my purse. The morning temperatures had been chilly as we left Sequim before daylight, and after about an hour on the road I began to smell the distinct odor of that paint. We were on the freeway, rolling smoothing along, so I reached down in the dark to check whether the gallon of paint was secure. To my dismay, the lid had slipped sideways and I stuck my hand directly into the can. It was still upright but had tipped sideways just enough to dribble a generous portion into my purse. This scenario was bursting with negative factors: I had nice clothes on, polyester in those days, black slacks and white jacket; I had paint all over my hand; it was dark; I was driving fast. I smeared the paint on the steering wheel as I slowed to a stop on the side of the road. Then I grabbed Kleenex, which was all I could find nearby, to wipe it off. Back in the camper, I had stashed a small pile of rags and towels that I had used for the final cleaning of the house. Thankfully, I was able to use those to clean up the bulk of the sticky mess. I replaced the lid securely back onto the paint can and carried it up the bank into the woods, setting it beside a pine tree. In my desperation, I didn't know what else to do with it. The floorboard had a rubber mat, which made that part easier to clean. I tried to wipe off the items inside my purse where the paint had poured in, but this was very thick, oil based paint; even if I'd had water available it would not have been sufficient. This type required paint thinner for proper clean-up. I knew that Gail would be worried about me and, as I hurried to wipe up the mess the best I could, I scolded myself. *"I'm so ashamed…how foolish for me to be so anxious to take this can of paint! Especially when Gail told me to leave it…what will he say now?"* I knew he couldn't turn around on this freeway so I had to catch up with him. I had barely jumped into the driver's seat and gotten back on the road when I saw him up ahead, running back to see what had happened to me. When I caught up to him I stopped and told him about the whole fiasco.

Gail was always so calm and, true to his nature, expressed no blame or criticism. "Oh, honey; don't worry about it. When we get to a gas station I'll get some gas in a can and we can use it to clean things up." I was so surprised, since he could have justifiably said, "I told you not to bring that paint!" He was feeling pretty humble about his own mistakes, though, and was genuinely sorry that this had happened to me. So I dropped him off at his truck and followed him to the next off-ramp where we were able to finish cleaning up the spill at a service station. I had to get rid of my nice, white jacket, and learn a hard lesson; but the dilemma was easily solved and we made good time the rest of the day with no mishaps—until midnight.

We had only stopped for meals and had all but completed our long journey, over six hundred miles, to Emmett, Idaho where we would stay with Gail's mother. Though it was a long day of driving, we'd had a peaceful trip and had stopped that evening at a restaurant in Oregon for dinner. I had taken my purse inside with me, stuffed with all the cash from the sale of guns and shop equipment Gail had given me before we left Sequim. Suddenly, about ten miles outside of Emmett, I panicked because I didn't remember having my purse with me when we got back on the road after dinner. I was petrified that I had left it in the restaurant. In the pitch black of midnight, on a country road after exiting Interstate 84 past Ontario, Oregon, I began to frantically feel around on the pickup seat and floor for my bag. In my fear, I lost my focus and drove off the road. I remembered Gail saying, "If you ever drive off the road, don't turn the steering wheel sharply to correct it or you will tip the camper over. Just hold it as straight and steady as you can until you stop." So I hung on because I was on the edge of a steep embankment. Holding the steering wheel as tight as I could, I kept it straight and came to a stop; but the camper was tipped dangerously to one side. Then I remembered what Gail had said about making it top-heavy by filling the cupboards with books. After the paint episode, I hoped that doing it my way would not cause a terrible accident; I was very frightened. I opened my door and leaped out toward the shoulder of the road, landing safely. As I stood on the side of the road wondering what to do, a lady pulled up in a car and said, when she saw my truck sitting precariously on the steep bank below, "Oh my! What can I do to help you?"

"My husband is in a big U-Haul up ahead, towing a car, and doesn't know that I've had an accident," I answered.

"I'll catch up with him and tell him!" she offered, and sped off into the darkness. In the meantime, a big truck coming toward me from the opposite direction stopped on the other side of the road. A man got out and said, "Looks like you've got some trouble here." Crossing the road, he smiled broadly and added, "I am just the guy who can get you out of that fix. I've done this a million times. Don't you worry;" and—seeing how very scared and upset I was—he gave me a reassuring pat on the shoulder. I had actually discovered my purse before I exited the vehicle. I had put it behind my feet on the floorboard against the driver's seat. Since I usually had it sitting beside me, I had not thought to feel for it under my feet. Despite my current predicament, therefore, I was at least relieved that all of our cash was safe and sound.

The lady that had first stopped to help had caught up with Gail and waved him down. She relayed the incident to him, but he could not turn his big rig around on this narrow country highway. He had to drive on into Emmett before he could find a spot big enough to turn around and come back for me. The guy in the truck stayed with me but explained, "I can get you back on the road but I want to wait for your husband because he needs to help me."

After a while Gail drove up with the U-Haul and I told him what happened. Once again, he responded with amazing patience and grace, "Oh, honey! Don't ever look for your purse while you're driving!" It was almost laughable, and when I asked him later why he was so kind about my blunders on that trip he answered, "After all the terrible mistakes I've made, how could I *ever* be upset with you?" The man that was helping us told me to go down and stop any traffic that might come up the road while he and Gail were pulling the camper off of the embankment. Then he hooked up the camper to his truck and told Gail to get in the pickup and throw it into reverse. He told him to give it the gas quickly and crank the wheel so that the burst of power and the direction of the tires would line up with his truck pulling hard from behind. Gail did exactly that, and in ten minutes we were out of danger! His strategy worked perfectly. Once Gail was up on the road with the camper I ran down to thank the kind stranger for his help and he was nowhere to be found. I looked up and down the road and asked Gail where he went but he didn't know. He was gone so suddenly that we always wondered if we had received supernatural assistance that night. Most people who are friendly enough to stop and help would hang around and say, "Well, looks like you're out of danger. Can I do anything else?" or have at least some kind of brief dialogue before taking off. Either way, whether human or angelic, God sent someone to our rescue in the middle of the night when we were on the brink of disaster. I waited in the pickup while Gail went down the road where he could find a wide place to turn the U-Haul around. Then I followed him to Hazel's house where we were to spend the night. She was waiting up but was not worried, knowing that it was a long trip and already expecting that we would arrive late. She was very excited to see us and to hear about our trip. The next day we headed for Boise, thirty miles away, to what we always called "the River House"; the place offered by our son-in-law's family for us to rent during our transition.

It's All Temporary

When we got there we were so excited. I had never had a house that was so convenient and roomy. All of our furniture fit perfectly; there were cupboards everywhere, and I found a place for everything. I was elated! The kitchen was big, too. There was a dishwasher, garbage disposal and everything we needed, much of which I had never had before. While I was putting things away Gail was trying to situate his gun-building equipment. The living room was so large that he used one end of it for his shop. The owners had built a new fireplace and long drapes hung at the windows. The master bedroom upstairs was so big that our bed looked small. It almost seemed like a country setting at first; the river was close by and there were no neighbors. The land was being developed, however, and right away construction crews were showing up to begin building new homes, which soon popped up all around us. Gail set up his shop to start his work. He already had the components for several more guns and wanted to finish them, but he needed a place to sight in his rifles. So after we were settled he found a place outside of Boise where he attempted to establish an area where he could accomplish this. He was very precise in his measurements and spent hours walking out various distances and setting up targets for his assessments. Before long, however, and much to his dismay, someone came and tore down all of his stakes and targets and posted a "Private Property" sign. He was disappointed because he could not sell a rifle without testing it first. Besides, his goal was to make a gun for each of the boys and one for me—which I had no desire to own but that, to him, would be a keepsake for me. I wanted to sound appreciative, but told him I didn't think we could afford $3,800 just for me to have a memento of his work.

In between his shop work, Gail was going often to Emmett to help his aging mother with projects around her house. While we were in Sequim, his sisters had moved her down to California where she would be close enough for them to care for her; but she had missed home and was too independent yet to be cared for. Hazel wanted to move back. When she had asked Gail about it he had quipped, "Well, Mama. I think you're old enough to make your own decisions;" which amused her greatly. So she had bought her house back and returned to Emmett a few years prior. Now, although she wanted to be on her own, she was well along in years and unable to maintain her home. She continually had projects for him to do and would call him to paint the eves or the fence or to fix the mailbox. Naturally, he was more than willing to help his dear mother and would spend the day in Emmett often saying, "Well, mom needs lots of things right now and I'm the only one here to help her." I found work cleaning houses right away and we both stayed quite busy.

Within these first months back in Idaho, we also made a trip to Post Falls. There was a facility there that provided accommodations and specialty counselling for ministers struggling with various problems. We had heard about it before our move and had registered for a session which was already paid for. After a whole week of interviews including every question they could think of, nothing materialized as a cause for Gail's recurring problems. Everything they questioned seemed to be in order: he loved his parents and had a good upbringing; he loved his wife and had a good marriage; he loved his children and they all loved him. So they finally concluded, "Well, all we can say is that we are very impressed that you were able to stick with it and keep moving on through all of this." They prayed for us and we went home with no more answers than we had before. Gail said, "They are very nice people and they tried to help us; but if I can't find answers for my own deliverance, how can we expect other people to?" He had always been open to counsel, advice, and prayers for deliverance by others. Additionally, Gail had always been a man of fasting and prayer himself, from the time he first entered the ministry as a young teen. Consequently, he was always discouraged when nothing seemed to change even though he was seeking God diligently; frustrated that he could not find freedom. We used to talk about it and I would say, "Well, you wouldn't do wrong things unless you wanted to." He just said, "Well, maybe it's true that my will is just weak; but I love the Lord and believe in His power to save and restore." After that week, however, he was never quite the same. He seemed more humble and more desirous of finding answers than ever before. Even though he had never been good about accountability, I encouraged him after that trip to seek out godly friends that he could talk to when he was having a struggle so that they could pray for him and stand with him to get through successfully. He promised that he would pursue that course of action.

Meanwhile, Gail's mother kept telling me that she was concerned about him and thought he needed to go see a doctor. I had told her that the doctors in Sequim had given him a clean bill of health; and that we could not go again because we had no insurance. So she offered to pay for a checkup. When we went to the appointment, the Boise doctor said the same thing as our medical professionals at Sequim. Gail was in great condition, his blood pressure was excellent, his weight was at one hundred and sixty-two, and his cholesterol was normal. Everything was fine so it seemed like the money was wasted. When we got the huge bill for all these tests, I gave it to Hazel and was relieved that she had offered to pay for it, yet hoped that her peace of mind was worth the cost! Still, I also wondered about my husband's health because he seemed weak and tired so much of the time. I shoveled all the snow around the house in the winter, carried wood inside for the fireplace, and did anything else I could to help out and keep him from working too hard.

We were glad to be close to Jim and Becca. They had married before our other children so by this time their kids were teenagers. Angie had just graduated from high school and enrolled in a college program at Boise State University. Jim had decided to go back into the Air Guard for more training and, during his six-month absence between Thanksgiving of 1992 and May of 1993, Gail and I were happy that we could be close to Becca and the kids. We spent many winter nights in our big, drafty house sitting around the fireplace. Gail always, throughout our marriage, read the Bible aloud to me, or other Christian books. He had been reading the biography of Cameron Townsend, the founder of Wycliffe Bible Translators, and talking about missions. He mused, "I would love to help my sons in their ministries; but I wish we could just go to a mission field and help some struggling missionaries who need support. Where could we find a mission field that could use our experience to help a younger couple?" He always loved and encouraged, exhorted and prayed for younger men. He was a good mentor in those ways. His attitude was very humble and his spirit peaceful; musing on whether there was another place where we could still be useful.

On February 1, 1993, another beautiful granddaughter was born to our son, Mark, and his wife, Diane. Anna Lanea was born on her daddy's birthday, much to his delight. They were in Portland so we were not close enough to take part in welcoming her to the world, but rejoiced with them across the miles. God had blessed us with eleven wonderful grandchildren, from newborn up to age eighteen, with little Sarah Elizabeth waiting for us in Heaven!

Our Final Days of Fellowship

A few months later the house we lived in was sold and we had to find another place to rent. We found a small house off of Maple Grove Road for seven hundred and fifty dollars per month. After settling in we both attended a workshop sponsored by the AARP that placed people over fifty-five into temporary jobs, with very minimal compensation, to see if they were a good fit for a permanent employee. I was doing Data Entry on a computer, typing eight-digit numbers all day long, and I couldn't stand it. Sitting in that office one day, I prayed aloud, "Lord, if you don't have a different job for me in this place, I'm quitting by the end of the week. I can't stand it." The final frustration was that, after spending a whole day putting in numbers, something happened to the system and all my work was lost. I'm a person who has to be productive, so I was finished with it and God saw my need. I walked out to get some coffee on my break and a supervisor said, "Eunice, how would you like to work for me? I need someone in Information and Referral and I think you might be just the perfect person!" It was an instant answer to prayer and I loved that job for several years thereafter! Gail had talked about wanting to retire. He was going to be sixty-two on his next birthday and, with his heart condition, thought he should retire but didn't know if we could make it. I was working at Senior Programs but he did not have a job at that time. I said, "Well, I have a good job now. I can work and you can fish and just do what you want to do."

"Really?" he was surprised. "You would be willing to let me do that?"

"Of course," I answered; "as long as we could pay our bills."

"Well," he continued; "maybe we could if we got a small enough house and got rid of some of our stuff, and my Gun Shop." Then Gail received a temporary assignment opportunity through the AARP with a delivery service called Pony Express. He drove a small truck and delivered packages around town all day. It was a very taxing job because they wanted him in a dead run all day long. He was always a good worker, but there were times at Pony Express when he had to stop and lean against his truck to breathe. I knew he was sick then; I could tell, even though the doctors had supposedly given him a clean bill of health. We lived only a few months at Maple Grove Circle. Two lives were about to change completely; one would begin again in Heaven, and one would start over on earth. Gail knew when he was going to die and kept talking about it. I didn't like it because I wanted him to talk about life. He would say things like, "Honey, when I die you're going to get along just fine. You're wise, and you're thrifty, and you have the kids. You have the Lord and he will be with you." I knew those things were all true, but I said, "Gail, please don't talk about death. Let's talk about life." He answered quickly, "Well, it's imminent."

We were co-hosting a home group at this time with other seniors who loved and appreciated us. Following our lifelong pattern, we made good friends and had wonderful Christian fellowship in our Boise church just as we had in all the places we had lived before. This was a consistent practice for us throughout our marriage, now going on forty-two years, even with the hard times in between. Our Seniors Home Group met every other week. Most of the meetings included singing choruses together, having prayer and fellowship, and often discussing a scripture verse or passage. We always had a potluck supper and several of us took turns hosting the group at our various residences. In November, Gail and I hosted the group and we had a wonderful Thanksgiving dinner. Gail carved the turkey and seemed to be doing well physically. He was joyful and accommodating to our guests, as always, and everyone had a wonderful time.

Finishing Well with our Family

In December of 1993, Gail wanted all the kids to come home for Christmas. He said it might be our last one with all of us together, but I didn't focus on that. I was simply excited about the possibility of having our whole family together again. We contacted David in Yuba City and Mark and Dorcas in Portland and asked them if they could come for a week. Then we began arrangements to accommodate all of them with their families. Our house on Maple Grove Circle was small, and although Jim and Becca lived in Boise their home was also too small for accommodating overnight guests. There was a couple at our church in Boise that found out our family was coming and offered to let us have access to their nice home while they were out of town for the holidays. We felt very blessed and we knew that it was the provision of the Lord. When everybody came, we housed David and Cheryl with their three boys. Mark and Diane along with Dorcas and Ed lodged with their families at the home of our generous friends. Our pastor there had also agreed to allow our family to use the church's Fellowship Hall for our family Christmas Dinner so that there would be room to set up long tables for our large family group—Gail and I, our four children with their spouses, and our eleven beautiful grandchildren. At the dinner, Gail talked to the kids with the preface, *"If this was our last Christmas together, I would want all of you to know…"* Later on, they all remembered that introduction distinctly; but in the moment, when your loved one says something like that, it is common to take it with a grain of salt because in your heart you don't want it to be true. We focused on this memorable time of being all together again, laughing, singing, telling stories and enjoying each other. We had also scheduled a photographer to come to the church and take pictures, so we have family portraits of that memory. Gail had to work most of the week, and seemed to be struggling with the exertion of his job. He was so weak that one of his coworkers said, "Okay, Bryan; get busy!" Gail responded, "I'm working just as fast as I can possibly work." He had evenings free, which provided enough time to enjoy the family and do some shooting with the boys. It was all wonderful, and after the kids packed up their families and headed back to their homes, Gail said, "This was one of the nicest visits we have ever had with all of our children and grandchildren together." We were so glad we had made the effort to make it happen. We sang and read the Bible together; we shared our lives with each other. I have a recording of it; but not a good one. I thought that the kids were getting tired of me making cassette tapes of everything, so I allowed them to intimidate me. Instead of passing the tape recorder around so everyone could speak into it, I simply sat it on a table across the room hoping the voices would pick up. After Gail's death, I regretted not having the courage to ask them to cooperate so we could have this memory of Christmas together. Who knew that we would never have another one, or that the beautiful portrait of Gail and I with our kids would become a memento of the last week that we spent together as a family?

The Perfect Day; the Ultimate Invitation

On New Year's Day, 1994 we had leftovers from our nice breakfast the day before. Our daughter had taken us to Elmer's, a favorite restaurant of Gail's. After all the kids had left to return to their homes from Christmas week, she had said, "Mama, even though we live right here in Boise, I realize that we don't get together as often as we should so I want to take you and Daddy to breakfast." Now we finished up our meal, had our morning devotions together and knelt for prayer. Gail always preferred to kneel when he prayed. Then he read for several hours more in the Cameron Townsend book, weeping over the sacrifice and dedication of this godly man and praying for lost souls. Then he asked me for a haircut. He always loved to have me cut his hair because he could relax while I combed, cut, and lovingly patted him all about the head and shoulders. We chatted about this and that, and decided to walk over to the home of some friends close by. It was a nice, crisp winter day, and on the way home he said, "Eunice, look how fast I'm walking! I feel better than I did before my first heart attack! I'm breathing deep and I feel so good!" We went to Café Ole for an early dinner and used a gift card I had recently received for speaking to a youth group led by one of my nieces. Later that evening Gail read for several hours and we prayed together for all the kids. Then he said, "Let's watch TBN for a while." The program highlighted events of the previous year and a special report about a new television station in Israel. Then a singer performed a popular country gospel song, "Higher Than I've Ever Been," and Gail wept openly, identifying with the lyrics about a bird with a broken wing that was expected never to fly again, and how the writer fell from grace and lost hope of ever rising above yesterday's sin. The song ended with the miracle of God's love that lifted him up above his past to fly higher than he had ever been.

The sun had set on day one of 1994. Gail wanted to go to bed and listen to our new Bible tapes as we fell asleep, and I gladly agreed. He had purchased the entire audio-Bible on cassette for my Christmas present. When he rose from his chair, he stood up, smiling, and softly exclaimed, "Well, honey; this is the end of a perfect day."

Little did we know that his Ultimate Invitation would come before he saw another sunrise. One definition of the word "invitation" is *"an offer to come or go somewhere, especially one promising pleasure or hospitality."*[2] In a few hours he would be beckoned to glory where he would meet the Savior face to face. He would rest from his labors on earth and be invited to bask in the pleasures of Paradise, escorted by angels into Heaven's matchless hospitality. We had already had a pleasurable day, and as we got ready for bed he said, "Before you turn the tape on, honey, I just want to tell you something. I just want to thank you for being such a faithful wife all these years. You could have divorced me so many times; but thank you for staying with me. You'll have a great reward in Heaven for all your sacrifice." Then, with a kiss goodnight, he said, "I wish I could cuddle you but when I lay on my left side, my heart really hurts. So I just want you to know before we fall asleep how much I love and appreciate you. I've never, ever, loved anybody but you."

We listened to Revelation chapters one through three. I was beginning to drift, but Gail kept exclaiming as he listened with comments such as, "My! Think what great rewards the overcomers are going to have!" Before Revelation Four began, I was fast asleep. At 3:30 am something woke me up. In those days I never got up in the night to use the restroom so I looked over at Gail to see if he was breathing. I had developed a habit of that during the days in Sequim when he would often stop breathing at night due, I believe now, to a condition called sleep apnea. He loved to sleep with his arms above his head and out of the covers. The doctors had told him to keep his arms down after his heart attack, but he was more comfortable with his arms up, and curled above his head. I saw that he was breathing soft and steadily, so I got up to use the restroom and got back in bed.

I had barely dozed off again when he began to gasp desperately for air. It was 3:45 am and I jumped up quickly to turn on the light and see if he was okay. I could tell that he wasn't because he didn't respond to me and his eyes were slightly open and fixed in a stare. I called Jim and Becca and told them to come quick because Daddy was dying. Then I called 911 and they had me stay on the line while they told me what to do. They wanted me to get him out of bed and onto the floor, which I didn't think I could do, but I did. I followed their instructions and they guided me through CPR, pressing my palms firmly on his chest and tipping his chin up to breathe air into his mouth. I had heard the death rattle before on a tape recording, so when the same eerie sound came from my husband's throat I recognized it instantly and knew that his spirit had left his body.

I stopped CPR, waiting in shock for the paramedics to arrive. When they arrived and came in to do their thing, I was disturbed that they didn't really try. They just stood around for about ten minutes with no effort to use the traditional methods for saving a life that I had always heard about, such as the paddles—or defibrillator. I suppose they knew he was already dead, since they told me there was nothing else they could do. Jim and Becca arrived as the paramedics loaded Gail onto the gurney and put him in the ambulance to transport him to St. Al's. I didn't think they would charge me for anything after he was dead, but they did. I didn't know what to say or do; but later learned that if a person dies at home the coroner is called to the house. I think they should have done that for me, under the circumstances; or at least given me a choice. Instead, I rode with Jim and Becca to the hospital and had to go through all the questions about his choice not to be resuscitated. Nevertheless, hospital staff still went through all their procedures and I was later charged for a $2,500 bill that included several heart kits and other things that are completely irrelevant once a person is deceased. I had a nurse friend that examined the bill and went with me to talk to the hospital administrator. God worked miraculously on my behalf so that I never had to pay it. When I explained what happened that night, the hospital administrator cancelled the charges, to the last dollar.

When the medical staff finally told us that he was gone and we could go in and say our goodbyes, his skin was cold and he was starting to turn blue. We had already called loved ones to pray, so we called them all again with the news that Gail was gone. My thoughts were not frantic or fearful at all. All I could think about were the amazing things he had said the night before and I thought, *He knew he was going to die.* I wasn't afraid and my tears were few at first, probably because I was still in shock. To be truthful, though, one of my first thoughts was,

Thank God; he made it safely into Heaven and I will never have to worry about him again. That very week he had said, "If not for all my problems, we would have had a perfect marriage." Satan had tried for almost forty-two years to break up our marriage and our home, and to destroy Gail and his ministry. Now the battle was over and the Devil didn't win. Gail had said many times, "If not for my wonderful, godly wife, I would surely be dead or in hell." Yet we had conquered through the power of the cross; and a life, a soul, a marriage and a family had been miraculously saved by God's grace. Gail had ended his earthly struggle in victory and joined the cloud of witnesses that cheers us from above. His father, one brother, his best buddy, Jim—who had actually died of a massive heart attack only two months after Gail's initial heart failure episode in Emmett— were all waiting for him. Now he and his dad, and his buddy, Jim, would be riding the ranges of Heaven together. There were happy thoughts sprinkled through the tears that I shed in the weeks following Gail's death. He had told me it was imminent. Now he was over the threshold, and I would live the rest of my pilgrim journey by myself, yet never alone. I knew that God's promises were true and that he would guide my every step as I lived out the remaining years of my earthly destiny.

Memorial of a Warrior

Gail's funeral was a well-attended celebration of his life. Friends and loved ones had come many miles to join us at the little church downtown Boise where our family had gathered barely a week before at our last earthly reunion. Now that their father was gone, all four of my children took their turn to stand at the pulpit and fight back the tears in order to give honor to him. I knew, and he had known, that they had all been gravely disappointed in him time and again during their adult years. I had given it to the Lord when I couldn't protect them anymore; when they got old enough to see his struggles and make their own judgements about them. I had hoped that they could be forgiving toward him, and I had trusted them to receive the same strength that God had provided to me through the years. Now I could see what God had done, not only in bringing my husband through to victory, but in bringing my children past the shame and disappointments to a higher ground of grace and mercy; a place of strength and maturity where they could share in sincerity about all the good things in their lives, about home, and about their dad and I.

Dorcas called her dad a warrior who triumphed over the battles in life, and who taught her that our heavenly father would always be near to guide her safely away from the pitfalls of her earthly pathway. She expressed appreciation for her daddy's patient listening skills, tender encouragement in difficult times, and solid counsel from the Word of God. She shared truths that impacted her life while growing up under her father's influence and spiritual guidance. Truths such as confidence in God's ever-present comfort and protection; the realization of the power of fervent prayer; a conviction that she and every other human being had a special purpose and destiny; the important lesson of determination—to never give up. She commended her father's great love for the

Word of God, which he was faithful to preach, to teach, to instruct his children in, and to leave a trail of proof that it would strengthen and sustain those who would love it as he did.

Mark said that we were celebrating the great life of a great man. He remembered his father as a man of prayer and a gifted communicator. "When I think of my dad in his greatest joy and most intense fulfillment of his life," he said, "I see him preaching the Word of God with his voice resonating and his hands raised high. That is my dad. He was a great preacher...With glowing eyes, inspiration, and eloquent words my dad could capture the eternal realities of God in a communicable fashion and make them known to the people...it was his passion." He spoke of his father's prophetic inspiration, his intentional striving for excellence, and his ability to humble himself before God; of his faithfulness in fasting for long periods of time in order to experience more of God's presence. He shared happy memories of spending time with his dad in the great outdoors, learning the lessons of life; of their genuine friendship—that he could tell his dad anything and expect to receive a listening ear and wise counsel without criticism. "My dad was always available...I loved him dearly. I learned everything from him and still do all the same things that he did. I hunt, and preach, and shoot a bow; I have his gun and his guitar. I'm a chip off the old block...deluxe!" Lessons learned from his dad, he said, were two-fold: Love God with all your heart, and never give up.

Rebecca said that her dad's loving memory would encourage her to finish her course with purpose and to press on, defying every opposition. Seeing God's power overcome her dad's life struggles taught her to cherish the cross of Christ and to live daily in the freedom that it brings. Her father's love for God's Word planted the same seeds in her own heart to pursue its treasures and lean upon its strength. The power of prayer in his life inspired her to cultivate prevailing prayer as a practice of her own, and to maintain unquestionable confidence in God's supernatural intervention. Her father's life story made her more determined to exercise faith and conquer doubt; to always embrace hope and resolutely castoff despair. To his memory she attributed the conqueror's creed built within her to never lie where one has fallen, stand firmly on the promises of God's Word, shouting VICTORY! in the face of the enemy, and raise the standard of righteousness, shining light into the darkness. His life example would aid her in seeking God expectantly, learning to recognize the anointing and to wait for it, and in carrying the torch of Truth responsibly. She ended her piece by sharing a song she had written for her dad's birthday; a song commending his accomplishments in both life and ministry, and culminating with the grateful expression, *"Of all the daddies in the whole, wide world, you were the one God chose for me."*

David talked about Solomon hearing the instruction of his father and said that the things Gail taught the kids would continue to enrich their lives. "Dad was an excellent teacher, whether it was around the dinner table or from the pulpit on a Sunday morning; behind the barn, or in a classroom setting.

Dad was a skillful and thorough instructor who so enjoyed teaching that those listening always enjoyed learning. I'll always treasure the memories of him laying his hand on my shoulder and saying, 'Now, son, let yer ol' dad teach ya somethin' here.'" He talked about his dad's work ethic and how he passed this value on to his kids. "He taught us how to milk the cows; get the best use out of a shovel; how to hobble a horse and gut a deer; how to make a fire in a rainstorm. He taught us how to 'quit your belly-aching' and 'bite the bullet'; how to strive for excellence; how to show up in the show-down; how to face adversity with courage and face difficulties in life without making excuses or becoming embittered." He thanked God for his father's spiritual instruction; about the purity and total reliability of God's Word as an answer for every situation life can bring; the power and priority of prayer, not as a religious exercise but as a dynamic reality that was powerfully effective in resolving man's dilemmas and securing God's favor in time of need; that God was sovereign, always in control over the details of human life, and completely trustworthy even when his ways are not understood by our human minds. He said that when he went to pastor in Yuba City as a green, young, inexperienced preacher, his dad told him, "You're going to come into many difficult and different experiences for which you are ill-equipped and untrained; but that doesn't make much difference because you have access to God, who knows it all. If you seek him, he will be found by you."

All our children knew what David put into words, "Dad was a sinner saved by grace and, like you and me, unworthy of God's forgiveness, unworthy of his mercy, and unworthy of his love; but always and immensely grateful for it. Dad was a trophy of God's saving grace." Then he played a cassette recording of Gail singing one of his favorite songs, "Unworthy", written by Ira Stanphill in 1959:

Unworthy am I of the grace that he gave;
Unworthy to hold to his hand;
Amazed that a king would reach down to a slave!
This love I cannot understand.

Chorus: Unworthy! Unworthy, a beggar in bondage and alone;
But he made me worthy, and now by his grace,
His mercy has made me his own.

My sorrow and sickness made stripes on his back.
My sins caused the blood that was shed.
My faults and my failures have woven a crown
Of thorns that he wore on his head.

Unworthy am I of the glory to come;
Unworthy with angels to sing.
I thrill just to know that he loves me so much!

A pauper, I walk with the King![3]

Mark, Dorcas and Becca sang a trio for the last song at Gail's home-going service, bringing all of us to the peak of true balance between this life and the eternity that awaits us all: "Until Then", written by Stuart Hamblen in 1958. This beautiful song was one of Gail's favorites, too. It expresses the truth that the heartaches of this life are stepping stones that take us higher; that this world is not our final home and one day we will behold the heavenly city where God resides. It tells how the things of earth begin to dim as we come closer to eternity, and that the hope we have helps us to carry on and keep singing until the day that God calls us home.

The final prayer was given by our aforementioned pastor from Portland, and the comments preceding his benediction drew our attention to the most powerful proof of conquest in Gail's earthly pilgrimage: "We've heard a powerful testimony of a man's life...the real success of a man is how much he loved his family...One can be a success in business or other areas, but a total failure in life according to the scriptures. God will judge us by how well we've done with our families...Gail and Eunice have some of the finest children that I've ever known. Today Gail is being crowned, not because of some great earthly success in the eyes of men, but because God is concerned about how we do with the seed he gives us; and Gail has done a marvelous job."

God's mercy and peace hovered over the crowd that gathered for this memorial. Good things were spoken, memories were cherished, and honor was given in abundance. For one whose journey had been fraught with marks and scars resulting from the universal battle between God and Satan, good and evil, all failures and losses were put to rest to focus instead on the great hope of the gospel—the mercy and forgiveness that comes through entrusting our lives to Jesus Christ alone; and the healing, restoration and reward that results in pressing through to victory. My husband, the father of our four children, had lost a number of battles along the way. He had been toppled, wounded, and imprisoned at times by Satan's schemes; but because he had refused to give up and had allowed God to fight for him, he had not lost the war. Now, those who were hurt the worst by his failures in life stood arm-in-arm to honor him the most at his death. Who could call an outcome like this anything but an amazing triumph? I was blessed beyond measure and my heart was full of thanksgiving to God.

Grace to the Mountain

When the angel spoke to Zerubbabel in Zechariah 4:6-7 (KJV), he gave the word of the Lord to him saying, *"..Not by might, nor by power, but by my spirit, saith the Lord of hosts. Who art thou, O great mountain? Before Zerubbabel thou shalt become a plain: and he shall bring forth the headstone thereof with shoutings, crying, Grace, grace unto it."* I had a mountain before me now; yet, when I looked back over my life with Gail I could see all the plains behind me that had been great mountainous obstacles when I first approached them. I had prevailed over every one, not by my own strength but by the power of the Holy Spirit in my life to enable me. I had remained victorious through every battle by depending on the Lord and believing that his grace would always be sufficient in my time of need. This mountain of living the rest of my life on my own would be no different. When resting in God's abundant grace, the size of the mountain is never a determining factor.

When Gail died, we had eighty-four dollars in our checking account and two hundred and fifty dollars in our savings. I knew I couldn't afford funeral expenses. Nonetheless, I immediately received $3,100 in the form of a $1,000 check from two different family members plus an insurance reimbursement. More checks began arriving in the mail from a multitude of family and friends, three hundred dollars here, fifty dollars there, until all the funeral bills were paid in full. The kids had all returned home to help with details and planning; everything had gone very smoothly. When our landlords heard about my husband's sudden death, they generously exempted me from my rental lease agreement with no fees. Help and grace surrounded me as God met one need after another. I told Mark I didn't know what to do with Gail's Gun Shop because I knew I couldn't afford the rent and had to get out of the house before it came due again. I wanted the kids to take everything they wanted, and as much as they could, so I could get into an apartment as soon as possible. Mark agreed to take care of the Gun Shop, and we had a giant garage sale besides. David wanted the camping and backpacking equipment and Jim and Becca took most of the garden tools. Ed and Dorcas only wanted a guitar, and all the kids looked through Gail's cherished library, gleaning whatever books they wanted to keep. I started looking for an apartment right away. After the kids left I cleaned out Gail's clothes immediately and began taking boxes of excess household goods to the second-hand stores. By this time I had cleared away everything I could live without, and had enough money to pay for the things I needed for my move.

True to my promise, I had found an available apartment in the newspaper and was able to be out by the end of the month as I had told the landlord I would. The rent was three hundred and fifty dollars a month, plus electricity costs. My wages were about $1000 per month from my Senior Programs job, so I would be able to make ends meet. At the funeral, our Boise pastor had told me that they would love to have me come on staff at the church for extra teaching and counseling help, but that they couldn't afford another position yet. That seemed like an exciting prospect for me; to be able to teach and counsel again, continuing my life's work and greatest joys in ministry.

My new apartment was off of Warm Springs and Walnut Avenue, and it felt very secure. I was on the first floor so I did not have to deal with stairs. The only thing that was difficult was taking my laundry across the street to the facility's laundry room, especially in Idaho's cold winter weather! My new location was close to work, making my morning commute fast and easy. I got acquainted with my neighbors right away and in October, after my granddaughter, Angie, was married, she and her husband moved into the same complex so I had family close by, and a growing family! The next year, August of 1995, Angie's first baby boy, Tristyn Peter arrived, making me a great-grandmother!

When the church was ready to hire me it was full-time work because I did all the hospital calls, a large percentage of the counselling appointments, and taught Bible studies. I was on call at all times, and all staff members were required to attend every church meeting, as well as regular staff meetings. I never had an office there because I did most everything off site, and they had a counseling office for me to use when I needed it. They paid me six hundred dollars per month and my widow's pension kicked in about three hundred and seventy-six dollars, nearly equaling my salary at Senior Programs; so I was able to quit that job and focus on what I loved—ministering to God's people. When I resigned from that position my co-workers gave me a lovely going-away party with many gifts and nice cards. Every one of them, twelve people in all, had come to Gail's funeral and heard the gospel message. That job had been the provision of the Lord, and now he was moving me through the next door of my destiny.

By November of 1996, my son, Mark, had decided to come home to Idaho and pastor a church. He and his little family pioneered a new work that began in Nampa and I started attending their meetings whenever I could squeeze them into my busy schedule. I missed Gail so much. I knew that he would have loved to serve as I was now in our Boise church, using his God-given gifts to bless the Body of Christ again under the gracious leadership of this pastor. Now especially, with Mark starting a church nearby, I remembered what Gail had said before he died about working with his boys. How he would have thrilled to offer his voice of experience to help his son in this strategic endeavor! How happy he would have been to witness Mark's pioneering of this new church as he took up the torch of something his father had done many times as a young minister himself; yet, God knew best. I was busy with my many duties at my home church while attending my son's services also; but Mark had decided that he needed to move to the Boise area where there was more opportunity. Then a loving, open-hearted pastor in the Boise Bench area offered to share his church building with Mark and Diane so they could hold their services on Sunday afternoons. We also had prayer meetings there on Saturday nights; but since the main service was on Sunday afternoon, I could still keep up with both churches for a while longer.

Meanwhile, I had heard about the Section Eight Low Income Housing program and had completed the application. It took months to process and be approved, but when the new apartments at Oak Park Village in Boise were built, I moved in. The rent was calculated according to income so I only had to pay fifty-seven dollars per month! It was an upgrade, since my first apartment complex was old and dark. These were new and modern. I had my own patio and storage unit. Angie and Pete had also moved to Oak Park earlier, so I was able to babysit for them once in a while.

The Toronto Blessing, or "renewal", as it was often called, was spreading across the country at this time and our pastor was one of many who had visited Toronto and returned with "the blessing". Being raised in Pentecost, and having years of experience watching the Holy Spirit move supernaturally in all types of healing and restoration, I understood this phenomenon. I knew that God's power moved in miraculous and mysterious ways. Nevertheless, although I was wholeheartedly open to the supernatural, I noticed that much of this new move appeared to be geared toward sensationalism—and I was not very comfortable with some of the manifestations that resulted. So I started volunteering on Wednesday nights to work in the nursery, as an option to sitting in every service. This eased my discomfort while still allowing me to faithfully serve my church. It was in 1998 that I finally went to my pastor and told him that I wanted to give my full support to my son's new work in town. He was so gracious—kind and understanding, just as I knew that he would be. "If it was my son, I would want to do the same thing," he assured me with his genuine smile. After taking time to thank me for all of my faithful service and telling me that I had done a wonderful job for them, he released me from my position with complimentary approval and well-wishes.

Working with My Boys

Leaving that position was a step of faith because it left me with only three hundred and seventy-six dollars a month and a weekly food box that I received from my volunteer work at a local Christian food bank. Additionally, the comfort and accommodation I had enjoyed for several years would be hard to replace. Even though I was excited about attending my son's church full-time, it took quite a while to feel like I belonged again. The setting was very different than what I had imagined. It was Mark's first pastorate and their approach to leading the flock was extraordinarily protective. In setting their ministry standards and church structure in place, they were remarkably mindful of the people learning to relate to them as pastors. So I stayed in the background, supporting them in any way that I could. I worked as a door greeter first, and I kept the nursery because the bulk of the new congregation was young families with small children. I invited many people to services by putting church bulletins in the Christian information packets that I shared with my neighbors. I even took some of my neighbor children to Sunday School with me, to the delight of their parents who were happy to have a relaxing Sunday morning at home. One man, whose little boy went with me each week, saw me outside one day and thanked me for it, saying that his son enjoyed going to church. I told him he was invited as well, and he responded that he was an atheist. I said, "Oh, come on now! You're not an atheist. Just look at the beautiful creation all around you!"

"Well…" he back-peddled; "I guess I'm not an atheist because I know that there is someone up there."

I rejoined with a sly smile, "Well then, why don't you call him God? That's who he is." He laughed and agreed that I was probably right.

Another little boy named Isaiah, with beautiful blue eyes, was only three years old when I started taking him to church. I had collected a few Christian cartoon videos and he would knock on my door often and ask if he could watch *Jonah*. I would always invite him in as long as his mother was apprised of his whereabouts. He usually wanted to stay and watch it again. One day he said to me, "You know somethin' Eunice? When you die you're gonna be an angel."

The church was growing by leaps and bounds and the work of the kingdom was advancing. Things were going well and I was glad to be there and witness the first years of Mark and Diane's church-planting. In July of 1999, however, I received a surprising telephone invitation from my younger son, David. He wanted me to come and work with him and Cheryl in Yuba City, California! He said that he valued my life-time experience in ministry and wanted to use my abilities in his church. At first, he said that he would love to have me as the receptionist; but I had instant flashbacks from answering phones at previous jobs and answered, "I'm not sure I would be very good at that." He laughed and said, "Mama, anything the Lord wants you to do would be welcome here." He also reminded me that his first son had been very small when Gail and I had suddenly uprooted our lives in Hoquiam, and that we had been able to live close to all the other kids' families since then. Now he had three boys and really wanted them to have some time with their grandma while they were still young. So I decided to go. Mark and Diane were sweet and supportive; they gave me a big going-away party at their house before I moved. My kids and many of the people from Mark's church helped me pack up my apartment. We left Boise in a small caravan with Jim driving the U-Haul while Becca and I drove my car. The U-Haul broke down on the way and it took a long time to get back on the road, but we finally made it to Yuba City where David had a whole crew of people waiting with welcoming smiles to help us unload the truck.

Highlights of Yuba

David had already helped me find an apartment so it was waiting for me. The social services were different in California, and I lost my Section Eight benefit. I had to pay almost one hundred and fifty dollars a month for rent and, though it may sound very inexpensive to most people, it was a lot compared to my Idaho benefit of fifty-seven dollars! I also paid my electricity and telephone bill on top of that. I qualified for a medical program that was very helpful, and I began receiving SSI which gave me another two hundred dollars a month. After I got settled in my new place I found out about a local Food Bank which gave additional support. God's provision was sufficient once again and my needs were met, despite the higher cost of living. Anyway, my attention was immediately consumed with the excitement of being involved in all that was happening at Glad Tidings, my new church home. Right away, David gave me an office of my own where I could take counseling appointments and keep all my books and files. It was so nice to have a place for my notes and teaching materials that I had kept over the years, thinking I might use them again. I was excited to get started offering my support in whatever capacity was needed, and I felt that I had a place here. I never had a dull day; I was productive and busy all the time while living in Yuba City. At first I got to send out all the visitor's cards and package my homemade bread to go with them. I had a bread making machine and the church secretary printed some nice labels for me. I wrote a card to each visitor who gave us contact information, and then delivered the card with the bread to their homes. People loved it. One man who is still there tells me every time I visit, "You're the reason I came to this church. I've been here ever since you brought me that loaf of homemade bread." The lady that had been asked to teach the Ladies' Bible Study had decided to take some time out to enjoy her grandkids, knowing how quickly that time would pass. So I was able to serve in that capacity for quite a while. I attended staff meetings once a week and had regular Leadership Retreats that I was also invited to. The services were great and we had many interesting special speakers. After about a year at Glad Tidings I had, true to my nature, developed quite a load of passengers that I transported regularly to church events. So the church traded my little car for a van, and gave me a gasoline credit card to help with fuel expenses. I was a full-time volunteer; but there were so many benefits included that I felt like I was part of the team. They valued my input and thanked me continually for everything I contributed. In between, I enjoyed planting and watering flowers in my daughter-in-law's beautiful yard; and popping in on my grandsons, who were being schooled at home.

Glad Tidings was a Missionary Church that reserved ample funding for spreading the gospel worldwide, and planned annual mission trips. They had a church-sponsored Bible college program for their young adults called Sold Out for Excellence. This group went on a mission trip every year. The young people would prepare dramas that depicted how the power of Satan could overtake a life and destroy it; then how the light of the gospel would come and enable them to be delivered through the power of Jesus Christ. It was very descriptive and they wore beautiful costumes. The drama would be performed multiple times on these mission trips, and followed up by a call to salvation where altar workers would talk to individuals about accepting Christ as their Savior.

When I first decided to go on a mission trip, David had come to me to ask if I would accompany the Sold Out group to Romania. He thought it was important for mature Christians to be present on these trips with our youth, and wanted some mothers to go along. I was seventy years old and on a limited income. I didn't know how I would raise $2500, so I did what the young people were doing and sent out letters asking for prayer and monetary support. I felt a little strange doing it but I knew that if the Lord wanted me to go the money would come in; and it did!

We traveled through France and Hungary and then drove in a bus all the way across Romania. We stayed in backward places where there were outhouses in lieu of restroom facilities. We were housed at a college building where the dorms were run down. The laundry room had deep, old-fashioned tubs in which to wash clothes but no place to hang them for drying. There was no place to set a bar of soap, or to hang a towel or a change of clothes. It was very unrefined, and often crude; with no trash cans available, the garbage was thrown in a pile in the corner of a room. We did lots of walking and saw some sites along the way. The dramas were vibrant and beautifully choreographed. The Sold Out team performed in city squares all across Romania. I was an altar worker along with others who were available to pray with responders. We also went to an orphanage in Deva and worked with some of the leaders there that David is still in contact with.

I stayed with a lady that was seventy-two years old. She lived on the tenth floor of a high-rise apartment with no elevators. They were built during the Communist regime when conveniences were taboo. She had to climb nine flights of steel stairs to get to her door. It was very hot weather that summer and there were thousands of mosquitos. Our church sponsored this orphanage, called The Yellow House. It was up on a hill and it was a nice facility with about fifty kids. When they had services they had to make their dining area into a conference room with seating and a pulpit. Then they would open it up to the public. Our hostess could not come to the services because she babysat people's children for her livelihood and was always busy with her job. She couldn't speak a word of English but others who could interpret told us what she was trying to say. She made meals for us while we stayed with her. For breakfast she served a chunk of fat with a bun or some bread, and sliced tomatoes or cucumbers. One or two days we had an egg, which was a great sacrifice for her to give. It was hard to eat some of those things but the young girl that stayed there with me would bring a baggie in her pocket to put the fat in to take away. We had been instructed to eat everything that was set before us so that we would not offend our hosts. As privileged Americans, we don't know how blessed we are to have such a large variety of foods. In Romania, we had the same food each day. Then we went to the orphanage to attend the church service and ate our next meal with the children. They had lots of good food because it was supplied by the Americans. We also went to regular churches to hold meetings. We were there for ten days and it was a life-changing experience, especially for the young adults.

There was also a group of missionary minded adults in the church that raised their own money to participate in regular mission trips. A talented and dedicated staff member at Glad Tidings led the first two trips that I went on. We went to Beijing, China and stayed in a hotel there. We each had to carry at least forty Bibles with us, and they were heavy ones. We packed them into our suitcases so we had to travel light and take fewer clothes. It was a very cold time of year with snow on the ground and zero temperatures. The smog in that part of China was much worse than Los Angeles. Once we were safely at our hotel destination, a group from the Underground Church came and put all the Bibles in vans to transport to safe storage. They were very happy for our team because we had a big group of fifteen, which represented a lot of Bibles donated to the Chinese church. Guides were always provided to take us into the places we visited.

Next we stayed in Hong Kong and made daily crossings over the border into China. We went through security areas about twice a day, miraculously, without being detained. It was a lot of walking, although sometimes we caught a bus or train. Since our backpacks were full of Bibles it was always unsettling to go through checkpoints each time. One time a girl was detained at a checkpoint where guards opened her suitcase and took a Bible they found on top of her clothes. The rest of the suitcase was full of Bibles as well; but since they didn't look underneath her clothing they did not confiscate those.

Then we flew down to Vietnam. We had to get new passports there and it took hours. A soccer tournament was being held in Ho Chi Minh City and it was crammed with wall to wall people, and motorcycles whizzing everywhere. Our hotel was across from a park where a huge screen was set up for crowds to watch the soccer game. There were 1,000 people sitting out in the park watching it. I thought the Vietnamese people were the most interesting I had ever seen. They rode bicycles everywhere. Many times I saw at least five people on one bike. They somehow attached a narrow board on top so the father, the mother, and a bunch of little kids could all ride on the same bicycle. It was fascinating! They are tiny people who can squat for hours without getting cramps in their legs. They were very agile and extremely skilled. I loved every minute of the mission trip to Vietnam. We went to a private room where a pastor came to talk to us. He had tried to escape Vietnam many times when he was young, but had never succeeded. His parents wanted him to get to America, but every time he tried he was caught, imprisoned, and beaten. Finally he met the Lord and decided that it must be God's will for him to stay in his own country and minister in the underground church. He was very dedicated, and thrilled to get all the Bibles we had brought with us. When we went out into the markets we were instructed to stay together. We had to be very cautious everywhere we went; but after the Bibles were all delivered we were able to relax. We always got to see some of the cultural sites and enjoy some fun activities at the end of the trip before flying back to America.

I went on two more trips like this, to China. Once we were in eastern China and traveled all day on a train across the country, just above Vietnam. I enjoyed the rhythm of the rocking train ride, and seeing all the little cities and unique villages along the way. One time we got to see where the Bibles were secretly stacked and stored. Different groups from various churches in the United States were involved in this Bible-smuggling project. We saw stacks of Bibles from various places that sent mission teams. The men that took us on this tour said that it was urgent for the Bibles to keep coming because they would be distributed quickly and they didn't want to run out. The Chinese Underground Church was growing and desperately needed copies of the Word of God for the many new converts that were coming to salvation through the message of Christ. My last trip to China included visits to Thailand and Laos, where I rode an elephant across a river! We walk for miles and miles to take all the Bibles to our designated meeting places. We went to a school in Thailand where we were allowed to give personal copies of the Holy Bible to every student. In this modern, post-Christian age, we would not even be able to do that in our own "one nation under God"! The smiling children dressed in their tidy uniforms were excited to receive our gifts.

I don't know where else I would have had such a great opportunity to experience international travel and missionary work. It was a great blessing to me.

Other highlights of my eight years in Yuba City included active exposure to the many community outreaches sponsored by Glad Tidings. Their church motto is, "Find a need and meet it. Find a hurt and heal it." They believe that "every member is a minister". Consequently, their schedule was brimming with outreach programs of all kinds that people were encouraged to participate in. At one time they had about seventy different community outreaches including Babies out of Bondage—church families caring for babies born to incarcerated mothers; Jail Services, T.I.P.—a Trauma Intervention Program that trained volunteers to work with the emergency services in the city.

I loved working with public school classrooms in a wonderful program called Character Counts. The Yuba-Sutter area had some very poor communities where drugs and criminal activity flourished, and the schools were in a dilapidated condition. Glad Tidings saw the need and met it. They reached out with work teams to clean up the property, paint picnic tables and trash cans, and plant flowers all over the school grounds. They did special things for the teachers and students as well, developing a caring and trustworthy reputation with school leadership. This relationship led to an open door inviting us to come and teach Character Counts in the classrooms. After training, we took our materials to present to students on a weekly basis for twenty to thirty minute lessons. Using parts of the Basic Youth Conflicts teachings, we used animal sketches to highlight strong qualities of a particular animal. Interesting illustrations and large, colorful posters made the object lessons come alive for the students. A famous personality, such as Abraham Lincoln, was also incorporated emphasizing a character quality that helped others or made a difference in the world. We took prizes and treats for the children. I volunteered in the Character Counts program every Wednesday for four years, going to four different schools during that time. Following several years of incorporating these character values into the schools, test scores were higher and the schools improved. It was amazing to see how God made ways to shine the light of Truth into dark places as our people learned to reach out in loving service to their communities.

A friend and I, sometimes with other ladies as well, started visiting rest homes to sing gospel songs to the elderly. We eventually had twelve homes that we visited each month. My favorite activity was my Ladies' Home Group. I facilitated it but the ladies took turns hosting our meetings. We always had a potluck and a Bible study. The church also had a very nice senior group. We had busses available for transportation, so our leaders would plan nice field trips to nearby attractions like the California State Railroad Museum in Sacramento, or a lunch boat tour on the Sacramento River. We visited Larsen Apple Barn where there were apple orchards producing a wide variety of apples. There was a deli onsite for lunch, and shops offering "apple everything" dotted the grounds like a carnival. Shopping for sunhats, dresses, and other non-edibles was also an option; it was a full day. Our leaders were excellent, and they thought of everything to make these trips comfortable and fun. They always brought a big cooler full of cold drinks and candy bars. We told stories and talked and had fun all the way. There were special summer outings, such as a BBQ on a house boat, and our Christmas parties were wonderful.

My friend who sang at the rest homes with me also loved to evangelize door to door. We even went to some parades that were sponsored by different religious groups and handed out gospel tracts. Yuba City is known for its wide representation of eastern religions. Large and ornate temples dot the landscape for Buddhist, Hindu, Muslim, and Sikh—the religion of the large Punjabi population residing in the Yuba-Sutter area. There were 30,000 Punjabis in that area who worshipped the goddess Shiva at their own temple. There was a large Muslim population as well, wearing their traditional costumes. Also, this area drew many New Age and occult groups that held activities there. God began using David and Cheryl in an active deliverance ministry for people who struggled with demonic oppression and possession of all kinds. Out of this ministry, the Isaiah 61 Conference was born, a teaching seminar on spiritual warfare that is now worldwide. The Isaiah 61 Conference has been presented in at least eighteen countries, and is held in California, Hawaii, India, and Finland annually. There were many people in the church who were trained to be on deliverance teams that prayed with people who came to the conference and wanted prayer for deliverance during the breaks or after services. Many attendees experienced blessing, spiritual enrichment, and lasting freedom.

I was involved in the church work days where a huge potluck lunch was provided mid-day for the volunteers who gave their time to work on the property. I was on a follow-up team for newcomers. Through these follow-up calls I had opportunity to provide prayer, encouragement, and counselling to people. One of these was the girl that eventually helped me with the rest home ministry. She was on her way to commit suicide when I first called her; but through prayer, encouragement, acceptance and friendship, she became a free and active member of our church. She attended Glad Tidings for the rest of her life and never missed a service. God does amazing things when we are willing to invest in the lives of others.

I had been living in Yuba City for over eight years when the winds of change began to blow once again in my life. I had thoroughly enjoyed all of my activities and involvements there, family times, and wonderful friendships. God had been so good to me and all my needs had been provided for. I had been able to support my son and daughter-in-law in their ministry and watch my grandsons growing up. A wide variety of service opportunities had enriched my life. I had been blessed to touch others in all walks of life through helps, prayer, teaching, exhortation and encouragement. As new priorities began to take shape and the vision and focus of the church began to adjust and grow, I began to wonder if God had some new priorities for me as well. I came to Idaho for Christmas during this period and talked to my daughter about it. I was somewhat in turmoil over what I should do and said to her, "If I only knew what the Lord wanted me to do it would be so much easier." She said to me, "Mom, you've served the Lord faithfully all of your life and you are a dedicated and trustworthy servant of the kingdom. If Jesus was standing here right now and you asked him what you should do, I really believe he would say, 'Well, Eunice, what would you *like* to do?'" She took me to look at some apartments just to get a feel for what was available, and when I got home I started sorting through my things in case I decided to move. At the same time, my mother had a stroke, and my sister, Lois, who lived with and cared for her in Caldwell, Idaho, was hospitalized with a sudden open-heart surgery that was unexpected. With these pressing circumstances, it became quite clear that I was needed elsewhere and I decided to come back home.

Home Again

I flew to Boise so that I could get to my sister and my mother right away. January was a terrible time to move, but all my wonderful friends and family in Yuba City finished packing up my apartment and my office at the church. As I remember, my son, David, drove my car and my son-in-law, Ed Mason— with my daughter, Dorcas—drove the U-Haul truck from Yuba City to Boise. They had to come over the Sierra-Nevada Mountains in a terrible snow storm, and had snow pack on the roads most of the way. I had secured an apartment in Boise, but it was smaller than my place in California, so Mark helped me purchase a storage shed. He arranged for it to be erected on Jim and Becca's property where I could keep some of my things that would not fit in my new residence. As soon as everything was unloaded, I left it all in boxes and went to stay with my mother and sister in Caldwell for a month. On the first of March, I came back to Boise to unpack and settle in. It was fun and exciting to be home again and to get everything set up. Becca had a big "Welcome Home!" party for me in the Community Room of my new senior apartment complex. I got acquainted with my neighbors and began to participate in some of the planned resident activities, which helped me build relationships and gave me many opportunities to witness and encourage others. The Lord is always faithful to give us plenty of occasions to share Christ and to love people if we are willing to be available.

I immediately became involved in Mark's church again, which was then being held in a gymnasium in Garden City while they were searching for a building. It was hard to find parking there, but Harvest Church was growing and everyone was enthusiastic about the future. I enjoyed getting acquainted with all the new people and spending time with my eldest son's family again. I wasn't involved in any ministry but all the services were very good. I participated in many small groups and took most of the classes that they encouraged the congregation to attend. I had been an active prayer counsellor at a local food bank before moving to California, so after a couple of years I became active in that outreach again. I volunteered one day per week, presenting a devotional for the staff members each time. I also continued my practice of door to door evangelism and handed out gospel tracts and Daily Bread pamphlets in neighborhoods all over Boise and Meridian.

Hearing my son preach was always my favorite church activity. In both of my sons' churches, my most important ministry was covering them with prayer; especially during the hard times of discouragement, which every pastor goes through. Since returning to Boise in 2008, I have thoroughly enjoyed watching my grandchildren grow in the Lord and develop their ministries in teaching and music, following in the footsteps of their parents, Mark and Diane. They are all very talented and enthusiastic about the work of God's kingdom, impacting many youth and young adults. It has been refreshing to watch so many young people who are fervent for the Lord and developing a passion for missions.

Happy Notes

This chapter, The Last Lap, was an account of extreme transitions; from Gail's and my last experiences together through several years of moves and changes as I discovered life on my own. My prayer is that this testimony will be instrumental in spreading the message that life will always include hardships but with God, all things are possible! I trust that that my readers will be encouraged to be faithful to God and never give up hope. Looking back on my married life I see that every time Gail had a big episode, though I prayed and cried and struggled to get through it, when it cleared up and things got back to normal I was always so glad that I had not given up. Even at Sequim, working in the church together, ministering to those people and hearing him preach again, I was so glad I had not given up on him. We were so happy there, and had so many good memories in between the brief storms. I think of all the kids doing well, and realize that—despite our disappointments—we all came through the storm with hope, and victory, and strength to move on. When the boys were in Bible College I remember being so grateful that God had enabled me to press through and not leave Gail. What would have happened to my boys? How would it have affected my kids? How might that outcome have changed their destinies, or the futures of my grandchildren? Many, many times I thought of that. We were so proud of our boys, and able to watch their blossoming ministries and enjoy it together. It was such a conundrum for someone with as much Bible knowledge as Gail had to be defeated by the enemy again and again. He had so much wisdom for counseling other people, and such a large capacity to mentor young men entering the ministry. His prophetic discernment, and powerful sermons; his great love for God and for the Truth were proof of the life of God within him. It was an excruciating mystery that I could have easily decided—many times—to live without; but I chose to walk with him through the valley.

Many young women that I have talked to—although they don't know the half of what I actually went through—have asked me, "How did you do it?" The answer has always been the same and very simple: "Only by the grace of God; because every day his mercies are new." If our hardships can be an example to someone else who needs hope or strength for the day, they are not wasted. In this day and age, many women might call me foolish, but look at my children now. Look at my life now; and look at my husband now! He waits for me at the Gates of Glory, free at last.

I attribute much of this success to a heart that was always happy in serving the Lord, whatever else was going on in my life. Gail was the love of my life, the only one I ever wanted to spend my life with. When he was doing well, we were a perfect match in every way and I wouldn't trade him for anything! With or without him, however, my happiness continued because it was centered on the big picture instead of just my own comfort. We can't afford to think only of personal things, but how our lives are affecting others. The Psalmist was remorseful when he said, *"I gave occasion for the enemies of the Lord to blaspheme."* I would never want anybody to stumble or become discouraged by hearing my story.

Many young women, especially under the influence of modern cultural norms, may lack the spiritual understanding to comprehend it. Some might think that if God would allow his child to go through something like this, then why follow him? That perspective would be unfortunate and incomplete because it puts the focus of the experience on *"what* I went through" instead of *"how* I came through it"! The purpose in sharing my story is to help people understand that there is a strong and successful way to get through anything with the Lord on their side.

I heard a famous preacher say once, "Life is only ten percent what happens to you and ninety percent how you handle it!" Most everybody knows that life will be difficult; what is more important is to know that we can do all things through Christ; for, when we are submitted to him, our weakness becomes another opportunity for his strength to prevail. When we stubbornly do life on our own, his strength is not a part of the equation. Therefore, when our own understanding and strength run out, there is nothing left to stand on, or to navigate with.

The Lord has always been faithful to me through the hard times, and those hardships always drew me closer to his side. My collection of poems has been a life saver so many times. This one comforted me often during those hard years:

I thank God for bitter things;
They've been a 'friend to grace';
They've driven me from paths of ease
To storm the secret place.

I thank Him for the friends who failed

To fill my heart's deep need;
They've driven me to the Savior's feet,
Upon His love to feed.

I'm grateful too, through all life's way
No one could satisfy,
And so I've found in God alone
My rich and full supply![1]
    —Florence White Willett

Another one talked about how we would understand better if we could see ahead and know what God was doing through all the hard times of our lives. We would have more confidence in his wisdom and more strength to endure our struggles. It ends with the line, *"I think that I could say that all God's ways are best."*

That's why I want to end this section with all the happy notes on the staff of my married life. Gail used to say, "You always wake up with a song!" He was amazed by this because he often had severe migraine headaches and, during his dark times, he woke up deeply depressed. For me, the songs were always there, and they ministered to my weary soul. I always felt like singing, no matter what was going on around me. Even when the tears flowed freely, I had music in my heart. The melodies came so quickly and easily to me that I always thought I could write a song of my own, but the lines just came as little snippets throughout the day. The only complete song I ever received was the one that I woke up singing one morning, "Jesus Has Triumphed in Me", and that one was written in my spirit! We can train our minds to focus on the good things. We are in control of our own thoughts and don't have to succumb to all the negative influence that Satan throws at us. We can block those fiery darts and take control of our thinking. The sound mind that God has given us is a powerful tool against the enemy's destructive tactics. One of his favorite tricks is making us feel that we *deserve* to react negatively. That's why the Bible exhorts God's people to be aware of Satan's devices!

In these twenty-four-plus years since my husband's home-going I have testified, in both verbal and written forms, of God's many blessings throughout the wonderful life I have lived, choosing to play all the happy notes on the staff of my heart. Regardless of the trials, I had many fond memories of life with Gail and much to be grateful for. He was very romantic and often expressed his feelings of love for me, which I knew were genuine. He could whistle love songs like a pro with the brightest notes precisely on pitch. Every year, he bought me the most beautiful and expensive valentine card he could find. Each one had tender, loving messages— along with his own written words about how thankful he was to have me for his own and how much he loved me. Other people even noticed his tender words to me and, although everyone knows that actions are more important, I would add that when the words are all you have, keep them. He was a tender and affectionate person most of the time, and he loved to hold my hand. I felt very secure when Gail was near. He was an "in-charge" person, a good leader and protector. As a light sleeper, he always woke up at the slightest sound, so I was never afraid of anything when he was with me.

Gail had a beautiful voice and I loved to hear him sing. Singing together was one of our chief enjoyments as he played along on his guitar and I, on my accordion. We both loved gospel songs and often sang together and played our instruments for an hour at a time. Our music was always a life-saving bond of friendship and comradery. It was also a highlight of all of our years of ministry together.

Gail was a great conversationalist and I loved talking to him. We thoroughly enjoyed a good discussion on many subjects of mutual interest. He was very articulate, whether speaking to a crowd, a family gathering, or just to me about his thoughts and feelings. He was also an excellent story-teller and everyone loved to sit around and listen to him. We always had great times with close friends and all of our relatives. I loved his hearty laugh, and all of our children did, too; it's one of our most cherished memories of him. We had lots of fun and laughter in our home; Gail was extremely witty and was gifted with a great sense of humor.

He loved his children and was a good daddy to them. He was always proud of them, enjoyed them thoroughly, and had close relationships with all of them, especially as they grew older. They always honored his wisdom on many and varied subjects of conversation and eagerly asked questions of him. To this day my children all speak endearingly, and often, about their father. Many times in conversations with me or with each other they have said, "I wonder what Daddy would say about this." Gail was very fatherly to young Christians as well, and helped many, many young men to grow in their faith. He was a good mentor, and an excellent counselor and teacher. He was loved and admired by those who sat under his ministry and leadership.

I loved his earnestness and intensity after God. His preaching was my "first impression" of him and it was a powerful draw in our relationship. I never got tired of listening to him and he was always my favorite speaker. Gail was gifted in communication. He had a grasp of vocabulary and pronunciation that made him a capable and effective preacher that everyone loved to hear. He spoke clearly and was very organized with his subject matter. He knew what he wanted to say and how to get the message across to his audience.

These natural talents were accentuated by a gift of utterance, or the Divine Unction. This anointing of the Holy Spirit empowered his presentation and caused him to excel in ministry. I feel like I remember every sermon that he ever preached. He made the truth so clear, it was nearly impossible to forget. One time in a Presbytery meeting, where he was receiving personal prophecy, a prophet exclaimed that Gail was a "teaching priest". His examples and illustrations were so picturesque and descriptive that he made the truth come alive to the congregation. Gail would tell me that it even amazed him when the anointing of the Holy Spirit was so evident in his meetings. The words came prophetically and spontaneously. He seldom used notes, beyond two or three points or scripture references. It was clearly supernatural; and many, many people told me through the years that Gail was the best preacher they ever heard. Some of our children later said that, whenever they were looking for churches to attend in the various places they lived it was always a challenge to find a good preacher because, "they were too spoiled by having Daddy to listen to."

I loved to hear Gail pray; he often prayed with a powerful anointing as if he were preaching or prophesying. He was also an excellent reader and loved to read the Bible aloud to me. He read it through several times through the years, in several different translations, as I listened and followed along. It was our favorite way to spend time together in the evening, and remained a common practice for us until the day that he died. I always loved the companionship with a man who had the same values and interests as I. We shared the same beliefs and theology and could talk for hours about the things of the Lord. We also shared the same work ethic and convictions about using all we had to the best of our ability. We were both content with what we had and held the same views about living simply and denying the grasping covetousness of a world that always wanted more than was needed. It was wonderful to have the support of someone who loved me and was concerned about my well-being. He often said, "Honey, are you working too hard? Don't you need to take a rest?"

In later years we enjoyed bicycle riding and long drives. Gail loved to go for a drive in the country, and I really missed that after he died. In the early days of our marriage we spent lots of time in the car traveling from meeting to meeting. Gas was cheap, so it was the most practical way to travel and we did lots of it. Gail was never one to get lost or disoriented; he could find his way anywhere. I guess we learned the art of packing and unpacking from our early days as traveling evangelists because we seemed to agree on what to take and what we could get along without. "Traveling light" with less baggage made for an easier trip. Each time we went, it was enjoyable and we seemed to have everything we needed. Consequently, we became good planners and had some fun-filled trips after our kids were older. We would plan the whole adventure: where to camp; when to stop; what to do; how much everything would cost. We made happy memories with our children and took lots of pictures.

Gail and I shared the same heart for reaching the lost with the gospel, which was the passion that drew us together in the first place. The glue that kept our relationship functioning through good times and bad was God's call upon our lives for ministry. Our greatest memories and accomplishments as a couple were the many fields of harvest where Gail and I worked together in Kingdom business. We were happiest shepherding the flock of God and pastoring groups of people. Most of them were wonderful, and showed deep appreciation for our service to them and for the Lord. True to his word, the message never returned void. God was faithful to change lives and heal hearts through our years of ministry. His vessels may be cracked and scuffed and we often need cleansing before use; but when God pours his life and power through us, great things happen because his intention is the eternal outcome and not our temporary, earthly accomplishment. Regardless of the trials of today, we must remember that all of our tomorrows are ahead of us. We can choose to let God reign every time a new day dawns!

CHAPTER FIFTEEN

Today, Tomorrow, and Always

My Here and Now

I have always been a busy person, but even our busyness changes over the years. My daily schedule at this time in my life is calm and secure. Never one to sit around in a robe and slippers, I always get dressed and ready for the day as soon as I rise in the morning. I prepare a hot beverage and sit at my tiny kitchen table for devotions and prayer. I've made a habit of reading the Bible through every year and I still find wonderful treasures that are new to me which feed the soul and spirit. After my devotional reading and time with the Lord in prayer, I will make breakfast to feed the body, keeping a balance of health in all areas. Then I check my calendar for scheduled appointments or obligations I have agreed to. Every day I make phone calls regarding my small groups, Bible studies, counseling, or touching base with neighbors and family. I call or visit my three older sisters every week, as well as my two sisters-in-law. Keeping in touch with my family has always been very important to me. I have maintained contact with Gail's family since he has been gone as well, through cards, letters, and telephone calls.

I make it my goal to do something to help or encourage somebody else. There are many opportunities to care for widows, or those who are sick and lonely. Since I've lived here I have used my sewing and cooking skills on a regular basis to help others. In a senior living complex such as mine, people experience many physical changes and challenges from week to week. I run errands for other residents and give them rides to their appointments or to the grocery store. Making custards or cookies to share with others in my building is a regular activity for me. In the winter I often make big pots of soups or stews that I can dish up and deliver to the units on my floor. Everyone is appreciative but to some, who are becoming too feeble to cook for themselves on a regular basis, a shared meal is a real gift.

I've found that there are many ways to be a blessing if that's what is in our hearts to do each day. I love to write notes, cards and letters of encouragement. Through the years, as God brought people to my mind, I would not only pray for them but often write a letter or send a card with inspirational poems or articles tucked inside. I have written hundreds of these, and still write ten to twenty cards each month. I am also inundated with mail from charitable organizations, mostly Christian ministries, that I like to read about, pray for, and support financially with my "widow's mites" that are dear to God's heart. It is a great joy to me to give whatever I can.

Anywhere we live, we can build a testimony and cultivate relationships, thinking about the people around us and what we can do to serve and encourage them. Most of them will be respectful and appreciative. My apartment complex has potlucks once a month and I've never missed one in the last ten years unless I was out of town. One time I baked four cakes for a birthday party in honor of all the residents celebrating birthdays that month. I enjoy serving in every way I can, from playing my accordion at the holiday celebrations to hosting on-site weekly Bible studies. After returning to Boise, I realized that I probably wouldn't have much more opportunity for ministry; but whenever I think about getting rid of the Bible study materials that I collected from all those years of teaching, someone requests another class! They are mostly for my lady friends but some of the men have also joined our studies from time to time. God's truth never returns void, and the Holy Spirit can work wonders through the written word given to others, even the elderly who are on their last lap of life. As a result of spiritual conversation with neighbors and friends, I have invited and transported many of them to church with me where they can enjoy a good message and an atmosphere of praise and worship. I often pray with people who call or stop by, encouraging them to take their burdens to the Lord.

I still love to sing more than anything else. I miss the old hymns of the church, and they remain my favorites. Although I no longer have the street meetings of my childhood days, or the Sunday night "sing-spirations" of my youth, I still sing my favorite songs at home, playing my own instruments. Whether the scripture choruses of the 70s and 80s played softly on guitar or some of the famous special numbers that rang true for generations of saints, the music refreshes my soul as much now as it ever has before.

God also gave me a heart for evangelism. From my earliest memories—of my daddy gathering all of us on a street corner to sing and testify to passers-by—until now, I have thrilled at giving the gospel by tract or conversation to any who will listen. Friends and family still save their Christian reading materials for me and, when I have a stack collected, I walk the neighborhoods to talk to people or leave my treasures of truth on their doors. Hostile receptions are few and far between; and I believe it is because the Holy Spirit goes with me and rejoices in the seeding of truth that may blossom later into the beautiful flower of Faith, drawing another soul to Jesus.

Opportunities for travel have been more than expected, too! Besides those unforeseen and remarkable mission trips I enjoyed through Glad Tidings in Yuba City, I have had opportunities to travel with family and friends. The spring following Gail's death, my two daughters took me on a nice trip to Atlanta, Georgia to visit all of our family there. It was wonderful to see all of them, and a special time to spend together with my girls. We also saw some beautiful gardens and had our portrait taken in Southern Belle costumes for a keepsake of our trip. I loved traveling with Gail, but I would never be interested in going alone; so my daughters and their husbands have taken me on several vacations with them in the years since his passing. They include me in lots of day trips, family dinners and outings with kids and grandkids, too. We always have a great time and I am always excited to go along.

In my older years, I enjoy seeing the news on the evenings I am home to keep up with world events and to "know the signs of the times." With the technological age in full swing, I also glean inspiration from the many programs on Christian television that offer good preaching and teaching. I've even gleaned from the Information Age and found many good websites where the gospel and Christian causes are promoted. I will often choose to read a variety of Christian periodicals, studies, articles, and biographies of famous Christians. We are never too old to glean from the lives of those who have gone before us.

One of my greatest joys right now is the legacy I will leave to all of my grandchildren. They don't know my story, but most of them know that I have maintained a lifelong testimony of Christian stability. I pray persistently for the ones who are not currently serving the Lord. They've had godly parents and Christian teaching all their lives and still the world draws them in to things that chip away at their strength of spirit and their focus on the things of God. My life is mostly lived, so now my joy is looking forward to Heaven. I think about it every day; because none of us knows how long we will live. The scripture says that it is "appointed" unto man to die; this means that our times are in God's hands and we will not go one minute before the day or the hour that he has set for our pilgrim journey to end.

A Changing World

I have witnessed profound changes in our world during my lifetime. Neighborhoods used to be peaceful, happy places to live where children could walk alone to nearby parks or school grounds and play safely with one another without fear of kidnapping or assault. All the kids walked or rode their bicycles to school unless they lived out in the country and had to ride the bus. They played ball, kick-the-can, and tag in vacant lots until after dark with no fear of harm. There was no such thing as a drug lord, and the neighbors knew each other on a first-name basis and were always available to help out. We could walk down to the corner mom and pop grocery stores and spend pennies on candy and bubble gum. A nickel could buy a package of gum, a big candy bar, or some ice cream; and it was usually earned from doing chores, so was not easily spent! Families were home together every evening for dinner and bed time was important. Night was for family time and rest; day was for work and school. Most mothers were able to stay home and did not work outside jobs; many of them sewed clothes for their families, and without so many modern appliances, the cooking and housework took much more time.

Now, advances in science, industry and medicine have brought us everything from modern appliances to medical cures we never thought possible for disease. We have vast communication systems through computers, cell phones and other electronic devices. The satellite systems and the space age have brought world news and the mysteries of the universe into our living rooms and made the weather more predictable than we ever imagined possible.

Family life, by definition, now seems a far cry from my rich and rewarding experience as a child. I grieve to look at our children today and see all the blessings that many of them will never know. Too many homes are filled with trauma, public education is infested with liberal philosophies, and the entertainment industry has almost single-handedly sponsored the moral decay of society in general. I acknowledge and appreciate all the conscientious people in education and industry who are standing for truth and right; but it is a bigger battle now than it ever was before. The rise of the ACLU has severely and adversely invaded our world with deception and false securities. They pretend to uphold liberty while robbing us of our most cherished freedoms. I have lived long enough to see the pendulum swing from one extreme to the other. My heart grieves to see blatant ravings of the atheist, while Christians are forced into silence; to see the radical aggression and promotion of sexual perversions in our society while the moral standards of Christian faith and conviction are assaulted, slandered, and even outlawed. I have lived long enough to see the horrible effects of The Year of the Child, the awful reaping of the Women's Liberation Movement, and the murderous results of the "Right to Choose" abortion laws; all of which have brought ruination and degradation to society on a global scale.

Politically, the New World Order is beginning to take place and our great American forefathers would be ashamed. I had great admiration for men like George Washington and Abraham Lincoln who honored God in their responsibilities of leading this nation. There have been a few that I greatly admired in modern times, like Ronald Reagan, and as a Christian citizen I always wanted to pray for our leaders as the Bible dictated we should do; but as evil becomes bolder and more blatant in the leadership roles of our society, it becomes a greater challenge! The Bible states clearly in Proverbs 14:34 that, *"Godliness makes a nation great, but sin is a disgrace to any people."* (NLT)

International news is bursting with reports of failing economies around the globe, and national sovereignty is weakening as currencies fail and dictatorial governments see opportunities to "save the day" and then keep the power. Every kind of crime and evil is on the rise as people toss their generational family and religious values to the wind in order to be independent of any authority or restriction from doing their own thing. Life has become about the "big I" while the ethics and wisdom of our forefathers, parents and pastors is disregarded as old-fashioned and restrictive. A fierce increase in hatred toward both Christians and Jews is now widespread, to the fulfillment of Bible prophecy. With end-time events happening worldwide, it is no longer difficult to imagine a one-world political, religious, and economic system falling easily into place in preparation for the rule of the Antichrist. People are worried and fearful about the future with governments falling apart and their daily lives regularly disrupted by natural disasters and unsettling changes. What we have learned from our history is that "we never learn from history"; and as it is so often said these days, "If we *don't* learn from history, it will most assuredly *repeat itself!*"

As a young person, I was never involved in any kind of public demonstration; but in 1980 Gail and I attended Washington for Jesus in Washington DC. A jet had been chartered and 87 people from Rhema Fellowship, where we pastored in Hoquiam, WA, went with us. We spent a week there, as referenced earlier in Chapter Eleven, participating in prayer rallies, marches, speeches, and youth meetings for the purpose of calling America to repentance and praying for our nation's leaders. We were so glad to be a part of something so important in our great country. In my later years I have been more active in peaceful demonstrations such as The Life Chain, opposing abortion, the Jesus March, and gatherings for prayer on the steps of our state capitol building annually. The nature of our desperate world calls us to stand up and be counted.

The world may look dim, but we have great cause to rejoice! In the spiritual realm, there is not only an increase of gross darkness but a great burst of God's powerful light of truth into the church. There is a networking of different denominations and a coming together of God's people from all walks of life. We are seeing unity on a grander scale and a willingness to lay down our differences and blend our strengths in order to work together in fulfilling the Great Commission of Matthew's gospel for evangelizing the world for Christ. At the same time, modern technological advances have made it possible for the explosion of the gospel message to reach the far corners of the earth. Masses of previously unreached people groups are being converted through the media. There are many Christian broadcasts on television that are seen all over the world and produce testimonies of people who come to Christ through their messages. I've heard wonderful Christian radio programs through the years, filled with gospel truth and light; many of these are still going strong.

God has always had plans to combat and defeat Satan's strategies. In the Bible, he used the heroes of the faith such as David, Joseph, Daniel, Paul, and John the Revelator. In the church there were many great men and women of God who gave their lives to the spread of the gospel and there are many doing the same today on a worldwide scale.

For Christians there is an element of excitement in the air because we know that God's promises are true. As we join together and rise up against the evils of our day, we know that God is on our side. In the battle for our families, our children, our churches and our neighborhoods, we are far beyond arguing human points of view. Instead we stand firmly on the eternal truth of God's holy Word and rejoice in our blessed hope--the return of our Lord and Savior, Jesus Christ. We are living in the end times, but I am watching for that last great harvest and ingathering of souls before the rapture of the saints. After he whisks His bride, the Church, away to his father's house, the world will be in worse turmoil than ever—the end of the End.

I pray for Jerusalem, because I see the nations aligning themselves against her, as the Bible foretold. Today the alliance of anti-Semitic nations with their vitriol and animosity is more blatant than ever! It sounds like the war of Ezekiel

38 and 39 is about to take place. Yet when Jesus comes back with ten thousands of his saints to reclaim the world he will forever change the landscape of the nations, bringing the lasting peace that no human cause or earthly government could ever hope to achieve without Him. His plan is victorious and eternal and all who make Christ their Lord of life will be part of His glorious kingdom!

Echoes from the Past

The more I look around, the more I miss about the "good ol' days". I miss the *simple life* of contentment and quiet living; having time together as a family to share freely about the wonderful miracles, healing and deliverances we have witnessed through the years. Sometimes I long to sing, laugh, and enjoy one another as we used to, without feeling rushed or anxious about someone's schedule. I miss the *commonness* of people taking the time to meditate, ponder, and listen to God without having every minute of the day crammed with agenda items. Those times of being at home with those we loved with no need or social expectation to constantly run here and there searching for entertainment have all but disappeared.

I miss being able to participate in the gathering of the saints freely without worrying that the schedule is being interrupted. I miss having ample time to pray around the altar after a church service"—just waiting on the Lord and listening for His voice without people thinking they need to "help". Giving exhortations or encouragement from the heart and sharing with each other what God has done used to be called "testimonies"; and time was set aside for this during services, usually on Sunday nights. There is no longer time, nor opportunity, to tell the next generation the things we have learned over a life-time; often it seems they can hardly bear to hear of the old landmarks of the faith. Traditional respect for one's elders is sadly lacking—even in the church—compared to what it used to be, and our standards or way of life are even rebuffed with defensive comments or mocking tones. Honor for our elders is seldom given where it is due.

Along with the things I miss, there are things I wish I had done differently. I would have complained less and praised God more. I would have never doubted or fretted, but trusted God fully. I would not have had such high expectations of frail and finite mortal men. I would have given my children more room to fail, without scolding. I would have prayed more and cried less. I would not have worried over finances—or anything else, for that matter! I would have conquered *all* fear; not just some fears. I would have meditated more and rejoiced in God's constant goodness. I would have done more journaling to record His blessing in our lives; the miracles of provision, healing and supernatural protection.

Life is short! There are always things we will wish we could have accomplished or experienced, but that we never had time to pursue. I always wanted to learn enough Spanish to have a simple conversation with Hispanic people, mostly for travel and witnessing. Most of the things I have really wanted to do, I've been able to learn in these latter years of living alone. I became quite tech-savvy (for a grandma!) so that I could write letters and use email on my computer and iPad, as well as texting photos and messages from my iPhone! I still practice my guitar, keyboard and accordion while singing all the old songs that I love, so that I can be ready to share at a nursing home or assisted living facility whenever a request is made of me. We all have the same amount of time; but how we choose to use it will either fill our life with fulfillment or regret. One thing remains constant for us all: there are no regrets for pursuing God's will. No one has perfect understanding, and as we live, we learn and grow; so everyone will wish a few things had been done differently. But God is pleased when we conscientiously carry out all that we *do* understand. So, in all these things, we can look back with gratefulness while still looking ahead with anticipation; for in God nothing is wasted. Every new experience can be a wholesome exercise in trusting Him and learning more of his ways. We can cherish the past without resenting the present; remember our training while still learning more; act honorably without recognition; speak reservedly, though there is much more to say; and be generous listeners whether or not we are heard. God's truth always marches on; His ways are far above our own.

Hopes for the Future

My wishes and expectations have never been for travel or adventure, such as many people in retirement dream of. Not only is my future growing shorter in earthly years, but I am quite content with the places I have already been and have no particular desire to go anywhere else. I can see so many travel programs on television, which is often a better view than being there in person! Travel, to me, is about who I am with rather than the place itself or the adventure; consequently, I would never travel alone just to go on a trip. When I am with people, anyplace is fun; from rides in the country to picnics in the park. Nevertheless, the Lord has allowed me to enjoy some of the most beautiful scenery in the world, travel on a cruise ship, and visit other countries despite my limited resources!

What I would really love to see, if the Lord tarries, is more of the gospel seeds that I have sown bear fruit unto eternal life. I'd like to know that people I have prayed for would be saved, and that all my family and loved ones would be obediently following the Lord. I would love to see all of my grandchildren more often, tell them my stories, and impart life lessons to them. I'd love to see them reach their full potential in God and be involved in the end-time harvest; or see some of them preach the gospel and carry the Torch through their dark world.

I would love to see a great spiritual revival in America, and a movement in our churches toward more spontaneous participation and less performance. The New Testament directs us all to share a psalm, a hymn, an exhortation and so forth, in turn as we are moved by the Holy Spirit. It seems tragic that our churches are so often focused on talent and position, singling out the elite few that are considered qualified to participate. I love hearing from the greater body of believers about God's blessing in their lives. The modern church has become ritualistic in so many ways, stuck in our ruts and routines that support a controllable church image, when it is the image of Christ in all of us that we should be supporting in our gatherings.

If I Could Tell Them...

My children are grown and gone, all raising families of their own. I have grandchildren and great-grandchildren from coast to coast! My role now is to love and pray for them all, support them in their endeavors and try to visit them whenever I can. But if I could spend time with them, I would tell them that Time is short! It is very possible that God will consummate His plan for the ages before any of my children reach the age I am today. We may be ruling and reigning with Jesus Christ in The Millennium someday soon! Acts 1:7 tell us, "... *It is not for you to know the times or the seasons, which the Father hath put in his own power."* (KJV) We await His glorious return, and it is important that we spread the gospel and be voices for God in this terminal generation. The world will continue to slide toward globalism in preparation for the coming of the Antichrist and Armageddon; but God's great plan will continue toward completion!

My greatest wish is for them to understand now what King Solomon finally discovered at the end of his life. Ecclesiastes 12:13(KJV) *"Let us hear the conclusion of the whole matter: Fear God and keep His commandments; for this is the whole duty of man."* So I would encourage them that the sooner they learn to seek the Lord, to walk in his ways, and live to please Him, the happier, safer, and more successful they will be. Faith in God is a gift to value. I pray that they may do the will of God in their generations, without the fear of man. Proverbs 29:25 teaches us that, *"The fear of man bringeth a snare; but whoso putteth his trust in the Lord shall be safe."* (KJV) I would exhort them to hold up the righteous standard; to never compromise with the world; to preach the whole counsel of God; to be an example to unbelievers of a Christian lifestyle; to honor their godly heritage and to live for Him without reservation. Yes, to be radical Christians! My advice to posterity is to be witnesses for the Truth, spreading the Light of the Gospel wherever they go.

I would coach them to read, love and obey the Bible, using it to chart their lives as the only road map to Heaven. The Bible is a valuable and priceless treasure, and 100% reliable! I would encourage them to resist the strong draw of the world in filling their lives and homes with temporal things, and instead to be content with what they have. Striving to "keep up with the Joneses" robs us of the time and energy we need to "contend for the faith" as Jude 3 exhorts us. I would remind them about Matthew 6:31-33, (NLT) *"So don't worry about these things, saying, 'What will we eat? What will we drink? What will we wear?' These things dominate the thoughts of unbelievers, but your heavenly Father already knows all your needs. Seek the Kingdom of God above all else, and live righteously, and he will give you everything you need."*

If I had the chance, I would always encourage them to be vigilant! The Message version of 1 Peter 5:8 warns, *"Stay alert. The Devil is poised to pounce, and would like nothing better than to catch you napping. Keep your guard up!"* I would remind them to pray much, trust God in everything, and to sing a lot! I would remind them to keep a happy heart and an optimistic, faith-filled attitude; to hold firmly to an awareness of God's continual presence wherever they go. I want them to remember that it will never be what they go through that will make or break them, but how they respond to life situations. I want them to believe that happiness is a choice; that they can be overcomers and triumph over any difficulty if they have faith in God and His Word, and keep a good attitude.

My hope, for all of us, is that we will live in peace and love with one another, allowing nothing to divide us. I pray that our lives will be godly and unspotted from the world, so that we will be able to keep the oil of the Holy Spirit in our lamps, always ready for Christ's imminent return. We cannot live as though this earth is our permanent home! I believe the Laodicean attitude, spoken of in Revelation 3 is prevalent; *"We are rich, and increased in goods and have need of nothing."* We can be so independent that we are not even aware of our need! Jesus said that we don't even see how poor, wretched, miserable, blind and naked we actually are. May the Lord anoint our eyes to see spiritually, with understanding and revelation; with Holy Spirit illumination and supernatural insight. It is our only hope for eluding the last day deceptions that will come upon our world. I want my children and grandchildren to be among the elect who identify with the message of the old gospel song that says this world is not our home! We are just passing through and our treasures are on the other side; we don't feel at home here anymore.

CHAPTER SIXTEEN

Keys for Living Happily & Victoriously

My Legacy of Take-away Treasures

My life has been a happy one because of the hope we have in Jesus Christ. God is faithful and will always keep His word and fulfill His promises. I hope this illustrated message of my life will remind all who read it that they, too, can know God and trust Him to guide their lives. Here are some valuable treasures from my life that I hope you will take into yours to help you live every day for God's glory and to make the best of every situation.

LIFE IS A JOURNEY: Life is a pilgrimage; we are just passing through on our way from darkness to light. Colossians 1:13 (NIV) *"For he has rescued us from the dominion of darkness and brought us into the kingdom of the Son he loves."* Since we are simply on a journey we should not get attached to the allurements of the present culture that could slow our progress. Instead, we should recognize the freedom that we have in Christ to travel light and stay safe and focused. There is great liberty in knowing that God's part is to lead and our part is to follow.

CONTENTMENT IS A GIFT: The scripture says that *"Godliness with contentment is great gain."* When we are willing to believe that righteousness, peace, and joy in the Holy Ghost are more important than earthly possessions, we are ready to receive God's free gift of being content with whatever we have! We can be happy with our family, home, church, friends, and neighbors. When we accept that God overrules in the affairs of men, even in difficult circumstances when it seems he is absent, we will find His purpose for everything. Fresh motivation will come with each new adventure, including a broader view, a greater anticipation, and a deeper purpose. This attitude enables us to thank God in everything. I learned that all material things are fleeting and uncertain; they cannot be trusted in, as they can be swept away in a moment. I learned that we don't need riches to make us happy, and that the ability to enjoy whatever we have is a great strength for navigating Life's pathway.

WILLINGNESS BRINGS ENTHUSIASM: When we are willing to be content, take challenges gracefully, and do what is set before us without complaint, we will find a new enthusiasm for life welling up within our souls. This joyful anticipation is also contagious and inspirational for others in our circle of influence. Thanking God for the little things fills life with more happiness and puts a damper on gloom. We don't have to resent our difficulties; we can use them to build strength of character!

PRIORITIZE SPIRITUAL GOALS: I learned that the best, and most reliable, ambitions are spiritual ones because *"only what's done for Christ will last"* as the old song says. God has given us life for His glory, not for our own achievements. Some people strive for years to find their purpose for living—reaching for fulfillment through careers, education, relationships, and other pathways—only to discover on their deathbed that the reason for this life was to prepare for Eternity! The Bible says that our lives are like a vapor, here today and gone tomorrow; like a weaver's shuttle, moving quickly; like water poured out on the ground, and absorbed; or like grass that grows up only to wither and die. Our existence is filled with many spontaneous demands of life that may prevent personal ambition, yet it is still possible to attain great fulfillment from living each day pleasing the Lord to the best of our ability in whatever our hands find to do. The powerful thing about spiritually-oriented goals is that there is no limit to higher vistas because God provides the grace and strength to keep stretching and reaching for more of Him all through life, and into Eternity. I believe we can, and should, continue to grow spiritually as long as we are alive. It is hard to see our own growth process because it seems to happen gradually over time, yet as I look back and see where God has brought me from, I can see how spiritual increase has happened all along the way. Looking forward, I know that as I apply my will to seek after God, study and obey His Word, and speak His truth wherever I am, I will continue to grow in God and learn more of His ways. There is never an end to learning!

VALUE THE HOLY BIBLE: My Bible is the most priceless treasure to me because it is God's holy Word; his love letter to his people—precious, unchangeable, and eternal! It is our map, our instruction book; God's Guide Book for Life. The Word shows us Jesus, and reveals to us the character of Almighty God. It is alive and powerful, working inside us to accomplish God's will in our lives. It illuminates the truth, so that we see clearly, and it gives us insight for everything in our lives as well as the lives of those who depend upon us. God's Word is the testimony of Truth to the world, the purity of God's judgement and justice over His creation. It is the most complete instruction for success. Proverbs provides ample wisdom for all of Life's situations and circumstances. The Psalms give inspiration for our pilgrim journey whether traversing great mountain peaks or dark valleys. The Parables of Christ in the Gospels give clarity and understanding on the principles of God's kingdom, and the book of Acts with its miracles and amazing exploits inspires us to seek the power that fueled the early church in spreading the gospel to the world. The New Testament epistles challenge us toward godly living, and The Revelation provides all we need to maintain a healthy fear of the Lord. The Old Testament narratives of Bible heroes and heroines of the faith guided my convictions from earliest childhood. I learned that if God could speak to Moses and part the Red Sea for him, He could do the same for me. I could be a friend of God as Abraham was, a shepherdess and a warrior as David, and I could pray as Daniel did and get amazing results.

I also realized that knowing what God says is not enough. We must put say and do together for success. We cannot attend church and expect to have a dynamic life. We must have our own cultivated relationship with the Lord;

spending time with Him in prayer and learning His Word to guide our lives. We can pray for eyes that see with revelation and spiritual understanding about what God is doing, ears that hear His voice, and a heart that wants to obey—a willing spirit that responds to Him. The Bible says, *"By the hearing of the Law shall no flesh be justified."* It is in responding to the Word that we find growth and fulfillment. Our faith must be our own, individually; not our parents' or the pastor's! Heaven and Earth will pass away, but God's Word will endure forever.

COUNT YOUR BLESSINGS: As the old hymn says, *"Count them one by one, and it will surprise you what the Lord has done."* Throughout the pages of this book I have recounted blessings from every period of my life. Soaking up every detail of the good times helps us to remember and relive our happiest memories. The surest way to live with no regrets is to focus on all the blessings of the past and then determine to pursue the best of life today! Rejoice in the positive elements of *now* because God is always doing a new thing in our lives that will produce more blessings to count in the future! Look for them; gather them diligently, and soon your blessings will far outnumber your troubles! On a comical note, if I had to choose only two blessings to keep: the first would be my Bible because it takes me where God wants me to go; the second would be my car because it takes me everywhere else I need to go!

IT'S ALL IN HOW YOU HANDLE IT: Life is not about what happens to you, but how you handle it! Each encounter, every unique set of circumstances, every tear God wipes away, and every victory He helps us gain in the countless struggles of life are what make us who we are! We can become overwhelmed thinking about the battle we are in. For no matter who we are, where we live, what we know, or what circumstances we have life is hard. Life is not only difficult by definition, but we also have an arch enemy bent on destroying us. Satan is not putting up his feet and ignoring our progress; he will try to discourage us at every turn. Starting today, however, if you will determine to look to Jesus in all things, and to remember that He has a purpose in every step of your life, one day—like me—you will look back and say, "God has given me a wonderful life!" God's gift of salvation, Christ in my heart, has become the balancing factor for setting the proper value on everything else in life. His ways are so perfect that he can make good out of anything that happens. He is the Master Potter, and he knows how to fix all the cracks and make his vessels solid, shiny, and secure; well-fitted for His amazing plans.

PURSUE PEACE AT HOME: Your home is your sanctuary; one of the only places on earth where you have the right and responsibility to decide how it looks. You can make it a safe place, and a place of peace. I learned that loving, laughing, sharing, working, and playing together builds a strong family foundation for all of life—for you as well as your children. I recognized the profound influence of a peaceful atmosphere in the home and the strong character that is built in a child by the balance of tender care, patience and grace. A deep sense of security is fostered in children by their parents' love; and they develop a healthy sense of wholeness from genuine acceptance and affirmation. That is why a Christian home is the most solid preparation and protection for any child growing up in this world. Church is important, and Christian schools are wonderful; but a godly family atmosphere in the home is the most powerful weapon we can give our children for a victorious life. It is the most constant influence and the most consistent teaching they will receive, if parents will take the challenge God has given them. That is why Satan has worked so hard to ruin it by tempting us to fill our lives with everything but time together at home learning God's way of living. The poem I have most identified with all these years, and one I have always remembered word for word is *The Old Family Altar.* It describes the feeling in the room and the power that was felt during family prayers each evening. I can testify from experience that there is nothing like it for a child's spiritual foundation.

TREAD LIGHTLY: I learned that our world system is actually hostile to God and to His heavenly kingdom; that my faith in Christ as Savior gave me citizenship in Heaven. We do not belong to this world but are only pilgrims passing through on our way to eternal paradise. We are warned in scripture that those who love the world and immerse themselves in its pleasures are devoid of God's love and light within. We are cautioned that even if a person gains the whole world he can lose his soul. If we remember that a healthy fear of God—to honor and revere Him and keep his holy word central to every aspect of life and relationships—is the safest and wisest perspective, we can have the deepest fulfillment and highest success of any available path on this earth. The hard part is learning to hold more tightly to Him than we do to our possessions, positions, and plans. It is a rewarding process well worth the ongoing effort.

LOVE NOT THE WORLD: I learned, on the other hand, that we can confidently associate with the world in order to shine the light of Jesus, without being immersed in the Christ-less culture around us. When Lois and I graduated from the eighth grade, our class had a noon dance in the high school gymnasium. For those who did not want to dance, there were table games and side benches on which to sit and watch. Our mother told us that since it was a class celebration, we should go and be a Christian testimony by cooperating while shining the light of Christ. She had us wear our prettiest dresses and we went to enjoy the party and visit with others on the sidelines. We didn't stay very long but it was a good experience and a way to show kindness and cooperation without legalism. Too often, Christians cannot find a proper line of separation between the culture and The Cross. Christ died to save sinners from the grasp of the world system. We need to love them and show respect for other people without diving into all the worldly attitudes and activities of our culture. Jesus showed us by example that we can reach out with love and care to those who don't know Him without becoming a part of the very system that separates them from His truth and love. We are the light of the world; that means it is a dark place, and we are meant to shine into that darkness so that others will be able to see which way to go. Going along with them will never help them find God's light. We must lead lovingly.

VALUE GOOD FRIENDS: I learned to value good friends and to nurture friendships. The Bible tells us in Proverbs 17:17 that *"a friend loves at all times."* The New Living Translation says, *"a friend is always loyal."* That's true friendship; someone who will be loyal to you through thick and thin. They will overlook your flaws, yet be honest in confronting you, too! Proverbs 27:17 tells us that, *"As iron sharpens iron, so a man sharpens the countenance of his friend."*(NKJV) They can see your faults and know your weaknesses, but they love you anyway! A real friend will enjoy your company, and feel comfortable around you. True friendships are completely reciprocal; the action comes from both sides. You are not the only one working to maintain the relationship, or making all the effort to get together. They will *make time* to spend with you, and you will have things in common with them that result in good fellowship. You do not feel drained every time they leave because the listening and support goes both ways. They will encourage you in your endeavors and listen to your heart. My daughter's best friend gave her a plaque that she keeps on her kitchen wall, which says it all.

"A friend hears the song in your heart,
and sings it back to you when you have forgotten the words."

A true friend is one of the sweetest gifts that God gives to us in the life. He knows how important it is, and He will provide for you if you will ask Him for a true friend. The best way to recognize a good friend is to practice being one yourself. Be a faithful, godly friend; and soon you will be thanking God for the good friends in your own life!

THE BEST CAREER PATH: I learned that the best career path is planned by the Lord. Proverbs 16:9 shows us that a man plans his way but the Lord orders his steps. This is especially true if we are looking to Him for direction in the first place! When we want God's will above everything else He is faithful to help us choose a pathway and then direct our steps. The best place to be is where God knows we will thrive. In the will of God there is peace and confidence, even in adversity. Good jobs are hard to find at times and there are seasons of difficulty in making a living; but no matter where we work God is there. When we live for Him and desire to spread the good news of Jesus every job is profitable because we are working for the Lord. As we "seek first the kingdom of God and his righteousness" everything else will fall perfectly into place for a happy, fulfilling life.

ADMIT SHORTCOMINGS: I learned that a willingness to recognize your own faults literally ushers in the grace to overcome them, because God exalts the humble and it takes humility to admit your wrongs and weaknesses! As our children were growing up society developed a popular slogan, *"If you don't like it, lump it!"* Later, as the secular world became more and more protective of human rights and The Big 'I' gained power and momentum, it was common to hear, *"I gotta be ME!"* The message of Jesus Christ to his followers was to seek humility and resist pride; that God resists the proud but gives grace to the humble. The apostle Paul said, *"I must decrease and He must increase,"* just the opposite of the world's view.

The older people get, and the more life experience they have, the easier it is to recognize their limits and short-comings. One of mine was to "zone out" whenever the conversation seemed unimportant to me. My natural tendency was to lose interest if the stories got too long and detailed or seemed irrelevant. Even in counseling, I would often fail to listen as closely as I should have, and then—to my chagrin—have to ask the person to "refresh my memory". The Lord was faithful to help me, however, by ensuring that my husband and three of my four children were very detailed personalities! Becca, as an adult, used to sense when my mind had strayed from our telephone conversation and say, "Mom, are you reading something?" or "Well, I can tell that you're busy so I'll let you go." God listens to each of us with greater patience and care than we could ever imagine possible. He can hone our listening skills to do the same for others, and balance our other short-comings as well.

RUN FROM EVIL: I saw a movie once of how a snake hypnotized a little bird, made it fly directly into its mouth, and then swallowed it. I hated that; it was so like the Devil! Yet we cannot blame him for the outcome when people choose to compromise their Christian standards and allow themselves to be drawn away by their own lust toward the things of this world. We, too, can be easily hypnotized and enticed right into Satan's web where we are unable to get ourselves free.

I suppose some of the strangest things I have encountered have been behavioral patterns in human beings. People can do such contradictory things. They can say one thing, yet do another; they can pretend to be a friend, but then betray you; they can be double-minded and unpredictable; they can open the door to the Devil so many times that he possesses them and controls their lives against their will. The more I have seen while traveling through life, the more deeply grateful and utterly amazed I am at God's sovereign protection. I am humbled to think that He kept me from exposure to so much defilement, harm, and danger that other people have been snared by and struggled for years to overcome! The vices offered by the world and its attractions seem to trap so many young people! Even though drugs, alcohol, and the sexual sins of our culture represent the obvious, there are many other temptations of the mind and heart that we must avoid as well. *"All have sinned"* the Bible clearly teaches us; yet we can be preserved from so many activities that open doors to satanic harassment just by listening to the conscience God created in us as a moral compass. The Holy Spirit teaches us how and where to draw the line on the world, and how easy it is to resist temptation when our spirit moves with God's Spirit and our desires are lined up with His eternal purpose. Serving the Lord is the most wonderful, safe, fulfilling and successful existence anyone could ever choose to live! I am so thrilled to belong to Jesus and be a part of the Family of God!

BEAUTY IS NOT SKIN-DEEP: I learned that beauty is *not* skin-deep! It comes from within; and I discovered that the more *time* we spend on inner beauty, the less *money* we feel a need to spend on the way we look. I've never spent much money on my outward appearance, but I've received lots of compliments about it anyway! (I would *never* say that; but my daughter is writing this!) I would classify myself as conservative or traditionalist in my style. I was never interested in the passing fads of the fashion world. I love suits and dresses, and jewelry; but I find almost everything second-hand. My willingness to be frugal with my clothing and accessories has actually resulted in three important benefits that will serve any woman well: 1) resourcefulness 2) contentment, and 3) confidence. When you already know who God says you are, there is no struggle for outer beauty because the beauty within will shine!

As for vitality, the best tips for a healthy life-style come from God:

- Keep a clear conscience
- Refuse anxiety; trust God instead
- Live by faith and practice contentment
- Choose to be joyful and to nourish a grateful heart
- Forgive everyone who has wronged you
- Consult the Great Physician *first* for every physical, emotional and mental need
- Following the *"prayer of faith, which heals the sick"*, use God-given common sense to ensure proper rest, a well-balanced diet (to the best of your ability allowing God to fill in the gaps), get plenty of fresh air and sunshine, get enough exercise by working hard and resisting idle entertainments.

FIRST THE NATURAL, THEN THE SPIRITUAL: I learned that God has surrounded us with beautiful analogies in the world to teach us His ways. I remember a winter day on the homestead when I opened the door and looked out at the freshly fallen snow. I saw that there was not one animal track and that my footprints to the outhouse would be the first impressions. I stepped out carefully, making a crisp, tidy pathway through the snow. Soon I spied the prints of a jack rabbit, and followed his trail. Then I discovered some bird tracks and followed theirs. The sun was so bright that the snow glistened like glitter. I stopped to listen, but couldn't hear even one sound across the fluffy, white countryside. I stood perfectly still, under the bluest of skies and surrounded by white, drinking it all in and thinking of a hymn we sang at church, "Whiter Than the Snow". I began to sing it softly and meditate on the words, grateful for Jesus' sacrifice that provided the cleansing from all sin. Then I remembered a poem, *The Beautiful Snow* that told a sad story of how a girl who was once pure like the snow had fallen in sin and become tarnished like dirty slush trodden underfoot. I was just a little girl learning from nature as God impressed truth upon my heart with nobody else around. The power of an object lesson, especially for a young person, should never be taken lightly; it will often last a lifetime!

THE BEST COUNSELLOR: I learned that the best counsel and guidance come from God's Word. It is the absolute and final authority for life and conduct, and His precepts lead us to happiness and success. When Jesus left this earth, he told his disciples that he would send the Comforter (KJV), and that *"...when He, the Spirit of Truth, has come, He will guide you into all truth..."* (John 16:13, NKJV). His ways are high above our ways, and His thoughts far above our finite human thinking. This is why we need to be baptized in the Holy Spirit in order to know God. I saw many Christians compromise, thinking they could live a little for God and a little for themselves at the same time; but the end of it was always the death of their vision and the ruination of their hopes and dreams—not to mention how many other people were affected by these selfish ambitions and resulting mistakes. This was because they did not take God seriously when he said in Romans 12:2 not to compromise with the ways of the world around us.

When we are filled with the Holy Spirit, our minds are renewed and we are not controlled by the philosophies of worldly wisdom. Romans 8:5-8 tells us, *"Those who are dominated by the sinful nature think about sinful things, but those who are controlled by the Holy Spirit think about things that please the Spirit. So letting your sinful nature control your mind leads to death. But letting the Spirit control your mind leads to life and peace. For the sinful nature is always hostile to God. It never did obey God's laws, and it never will. That's why those who are still under the control of their sinful nature can never please God"* (NLT).

It is a blessing and comfort to have godly family, friends and leaders to support the truth and to give words of confirmation to us when we are seeking direction. Our birthright, however, is the *direct* guidance of the Holy Spirit through regular communion with him and through God's Word. If we are diligent to learn God's ways, we will usually know what He wants us to do, and can wait for confirmation and circumstantial evidence to line up with it. Romans 12:2 clearly directs us, *"Don't copy the behavior and customs of this world, but let God transform you into a new person by changing the way you think. Then you will learn to know God's will for you, which is good and pleasing and perfect."*(NLT)

As our minds continue to be renewed by the Holy Spirit, we retain God's righteousness as our guide because we are becoming like Him. *"The integrity of the upright will guide them, but the perversity of the unfaithful will destroy them."* Proverbs 11:3 (NKJV) Many times in life, we must make decisions on our own; and at those times we must have the confidence of knowing that our steps are being ordered by the Lord and that we can count on Him to guide us truly as the Good Shepherd of our souls. Having a strong trust in the Lord will enable positive decision-making in everyday life. The inability to make decisions without anxiety merely exhibits a lack of trust in the God, who holds your future in His great and loving hands. These days it is accepted social behavior to blame a lot of things on "stress"; but anxiety is old fashioned fear dressed up in modern vernacular. Fear is a tool of Satan to prevent God's best in our lives, and it should be resisted and banished at every turn. When the Lord tells us that we can do *"all things through Christ"* (Philippians 4:13), then we can do all things through Christ! One of my favorite sayings regarding that scripture is,

"*All* means 'all'; and that's all 'all' means!" At this point, all of our "I can'ts" are plainly exposed as "I won'ts", and it is time to become "*doers of the word and not hearers only*" James 1:22. Of course, this is a whole different sermon!

THE REAL CHURCH: I learned to love the Body of Christ, the real Church with a capital 'c'. The church is a safe place because it is the environment that God himself has chosen to use for nurturing our spiritual growth and maturity. We tend to "shop" for churches that are comfy and skin-deep. We like the ones that demonstrate our personal preferences for worship and teaching, personality and entertainment. Then we naively assume that these Christian gathering places will be free of all discomfort and offense—the 'o' word. But offense will happen wherever other finite human beings are present because it's part of the world we live in. I quoted a favorite maxim of Gail's in another chapter, but it bears repeating here: "If you ever find a perfect church, don't join it; you will ruin it!" The church is vital and important because God ordained it as a place for His people to learn and thrive together. He never meant for any of us to go through life alone." Psalm 68:6 says that He "*sets the solitary in families*". Why do you suppose? In Romans 14 where the apostle Paul is talking about personal preferences and showing deference one to another, verse seven reminds us that "*None of us lives for ourselves alone...*" We are all influenced by those around us, and we have a circle of influence where we have an impact on the lives of others as well. My family and Christian friends have enriched my life, imparting truth, balance, and encouragement. I value and appreciate—and give credit to—those who have affected my perspectives and desires in the most positive ways. God uses us to help others, and others to help us because that's what family is about, and the church is where much of this interaction takes place. We all have rough edges and idiosyncrasies that we need to work on; but secluding ourselves away with our Bible and tea is not the answer. Yes, the Holy Spirit is the best counsellor and God's Word has all the answers; but it's not all about what we get; it's actually more about what we give and contribute! We can never forget that the Body of Christ is close to the heart of God; close enough for Him to defend. One of the things God hates is someone who causes discord in His family. His desire is for us to love each other the same way He loves us; unconditionally and without expectation. Tough to carry out at times, but we can do whatever He wants us to do because the strength to succeed will be his.

HOSPITALITY IS BIBLICAL: Speaking of interaction with others, did you know that hospitality is a biblical principal? We were never meant to keep all our blessings to ourselves; and we all know from raising a child, or being one, that sharing cannot be learned when there is nobody around to share with! Society may call it "entertaining" which can intimidate people; but putting on an impressive show is not what we are talking about. The tips for success that I give you here are the simple things I discovered throughout my own life and experience. You can do this!

- Enjoying life and serving people is what turns entertainment into true hospitality

- Never get ruffled. The whole point is to enjoy
  it and enjoy others. Be yourself!

- Stay calm and do things as you are able,
  keeping your plans on the simple side

- Whatever the menu, or occasion, people have a great time
  if the hostess is relaxed. Soup and sandwiches in a peaceful
  home are better than prime rib in a chaotic environment!

- Have things ready, and food prepared, in advance as much as possible

- Allow guests to help if they ask, or if you can use a hand with something

- Be cheerful! This shows your guests you are glad they came
  instead of making them wonder if you can't wait until it's over

- Focus on your plan until your guests arrive; then
  focus on them! Their comfort is more important than
  how your agenda is playing out. Be flexible!

WE REAP WHAT WE SOW: "You will reap what you sow" was the most valuable advice from my childhood. We sang a song about the reaping day that made a great impression on me! Galatians 6:7-9 was a beacon light in our home, guiding us through life: "*Do not be deceived: God cannot be mocked. A man reaps what he sows. Whoever sows to please their flesh, from the flesh will reap destruction; whoever sows to please the Spirit, from the Spirit will reap eternal life. Let us not become weary in doing good, for at the proper time we will reap a harvest if we do not give up.*"(NIV) Sowing and reaping is a principle of life, no matter who you are; and it affects everything because it is about choices. This principle affects our progress, our goals—both natural and spiritual, our relationships, our hopes and dreams, and our day to day existence. The treasure you must keep is the knowledge and determination to make it work for you, and not against you, for the rest of your life.

SUPERNATURAL INTERVENTION: I learned that Jesus never fails, that He is all-powerful and knows all things. Many things are hard, even impossible, for us; but nothing is impossible for Him. God has endowed us with knowledge, ability, and a free will but we are still very small and incapable in the face of many obstacles that loom ahead on our pathway of life. We need the constant input of the supernatural in our lives. I believe in salvation, the Baptism of the Holy Spirit, and healing—all supernatural experiences given by God for sustenance and comfort to His people. I know first-hand that the Lord will give supernatural provision where it is needed in substance and finances, wisdom and guidance, and every aspect of our lives. We have the privilege of approaching the very throne of God with our petitions and knowing that He hears and is able to answer completely. God is good, and He promises that nothing can separate us from His love. He can and will do whatever is needed in our lives, and for our good.

THE HOPE OF HEAVEN: This thrilling expectation is the inner, bubbling joy of every saint, looming ever closer as the days go by. Christ has promised to return for His own and throughout the ages Christians have eagerly looked for His coming. The hope of Heaven has sustained many a patient with terminal illness, many missionaries struggling on a foreign field, many dedicated Christians persecuted for their faith, many a soldier on the battlefield, and many helpless victims of the evils in our society. All of these scenarios cause people to look upward with thoughts of a better place where no pain or sorrow will ever reside. Revelation 21:4 and 7(KJV) comforts the weary with these words: "*And God shall wipe away all tears from their eyes; and there shall be no more death, neither sorrow, nor crying, neither shall there be any more pain: for the former things are passed away... He that overcometh shall inherit all things; and I will be his God, and he shall be my son.*" Not only is a place of peace, security, and rest promised, but a place of great excitement and activity for eternity! As a child, I thrilled at the thought of seeing King David some day; or Daniel; or Joseph. As I grew older I identified more with Paul the apostle and John the Revelator. I was so inspired by their lives and dedication! I've thought so much about Mary, the mother of Jesus, with the contradictions and sorrows she bore; about talking to her and hearing her heart. I can't keep from loving Peter and appreciating his absolute transparency; about the great apostle he became. All of the Patriarchs intrigue me; to think of sitting down in the Kingdom of God with Abraham, Isaac, and Jacob; hearing all about their life experiences. I can't wait to see Elijah and Elisha, John the Baptist and, most of all, I want to see Jesus and look into his loving eyes. I want to see him smile with open arms and say to me, "Well done, thou good and faithful servant. Enter into the joy of the Lord!"

The mysteries of God's Word will never be fully understood in this life; yet every day of every year along our Pilgrim Journey we can be filled and thrilled with its promises, precepts, and power. How blessed we are to know the truth of Romans 8:38-39: "*For I am persuaded, that neither death, nor life, nor angels, nor principalities, nor powers, nor things present, nor things to come, nor height, nor depth, nor any other creature, shall be able to separate us from the Love of God, which is in Christ Jesus our Lord.*" (KJV) We are challenged to be constantly aware of Christ's imminent coming and to live accordingly. Psalm 90:12 (KJV) "*So teach us to number our days, that we may apply our hearts to wisdom.*" We have finite minds that understand only what has a beginning and an end; but some day we will transcend the barriers of time and space to be forever with the one who planted this hope in our hearts. We must watch and wait; live carefully; for one of these days will be our last on earth, and Eternity will be our new home.

Happily Victorious

God's Word is filled with songs of the soul and spirit; with "Wonderful Words of Life" as the old hymn describes. Looking back over my life I see why the love of music and poetry was written on my heart at birth. It is plain to see the reason that I have collected inspiring poems, songs, and stories all through the years and filled scrapbooks with them. I see now why I have cherished the old hymns so, and why one of my greatest thrills was always to pick up a musical instrument and fill the room with some sweet refrain. It is because God knew that these things would be my pathway to peace. Music touched my spirit and drew me to Jesus. I could always remember words to songs and poems; the rhythm, meter, melody and rhyme refreshed my soul. Often I would awake in the morning with a song on my lips, spilling from my heart. Spiritual songs, often written from the cries of one's soul, convey truths in such a way as to bring deliverance to the captive, refreshment to the weary, cleansing to the soul, and healing to the broken heart.

In many of my darkest days, the hymns of the faith and anthems of the redeemed have lifted my spirits and renewed my hope. When my faith was tried and hope seemed to wane, I sang about the mighty name of Jesus on which my hope was built, "The Solid Rock".

Music was my manna in the wilderness, my water in the desert. When the Winds of Adversity blew cold in my soul God always sustained me with a song. I knew from experience that I could have a melody deep in my heart even when it was breaking. God was always faithful to give me A Song in the Night.

Telling one's story may include accounts of various struggles and heartaches, true to life. Yet, in the telling, there must remain a thread of hope lest the meaning be lost in the chaos of trauma. However sorrowful or unfair our experience, the outcome should somehow convey joy and peace; because God is good and his mercies are new every morning. We who claim to be his children must ultimately learn to extol his greatness above all else, for even Job—following the loss of everything he valued except his very breath—said of God in Job 13:15 (KJV) *"Though he slay me, yet will I trust in him…"*

There are millions of stories to be told that readers, through their own experiences, may relate to; but I want this one to be more than that. If you have read about my life and laughed and cried and identified with certain elements, my hope is that you will also come away with useful benefits and lasting truth. I want you to see that whatever life throws at you can be navigated with faith and become a strong stepping stone to take you higher. Have you endured groundless shame through the faults of others? You can remove it with the sponge of Grace so that what remains is not a blemish or scar, but a shining testimony. How much healthier you will be to take your trying times of poverty or lack and turn them into eyes of compassion for others in need, rather than succumbing to the blindness of resentment about your "lot in life". How worthwhile the telling of one's hardships would be if the outcome could be another's hope for triumph—not the dread of defeat. In Christ, we always have a happy ending, and mine was built upon the counting of blessings. What you will find, if you will do the same, is that in the sorting out of all your troubles you will also find blessings if you are willing to look for them. When the sorting is completed you may be surprised to find that your Blessing Heap will far outweigh your Pile of Woes, for this is the reward of a grateful heart. No human life will finish its course unscathed, for the Lord warns that life will be full of troubles. But ours is the choice that determines how to handle them; and ours is the voice that decides to appeal to the Lord of Heaven's Armies for ongoing assistance.

Nearing eighty-five at the writing of this book, I am still "happily victorious" as my mother exhorted me to be so many years ago—true to the meaning of my name. What joy I have found in choosing to focus on my blessings and giving all of Life's problems to the Lord. Our lives on earth need not be trumped by the burdens when our experience is just as likely to be enhanced by the blessings. Although Life is guaranteed to take turns we don't expect, we always own the power to decide where to camp and when to move on; what to embrace and what to refuse—unless we choose to relinquish this God-given right. Rejoice in the Lord always! Trust him with your heart and cultivate close communion with him above all other relationships. Meet each new day with hope and gladness; and you, too, will have "A Song in the Night".

Tributes to a Wonderful Mother
— From Her Children —

From Dorcas, firstborn:

I am so grateful that God gave me Eunice Christina Bryan as my beloved mother. She is the one who first introduced me to Jesus as a child and prayed with me to accept Christ as my Savior at the age of five. I was always amazed at how much Scripture my mother could quote and she regularly taught me how the word of God applied to our lives. Because of her loving guidance I never wanted to leave God and go my own way. I know that my life has been rewarding and happy because I have not suffered the sorrows and regrets that plague the lives of those who wander away from God.

My mother has always been one of my best friends and confidants. I could share any concern with her and know that I would be lifted up in earnest prayer. I knew that my mother loved me with faithful devotion no matter what my carnal nature might produce. I could completely trust her; but she was consistent to correct me when I needed adjustment that would bring me back into alignment with the heart of God. As an adult I value the disciplines she displayed; those simple disciplines that keep us from disobedience to God and bring His favor upon our lives.

Mom showed me by her example how to love other people, and how to worship the Lord in song and in action. She was, and is, continually serving people that are blessed to know her. I saw unselfishness, kindness, and mercy demonstrated to me on a regular basis. One of the most enjoyable things we did consistently was to sing together as a family. Mom usually played her accordion, Dad and my brother, Mark, played guitar, my youngest brother, David, played bass guitar, while Mom, Becca, and I sang as a trio. I loved the gospel choruses, special songs, and worship that we shared to encourage other people, groups, or churches. Mama also taught us many children's songs that were filled with godly principles to live by. I am sixty-five years old at the writing of this book, but my heart is still made glad by all of the songs I learned from my joyful, dedicated mother.

Although life circumstances were not always kind to her, she never groveled in discouragement. Instead, she turned her heart to the God she loved and trusted, to the Bible for its words of encouragement and wisdom, and to songs of praise and worship that soothed her soul. She was a true overcomer!

Mom, you will always be my hero, and the best example of a solid Christian that I have ever known. Your faith and confidence in God are unwavering, and I will be forever grateful for, and indebted to you—my awesome Mom!

From Becca, second daughter:

Mom, weaving the story of your life with the words and music of your heart has been one of the greatest joys I have ever experienced. You have always been a priceless treasure to me, and this endeavor has made me love you even more! As the chapters came together I was amazed to see how much of you has become a part of me. I am so grateful to have you as my mom! Thank you for your wisdom about life, for all you taught me about God and about people. Thank you a thousand times for loving my daddy, for being dedicated to his success, despite the odds, and for choosing to do it with as much joy as possible. You have shown us all what it means to make each day worthwhile, living with purpose no matter what others choose to do or what life brings our way. God is the Author of life and by his grace we, too, will live joyfully and finish well!

From Mark, firstborn son:

My mother has been a joyful, godly, hardworking Christian her whole life. I've never seen her any other way than loving God, loving his people, and joyfully serving in the church. The most consistent gospel witness I've ever known, she aims to guide every conversation back to the Bible and God at the first opportunity. My mom is always happy, and taught us to be happy; even during chore time when a common tune around the house was, "Whistle while you work, its lots of fun, whistle while you work, you'll get everything done". It was hard to have a sour attitude around mother; her example shaped us, and her strong discipline left no room for mopish attitudes!

She loved to sing, and most every day of her life was filled with music. She taught herself to play the guitar, the piano, and the accordion, as well as other instruments such as the ukulele and Autoharp. She collected gospel songs, typed or written out, to put into her home-made song books. She and dad sang duets, as she played her accordion and Dad, his guitar. Later we sang as a family, or she and the girls sang as a trio while Dave, dad and I accompanied them on our instruments. Even in her eighties she now remembers more words from old songs and poems than anyone I know. She can remember poems she learned at five years of age!

Mama prays, and prays, and prays fervently! When we lived on the farm in Emmett I remember coming home from high school, walking in the front door from the screened porch. As I came into the front room she would be kneeling on the floor, over her open Bible, crying out to God with tears streaming. Not hearing me walk in, she would look up apologetically to explain, 'Oh I'm sorry son, I was just praying'; and praying she was! I will never forget the picture of my godly mother on her knees, and the sense of urgency in her voice, as she poured out the deep burdens of her soul to the great God of Heaven. I have a praying mom; not just 'bless-the-food', or 'now-I-lay-me-down-to-sleep' but real soul-searching, family-shaping, world-changing prayer!

Unless one can love God too much, I see no outstanding fault in my mother's life. An example of the true believer in every way, she gives all of her heart, soul, mind and strength to loving the Lord and doing his work. Thanks, mom, for always exemplifying the virtues of Christ in our home, to our family and friends through the years. I will ever be thankful and always feel fortunate to have been born to such a wonderful, joyful, godly, prayerful Christian woman as my dear mother.

From David, lastborn:

Memories of my mother, innumerable and precious, would be difficult to abbreviate and commit to text. So let me attempt to share only a few. My earliest memories of my mother were introductions to God. Some might say their mother was "like God"—but I remember being pleased to discover that God was "like my mother!" Always helpful; always encouraging; never condemning; never disconnected or aloof; always inspiring me toward greatness and, in the words of Scripture, "a very present help in time of need!" I remember as if it were just yesterday the angelic visitation I experienced as a young child, told in Chapter Nine of this book. The overwhelming sense of what I recognized as "my mother's" gentle, loving presence hovering over me was, in fact, a heavenly being! When I finally turned to see why she stood so close and so quietly, it was an angel with a radiant countenance and dazzling white robes that lovingly watched over me as I played! I will always remember the genuine love and joy we shared as Mama told me how special I was that God had allowed me to see my Guardian Angel! She pulled me up onto her lap and opened a storybook that showed an angel looking over the shoulder of a little boy, just about my age. She said, "See, David! You have an angel sent from God to watch over you, just like the one in this picture! Your Guardian Angel keeps you safe from harm and danger, and will protect and watch over you all your life!" In blissful amazement I asked if all children had guardian angels, and she said, "Yes… I think so; but not many are allowed to see them! This means that God has a very special and wonderful plan for your life, David; so he has allowed you to see the angel that he sent to watch over you!" Though it may sound like just another kid's story, a lasting sense of spiritual calling and significance was imparted to me that day.

Soon after, Mama was getting me ready for my first day of Kindergarten. She had already prepared me to succeed by telling me how wonderful it would be, and how well she knew I would do in school. Kneeling before me, checking to see that everything was in order, her express enthusiasm about my imminent success was infectious. She told me how excited she was for me! How God had blessed me with talents and abilities that she knew would give me favor with my teacher. I remember my little heart nearly bursting with excitement while listening to her descriptions about how much I would love it and how many new, fun friends I would soon have. On the small, still-mostly-blank canvas of my little mind, she was painting a picture of happiness, fulfillment and overwhelming success! I remember coming home a few hours later thinking, "Mama was right! It was so much fun! My teacher loves me! I have lots of new friends! This is going to be magnificent!" Only as I grew to maturity did I come to fully appreciate the preciousness of the gift my mother gave me. When my self-image was new and wet—still malleable and easily influenced—my mother's words of faith and goodwill shaped my tiny world-view and my own self-image to expect the very best out of life!

Thank you, Mama! Only God himself knows how much your words of faith, hope and love have shaped my soul! My tribute to you was best put years ago by that sage orator, Abraham Lincoln, who said, "All that I am—or ever hope to be—I owe to my Angel Mother!"

Endnotes

Chapter 1 Ancestry: My Beginnings

1. Helen Olson, Manuscript (Owyhee County Historical Society Pioneer Family Program, 1991), 1
2. William Mussell, Genealogy Record #12 (from census, church, Family Bible, family sources)
3. *Owyhee Outpost* #32 (OCHS Press, 2001) 18
4. Olson, (OCHS Pioneer Family Program), 1
5. Jacob Mussell Diary, *Biography*, 2
6. O.C. McProud, *Interview of Jacob Mussell* (Owyhee Chronicle, Homedale, October 3, 1946), 1
7. Olson, (OCHS Pioneer Family Program), 1
8. O.C. McProud, *Interview*, 2
9. Mussell Diary, *Biography*, 2
10. Jacob Mussell Diary, *Looking at Life after it Has Happened*, 1
11. Mussell, *Looking at Life*, 2
12. Helen Olson, photo article submission on Jacob Mussell, column 1
13. Mussell, *Looking at Life*, 4
14. Olson article, column 1
15. Olson article, column 2
16. Helen Olsen, manuscript *Mussell Ferry Stage Stop*
17. James L. Huntley, *Ferryboats in Idaho*, (The Caxton Printers, 1979), 176
18. Huntley, *Ferryboats*, 178
19. Mussell, *Looking at Life*, 4
20. Olson article, column 2
21. Olson article, column 3
22. Addie Mussell Diary, *Life Review – Journal I*, 8-9
23. A. Mussell Diary, *Journal I*, 1-2
24. A. Mussell Diary, *Journal I*, 3-4
25. A. Mussell Diary, *Journal I*, 5-6
26. A. Mussell Diary, *Journal I*, 17
27. A. Mussell Diary, *Journal I*, 19
28. http://www.gfaschools.org/about/history
29. A. Mussell Diary, *Journal I*, 23

Chapter 2 Vern and Addie

1. Addie Mussell, *Record of Places Lived*, #1-12

Chapter 3 Life According to Me

1. Addie Mussell, *Record of Places Lived*, #13
2. Listen and Sing, Boston; New York: Ginn and Company, 1936
3. The Umbrella Man, *Flanagan & Allen*, 1939
4. Vom Bruch, Harry, *Glad Gospel Songs-pg 69*, 1937, public domain
5. Addie Mussell Diary, *Life Review – Journal III*, 23-24
6. Ludgate, Rev. J.C., public domain
7. Mussell, *Places Lived*, #18-19
8. Wikipedia: https://en.wikipedia.org/wiki/Zoot_suit
9. A. Mussell Diary, *Journal III*, 25-26
10. https://en.wikipedia.org/wiki/Figueroa_Street
11. Mussell, *Places Lived*, #21
12. Ibid.

Chapter 4 Growing Up
1. Addie Mussell, *Record of Places Lived*, #27
2. Crosby, Fanny J., public domain
3. Oelander, Anna, Glad Gospel Songs-pg. 63, 1937, public domain
4. Mussell, *Places Lived*, #28
5. Mussell, *Places Lived*, #29
6. Mussell, *Places Lived*, #30
7. https://en.wikipedia.org/wiki/Schoenoplectus_acutus
8. Featherstone, William Ralph, public domain

Chapter 5 Treasures from my Tapestry
1. Flint, Annie Johnson, Hope Publishing Company, public domain in U.S. only
2. Faris, Lillie Anne, 1927, Standard Bible Story Readers

Chapter 6 Life with Gail
1. https://www.dictionary.com/browse/shivaree

Chapter 7 Feathering the Nest
1. https://www.britannica.com/science/sulfonamide
2. https://serc.carleton.edu/earthscope_chronicles/danielle_harmony.html

Chapter 9 Regrouping for Growth
1. https://lrm1948.blogspot.com/2013/05/david-schoch-prophet-of-god.html

Chapter 10 Ranch Life
1. https://en.wikipedia.org/wiki/Ore-Ida
2. Rebecca Bryan-Howell, lyrics to "Home Again", 1985, used by permission

Chapter 12 Unsettled Weather
1. Eunice Bryan, lyrics to "Jesus Has Triumphed in Me", 1984, used by permission
2. Edwin Markham, *The Shoes of Happiness, and Other Poems*, (New York: Doubleday Page & Co., 1915)
3. Mark T. Bryan, lyrics to "He's Ever Interceding", 1985, used by permission.
4. Buffum, Herbert, 1930, Buffum Music Publishing

Chapter 13 Last Chance to Thrive
1. https://en.wikipedia.org/wiki/Sequim,Washington

Chapter 14 The Last Lap
1. Henry Jackson van Dyke Jr., public domain
2. Encarta Dictionary, English (North America), online
3. Stanphill, Ira F. Copyright ©1959 New Spring Publishing Inc.(ASCAP) (adm. at CapitolCMGPublishing.com) All rights reserved. Used by permission.
4. Florence White Willett, public domain

CPSIA information can be obtained
at www.ICGtesting.com
Printed in the USA
FSHW012000301218
54763FS